Fragments of Modernity

Studies in Contemporary German Social Thought
Thomas McCarthy, General Editor

Theodor W. Adorno, *Against Epistemology: A Metacritique*
Theodor W. Adorno, *Prisms*
Karl-Otto Apel, *Understanding and Explanation: A Transcendental-Pragmatic Perspective*
Richard J. Bernstein, editor, *Habermas and Modernity*
Ernst Bloch, *Natural Law and Human Dignity*
Ernst Bloch, *The Principle of Hope*
Hans Blumenberg, *The Legitimacy of the Modern Age*
Hans Blumenberg, *Work on Myth*
Helmut Dubiel, *Theory and Politics: Studies in the Development of Critical Theory*
John Forester, editor, *Critical Theory and Public Life*
David Frisby, *Fragments of Modernity: Theories of Modernity in the Work of Simmel, Kracauer and Benjamin*
Hans-Georg Gadamer, *Philosophical Apprenticeships*
Hans-Georg Gadamer, *Reason in the Age of Science*
Jürgen Habermas, *Philosophical-Political Profiles*
Jürgen Habermas, editor, *Observations on ''The Spiritual Situation of the Age''*
Hans Joas, *G. H. Mead: A Contemporary Re-examination of His Thought*
Reinhart Koselleck, *Futures Past: On the Semantics of Historical Time*
Claus Offe, *Contradictions of the Welfare State*
Claus Offe, *Disorganized Capitalism: Contemporary Transformations of Work and Politics*
Helmut Peukert, *Science, Action, and Fundamental Theology: Toward a Theology of Communicative Action*
Joachim Ritter, *Hegel and the French Revolution: Essays on the Philosophy of Right*
Alfred Schmidt, *History and Structure: An Essay on Hegelian-Marxist and Structuralist Theories of History*
Carl Schmitt, *The Crisis of Parliamentary Democracy*
Carl Schmitt, *Political Romanticism*
Carl Schmitt, *Political Theology: Four Chapters on the Concept of Sovereignty*
Michael Theunissen, *The Other: Studies in the Social Ontology of Husserl, Heidegger, Sartre, and Buber*
Ernst Tugendhat, *Self-Consciousness and Self-Determination*

Fragments of Modernity

Theories of Modernity in the Work
of Simmel, Kracauer and Benjamin

David Frisby

The MIT Press
Cambridge, Massachusetts

First MIT Press edition, 1986
First published in paperback, 1988

©David Frisby, 1986

Library of Congress Cataloging-in-Publication Data

Frisby, David.
Fragments of modernity.

(Studies in contemporary German social thought)
Bibliography: p.
Includes index.
1. Modernism (Aesthetics)   2. Culture — Philosophy.
3. Simmel, Georg, 1858–1918 — Views on modernism (Aesthetics)   4. Kracauer, Siegfried, 1889–1966 — Views on modernism (Aesthetics)   5. Benjamin, Walter, 1892–1940 — Views on modernism (Aesthetics)
I. Title.   II. Series.
BH301.M54F75   1986   700'.1   85-23707

ISBN 0-262-06103-1 (hard)
ISBN 0-262-56046-1 (paper)

Phototypeset by Dobbie Typesetting Service, Plymouth, Devon
Printed in Great Britain by Page Bros (Norwich) Ltd

Contents

Acknowledgements   vii

Introduction   1

1 *Modernité*   11

2 Georg Simmel: *Modernity as an Eternal Present*   38

3 Siegfried Kracauer: *'Exemplary Instances' of Modernity*   109

4 Walter Benjamin: *Prehistory of Modernity*   187

Conclusion   266

Notes   273

Bibliography   309

Index   318

Acknowledgements

I wish to thank the staff of the following libraries who provided material for this volume: Glasgow University Library, the British Library, the Bodlean Library Oxford, the Universitätsbibliothek Heidelberg, the Universitätsbibliothek Konstanz and the Universitätsbibliothek of the Free University, Berlin. In particular, the staff of the Deutsches Literaturarchiv (Marbach/Neckar) were especially helpful in guiding me through the Siegfried Kracauer Nachlass. Also in this connection, I am very grateful to Inka Mülder who made available to me her then unpublished thesis *Erfahrendes Denken* on Kracauer.

The research for this study was made possible by the generous support of the Alexander von Humboldt Foundation who awarded me a fellowship at Heidelberg University (1980–1) and at Konstanz University (1982/1983/1984). And here I wish to thank Wolfgang Schluchter (Heidelberg) and Horst Baier (Konstanz) for their hospitality and assistance. Thanks are also due to the students who attended my seminars on Social Theories of Modernity in the summer semesters of 1981 (Heidelberg) and 1982 (Konstanz). A term as Snell Visitor at Balliol College, Oxford, enabled me to further clarify the outlines of this study and I am grateful to the Master and Fellows for their hospitality.

Some parts of this study go back to papers which I presented at recent conferences. In particular, mention should be made of the conference on 'Antiquity and Modernity' (1984) organized by Wolfgang Schuller at Konstanz University and two conferences on Simmel (1982) and the foundation of sociology in Germany (1984) organized by Otthein Rammstedt and H. Jurgen Dahme at Bielefeld University. I have benefited greatly from discussions with participants at the latter. A further paper on Benjamin's prehistory of modernity was presented to a conference on the

Frankfurt School (1984) organized by the Alexander von Humboldt Foundation.

Finally, I wish to thank Pru Larsen for typing the manuscript and, as usual, offering invaluable stylistic advice.

David Frisby, Glasgow 1985

The author and publisher are grateful to the following for permission to quote previously published material in this book.

Harcourt Brace Jovanovich Inc. for extracts from Walter Benjamin's *Charles Baudelaire* and *One Way Street*.

Routledge and Kegan Paul for extracts from Georg Simmel's *The Philosophy of Money*.

Simon and Schuster Inc. for extracts from Marshall Berman's *All That Is Solid Melts Into Air*.

Suhrkamp Verlag for extracts from Walter Benjamin's work including *Briefe* 2.

Dr Siegfried Unseld and Suhrkamp Verlag for extracts from the work of Siegfried Kracauer.

Verso and New Left Books for extracts from Walter Benjamin's *Charles Baudelaire* and *One Way Street* and Marshall Berman's *All That Is Solid Melts Into Air*.

Introduction

Left to itself . . . life streams on without interruption; its restless rhythm opposes the fixed duration of any particular form. Each cultural form, once it is created, is gnawed at varying rates by the forces of life. As soon as one is fully developed, the next begins to form; after a struggle that may be long or short, it will inevitably succeed its predecessor.

Georg Simmel

. . . as if the present lasts for an eternity.

Siegfried Kracauer, *Georg*

The destructive character sees nothing permanent. But for this very reason he sees ways everywhere. Where others encounter walls or mountains, there too, he sees a way. But because he sees a way everywhere, he has to clear things from it everywhere. Not always by brute force; sometimes by the most refined. Because he sees ways everywhere, he always positions himself at crossroads. No moment can know what the next will bring. What exists he reduces to rubble, not for the sake of the rubble, but for that of the way leading through it.

Walter Benjamin

This study deals in large measure with three writers' approaches to the study of modernity. It is intended as not merely an account of the substantive analysis of modernity in the writings of Georg Simmel (1858–1918), Siegfried Kracauer (1889–1966) and Walter Benjamin (1892–1940) but also a discussion of the methodological problems that arise out of any study of modernity. Hence their diverse analyses of modernity – provisionally understood as the modes of experiencing that which is 'new' in 'modern' society – are intimately connected with diverse methodological presuppositions. What their analyses of modernity have in common is an orientation – often

1

unwittingly – towards that which Baudelaire, as the originator of the modern concept of *modernité*, characterised as 'le transitoire, le fugitif, le contingent'.

The theme of modernity itself has once more moved towards the centre of discussion in social theory and, with the presumed arrival of post-modernity and post-modernist movements, it has become a topic for discussion in the literary and aesthetic realms too. This is evident from the debate surrounding Habermas's interventions into a theory of modernity as well as critical studies by Berman on modernity and by Lyotard on post-modernity, quite apart from the continuing debate on earlier critiques of modernism by Lukács and others in the aesthetic sphere which themselves presuppose a theory of modernity.

Yet such contemporary discussions and debates in these areas are hardly new. Over a century ago, Baudelaire, Marx and Nietzsche, in their different ways, all sought to investigate and adopt a critical stance towards that which is 'new' in 'modern' society and its cultural manifestations. Furthermore, the establishment of sociology as an independent social scientific discipline in the closing decades of the nineteenth century – and the debates which this process generated then and continues to stimulate today – is hardly intelligible without our recognition of its attempts to delineate the new modes of experiencing the social world which modern society had generated.

Unfortunately, the recent rediscovery of the theme of modernity in the 'classical' texts of sociological theory has so far given undue emphasis to the one sociologist who was in many respects a most determined anti-modernist, namely, Max Weber. Although this did not prevent Weber from providing a social theory of modernity that centred around the process of rationalization and its consequences for the individual – especially, according to Habermas, the attendant loss of meaning and loss of control – his treatment of modernity hardly does justice to the important changes in experience that capitalism inaugurated. The concentration upon the theme of modernity in Weber's work has meant that its significance in the writings of the other sociologists of his generation such as Ferdinand Tönnies, Emile Durkheim and Georg Simmel has only just commenced.

This study of modernity quite deliberately takes up the work of three writers whose work on modernity commences from a different focal point. It starts out with the social theory of modernity developed by Georg Simmel, perhaps the first sociologist of modernity in the sense which Baudelaire had originally given it. The main outlines of Simmel's theory of modernity were already elaborated in his *Philosophy of Money* (1900),[1] several years before Weber commenced his reflections upon modernity.

In the case of Siegfried Kracauer, for whom Simmel originally opened 'the gateway to reality', we have an instance of a writer whose early work seems to take up a theme in his analysis of modernity that derives directly from Weber, namely the domination of instrumental reason and the consequences of the process of rationalization. However, a closer examination suggests that Kracauer's discussion of a restricted form of intellectual reasoning (*ratio*) can just as easily be derived from a close reading of Simmel's *Philosophy of Money* – and Kracauer wrote extensively upon Simmel – and from the elaboration of some central themes in Lukács's *History and Class Consciousness* (where, of course, Weber's mediating influence should not be underestimated). Further, Kracauer's early quasi-existentialist position bears testimony to the works of Kierkegaard, whose writings were in vogue in Germany in the years immediately after the First World War. Finally, it is clear that, at the substantive level, Kracauer was concerned from the mid-1920s onwards with the capitalist process of rationalization in Germany that was under way after the instigation of the Dawes Plan in 1924 and which was accelerated with the deepening capitalist crisis in the later Weimar years. In the light of Kracauer's increasingly Marxist orientation, it was not difficult for him to regard this process of rationalization as ultimately an irrational one, though on grounds that were by no means derived from Weber's standpoint.

Whereas Benjamin's early work displays an often quite bewildering conjuncture of sources, his attempt to generate a social theory of modernity that is implicitly announced in *One-Way Street* (1928)[2] and continued in what has come to be known as the 'Arcades Project' is certainly one that owes nothing to Weber's theory of modernity, despite the fact that it developed important sociological dimensions. Indeed, in the notes to this project only one sociologist is frequently cited: Georg Simmel. The Arcades Project took its original impetus from Aragon's surrealist vision of the Passage de l'Opéra in his *Le Paysan de Paris*. Benjamin's theory of modernity was to later have its source in the prehistory of modernity, one of whose central locations was the Parisian arcades of the earlier part of the nineteenth century. They were to be conceived as the threshold to a primal world of fantasy, illusion and phantasmagorias that expressed the dream world of capitalism.

If it is the case, therefore, that the three attempts at an investigation of the social dimensions of modernity owe little to Weber's analysis of modernity, understood as the delineation of what distinguishes modern western societies from earlier forms of society and from other civilizations, then what is this modernity that they were investigating? In their different ways, Simmel, Kracauer and Benjamin were all concerned with the new modes of the perception and experience of social and historical existence set in train by the upheaval of capitalism. Their central concern was the discontinuous experience of time, space and causality as transitory, fleeting and fortuitous or arbitrary – an experience located in the immediacy of social relations, including our relations with the social and physical environment of the metropolis and our relations with the past.

Such disjunctions, dislocations and disorientations were also taken up in a variety of ways in the literary and artistic movements that even by the late nineteenth century were assembled under the umbrellas of 'the modernist tradition', 'the modern movement' and 'modernism'. One feature which the works of Simmel, Kracauer and Benjamin have in common, at least with regard to their investigations of the social dimensions of modernity, is the expression of a strong aesthetic interest in literary and artistic modernism that reacts upon and informs their visions of modernity.

Simmel wrote frequently upon the literary and artistic movements of his time – upon naturalism and somewhat more indirectly upon the *art nouveau* (*Jugendstil*) movement – and some central figures in art, such as Arnold Böcklin and Rodin, and literature, such as Hauptmann and, more extensively, Stefan George, as well as corresponding with writers such as Paul Ernst and Rilke. More importantly, it is not difficult to see aesthetic movements such as impressionism manifesting themselves in Simmel's own style and mode of presentation. In Kracauer's case, his one novel, *Ginster* that was published anonymously during the Weimar period, was itself hailed as an important modern literary work. A whole range of his contributions to the *Frankfurter Zeitung* and other journals testifies to his critical response to the literary, artistic and, significantly, architectural avant-garde of the period. Of particular note are perhaps his receptions of Kafka, Tretjakov, Döblin, Brecht and, elsewhere, his critical response to the *neue Sachlichkeit* (literally, new objectivity) movement. Above all, Kracauer proved himself to be one of the outstanding film critics of the Weimar period. For Benjamin, too, one must speak not merely of an interest in aesthetic movements such as modernism but also his active participation in their reception. Aside from his early literary criticism and his translations of Baudelaire and Proust, together with his reception of Kafka, Lesskov, Malraux and many others, his reception of surrealism and the extensive discussion of Brecht's dramatic and political programme bear directly and indirectly upon his own construction of a social theory of modernity. Above all, however, the centrality of Baudelaire's work for the Arcades Project testifies to a crucial source of his insights into the world of modernity in the nineteenth century. All this is quite apart from both Kracauer and Benjamin's interest and participation in new mass media such as film and radio.

Not surprisingly, therefore, the search for a social theory of modernity is fused with that of a concern for the aims and sometimes techniques of modernism in all three writers. Indeed, none of them can be reduced to the simple category of social theorists of modernity and least of all can they be readily incorporated into a single profession such as sociology. Nonetheless, it is their contributions to a social theory of modernity that is at issue here. And of the three writers, Simmel's inclusion requires least justification. If Simmel's contribution to a theory of modernity has, until recently, largely been neglected, then that of Kracauer has – along with his other contributions to social theory – been almost totally ignored. It is not merely that Kracauer's contribution to critical theory has been overshadowed by that of other members of the Frankfurt School circle but that some of its members – notably Adorno – seriously undervalued it. This is especially unfortunate since, if the metropolis is one of the key sites for the changing modes of experiencing modernity, then Kracauer must be judged to be one of its most sensitive excavators, both in relation to the deciphering of the significance of social space and in relation to the varied configurations of its inhabitants. In particular, and as a kind of critical cultural materialist, Kracauer analysed the culture of modernity in its extremes in the vanguard city of Berlin in Weimar Germany. His ability to decipher the signifiers of social space was matched only by that of Benjamin whose social analysis of modernity focused upon the ambitious attempt to reconstruct the prehistory of modernity in the capital of the nineteenth century: Paris. Despite the fact that Benjamin's projected investigation of modernity is incomplete, it remains one of the most original interventions into this area. For this reason, his project must, like that of Simmel and Kracauer, be reconstructed.

What is distinctive about the three authors' investigations of modernity, and the specific nature of modern life experience, is that they do not commence from an analysis of society as a whole or from a structural or institutional analysis. In this respect, their analyses have little in common with theories of modernization that have become commonplace in sociology in the twentieth century. Nor, as in the case of social theories of modernism in the literary and artistic sphere, do they have much in common with those theorists such as Lukács who start out from the primacy of the totality of modern society. Rather, all three authors start out from the apparent fragments of social reality. Indeed, this they share with the modernist movement itself.

In turn, this implies that they confront interesting methodological problems that derive, in part, from the object of study itself. If one starts out from Baudelaire's notion of modernity as the fleeting, the transitory and the arbitrary, then there can be no fixed, secure object of study in the accepted sense. The object of study is thus determined not merely by a particular mode of viewing modern life but by the new mode of experiencing a new social reality itself.

In Simmel's case, for instance, the starting point of his analysis of modernity is not the social totality. Rather, it commences with 'the fortuitous fragments of reality'. In other words, the key to the contemporary analysis of modernity does not lie in the direction of an investigation of the social system or even its institutions, but in 'the invisible threads' of social reality, in diverse 'momentary images' or 'snapshots' (*Momentbilder*) of modern social life that are to be viewed *sub specie aeternitatis*. Yet such a mode of procedure does not necessarily exclude access to the social totality. In the preface to his important work, *The Philosophy of Money* (1900) – which is one of the major sources for his theory of modernity – Simmel states quite explicitly that 'the unity of these investigations lies . . . in the possibility . . . of finding in each of life's details the totality of its meaning'.[3]

In Kracauer's essay 'The Mass Ornament' a similar starting point for his analysis can be discerned. There he states that 'the place which an epoch occupies in the historical process is determined more forcefully in the analysis of its insignificant superficial manifestations than from the judgment of the epoch upon itself'.[4] Yet these 'insignificant superficial manifestations' are not to be understood as typical forms of expression of social reality. They play a very different role than is the case in an orthodox empirical analysis of social reality. In the preface to his fascinating study, *White Collar Workers* (*Die Angestellten* – 1930), Kracauer insists that 'quotations, conversations and observations on the spot form the rudiment of the study. They are not to be taken to be instances of this or that theory but as

exemplary instances of reality.[5] Kracauer's analysis of modernity is
to be found not merely in this study but also in his early unpublished
study, *The Detective Novel* (1922–5) and his later 'societal biography'
of Jacques Offenbach (which he was working upon at the same time
as Benjamin was engaged upon his Arcades Project) which Kracauer
published in 1937.[6] Above all, his analysis of modernity is to be found
in a richly diverse collection of shorter texts (of which 'The Mass
Ornament' is one) that he published largely in the *Frankfurter Zeitung*
during the Weimar period.

Although Walter Benjamin is the only one of these three authors
who quite explicitly goes in search of a theory of modernity, his whole
project remains to be reconstructed. Work on this theme commenced
in the late 1920s and is evident in his *One-Way Street* (1928), the 'first
of Benjamin's writings in the context of his planned prehistory of
modernity' (Adorno).[7] This whole cycle of work, usually referred to
as the 'Arcades Project', remained incomplete and almost totally
unpublished at his death in 1940. A small part of that work on
Baudelaire has been assembled in English in *Charles Baudelaire:
A Lyric Poet in the Era of High Capitalism.*[8] Benjamin's 'prehistory of
modernity' – itself no orthodox 'historical' project – was to be captured
in 'dialectical images' of modernity. It too was to take fragments as
its starting point from 'Paris – Capital of the Nineteenth Century'.
Indeed, the Arcades Project as a whole has been viewed as merely
a collection of fragments, as a complex montage, to such an extent
that Adorno could declare that 'the whole . . . is hardly capable of
being reconstructed'.[9]

Whilst one may challenge Adorno's judgement on the Arcades
Project, it does remain true that the social theories of modernity need
to be reconstructed not merely in Benjamin's work but also in that
of Simmel and Kracauer. Nonetheless, their work is replete with social
analyses of modernity. Benjamin's focus of attention in the Arcades
Project lay in mid-nineteenth century Paris, Simmel's in what one
may term a sociology of modes of experiencing modernity around
the turn of the century in Berlin, and Kracauer's with Weimar
Germany, and especially with 'the newest Germany' (*Die Angestellten*)
in the Berlin of the 1920s and early 1930s (by then for many people
in Europe *the* city of modernity just as, for Benjamin, Paris was '*the*
city of modernity' a century earlier). Sometimes, their analysis extended
beyond these spatial and temporal locations. Benjamin, for instance,
hoped to extend his analysis of modernity down to the turn of the century
in an attempt to show both 'how far *Jugendstil* [art nouveau] appears

already formed in Baudelaire's concept of the new' and to what extent 'Nietzsche's Will to Power (the eternal return)' is prefigured in Baudelaire's 'idée fixe of the new and the ever-same'. The relevance of Kracauer's 'societal biography' of Jacques Offenbach, 'a phantasmagoria of the Second Empire', lay not merely in the fact that this society was 'the immediate predecessor' of modern society but also that the 'motifs in the most diverse spheres' of that earlier society 'still continue to assert themselves today'.

Thematically, Kracauer's Offenbach study – though not his most successful social analysis – is intimately connected with Benjamin's investigation of the Second Empire. In Simmel's case, the connections are indirect. Simmel shared many of the aims of the *Jugendstil* movement at the turn of the century and was deeply indebted to Nietzsche. Indeed, it is at least plausible to inquire how far his sociology of modernity seeks to show how 'the new' is, in fact, 'the ever-same', especially since at least one of his students discerned that 'Simmel dealt with problems *sub specie aeternitatis* while feigning to deal with them *sub specie momenti*' (Arthur Salz).[10]

At the biographical level, the relationship between the three writers suggests that our choice is not an arbitrary one. Simmel attracted as students many who were later to become some of the most original critical social theorists, such as Georg Lukács and Ernst Bloch. He also attracted the young Kracauer who, at one point, considered writing his doctoral dissertation under Simmel. Although this did not take place, Kracauer has left us with one of the most sensitive but critical appreciations of Simmel's social theory by any of his students.[11] Kracauer's own analysis of modernity owes not a little to Simmel. In Weimar Germany, Kracauer himself had an extensive network of connections with the younger generation of critical social theorists. Aside from his close friendship with the young Adorno and his sometimes uneasy but productive relationship with Bloch, Kracauer was on relatively close terms with Benjamin. As an increasingly prominent reviewer in the *Frankfurter Zeitung* in the late 1920s, Kracauer was responsible for placing a number of Benjamin's short pieces in the newspaper as well as producing one of the most illuminating reviews of Benjamin's *One-Way Street*. For his part, Benjamin was impressed by Kracauer's critical pieces in the *Frankfurter Zeitung* and especially by *Die Angestellten*, which he reviewed twice. Sometimes, as when Benjamin was working on the *exposé* for his Arcades Project during his Paris exile, relations became somewhat strained. However, what they did share in this period of exile was an uneasy and unsatisfactory relationship to the *Institut für Sozialforschung* (Institute for Social Research) or, as Kracauer termed it (according to Bloch), the *Institut für Sozialfälschung* (Institute for Social Falsification).

Benjamin's contact with the work of Simmel is also worthy of note. Although Scholem confirms that Benjamin was already acquainted with Simmel's work prior to the First World War and that in 1920 he hoped to apply for admission to 'Troeltsch's seminar on Simmel's philosophy of history' (though only as a means of using the library!),[12] evidence of Simmel's influence on Benjamin's early work is difficult to find. One important location is *The Origins of German Tragedy*, where Benjamin secured the vital concept of 'origin' from Simmel's study, *Goethe*.[13] A much later reference occurs in the first draft of his essay on Baudelaire 'The Paris of the Second Empire in Baudelaire'. Adorno, in his highly critical remarks on this first draft, criticized the use of Simmel's writings.[14] It is apparent from Benjamin's reply that he disagreed with Adorno's 'askance view of Simmel' and that he had found his reading of *The Philosophy of Money* highly stimulating.[15] Indeed, as we can now see from the recently published notes on the Arcades Project,[16] there is one sociologist whose work is cited, often critically, on many occasions – that of Georg Simmel. Interestingly, in the light of the construction of a social theory of modernity, there is not a single reference to the work of Max Weber.

Aside from these methodological, thematic, biographical and textual connections between Simmel, Kracauer and Benjamin, there is something which unites all three authors. In their various ways, they were all outsiders, strangers in their own society. Simmel's role as a 'stranger in the academy'[17] (Coser) and his preoccupation with various forms of distance, including social distance, has often been remarked upon. Kracauer's early personal reserve – perhaps the result of a very bad stutter – and his sense of a deep estrangement is captured in his highly autobiographical novel, *Ginster*. Both Kracauer and Benjamin, despite their personal contact with Adorno, remained very much on the margins of the Frankfurt Institute in its exile years and, in Kracauer's case, even in the US exile and the post-war phases too. Benjamin's marginality is manifested with regard to his relations to the academy – witness his rejected Habilitation thesis and the hostility of those such as Horkheimer to its possible resubmission in Frankfurt – and in his extensive publications outside the 'academic' sphere. This characteristic he shares with Simmel. But more than Simmel or Kracauer (who also experienced real hardship in the Paris exile years), Benjamin's later life appears as a constant struggle for the existence minimum. All three, as outsiders, could experience modernity in a critical manner, they could all view their society as strangers.

1

Modernité

I am not astounded that Megalopolis which the Arkadians founded
in all eagerness, and for which Greece had the highest hopes,
should have lost its beauty and ancient prosperity, or that most
of it should be ruins nowadays, because I know that the daemonic
powers love to turn things continually upside down, and I know
that fortune alters everything, strong and weak, things at their
beginning and things at their ending, and drives everything with
a strong necessity and according to her whim. Mycenae which led
the Greeks in the Trojan War, and Nineveh, seat of the Assyrian
Kingdom are deserted and demolished . . . The sanctuary of Bel
survives at Babylon, but of that Babylon which was the greatest city
the sun saw in its time, nothing was left except a fortress wall, like
the one at Tiryns in the Argolid. The daemonic power annihilated
all these, and Alexander's city in Egypt and Selenkos's city on the
Orontes were built yesterday and the day before, and have risen to
such greatness and such prosperity because Fortune is favouring
them . . . This is how temporary and completely insecure human things
are . . .

Pausanias *Guide to Greece*
(Second Century AD)

l'évolution social prend la form d'une *désagrégation spontanée*.

Ferdinand Tönnies

One thing distinguishes modernity from all that is past and gives
it its particular character: knowledge of the eternal becoming
and disappearance of all things in ceaseless flight and insight
into the connectedness of all things, into the dependency of
each thing upon every other in the unending chain of what
exists.

Hermann Bahr

I

The social theorist who goes in search of a theory of modernity is soon confronted with a paradoxical situation. Social and political theory abounds with attempts to grasp that which is 'new' in 'modern' society. There is no lack of theories of modernization and the process of modernization, many of which take as their starting point the very 'modern' society within which they themselves are located. In particular, sociology now abounds with theories of modernization that refer in large part to the transformation of political, economic and social systems or sub-systems. Sometimes, as Habermas has pointed out with respect to recent neo-conservative social theories of Daniel Bell and others, they are combined with a denunciation of the culture of modernity in order to assert the existence of post-modernity, post-industrialism, post-capitalism.[1] Such theorists betray a desire 'to get rid of the uncompleted project of modernism, that of the Enlightenment'. Lyotard suggests that, for its part, Habermas's critique of modernity rests upon the view that

> if modernity has failed, it is in allowing the totality of life to be splintered into independent specialities which are left to the narrow competence of experts, while the concrete individual experiences 'desublimated meaning' and 'destructured form', not as a liberation but in the mode of that immense *ennui* which Baudelaire described over a century ago.[2]

This is argued by Lyotard in the context of answering what exactly is '*le postmoderne*'. The literary and artistic context within which the question is posed in turn suggests that Lyotard has already fused modernity with modernism in the aesthetic sphere. His answer is that post-modernism 'is not modernism at its end but in the nascent state, and this state is constant',[3] whilst '*post modern* would have to be understood according to the paradox of the future (*post*) anterior (*modo*)'.[4] The implication of Lyotard's argument is that modernism has *not* been superseded. But perhaps a virtue of Lyotard's discussion is that, unlike much aesthetic discourse on modernism, it is not confined to the attention of those who deal solely with art and culture.

The problem faced by a social theory of modernity in this context is that modernity itself becomes subsumed either under modernization or modernism or it disappears altogether as an object of investigation.

The splintered and thereby precarious concept of modernity must itself be reconstructed out of its earlier conceptualizations. It would be possible to commence with that academic discipline which, in the late nineteenth and early twentieth centuries, during its struggle to assert itself as an independent discipline often took as its object of study that of which it was a product – modernity. Certainly, the sociology of this period does confront the problem of distilling what is new, what is modern in modern society. Most often, it performed this task by juxtaposing what is new with its opposite. Such a reading of sociology in this period would provide us with Tönnies's contrast between *Gemeinschaft* and *Gesellschaft*, Durkheim's opposition of societies based upon mechanical and organic solidarity, Simmel's less pronounced contrast between a society with a non-money economy and a developed (capitalist) money economy and Weber's contrast between all previous 'traditional' societies and those based upon modern western rationalism (modern western capitalism).

With pessimistic hindsight, it has been fashionable in much modern sociological discourse to read all these polarities as if they were grounded in a philosophy of history thesis as to the inevitable transition from one to the other in such a way that the source of their dynamic – be it functional differentiation, rationalization, etc. – not merely produced only negative consequences but obscured the complexities of the 'present' societies and any counterveiling tendencies operating within them. Yet, to take but one example, and perhaps the least understood, Tönnies emphasized time and time again not merely that features of *Gemeinschaft* and *Gesellschaft* exist side by side in contemporary society but – and this is a crucial thesis of modernity theories – that *Gesellschaft* 'is only a transitional and superficial phenomenon' which one goes into 'as into a *strange* country'.[5] Any reading of such social theories which took the modern society they delineate as being a fixed end state (development or 'progress' only existing up to the present) would fail to see the emphasis upon the transitory nature of the 'new', sometimes even the recognition that the 'new' was already doomed.

Thus, it is important to remember that this transitory nature of the new in notions of modernity was associated with crucial changes in time consciousness – and especially a challenge to the notion of unilinear progress – in such a way that the study of modernity could become 'a reconnaissance into an unknown realm, that carries with it the risk of sudden, shocking confrontations' (Habermas).[6] One possible implication was to see society and social relations in a state of flux, in motion, in ceaseless movement.

Although this view of society took many varied forms in the course of the second half of the nineteenth century and became a central feature of 'modernist' artistic and literary movements in the twentieth century, it is clearly not possible to outline all these developments here. Instead, the treatment of some of the key dimensions of modernity will be extracted from the works of three writers, all of whom play an important role in the subsequent delineations of modernity in the writings of Benjamin and to a lesser extent those of Simmel and, more marginally, Kracauer.

In Benjamin's projected 'prehistory of modernity' that was to focus upon 'Paris – Capital of the Nineteenth Century', one figure came to dominate his study, that of Charles Baudelaire. His work provided Benjamin with a 'fresco of modernity'. Yet Baudelaire is significant in the much more specific sense that he gave the concept of *modernité* its modern meaning in his essay 'The Painter of Modern Life' (written 1859–60 and first published in 1863). Its focus lay in the newness of the present, indeed even to the extent of identifying modernity as that which is new. A second contemporary figure who may be described as a hidden analyst of modernity is, of course, Marx, for whom modernity is a historical phenomenon. Marx's analysis of the dialectics of a society based upon commodity production not merely sought to grasp what was new about capitalist society but, in searching for the dynamics of that social formation, came to recognize it as historically transitory. In the later decades of the nineteenth century, another writer engaged in what can only be described as a radical critique of modernity in which modern society was viewed as decadent. Modernity, for Nietzsche, came to be 'the eternal recurrence of the ever-same'. Even this cursory glance at these three writers provides us with conceptions of modernity as the new, the historical (and transitory) and the ever-same. It is to their contributions to the delineation of the elusive concept of modernity that we now turn.

II

La modernité, c'est le transitoire, le fugitif, le contingent, la moitié, de l'art, dont l'autre moitié est l'éternel et l'immuable.

Charles Baudelaire

The true painter, will be the man who extracts from present day life its epic aspects and teaches us in lines and colours to understand how great and poetic we are in our patent-leather shoes and our neckties.

May the real pioneers next year give us the exquisite pleasure of being allowed to celebrate the advent of the truly *new*.

Charles Baudelaire

'No matter what party one may belong to', wrote Baudelaire in 1851, 'it is impossible not to be gripped by the spectacle of this sickly population which swallows the dust of the factories, breathes in particles of cotton, and lets its tissues be permeated by white lead, mercury and all the poisons needed for the production of masterpieces . . .; of this languishing and pining population to whom *the earth owes its wonders*; who feel *a purple and impetuous blood coursing through their veins*, and who cast a long, sorrow laden look at the sunlight and shadows of the great parks.' This population is the background against which the outline of the hero stands out. Baudelaire captioned the picture thus presented in his own way. He wrote the words *la modernité* under it.

Walter Benjamin

When Baudelaire introduced the concept of *modernité* in his 'The Painter of Modern Life',[7] he confessed to the reader: 'I know of no better word to express the idea I have in mind.' He viewed modernity as both a 'quality' of modern life as well as a new object of artistic endeavour. For the painter of modern life, this quality is associated with the notion of newness, with *nouveauté*. Its significance 'as a conscious aim of artistic production' is emphasized by Benjamin:

In Baudelaire's work, the concern is not with the attempt, common to all the arts, to call into life new forms or to gain access to a new side of things but with *the fundamentally new object whose force lies solely in the fact that it is new*, regardless of how repulsive and wretched it may be. [My emphasis.][8]

This proposed aim of modern painting – which Baudelaire detected in the work of Constantin Guys and elsewhere in Goya and Daumier – coincides with Baudelaire's own artistic intention. However, this should not lead us to assume that even in 'The Painter of Modern Life' or elsewhere in Baudelaire's writings there exists a theoretical 'analysis' of modernity. As Oehler remarks with reference to Baudelaire's earlier writings:

In the search for his conception of modernity, specific guiding images remain before him, but he is not in a position . . . to anticipate theoretically his own advance beyond these preconceptions. This further step is only indicated by scenes and sketches that Baudelaire continually adds to his argument either without comment or even in a misleading manner.[9]

Some of these guiding images are to be found, of course, in Baudelaire's poetry too and are the subject of Benjamin's analysis almost a century later.

At the heart of Baudelaire's 'phenomenology of modernity' there lies the newness of the present. Baudelaire says: 'the pleasure which we derive from the representation of the present is due not only to the beauty with which it can be invested, but also to its essential quality of being present.'[10] But this presentness is of a transitory nature and this feature gives to modernity its distinctive character since 'by modernity I mean the ephemeral, the fugitive, the contingent, the half of art whose other half is the eternal and the immutable'.[11] Indeed, beauty itself is not merely 'made up of an eternal, invariable element' but also 'a relative, circumstantial element, which will be . . . the age, its fashions, its morals, its emotions'.[12] Nonetheless, as Jauss has argued, this aesthetics of the absolutely new was not merely a later variant of the ancient antithesis of the temporal and the eternal:

> Just as the transitory, momentary and contingent can only be one half of art that requires of its other half the constant, timeless and universal, so also the historical consciousness of modernité presupposes the eternal as its antithesis . . . timeless beauty is nothing other than the idea of beauty in the status of past experience, an idea created by human beings themselves and continuously abandoned.[13]

Baudelaire's conception of modernity and the tasks set for the modern artist 'liberate the poetic precisely in the fashionable and historical dimensions which classical taste left out of its account of the beautiful'.[14]

Yet this very task which Baudelaire set the painter of modern life, namely to capture 'the ephemeral, contingent newness of the present' poses a particular problem of method since 'in trivial life, in the daily metamorphosis of external things, there is a rapid movement which calls for an equal speed of execution from the artist'. It requires a special skill, even a new kind of artistic function: 'Observer, philosopher, *flâneur* – call him what you will; but . . . you will certainly be led to bestow upon him some adjective which you could not apply to the painter of eternal, or at least more lasting things' since 'he is *the painter of the passing moment and of all the suggestions of eternity that it contains* [my emphasis].'[15]

This prompts us to ask what distinctive experiences the painter of modern life can call upon, what is his social milieu? As 'a passionate lover of crowds and incognitos' and as a 'man of the world', he resembles Poe's 'Man of the Crowd' who, convalescing from a recent illness, seeks to remember everything in the midst of the urban throng and for whom 'curiosity has become a fatal, irresistible passion'.[16] The capacity for capturing *la nouveauté* resembles this post-illness ability to see everything anew. In like manner, it has affinities with the experience of childhood since 'convalescence is like a return towards childhood. The convalescent, like the child, is possessed in the highest degree of the faculty of keenly interesting himself in things, be they apparently of the most trivial . . . The child sees everything in a state of newness; he is always *drunk.*' In this respect, then, 'genius is nothing more nor less than *childhood recovered* at will – a childhood now equipped for self-expression with manhood's capacities and a power of analysis which enables it to order the mass of raw material which it has involuntarily accumulated.'[17]

Armed with the naive gaze of childhood and the obsession with form of adulthood, the artist of modern life goes in search of its fleeting beauty. Where does he look to? Baudelaire's answer is unequivocal:

> The crowd is his element . . . His passion and his profession are to become one flesh with the crowd. For the perfect *flâneur*, for the passionate spectator, it is an immense joy to set up house in the heart of the multitude, amid the ebb and flow of movement, in the midst of the fugitive and the infinite. To be away from home and yet to feel oneself everywhere at home; to see the world, to be at the centre of the world, and yet to remain hidden from the world . . . The spectator is a *prince* who everywhere rejoices in his incognito.[18]

Entry into the crowd is as though entering 'a magical society of dreams' or 'as though it were an immense reservoir of electrical energy'. The artist himself is like 'a mirror as vast as the crowd itself' or 'a kaleidoscope gifted with consciousness' that reproduces 'the multiplicity of life and the flickering grace of all the elements of life . . . at every instant rendering and explaining it in pictures more living than life itself, which is always unstable and fugitive'.[19]

But despite the transitoriness of the crowd, the artist of modern life seeks out its eternal beauty while not neglecting its slightest and newest modification. On the one hand, 'if a fashion or the cut of a garment has been slightly modified . . . his eagle eye will have already spotted it from however great a distance'. Yet on the other hand, the artist of modern life 'marvels at the eternal beauty and the amazing harmony of life in the capital cities, a harmony so providentially maintained amid the turmoil of human freedom. He gazes upon the landscapes of the great city – landscapes of stone, caressed by the mist or buffeted by the sun.' The resulting 'phantasmagoria' of modern life that has been distilled from nature results from 'a perceptiveness acute and magical by reason of its innocence'.[20]

Yet this very perceptiveness suggests that the painter of modern life is not merely a *flâneur* since he 'has an aim loftier than that of a mere *flâneur*', namely the systematic search for modernity. His task is that of 'seeking out and expounding the beauty of *modernity*'. The artist must grasp 'this transitory, fugitive element, whose metamorphoses are so rapid'. Only the artist of modern life can release this beauty from its most trivial externalities since, 'for most of us . . . for whom nature has no existence save by reference to utility, the fantastic reality of life has become singularly diluted'.[21] The artist, on the other hand, concerned with 'the *outward show of life*, such as it is to be seen in the capitals of the civilised world', is able 'to express at once the attitude and the gesture of human beings . . . and their luminous *explosion* in space'.[22]

Where, then, is this elusive modernity located, if not merely in 'the landscapes of the great city', with their threatening crowds and 'pomps and circumstances'? Baudelaire chose to emphasize its location in the fleeting beauty of *fashion*, 'a symptom of the taste for the ideal which floats on the surface of all the crude, terrestrial and loathsome bric-a-brac that the natural life accumulates in the human brain', 'an ideal for which the restless human mind feels a constant, titillating hunger'.[23] In fact, fashions retain 'the moral and aesthetic feeling of their time'. Again, the artist's task is 'to extract from fashion whatever element it may contain of poetry within history, *to distil the eternal from the transitory* [my emphasis]'.[24] And here we may concur with Oehler that fashion is not merely a feature of modernity for Baudelaire; rather, 'for him fashion is the salt of modernity'.[25] It is also the starting point for his aesthetics since

> it contains a dual attraction. It embodies the poetic in the historical, the eternal in the transitional; in it there arises beauty not as a permanent trustworthy ideal but as the notion that the human being

himself makes of beauty, in which he betrays the morality and aesthetics of his epoch and which, like the latter, permits him to be what he wishes.[26]

The centrality of fashion which we ourselves create and within which 'the eternal part of beauty will be veiled' challenges the timeless notion of beauty and renders it historical. Now the eternal lies in the transitory, in the temporal, 'for almost all our originality comes from the seal which Time imprints on our sensations'.[27]

In turn, the total devotion to fashion is to be found in a fast disappearing social type, the dandy who, 'even if blasé, has no other occupation than the perpetual pursuit of happiness'. In possession of time and money in quantity, 'these beings have no other calling but to cultivate the idea of beauty in their persons'. As 'a kind of cult of the self' dandyism is also 'a kind of religion'. It flowers, says Baudelaire, in periods of transition from aristocracy to democracy. It is 'the last spark of heroism amid decadence', 'a sunset; like the declining daystar, it is glorious, without heat and full of melancholy'.[28] Dandies are, as Lefebvre remarks, 'spontaneous (as opposed to professional) artists'.[29] Baudelaire saw dandyism as the last heroic stand against bourgeois *ennuï*. He did not live to see its resurgence in the aestheticism and decadence of the fin de siècle. The artistic production of this second phase constituted, for Benjamin, the second moment of modernity, the analysis of which he was unable to complete.

Baudelaire's essay on the painter of modern life gives little indication of the dark side of modernity that is already indicated in the title of his most famous series of poems *Les Fleur du Mal*. It is there, in *Spleen* and other writings, that the images 'pregnant with dreams and evocations' of 'the savagery that lurks in the midst of civilisation' are to be found. There, too, is to be found a historical dimension of Baudelaire's work, one that – as Oehler and Sahlberg have shown – is more political than even Benjamin's interpretation would suggest.[30] Baudelaire's poetic filtering of the 'harsh refuse of modernity' (Oehler) and his capacity for 'extracting *beauty* from evil' possess an important aesthetic function: 'The negative beautiful dimensions of modern reality are the *materia prima* of the utopian art propagated by Baudelaire, a necessary transitional stage on the way to the absolutely new.' But as Oehler goes on to indicate, this aesthetic aim is also a critical one, especially in his work up to and around the Revolution of 1848: 'The essence of modern aesthetics, that Baudelaire sketched out on the eve of the 1848 Revolution, consists however no longer merely in a romantic adherence to negativity; it is a dialectical transcendence and supercession by means of two "fundamental literary qualities: surnaturalism and irony", of that bourgeois newness which was soon to bore everyone.'[31]

Having liberated modern aesthetics from its mesmerism with a timeless past, Baudelaire did not intend that the presentation of modernity would replace it with the aesthetics of a timeless present. Indeed, he intended the aesthetic representation of the 'modern' world, often as its opposite, one that would reveal the 'harsh refuse of modernity', 'the savagery that lurks in the midst of civilisation' and its 'living monstrosities'.[32] Such a view of modernity was to commend itself subsequently to Benjamin, for whom there was no object of civilization that was not, at the same time, the product of barbarism.[33]

Baudelaire's introduction of the concept of *modernité* and his presentation of its temporal, spatial and causal (reduced to the fortuitous) dimensions, however unsystematic, proved to be central to both the future debate on modernism (and the modern hero) and, especially in Benjamin's work, the attempt to generate a social theory of modernity. The location of *modernité* in various modes of experiencing modern metropolitan life and the problem of its artistic representation unwittingly created problems for those social theorists who wished to examine the fleeting, transitory and the fortuitous in modern social life. The dialectic of the transitory and the eternal, already present in Baudelaire's aesthetics, was transposed by the social theorist of modernity into dimensions of social life itself.

III

The reform of consciousness consists entirely in making the world aware of its own consciousness, in arousing it from its dream of itself, in explaining its own actions to it.

                                        Karl Marx, *Early Writings*

Constant revolutionising of production, uninterrupted disturbance of all social relations, everlasting uncertainty and agitation distinguish the bourgeois epoch from all earlier ones. All fixed, fast-frozen relationships, with their train of venerable ideas and opinions, are swept away, all new-formed ones become obsolete before they can ossify. All that is solid melts into air, all that is holy is profaned and men

at last are forced to face with sober senses the real conditions of their
lives and their relations with their fellow men.

Karl Marx, *Communist Manifesto*

Value . . . does not have its description branded on its forehead.
Rather, it transforms every product of labour into a social hieroglyphic.
Later on, human beings try to decipher the hieroglyphic, to get behind
the secret of their own social product, for the determination of useful
objects as values is as much their social product as is their language.

Karl Marx, *Capital*

Baudelaire was not alone in sensing the transformation of modern
experience into the temporally fleeting and the spatially transitory
and the concomitant appearance of events as arbitrary and fortuitous.
Berman has argued that we should give due recognition to Marx as
'the first and greatest of modernists'[34] and not merely see him as a
major contributor to theories of modernization. Berman maintains
that crucial aspects of modernity and critical reflection upon them
are contained in Marx's work. How far is this the case?

Certainly there is evidence of an analysis of the internal dynamic
of modernity in Marx's account of the 'unleashing' of productive
forces, production relations and social relations in general. In the
Communist Manifesto (1848)[35] – 'the archetype of a century of
modernist manifestos and movements to come' (Berman)[36] – Marx
radically characterizes the 'new' historical configuration of capitalism
as one in which 'constant revolutionising of production, uninterrupted
disturbance of all social relations, everlasting uncertainty and agitation
distinguish the bourgeois epoch from all earlier ones'. Marx concludes
that this permanent sweeping away of all earlier fixed relationships
and the rapid disappearance of all newly formed ones leads to a
situation in which human beings for the very first time can confront
'the real conditions of their lives and their relations with their fellow
beings'. Berman poses an opposite possibility, namely that
'"uninterrupted disturbance, everlasting uncertainty and agitation",
instead of subverting this society, actually serves to strengthen it'.[37]

Certainly this vision of a '*révolution en permanence*' (Proudhon) is an
impossible one for those who seek to dominate such a society. Any
society which requires for its dynamic the revolutionizing of production
as a permanent (or even periodic) process requires at the same time
the stabilization of some social relations that are necessary for this
mode of production. Alongside a need for the permanent adaptability
of individual personalities (secured not merely by virtue of work

discipline), there is a corresponding necessity to maintain crucial relationships between capital and labour. In other words, not everything is allowed to be swept away and, as we shall see, not all illusions are permanently dissolved.

Confronted with this revolutionizing of 'the instruments of production, and thereby the relations of production, and with them the whole relations of society',[38] what is the role of those sciences devoted to the study of society? One possibility is to go in search of the 'laws of motion' of this society that is in permanent flux. Marx's option, to uncover the dynamic of capitalist society and apply that knowledge to that society within 'the vanguard of movement' with the aim of its transformation, was not the only one available. To take but one contemporary example, Lorenz von Stein could assert, in the light of the complex of movements in modern society, that 'the life of European society is such an infinitely multifarious, restless to and fro', whose movements themselves were caught 'in the threads that lead through the labyrinth of movement' in such a way that 'most see nothing of the motions of things and the law of this life'. One of the ways out of this 'labyrinth of movement' lay for Stein in a 'System of Statistics', 'whose foundation is the fact of moving energy'.[39] The subsequent history of the social sciences suggests that another option lay in seeking out the sources of stabilization and integration in modern society.

Even Marx's search for the 'laws of motion' of capitalist society proved more difficult than his early work suggested. Whereas in 1848 Marx could assert that the fundamental relations in bourgeois society had been rid of their 'religious and political illusions', or that 'the bourgeoisie has stripped of its halo every occupation hitherto honoured and looked upon with reverent awe' and has 'torn away' the 'sentimental veil' from the family, he was much less certain two decades later that social relations had been stripped of their illusions. Rather than people being 'forced to face with sober senses' their real conditions and social relations, the latter appeared only in their fetishized form. The task of a critical social science – in contrast to a 'vulgar economy' that merely reproduced the ways in which relations 'appear' to its participants – lay in a confrontation with the 'secret' of 'the fetishism of the commodity' and its 'mysterious character' in order to 'decipher the hieroglyphic' of the commodity form. As Benjamin was later to recognize in his 'prehistory of modernity', the commodity form not merely symbolizes social relations of modernity, it is a central source of their origin. The 'phantasmagoria' of the world of commodities is precisely a world in motion, in flux, in which all values are transitory and all relations are fleeting and indifferent. In part this was also recognized by Simmel in his analysis of the consequences of the mature money (implicitly capitalist) economy. But though this world of commodities appears to be permanently transitory, it goes together with 'the continuous reproduction of the same relations – the relations which postulate capitalist production'.[40] It thus provides Benjamin with one of his images of modernity as the dialectic of the new and the ever-same.

But before raising some aspects of the theory of commodity fetishism, it should be emphasized that Marx's analysis of the commodity bears directly upon a methodological approach to modernity that takes as its starting point the fragment of social reality. Marx commences his most fully developed analysis of the capitalist system as a whole in *Capital* with an examination of its seemingly most insignificant element – the commodity. As Marx himself acknowledged, 'the understanding of the first chapter . . . will . . . present the greatest difficulties'.[41] Economic investigations, Marx argues, have been more successful at the 'analysis of forms which are much richer in content and more complex' than the value form, in part because 'the complete body is easier to study than its cells'. Yet,

> for bourgeois society, the commodity-form of the product of labour, or the value-form of the commodity is the economic cell-form. To the superficial observer, the analysis of these forms seems to turn upon minutiae. It does in fact deal with minutiae, but so similarly does microscopic anatomy.[42]

By commencing with the 'elementary form' in which 'the wealth of societies in which the capitalist mode of production prevails appears', Marx sought to unravel the 'secret' of the value form. This seemingly insignificant fragment of capitalist production appears to us as something that we might indeed easily overlook: 'A commodity appears at first sight an extremely obvious, trivial thing. But its analysis brings out that it is a very strange thing, abounding in metaphysical subtleties and theological niceties.'[43]

One of the prices to be paid for the phenomenal development of the productive forces under capitalism is that what is actually occurring in capitalist transactions is not merely veiled but appears to us in an inverted form. Whereas in earlier forms of society, the social relations of production are 'much more simple and transparent', under capitalism the products of labour, for instance, are surrounded by 'mystery', by 'magic and necromancy'. Indeed, the 'finished form of the world of commodities – the money form – . . . conceals the social character of private labour and the social relations between the individual workers, by making those relations appear as relations between material objects, instead of revealing them plainly'.[44] Mesmerized, as it were, by the fleeting and arbitrary relations between what is exchanged, it becomes all the more difficult to recognize that 'in the midst of the accidental and ever-fluctuating exchange relations between the products, the labour-time socially necessary to produce them asserts itself as a regulative law of nature'.[45] In other words, that which appears as arbitrary and fleeting hides the ever-same.

Stated differently, 'the mysterious character of the commodity-form' arises from the fact that

> the commodity reflects the social characteristics of men's own labour themselves, as the socio-natural properties of these things . . . As against this, the commodity-form, and the value-relation of the products of labour within which it appears, have absolutely no connection with the physical nature of the commodity and the material [*dinglich*] relations arising out of this. It is nothing but the definite social relation between men themselves which assumes here, for them, the fantastic form of a relation between things.[46]

One implication of the existence of this new 'veil' which envelops social relations within the capitalist mode of production is that their analysis cannot remain confined to 'their form of existence as it appears on the surface, divorced from the hidden connections and the intermediate connecting links'.[47] It cannot remain with the 'banal and complacent notions held by the bourgeois agents of production about their own world'.[48] A critical analysis must investigate 'the real internal framework [*Zusammenhang*]' of these relations.[49]

The starting point of that analysis is the seemingly insignificant cell of the commodity and the commodity form, but not conceived as an entity that is merely to be described in its phenomenal form, as if it were a natural product. The commodity form possesses a historical specificity that is often overlooked, even within classical political economy. Marx maintains that

> The value-form of the product of labour is the most abstract, but also the most universal form of the bourgeois mode of production; by that fact *it stamps the bourgeois mode of production* as *a particular kind of social*

production of a historical and transitory character. If we then make the mistake of treating it as the eternal natural form of social production, we necessarily overlook the specificity of the value-form, and consequently of the commodity form together with its further developments, the money form, the capital form, etc. [My emphasis.] [50]

Thus, whereas we have already seen that Marx's analysis of the commodity locates one dimension of modernity in the continuous appearance of new commodities which hides the reproduction of the same relations of production, Marx here points to the fact that this particular mode of production hides its 'historical and transitory character' in the illusion of 'the eternal natural form of social production'.

Further, the commodity form extends its 'necromancy' throughout bourgeois society, creating 'the riddle of the money fetish' of 'the magic of money', 'the perfect fetish' of 'the consummate automatic fetish' of interest-bearing capital and 'the *most fetishistic* expression of the relations of capitalist production' in 'the form of revenue and the sources of revenue'. The riddles of the hieroglyphics of c – m – c, M – M' and the 'Trinity Formula' of Rent (Land) – Interest (Capital) – Wages (Labour) only 'become visible and dazzling to our eyes' when we reject the standpoint of 'the participants in capitalist production' who 'live in a bewitched world'. [51]

The 'mystery' of the universal equivalent is resolved once money is seen as 'the direct incarnation of all human labour'. By means of money,

Men are henceforth related to each other in their social process of production in a purely atomistic way. Their own relations of production therefore assume a material shape which is independent of their control and their conscious individual action. This situation is manifested first by the fact that the products of men's labour universally take on the form of commodities. The riddle of the money fetish is therefore the riddle of the commodity fetish. [52]

Yet it is not merely the commodity and money which appear in a fetishized form in capitalist society. Capital itself appears in a fetishized form but neither when it is located in the production where 'the relation of the capitalist to the worker is always presupposed and assumed' nor when it appears in the circulation process as merchant capital, where at least profit 'is explained as a result of exchange, that is, as arising from a social relation and not from a thing'. Rather, when capital appears as interest-bearing capital or money capital, it appears as 'capital in its finished form . . . and therefore yields a definite profit in a definite period of time'. Money capital here 'becomes very much obscured, something dark and mysterious'. In other words, when money capital as $M - M'$ hides $M - C - M'$, it becomes 'the consummate *automatic fetish*, the self-expanding value, the money-making money, and in this form it no longer bears any trace of its origin. The social relation is consummated as a relation of things (money, commodities) to themselves,'[53] and 'instead of the real conversion of money into capital, there appears only the empty form of this process'.[54] Marx takes the riddle of 'the perfect fetish' a stage further to the point at which 'capital which yields "compound interest"' becomes 'the complete *objectification, inversion* and *derangement* of capital as interest-bearing capital', 'the incomprehensible form of capital'. Here, 'it appears as a Moloch, demanding the whole world as a sacrifice belonging to it of right, whose legitimate demands, arising from its very nature, are however never met and are always frustrated by a mysterious fate'.[55]

'This bewitched and distorted world' of the capitalist mode of production which creates one 'mystical being' after another, is completed in what Marx terms the 'Trinity Formula': 'Capital-profit (profits of enterprise plus interest), land-ground rent, labour-wages, this trinity form holds in itself all the mysteries of the social production process.'[56] Indeed, it is 'this economic trinity as the connection between the components of value and wealth in general and its sources' which

> completes the mystification of the capitalist mode of production, the reification of social relations, and the immediate coalescence of the material relations of production with their historical and social specificity: the bewitched, distorted and upside-down world haunted by Monsieur le Capital and Madame la Terre, who are at the same time social characters and mere things.[57]

For those 'who feel completely at home precisely with the *alienated form* in which the different parts of value confront one another', including those who inhabit 'the *graveyard* of this science' of political economy, 'the different forms of surplus-value and configurations of capitalist production do not confront one another as alienated forms, but as heterogeneous and independent forms, merely different from one another but not *antagonistic*'.[58] Hence, these 'factors of production' and the different revenues,

> do not stand in any hostile connection to one another because they have no inner connection whatsoever. If they nevertheless work together in production, then it is a harmonious action, an expression of harmony . . . Insofar as there is any contradiction between them, it arises merely from competition as to which of the agents shall get more of the value they have jointly created.[59]

Only the most critical analysis, which accepts that 'all science would be superfluous if the form of appearance of things directly coincided with their essence', is capable of illuminating the 'metamorphoses' of the elements of the capitalist mode of production in order to reveal their 'hidden' 'inner connections'.

When all this is conceded, it becomes clear that Marx himself was not a modernist in the sense of identifying with the experience of modernity that he outlined. When Habermas maintains, for instance, in relation to the project of modernity that 'in the over-evaluation of the transitory, the fleeting and the ephemeral . . . there is expressed just as much the desire for an untarnished, still intact present',[60] then this in no way applies to Marx's account of modernity, which neither expresses this secret desire for present-day society nor hides an 'abstract opposition to the past'. The capitalist society which Marx analysed was, for him, doomed to be transitory. And in so far as European Marxist orientated socialist movements retained this perspective in the late nineteenth century and beyond, they became the 'spectre' that 'haunted' sociology's own analyses of modernity.

Indeed, to the extent that Marx identifies the 'origins' of the experience of modernity in capitalism, his analysis suggests that these 'origins' were themselves almost totally obscured to its participants. If the mystified world of commodity exchange did create the impression of a fleeting, transitory, arbitrary and indifferent constellation of social relationships, the mere experiencing of these relations did not open up the possibility for the realization of the transitory nature of capitalist society as a whole. Rather, as a seemingly eternally self-reproducing natural process, it cast a veil over precisely this transitory dimension at another level. The dialectic of modernity remained hidden by vulgar political economy and remained hidden to the participants in the 'bewitched world' of capitalist relations. The eternal and the natural and the harmonious masked the transitory, the historical and the contradictory.

IV

The madly thoughtless shattering and dismantling of all foundations,
their dissolution into a continual evolving that flows ceaselessly away,
the tireless unspinning and historicising of all there has ever been by
modern man, the great cross-spider at the node of the cosmic web –
all this may concern and dismay moralists, artists, the pious, even
statesmen; *we* shall for once let it cheer us . . .

                              Friedrich Nietzsche, *Untimely Meditations*

ON MODERNITY

What does us credit

If there is anything that does us credit, then it is this: we have located
what is *serious* somewhere else: we take seriously the *meanest* things that
are ignored in all ages and left aside – conversely we provide the
'beautiful feelings' cheaply.

. . . We have discovered the 'smallest world' as the universally decisive
one . . .

. . . we have taken seriously all the *necessities* of existence and *ignore* all
'soulful beauty' as a kind of 'light-heartedness and frivolity'.

That which has hitherto been most ignored is placed above all else.

                              Friedrich Nietzsche, *Nachgelassene Fragmente*

The significance of the notion of the eternal return lies in the fact that
the bourgeoisie no longer dares to look the impending development
of the mode of production which it set in motion in the eye.
Zarathustra's notion of the eternal return and the motto of the cushion
cover, 'Just a short nap', complement one another.

                              Walter Benjamin, *Zentralpark*

Marx was not alone in viewing contemporary society as riddled with
mystification and illusion. From a very different perspective, this was
also the conclusion reached by Friedrich Nietzsche. But Nietzsche's
critique of contemporary society and of modernity – about which he
often quite explicitly spoke – commences from quite other premises,
even though at a formal level there are some remarkable parallels with
Marx's critique. Indeed, to reverse the comparison, there are some
aspects of Marx's analysis of the contemporary situation which, in
the context of the crisis of 1848 and its aftermath, read like Nietzsche's
vision of the crisis which he detected several decades later. Hugo
Fischer,[61] for example, cited a passage from Marx's *Eighteenth*

Brumaire where he sums up 'the peculiar physiognomy of this period' of revolution in France in 1848 as one in which 'if any section of history has been painted grey on grey it is this. Men and events appear . . . as shadows which have become detached from their bodies.'[62] It was a period possessing 'the most variegated mixture of crying contradictions':

> a republic with imperialist trappings, which is nothing but the combined infamy of two monarchies . . .; alliances whose first condition is separation and struggles whose first law is their indecisiveness; wild and empty agitation in the name of tranquillity, the most solemn preaching of tranquillity in the name of revolution; passions without truths, truths without passion; heroes without deeds of heroism, history without events; a course of development apparently only driven forward by the calendar, and made wearisome by the constant repetition of the same tensions and relaxations; antagonisms which seem periodically to press forward to a climax, but become deadened and fall away without having attained their resolution; exertions pretentiously put on show and bourgeois terror at the danger that the world may end, and at the same time the pettiest intrigues and courtly comedies played by the world's saviours.[63]

But whereas for Marx this constituted a rhetorical description of the development of a crisis in a revolutionary situation and whereas for him the 'superficial appearance' of this crisis 'veils the class struggle', for Nietzsche it could describe the permanent present of decadence, the total decadence of modernity with its lack of genuine passions, its false truths, its empty historicism, its eternal recurrence of the ever-same that, at the same time, did not veil or mask anything lying beneath it. Rather, modernity *is* this present, this inversion of all values, this world of masks and illusions.

Modernity as decadence 'announces the permeability of present day life'. Decadence is, Fischer argues, 'the deepest and most apposite characterisation of the provisional character of all arrangements, all world views, all political and social forms of our present time.[64] It is intimately bound up with 'present' reality. Its analysis was Nietzsche's task, the analysis of the 'forms of human decadence' that arise out of the decay of *'organising* force, of "willpower"'. What is left is an empty shell of convention and appearance: 'The phenomenon of modern man has become wholly appearance; he is not visible in what he represents but rather concealed by it.'[65] His analysis of modernity was not merely a description of the forms of decadence in the present but a critique of them. This was sometimes explicitly stated as in *Beyond Good and Evil* where Nietzsche announces that 'this book is . . . in all essentials a critique of modernity' – an aim that could well describe most of his published works as well as his unpublished fragments.

If the starting point of Nietzsche's analysis of modernity lies in his critique of the present, then it does not lie with the science of modern society: sociology. Sociology is itself evidence for 'the unconscious effect of decadence upon the ideals of science'; sociology 'only knows the *decayed-form* of society from experience', and is itself a symptom of the 'herd instinct'.[66] It merely looks upon the destructuration of its own object – society. In fact, '*modern society* is not "society", not a "body", but a sick conglomerate of components'.[67] As an illusory science, sociology investigates 'the illusory world', along with other sciences. If we are to study the modernity of the present then we must seek another approach and another object. Nietzsche replaces sociology with a study of structures of domination and society with the cultural complex, with modern culture as a whole.[68]

This modern culture, with its 'modern ideology', its false spokesmen for 'modern ideas', is characterized through and through by its decadence, by the disintegration of all genuine values. In their place stand illusions: 'viewed from any position, the *illusory nature* of the world in which we believe to live is the most certain and secure thing which our eyes can still catch hold of'.[69] In large part, therefore, Nietzsche's critique of modern ideology is 'in all basic respects a critique of modernity' and a difficult search for an alternative. This does not lie unambiguously in a juxtaposition of a false present with a true past. Any alternative does presuppose an unpleasant recognition of the real nature of the modernity of the present, in order to conceive of 'a culture which corresponds to real needs' and instead of belonging to a 'retinue of slaves whose task it is to satisfy its *imaginary needs*' in a 'soulless or soul-hardened society', in 'an entire merely decorative culture'.[70]

Looked at more closely, this modern culture seems to be afflicted with a terrible sickness. When the genuine philosopher for the future thinks of

> the haste and hurry now universal, of the increasing velocity of life, of the cessation of all contemplativeness and simplicity, he almost thinks that what he is seeing are the symptoms of a total extermination and uprooting of culture. The waters of religion are ebbing away and

leaving behind swamps or stagnant pools; the nations are again drawing away from one another in the most hostile fashion and long to tear one another to pieces. The sciences, pursued without any restraint and in a spirit of the blindest *laissez-faire*, are shattering and dissolving all firmly held belief; the educated classes and states are being swept along by a hugely contemptible money economy. The world has never been more worldly, never poorer in love and goodness . . . Everything, contemporary art and science included, serves the coming barbarism. The cultured man has degenerated to the greatest enemy of culture, for he wants lyingly to deny the existence of the universal sickness and thus obstruct the physicians.[71]

Confronted by 'the weakness of the outlines and the dullness of the colours in the picture of modern life', by 'the whole noisy sham-culture of our age', individuals exhibit a 'restlessness', 'they think with a precipitancy and with an exclusive preoccupation with themselves' which suggests that they are dimly aware of 'absolutely fundamental convulsions', of the 'absolutely unavoidable . . . atomistic revolution', 'in the age of atoms, of atomistic chaos'. This fragmented universe is indeed a frail construct since 'everything in our modern world is so dependent on everything else that to remove a single nail is to make the whole building tremble and collapse'. Hence, we cannot be unaware of 'the uncanny social insecurity which characterises our own times'.[72]

What modern culture symbolizes is, then, the fleeting, the transitory and the fortuitous nature of modernity. All modern culture

requires extreme mannerliness and the newest fashions, inward hasty grasp and exploitation of ephemera, indeed of the momentary: and absolutely nothing else! As a result, it is embodied in the heinous nature of journalists, the slaves of the three M's: of the moment (*Moment*), of opinions (*Meinungen*) and of fashions (*Moden*); and the more an individual has affinities with this culture the more will they look like journalists.[73]

Nietzsche contrasts this symbolic social type of modernity with the genuine philosopher whose aim is to secure people for 'all blows and sudden eventualities of fate and to arm them against any surprise'. In so far as philosophy should prevent people from 'taking the fleeting moment too seriously', 'it is the greatest enemy of that haste, that breathless grasp of the moment, that excessive hurry which breaks all things too early from their branches, that running and hunting which now digs furrows in people's faces and, as it were, tattoos everything that they do'.[74] Modern art, too, mirrors this 'modern way of living . . . as a reflection of its hurried and over-excited worldliness, as an ever broader means of distraction and diffusion, untiring in the constant change in excitements and titillations, as it were, the spice shop of the whole West and East, equipped for any taste . . . regardless of whether someone exhibits good or bad "taste" within it'.[75] Modern art is thus a 'flight from boredom'. Modern life itself is an indication of how little human beings have gone beyond '*education through the fortuitous*'.

But just as a genuine philosophy may counter the decadence of modernity, so too, at least in *The Will to Power* and elsewhere, art can also serve as a counter-movement to the 'forms of human decadence', in so far as it contains positive force.[76] As early as his *Untimely Meditations*, Nietzsche speaks of 'the redemption of art, the only gleam of light to be hoped for in the modern age'.[77] It can also be countered precisely in the fleeting moment itself in so far as we possess 'the capacity to feel *unhistorically* during its duration. He who cannot sink down on the threshold of the moment and forget all the past . . . will never know what happiness is.'[78] For those who possess a suprahistorical capacity, 'the world is complete and reaches its finality at each and every moment'.[79] This capacity is not in the possession of the levelled, chaotic masses of modern society, only those who possess outstanding gifts of excellence (*Vornehmheit*). They alone can grasp this eternal moment. Nietzsche confesses that he would 'gladly exchange a couple of Goethe's "outlived" years for whole cartloads of fresh modern lifetimes . . . and thus be preserved from all and any up-to-date instruction from the legionaries of the moment'.[80]

The context for such reflections is Nietzsche's critique of the relationship between modernity and history. If modernity is characterized by an emphasis upon a transitory fleeting present, then it also takes on another seemingly contrary feature, namely, 'the oversaturation . . . with history', '*the malady of history*' which 'has attacked life's plastic powers, [since] it no longer knows how to employ the past as a nourishing food'.[81] The antidote to the historicist 'sickness', brought upon by a surfeit of scientist history which 'sees everywhere things that have been, things historical, and nowhere things that are, things eternal' and which has robbed 'man of the foundation of all his rest and security', his belief in the enduring and the eternal, lies in the unhistorical and the suprahistorical. They constitute the counterpoint to modernity. As Nietzsche declares, 'by the unhistorical I designate the art and power of forgetting and of enclosing oneself within a bounded *horizon*; I call "suprahistorical" the powers which lead the eye away from becoming towards that which bestows upon existence the character of the eternal and stable, towards *art* and *religion*.'[82] The echoes of Baudelaire's aesthetic reflections are unmistakable here.

Is there then any genuine historical knowledge of the past? If it exists then it can only do so *'out of the fullest exertion of the vigour of the present'* and not the empty present of the 'essentially subjective' modern culture. Indeed, 'when the past speaks it always speaks as an oracle: only if you are an architect of the future and know the present will you understand it.'[83] But this does not imply that the 'architect of the future' can opt for a 'reversion' to the past. The way forward is only through the present: 'There is nothing for it: one *has* to go forward, which is to say *step by step further into decadence* (– this is *my* definition of modern "progress" . . .).'[84] That modern belief in progress is precisely what gives a false significance to the past. It sets it out in grand propositions and in an irresistible grand course of things. Nietzsche, however, affirms his 'hope that the significance of history will not be thought to lie in its general propositions, as if these were the flower and fruit of the whole endeavour, but that its value will be seen to consist in its taking a familiar, perhaps commonplace theme, an everyday melody, and composing inspired variations on it, enhancing it, elevating it to a comprehensive symbol, and thus disclosing in the original theme a whole world of profundity, power and beauty'.[85] Hence, Nietzsche will seriously take up 'the *meanest* things that are ignored in all ages', 'the "smallest world"'.[86] In other words, he will take up the insignificant fragment.

What this implies is, of course, that the genuine totality no longer exists. This Nietzsche emphasizes in relation to whole realms of modern existence – social, political, moral, individual, and so on. He gives it a dramatic emphasis in his characterization of *'literary* decadence' which consists in the fact that

life no longer lives in totalities. The word becomes sovereign and springs out of the sentence, the sentence takes over and obscures the meaning of the page, the page gains life at the cost of the whole – the totality is no longer totality. But that is the image for any decadent style: everytime the anarchy of atoms, the disintegration of the will, to express it morally, 'freedom of the individual' – enlarged into a political theory, *'equal* rights for all'. Life, *equal* liveliness, the vibrance

c

and exuberance of life driven back into the smallest form, the
remainder *impoverished* of life. Everywhere paralysis, drudgery, torpidity
or enmity and chaos . . . The whole no longer lives any more; it is
compounded, calculated, artificial, an artefact.[87]

Nietzsche's critique of literary decadence thus also holds for the whole
contemporary social fabric. As a 'criticism of modernity', he
emphasizes the fact that 'our institutions are no longer fit for anything . . . But the fault lies not in them but in *us*.'[87] This is because
'one lives for today, one lives very fast – one lives very irresponsibly:
it is precisely this which one calls "freedom"'. That which *makes*
institutions institutions is despised, hated, rejected.' Indeed, 'the entire
West has lost those instincts out of which institutions grow, out of
which the *future* grows'.[89]

What then, of the future? In his later writings, especially, Nietzsche
developed his much disputed doctrine of 'the eternal recurrence of
the ever-same'. It presupposes a conception of time as discontinuous,
the denial of duration, the irreversibility of time. The doctrine of
eternal return contains two possibilities. The first, negative possibility,
is that of permanent duration:

> Duration with an 'in vain', without goal or purpose, is a most *paralyzing*
> thought . . . Let us think this thought in its most terrible form:
> existence, as it is, without meaning or aim, but inevitably recurring,
> without a finale, into nothingness: 'the eternal recurrence.' This is
> the most extreme form of nihilism: nothingness (meaninglessness)
> eternally![90]

This is the nihilistic moment of modernity which, in a different context,
Max Weber sought to confront. The affirmation of recurrence is
countered by modernity's affirmation of each moment of existence.
In the context of the process of movement within the existent,
Nietzsche poses this second possibility:

> Can we remove the idea of purpose from the process and *still* affirm
> the process? – That would be the case if something within that process
> were *attained* in every moment – and always the same . . . *Every
> fundamental characteristic* which underlies every event, which expresses
> itself in every event, would have to drive the individual to affirm
> triumphantly every moment of existence in general, if the individual
> experienced it as *his* fundamental characteristic.[91]

In every moment is contained eternity. Indeed, 'the *infinitely small moment* is the higher reality and truth is a lightning flash out of the eternal flux'.[92] This *leitmotif* that came to dominate aesthetic discussion at the turn of the century, is expressed more dramatically by *Zarathustra* in which he conceives of the gateway to eternity in the moment itself. Zarathustra and the dwarf behold a gateway which

> has two faces. Two roads came together here: no one has yet ever followed either to its end. This long lane backward continues for an eternity. And that long lane forward – that is another eternity. They contradict each other, these roads. They directly abut one another. The name of this gateway is inscribed above: 'Moment' . . . And are not all things knotted together so firmly that this moment draws after it *all* that is to come? *Therefore* – itself too? For whatever *can* run its course of all things – also into this long lane *outward* too – it must run it once more! And this slow spider which crawls in the moonlight, and this moonlight itself, and I and you in the gateway, whispering together, whispering of eternal things – must not all of us have been there before? And return and run in that other lane before us, in that long, dreadful lane – must we not eternally return?[93]

The same can thus be attained at any moment in the 'abyss of midday', not in the masked everyday world of modernity but in 'the magic of the extreme', not in the world of mediocrity but in the moment beyond herd existence.

This possibility, however, was continually threatened by the forces of modernity themselves. Nonetheless, those deeply influenced by Nietzsche such as Simmel saw the significance of his doctrine in the relevance for the individual in modern society as lying in a moral imperative. We should live as if we wished to realize 'the ideal lines of development' that extend 'beyond this momentary reality' of our existence, 'as if we lived for eternity, i.e. as if our eternal return did exist'.[94] Leaving aside the extent to which this is a reformulation of Nietzsche's doctrine, there is certainly a whole complex of strands of thought linking Nietzsche with Simmel – the significance of the 'pathos of distance', the emphasis upon excellence and differentiation and sometimes a form of aristocratism, the significance of the fragment and a constellation of judgements upon modernity.[95]

In contrast, Kracauer's analysis of modernity seems to have little affinity with Nietzsche's judgements upon it, until we introduce the mediating role of Simmel and especially Max Weber. Weber's delineation of the consequences of modern social development itself owes not a little to Nietzsche's work. If the loss of meaning and the loss of individual control are two of the major consequences of the process of rationalization in modern society, then the first of these is certainly of central concern to Kracauer. This search for a lost meaning was often expressed by Weber, sometimes drawing on echoes of a vision of empty duration that Nietzsche had earlier brought to life:

> As intellectualism suppresses belief in magic, the world's processes become disenchanted, lose their magical significance, and henceforth simply 'are' and 'happen' but no longer signify anything. As a consequence, there is a growing demand that the world and the total pattern of life be subject to an order that is significant and meaningful.[96]

In a variety of ways, Kracauer too went in search of lost meaning within modernity.

If we turn to Benjamin's analysis of modernity, then it is difficult to underestimate the significance of one aspect of Nietzsche's work – however reinterpreted – for his prehistory of modernity.[97] Benjamin himself acknowledged the decisive importance of Nietzsche's doctrine of the eternal return of the ever-same for his understanding of the historical content of Baudelaire's aesthetic experience. Together with Benjamin's discovery of Blanqui's *L'éternité par les astres*,[98] Nietzsche's doctrine proved decisive for his own theory of modernity located as it was in the experience of a society based upon commodity production in which the ever new commodity whose newness was clothed in the latest fashion announced, in fact, the significance of the ever-same production of exchange value necessary to keep such a mode of production in existence. Elsewhere, in his analysis of the experience of history in the nineteenth century, Benjamin also drew upon Nietzsche's critique of historicism.[99]

Above all, however, it is Benjamin's adaptation of Nietzsche's doctrine of the eternal recurrence that is most striking. When it is recognized that one cannot decree for the world 'the capacity for *eternal newness*', then, equally, it must be conceded that 'the world . . . lives from itself: its excrements are its nourishment'.[100] The response to the fact that 'the world . . . lacks the capacity for eternal newness' is a varied one. For Marx, the capitalist mode of production up to the point of its disintegration produces nothing new other than 'new' commodities. Benjamin adopts Nietzsche's doctrine for a way into the historical configuration which Marx's insights into commodity exchange and fetishism provide. Benjamin hoped to investigate the historical connection between those who took up the doctrine of the ever-same. In 'Zentralpark' he declared that

> It must be elucidated and emphasized how the idea of the eternal return crops up roughly simultaneously in the world of Baudelaire, Blanqui and Nietzsche. In Baudelaire, the emphasis lies upon that which is new that is gained with heroic striving from the 'ever-same', in Nietzsche, upon the 'ever-same' which the human being awaits with heroic composure. Blanqui stands much closer to Nietzsche than to Baudelaire but resignation predominates in his case. For Nietzsche, this experience is projected cosmologically in the thesis: nothing new will ever appear.[101]

In the end, it was only Baudelaire's presentation of the doctrine which Benjamin worked upon in any detail. It is, for him, Baudelaire 'who conjures up the phantasmagoria of modernity out of the calamity of humdrum existence'.[102]

2

Georg Simmel

Modernity as an Eternal Present

The essence of modernity as such is psychologism, the experiencing
and interpretation of the world in terms of the reactions of our inner
life and indeed as an inner world, the dissolution of fixed contents in
the fluid element of the soul, from which all that is substantive is filtered
and whose forms are merely forms of motion.

Georg Simmel

Simmel is a child and favourite of modernity with all its dreadful
sicknesses and weaknesses.

Ernst Troeltsch

The gateway to the world of reality was first opened for us by Simmel.

Siegfried Kracauer

Your askance view of Simmel. Is it not time that we recognised the
inklings of cultural bolshevism in him?

Walter Benjamin to Adorno

I

It has been suggested recently that Simmel 'intimates, but never really
develops, what is probably the closest thing to a twentieth-century
dialectical theory of Modernity'.[1] However, what Berman has in
mind here is largely the outcome of Simmel's theory of the inevitable
clash between subjective and objective culture as he developed it in
his later and especially in his wartime writings.[2] Although this theme
is present from his early writings onwards and is thus not confined
to his essay on the tragedy of culture, Simmel's preoccupation with
modernity surely deserves a much wider focus. In the context of

38

Simmel's social theory as a whole, it is plausible to argue, in the sense in which Baudelaire understood modernity, that Simmel is the first sociologist of modernity. More than any of his contemporary sociologists, he came closest to expressing and analysing the modes of experiencing the 'new' and 'modern' life-world. This may in part be due to his strong aesthetic interest in modernity – which would bring him closer to Baudelaire – as well as his own mode of presentation of modern experience which suggests that he himself was a modernist.

The location of his analysis at the level of modes of experiencing reality has its origins in the distinctive nature of his sociology. The earlier interest in social interaction and, even in the early 1890s, the definition of sociology as the study of forms of social interaction (and later of sociation) was combined with Simmel's original interest in emotional and psychological states derived from the study of the *Völkerpsychologie* of Lazarus and Steinthal.[3] This acute analysis of the experiences of modern, and largely urban, life was often commented upon by Simmel's contemporaries. It was an analysis that not only related very directly to his own position within Berlin at the turn of the century but was also capable of capturing the nuances of its bourgeois culture.

Indeed, if we look to the judgements of his contemporaries, there is ample support for the thesis that Simmel possessed the capacity for capturing the basic experiences of modernity in a way that few of his contemporaries could equal. His students 'scented the instinct for the times' and his 'interpretation of the times from the modernist perspective [*Zeitdeutung von Modernen aus*]'.[4] Other contemporaries maintained that he was 'the only genuine philosopher of his time, the true expression of its fragmented spirit'.[5] Another saw his *Philosophy of Money* as 'a philosophy of the times'.[6] Yet this capacity for capturing the essential nature of modernity was reflected not merely in his substantive analysis of modernity but also in the mode of presentation itself. A reviewer of his *Soziologie* discerned that

> Modernity has found here a dynamic expression: the totality of fragmentary, centrifugal directions of existence and the arbitrariness of individual elements are brought to light. In contrast, the concentric principle, the monumental element is not attained.[7]

More negative is Troeltsch's judgement that, as a creature of modernity, Simmel embodied 'its dreadful sicknesses and weaknesses',[8] which for Troeltsch meant, amongst other things, 'the

transformation of history into a somewhat free game of fantasy . . .
This was the most basic essence of modernity.'[9]

What Simmel's contemporaries did discern, in their various ways,
was the extent to which at least one aim of his social theory was the
analysis of the present. His response to modern modes of experiencing
social reality is emphasized by Becher:

> Simmel's alert, critical mind not only allowed the contemporary
> cultural currents to pass through it but also, simultaneously, as a
> sociologist and philosopher of culture, to question their content. In
> so doing, he 'elevated the social reality of the *present* into scientific
> consciousness'.[10]

Yet the manner in which Simmel engaged in a critique of contemporary trends is a very distinctive one, possibly one that is in many
respects far removed from 'scientific consciousness'. The critique takes
place within the context of an aestheticization of reality that led Simmel
to distance himself from the practical consequences of his critique.
Simmel might shock the bourgeoisie – an aim imputed to his work
by Troeltsch – but, at the same time, leave them undisturbed. In
Benjamin's terms, the shock of the new is countered by experiencing
it as the ever-same. What seems to be viewed *sub specie momenti* is
actually interpreted *sub specie aeternitatis*. Nonetheless, Simmel did bring
the experience of modernity, very much as Baudelaire had understood
it, into the realm of sociological investigation. In so far as he was the
first to do this, we may justly claim Simmel as the first sociologist
of modernity.

II

However, it is here that the problems begin. If Simmel can be credited
with the development of sociology as a form of analysis of the present
(*Gegenwartsanalyse*), even with seeking for a sociology that is a science
of the present times (*Gegenwartswissenschaft*) – though, however, much
this is implicit in his analysis of the present, it was never expressed
as an explicit aim – then we need to examine the distinctive nature
of this analysis of the present. Secondly, if it can be shown that Simmel
provides us with the first sociology of modernity in Baudelaire's sense
of *modernité*, then how is it possible for sociology to analyse 'le
transitoire', 'le fugitif' and 'le contingent' and to capture 'the fleeting

beauty of modern life'?[11] The methodological problems posed by an
analysis of the fleeting and transitory suggest that Simmel had
embarked on no orthodox sociological project. Indeed, like
Baudelaire's painter of modern life, such a project may well be
predicated upon a particular form of experiencing social reality on
the part of the 'painter' or sociologist of modernity. And if this is
the case, then the recognition of Simmel's sensitivity towards modern
contemporary life, towards 'the specifically modern aesthetics of the
style of life'[12] and the 'seismographic accuracy'[13] of its presentation
carries with it a necessary confrontation with the reflexivity of his
analysis since the mode of accounting for *modernité* also belongs to the
modernist tradition itself. Only when these problems have been
confronted can we turn to Simmel's substantive social theory of
modernity.

If we start out from the assumption that around the turn of the
century an implicit aim of Simmel's social theory was an analysis of
the present, then we must examine the nature of this analysis. It does
not take the form of a 'prehistory of modernity' as in Benjamin's study
of modernity. Simmel's account of modernity is not grounded in a
historical investigation of the important changes in German society
around the turn of the century. In this respect, his analysis has little
in common with that of his contemporaries such as Werner Sombart
or Max Weber. There exists no systematic historical analysis of any
of the phenomena that he describes. Even at the individual level, it
is not only the case that Simmel viewed the historical location of
particular figures as uninteresting (as in the case of individual figures
such as Rembrandt whose life and work he analysed in detail)[14] but
also his own writings exhibit a complete absence of references to earlier
contributors to the field of study. At the substantive level, Kracauer
pointed out that of Simmel's social fragments and vignettes 'none of
them live in historical time'; rather, each is transposed into 'eternity,
that is, into the sole form of existence in which it can exist as pure
essentiality and can be contemporary with us at any time'.[15] Even
in his major text, *The Philosophy of Money*, one of the most important
sources for his theory of modernity, the analysis of contemporary
society is located in a historical constellation that is given no more
definite features than that of a mature money economy. Even his
remarkable analysis of the alienating consequences of the modern
division of labour in the same work is located within the context of
a permanent and accelerating opposition between subjective and
objective culture.

However, there does exist a neglected and isolated exception to this lack of a historical analysis of modernity. In an article entitled 'Tendencies in German Life and Thought since 1870' (1902)[16] published shortly after his *Philosophy of Money*, Simmel provides us on one of the very few occasions, with his 'diagnosis of the times'. There Simmel seeks to locate important tendencies in 'the spirit of the times' in such a manner that suggests a biographical identification with them. In other words, it unconsciously traces significant stages in the development of Simmel's own response to the modernity of German society after 1871, to a society which, in a very explicit sense, was 'new'. It is thus useful to examine this article briefly since it serves to locate Simmel's own substantive theory of modernity in the light of his own development.

One fundamental process 'during the last seventy years' – which had preoccupied Simmel since its first announcement in *Über sociale Differenzierung* (1890) – was 'the increased externalisation of life that has come about, with regard to the preponderance that the technical side of life has obtained over its inner side, over its personal values'.[17] In other words, the central tendency has been the domination of objective over subjective culture. But rather than see this process in a unilinear manner, Simmel maintains that the various periods of development in Germany 'stand in very complex relations to this tendency' which will include 'the degree in which they embody it or compel reactions against it'. After German unification and the Franco-Prussian War, political and economic forces encouraged the development of 'a practical materialism' and 'the *material* enjoyment of life' whose consequence 'from the psychological point of view . . . was an externalisation of interests' – including not merely improved immediate surroundings but also 'the adornment of buildings', 'the greater amount of travel', etc. The economic growth of the years immediately succeeding German unification (*Gründerjahre*) stimulated the subordination of all things to material interests, resulting in the domination of technique as 'the sole concern of most producers and consumers' whilst 'forgetting that *technique* is a mere means to an end'. Technical perfection was extolled 'as though the electric light raised man a stage nearer perfection, despite the fact that the objects more clearly seen by it are just as trivial, ugly, or unimportant as when looked at by the aid of petroleum'.[18] In the arts, however, Simmel points to new techniques, as in painting (impressionism) which have been beneficial.

However, this 'rapid development of external civilisation', facilitated by large-scale industrial development, 'has assisted the outbreak of the greatest popular movement of the century, namely, the rise of the Social Democrats'. Their 'idealised picture of the future . . . is an essentially rational one in the highest degree: extreme centralisation, nicely calculated adjustment to each other of demand and supply, exclusion of competition, equality of rights and duties'. Alongside the genuine 'ethical impulses of justice and sympathy' on the part of 'the more highly educated', Simmel discerns more confused motives for an interest in socialist ideas:

> Many persons are actuated by a diseased longing to experience new sensations, and they feel the power of attraction that everything paradoxical and revolutionary is always capable of exerting upon numerous members of a nervously excitable and degenerate society. With this is often connected a fantastic and effeminate mental state, a vague desire for unity and universal brotherhood; in other words . . . – we might call it parlor socialism – a coquetting with socialistic ideals whose realization would be mostly unendurable to these very dilettanti.[19]

But Simmel sees the interest in socialism having declined among non-working class groups once the Social Democrats became 'a reform party on the basis of the existing social order'.

Simmel sees the interest in social issues as emanating from another source, in part in the philosophy of Schopenhauer embodying the notion that there is no final end in life, only the human will. Hence, 'the lack that men felt of a final object, and consequently of an ideal that should dominate the whole of life, was supplied in the eighties by the almost spontaneous rise of the idea of social justice'. This also had its origin in 'the decline of Christianity which had supplied a *final object* to life – 'above everything relative, above the fragmentary character of human existence, above the limitless structure of means and means to means'. This 'yearning after a final object' in a context which 'no longer renders possible its attainment' produces

> specifically modern feelings, that life has no meaning, that we are driven hither and thither in a mechanism built up out of mere preliminary stages and means, that the final and absolute wherein consists the reward of living, ever escapes our grasp.[20]

In the 1880s, Simmel maintains that this absence was filled with the ideal of social justice and a sense of serving society as a whole, a sense 'that the individual was but the crossing-point of social threads and that he, by a devotion to the interests of all, merely discharged an obligation of the most fundamental character'.

Yet Simmel also detected 'the rise of an opposite ideal, that of individualism, which about the year 1890 began to compete with the socialist ideal'. Possibly speaking for himself – at least in the early 1890s – Simmel refers to those 'who are in every way individualists by conviction . . . and who at the same time belong to the social-democratic party, because they regard socialism as a necessary transition stage to a just and enlightened individualism'. This conviction is sometimes stimulated by serious doubts as to 'the physical and spiritual excellence of the higher classes' who 'seem in many cases to be so decadent, so exhausted and neurasthenic as to be unable to bear the future upon their shoulders'. In this context Simmel even speaks of an 'internal migration' of 'the proletarian elements' into such positions in order that society may preserve itself.

A primary source of this new 'enlightened individualism' was the philosophy of Nietzsche which gained popularity in the 1890s, often amongst those who saw in his ideas 'the justification of an unrestrained egoism, and who considered that they gave an absolute right to develop in the highest degree the personality of the individual in defiance of all social and altruistic claims'. It was particularly attractive to the new youth movement and those who sought a false individuality. At the end of the first part of this article, Simmel draws attention to the inevitable conflict between the maintenance of the highest values of mankind and 'the cry for a levelling' as 'a reaction against the dismemberment of society, against the established division of labour'. Somewhat cryptically, Simmel notes that the reconciliation of the two goals 'may require diametrically opposed measures'.

Thus, alongside differentiating tendencies in modern society, there have simultaneously arisen 'levelling tendencies' manifested, for instance, in the women's movement, to which Simmel elsewhere devotes considerable attention.[21] A further tendency is the growing centralization of church and state and a consequent search by individuals for some secure area 'beyond all the oscillations and the fragmentariness of empirical existence' in order to escape from 'life's complexity and constant unrest'. Here, at the heart of the modernist experience, Simmel argues that for many people

this longing assumes an aesthetic character. They seem to find in the
artistic conception of things a release from the fragmentary and painful
in real life . . . Unless I am deceived, however, this sudden increase
in fondness for art will not long endure. The transcendental impulse,
disillusioned by a fragmentary science that is silent as to everything
final, and by a social-altruistic activity that neglects the inner, self-
centred completion of spiritual development, has sought an outlet for
itself in the aesthetic; but it will learn that this field also is too
limited.[22]

In other words, Simmel reiterates what was implicit in *The Philosophy
of Money* namely that an aesthetic retreat from reality cannot be a final
one.

Nonetheless, Simmel still maintains as an aim of social analysis
the capacity

to experience in the individual phenomenon, with all of its details,
the fullness of its reality. To this end, . . . a certain retreat from the
phenomenon is necessary, a transforming of it which renounces the
mere reflection of what is given in nature, in order to regain, from
a higher point of view, more fully and more deeply its reality.[23]

This implies a rejection of naturalism in art and also in the historical
sciences which, Simmel argues, have passed beyond 'the history of
princes and of particular leading persons' as immediate historical facts.
Instead, interest has shifted to 'the history of the masses', to 'the totality
of social forms and . . . their evolutions'.

Interestingly enough, this 'diagnosis of the times' appeared only
in English and not in German. For his German contemporaries it
therefore provided a kind of hidden historical location for his analysis
of the 'new' in modern society. The economic and social location of
modernity – as one of Simmel's central preoccupations around the turn
of the century – is to be found in his *Philosophy of Money* and the works
which surround it. There Simmel seeks out the fleeting, transitory
and contingent elements of modernity as Baudelaire identified them.

But, as Baudelaire maintained, only 'the painter of the passing
moment' was able to capture modernity. If modernity as a distinctive
mode of experiencing (social) reality involves seeing society and the
social relations within it as (temporally) transitory and (spatially)
fleeting then this implies, conversely, that traditional, *permanent*
structures are now absent from human experiences. The emphasis
which Baudelaire also places upon 'le contingent' is present in

Simmel's explicit concern with that which is fortuitous and arbitrary in modern social life. The transitory, fleeting and fortuitous elements of social interaction must be a central concern for the painter of modern life who is true to the 'passing moment'. In other words, to borrow a phrase from Tönnies, 'l'évolution sociale prend la forme d'une *désagrégation spontanée*'.[24] What this implies is that the social theorist is presented with the distinctive problem of locating and capturing the fleeting and the transitory. This is a methodological problem faced not merely by Simmel but also by Kracauer and Benjamin.

III

If the direction of Simmel's account of modernity is hardly ever found in a historical analysis of modern society, where is it located? In the opening passage of 'The Metropolis and Mental Life' (1903), Simmel declares his aim as one in which 'the products of specifically modern life are questioned as to their *inner nature*, as it were, the body of culture as to its soul [my emphasis]'.[25] This can be seen to be the task of his sociology of modernity. But this aim is given a more concrete expression in one of the few – if not the only – definitions of modernity provided by Simmel:

> The essence of modernity as such is psychologism, the experiencing [*das Erleben*] and interpretation of the world in terms of the reactions of our inner life and indeed as an inner world, the dissolution of fixed contents in the fluid element of the soul, from which all that is substantive is filtered and whose forms are merely forms of motion.[26]

Modernity is thus a particular mode of lived experience within modern society, one that is reduced not merely to our inner responses to it but also to its incorporation in our inner life. The external world becomes part of our inner world. In turn, the substantive element of the external world is reduced to a ceaseless flux and its fleeting, fragmentary and contradictory moments are all incorporated into our inner life. Viewed in this manner, modernity presents a distinctive problem for its analysts: how is it possible to capture the fleeting, fragmentary social reality that has been reduced to individual inner experience? Only once this modernity has been grasped can we pursue the search for its causes.

One answer is provided in Simmel's essay on Rodin, from which this definition is taken. We should look to those forms of human expression which can capture the fleeting nature of inner experiences. It is modern art that captures 'human beings in the stream of their life' and which emphasises 'the increased dynamic nature [*Bewegtheit*] of real life' since 'art not merely mirrors a world in motion, its very mirror has itself become more labile'.[27] Unlike naturalism, modern art does not overlook the fact that 'a style, in which the meaning of our life directly lives, is much more fundamentally true and true to reality, than all copies; it not only *possesses* truth, it *is* truth'.[28] Simmel's admiration for Rodin's art stems, in fact, both from its embodiment of modernity and its resolution of modernity's contradictions. Rodin captures modernity in 'the impression . . . the impression of the supra-temporal, the timeless impression'.[29] The search for the timeless impression in Simmel's theory of modernity is encapsulated in the title of a number of pieces he wrote for *Jugend:* 'Snapshots *sub specie aeternitatis*'.[30] But the real achievement of Rodin's art lay, as we shall see, in its resolution of the contradictions of modernity.

But however much the aesthetic dimension is important for Simmel's delineation of modernity, it is clear that the work of art is not the starting point for Simmel's analysis of modernity, however much it may have been the source for many of its insights into modernity and however much Simmel's accounts of the work of art provide us with insights into his 'method'. Nonetheless, it is worth pointing out in this context the contrast between Simmel's approach and that of his contemporary Max Weber. In 'Science as a Vocation', Weber explicitly contrasts science and art on the grounds that 'scientific research is harnessed to the launching of progress. In the sphere of art, in contrast, there exists – in this sense – no progress.'[31] This is because 'a work of art, that is a true accomplishment, will never be surpassed, it will never become obsolete. In contrast, each of us in the scientific realm knows that that which he has worked on will become obsolete in ten, twenty or fifty years.'[32] Weber goes on to suggest that scientific progress proceeds through the steady accumulation and refutation of knowledge. The instruments of scientific research, which ensure an even greater precision and progress, comprise 'the concept' and its refinement and 'the rational experiment as the means for a reliably checked experience'. Although Simmel was concerned with conceptualization and with intellectual experiments in the sense of typification of forms of human sociation,

his contemporaries, including Weber, lamented the absence of clarity
with regard to both. Indeed, they tended to characterize his work as
lacking systematization and clarity and consistency of conceptualization. Hence, Becher has correctly argued that 'expressions such as
"mode of observation", "viewpoint", "standpoint", "research
tendency" would be more accurate here. This would also correspond
with Simmel's perspectivism. The concept of "method", taken in
its strict sense, is false.'[33]

IV

If we accept this claim, then we must look elsewhere for the starting
point of Simmel's analysis of modernity. Simmel's approach to his
object of study as well as his most sustained account of modernity
is to be found in *The Philosophy of Money*. Here, from the very outset,
Simmel rules out the possibility of some naive accumulation of
empirical knowledge as an end in itself since

> the ever-fragmentary contents of positive knowledge seek to be
> augmented by definitive concepts into a world picture and to be related
> to the totality of life.[34]

Hence, 'the very standpoint of a single science, which is also based
on the division of labour, never exhausts the totality of reality'. Yet
in *The Philosophy of Money* at least, Simmel is in no doubt that this
totality is apprehendable.

In turn, this totality is not an abstract postulate but is approachable
from specific individual phenomena and problems. It is not the starting
point of his analysis, rather its goal. Hence, in his investigation of
money, Simmel maintains that he must 'regard the problem as
restricted and small in order to do justice to it by extending it to the
totality and the highest level of generality'.[35] In this respect, the
specific object of study, money

> is simply a means, a material or an example for the presentation
> of relations that exist between the most superficial, 'realistic'
> and fortuitous phenomena and the most idealised powers of
> existence, the most profound currents of individual life and
> history.[36]

Simmel's intention 'is simply to derive from the surface level of economic affairs a guideline that leads to the ultimate values and things of importance in all that is human'.

The starting point of his analysis is thus 'what is apparently most superficial and insubstantial'. Indeed, the unity of the whole study lies 'in the possibility . . . of finding in each of life's details the totality of its meaning'. In this respect, it follows the same method as art – in contrast to philosophy's concern with 'the totality of being' – which 'sets itself a single, narrowly defined problem every time: a person, a landscape, a mood'. It is Simmel's conviction that 'it is possible to relate the details and superficialities of life to its most profound and essential movements'.[37]

It follows from all this that empirical scientific research is restricted in the sense that it cannot approach the totality that alone gives meaning to 'each of life's details'. Hence,

> Science always finds itself on the path towards the absolute unity of the conception of the world but can never reach it; regardless of the point from which it starts, it always requires from that point a leap into another mode of thought – of a religious, metaphysical, moral or aesthetic nature – in order to expand and integrate the inevitably fragmentary nature of its results into a complete unity.[38]

Of these other modes of thought, it is the aesthetic perspective or *'Anschauungsweise'* to which Simmel himself most often has recourse.

Indeed, elsewhere, Simmel seems to suggest that the interactions between individuals and society as a whole constitute a totality that is only apprehendable aesthetically:

> The totality of the whole . . . stands in eternal conflict with the totality of the individual. The aesthetic expression of this struggle is particularly impressive because *the charm of beauty is always embedded in a whole*, no matter whether it has immediate distinctiveness or *a distinctiveness that is supplemented by fantasy as in the case of a fragment. The essential meaning of art lies in its being able to form an autonomous totality, a self-sufficient microcosm out of a fortuitous fragment of reality that is tied with a thousand threads to this reality* [My emphasis.].[39]

Some fragments of our existence and, more especially, some modes of apprehension are more capable of grasping the totality. Simmel's sociological texts are richly populated with these fortuitous fragments of reality, with seemingly superficial social phenomena, with snapshots, with a myriad of social vignettes.

What this also suggests is that the aesthetic totality may itself exist as a fragment. Such a principle was later elevated into a universal principle in his later philosophy of life (*Lebensphilosophie*). In his study of *Rembrandt* (1916), for example, Simmel maintains that 'each moment of life is the totality of life',[40]

> because life is thereby nothing other than continuous development by means of material oppositions, because it is not composed from individual pieces and its totality therefore does not exist outside of the individual element.[41]

However, at the time of publication of his *Philosophy of Money*, Simmel had not yet fully developed his philosophy of life and his interest in sociology was still much in evidence.

Nonetheless, there are passages in this work which suggest that Simmel's 'categories for interpreting the world' are already grounded in an essentialism that is far removed from an empiricist framework for the apprehension of social reality. Rather than viewing Simmel's philosophy as located within a neo-Kantian paradigm,[42] certain crucial arguments suggest a very different alternative, as when Simmel maintains that

> If we describe the sum total of fragments that make up our knowledge at any one moment in relation to the goal we want to attain . . . then we can do so only by presupposing that which lies at the basis of the Platonic doctrine: that there is an ideal realm of theoretical values, of perfect intellectual meaning and coherence, that coincides neither with the objects . . . nor with the psychologically real knowledge that has been attained. On the contrary, this real knowledge only gradually and always imperfectly approximates to that realm which includes all possible truth.[43]

Yet it is not merely that our fragments of knowledge approximate imperfectly to the totality. Rather, Simmel views the human subject as playing an active role within this totality:

> the formula of our life as a whole, from the trivial practice of everyday to the highest peak of intellectuality, is this: in all that we do, we have a norm, a standard, an ideally preconceived totality before us, which we try to transpose into reality through our actions.[44]

Even more explicitly, Simmel sees an essential quality of our action as being that we follow some prefigured possibility and, as it were, carry out an ideal programme. *Our practical existence, though inadequate and fragmentary, gains a certain significance and coherence, as it were, by partaking in the realisation of a totality* [My emphasis.].[45]

Precisely how that totality is realized is not clarified by Simmel.

Elsewhere, Simmel takes the problematic relationship between the universal and the particular to be a feature of modern times in so far as 'the evolution of the modern naturalistic spirit tends to dethrone universal concepts, and to emphasise singular instances as the only legitimate content of conceptions'.[46] Yet Simmel maintains that the importance of universals 'has not altogether disappeared'. Indeed, he asserts that

> we would attain a completely satisfying relation to the world only if every aspect of our world view reconciled the material reality of singular instances with the depth and scope of a formal universality. Historicism and a sociological world view are attempts to confirm universality and yet to deny its abstractedness, to transcend the singular instance, to derive the singular from the general without sacrificing its material reality; for society is universal but not abstract.[47]

By the time of writing this passage, Simmel had clearly moved away from his earlier psychologistic naturalism towards a preoccupation with social forms and 'a formal universality'. But although this passage is illustrative of his indebtedness to Platonism, it is in fact the reverse position which is his sociological starting point, namely the derivation of the essence of social phenomena from a particular instance. In other words, social reality is viewed *sub specie aeternitatis*.

It should already be evident that he sees some fragments of our existence and, more especially, some modes of apprehension as being more capable of apprehending a totality. We already know that, for Simmel, art forms 'an autonomous totality' out of fortuitous fragments of reality. In the preface to *Philosophy of Money*, Simmel emphasized that the empirical realm could never be capable of realizing this totality. The empirical needs to be located within a totality that it is itself incapable of creating. Hence, in a passage which unwittingly takes up a theme of Benjamin's later works, Simmel insists that

> even the empirical in its perfected state might no more replace philosophy as an interpretation, a colouring and an individually selective emphasis of what is real than would the perfection of the mechanical reproduction of phenomena make the visual arts superfluous.[48]

Indeed, Simmel maintains that the whole of his study of money is grounded in a world picture 'which I consider to be the most appropriate expression of the contemporary contents of science and emotional currents'.[49] Even from the preface we can surmise that Simmel favours a 'relativist interpretation' of social phenomena. This is confirmed in his theory of value as well as in the text as a whole. He also favours a perspective that we must term modernist.

Simmel is insistent in his *Philosophy of Money* that 'not a single line of these investigations is meant to be a statement about economics'. Almost as explicit is Simmel's lack of concern with 'the historical phenomena of money' even though this is his stated concern in the second part of his text. This becomes clear when we learn that this historical dimension has as its basis 'feelings of value', an analysis of 'praxis in relation to things and the reciprocal relationships between people'. Simmel's concern is, rather, with the effect of money 'upon the inner world – upon the vitality of individuals, upon the linking of their fates, upon culture in general'. The historical dimension is replaced by a phenomenology of human emotions.

Such preliminary remarks should suggest that the totality within which the fragments of social life are to be located or even the totality that they themselves are is not historical. Rather, this totality, this whole, rests upon the 'attitude' of the human observer. In seeking to demarcate Simmel's thought from the post-First World War generation, Margarete Susman points out that

> for Simmel, the philosophical perspective was always a view from the centre into the totality, which was only able to extract a single sector from the whole. This relationship of the individual to the totality Simmel termed the 'attitude' of the thinker. This attitude signifies for him the relationship of a mind to the totality of the world.[50]

Susman points out that this notion of attitude towards the world is fundamentally mystical and 'obtains a metaphysical justification only through the feelings'.

Though the notion of 'attitude' to the world belongs, more accurately, to Simmel's later philosophy, it also plays a subterranean role in his *Philosophy of Money*. We have already pointed out that Simmel did not view empirical knowledge as alone providing the key to the totality. In keeping with the later notion of our 'attitude' to the world, Simmel maintains that, psychologically, what we refer to as verification of empirical phenomena is merely a function of the creation of a specific 'feeling' for the object in question. He refers to the theory according to which everything held to be true is a certain *feeling* which accompanies a mental image; what we call proof is nothing other than the establishment of a psychological constellation which gives rise to such a feeling. No sense perception or logical derivations can directly assure us of a reality.[51]

Such intuitionism as the basis for grounding knowledge is hardly the firmest foundation for the development of a sociology of modernity. However, it could form the starting point for what we might term a sociological impressionism that is rooted in an aesthetic stance vis-à-vis social reality.

This brief examination of Simmel's emphasis upon the relationship between the aesthetic mode of apprehension and the totality should leave little doubt that Simmel viewed the aesthetic perspective as a legitimate one for acquiring insights into social reality. In evaluating Simmel's work, we should take this aesthetic dimension seriously and clearly distinguish it from a tendency towards the aestheticization of reality since the two are not synonymous. Indeed, in some respects, the aesthetic dimension in theorizing can be seen to be coterminus with modernity itself. Bubner, for instance, maintains that 'the *autonomous development of the arts* in fact dates from the middle of the previous century, which we have since become accustomed to characterise as modernity without an end to this development being perceived'.[52] Furthermore, Bubner highlights a tendency that is also apparent in Simmel's work, namely the tendency to see art as 'not so much an object' but rather that 'art serves as a medium in which philosophy seeks to make certain its own theoretical status'. In the context of Simmel's social theory of modernity, the aesthetic dimension also provides a degree of 'self-understanding' with regard to its own role in delineating modernity. One might even maintain that this aesthetic dimension makes Simmel's social theory of modernity possible.

If Simmel's social theory exhibits a somewhat problematic relationship towards the possibility of grasping the totality of existence, how does he view the role of the fragment in this context? More specifically, with the aim of understanding *modernité*, what is the justification for starting out from 'a fortuitous fragment' of reality, from 'each of life's details', from a 'snapshot' or 'fleeting image' of social interaction? Why not commence with 'the social structure' as a whole, with the 'social system' or with the central 'institutions' of society? In Simmel's case, the second of these questions is the easier to answer.

Concepts such as 'social structure', 'social system' and even 'social institution' play a very subordinate role in his sociology. From his early works onwards, Simmel was at pains to avoid the reification or hypostatization of 'society'. Already in 1890, Simmel was insisting that 'society is not an entity fully enclosed within itself, an absolute entity, any more than is the human individual. Compared with the real interactions of the parts, it is only secondary, only the result.'[53] Instead, Simmel commenced from 'a regulative world principle that everything interacts with everything else, that between every point in the world and every other force permanently moving relationships exist'.[54] This is not merely a heuristic principle but also a substantive feature of modernity since 'the dissolution of the societal soul into the sum of interactions of its participants lies in the direction of modern intellectual life itself'. Sociology should therefore not concern itself with a reified notion of society but with 'what is specifically societal; the form and forms of sociation as such are distinct from the particular interests and contents in and through which sociation is realised.'[55] Thus, from the outset, it is social interaction and forms of sociation and, later, 'the phenomenological structure of society' (1908) that constitute the key elements of sociology.[56]

If one of the features of modernity is that social reality is felt to be in a state of ceaseless flux, then the concepts that can best express this fluid reality must be relational concepts. Interaction (*Wechselwirkung*) and sociation (*Vergesellschaftung*) are key concepts for Simmel and what interests him is relationships between phenomena. Society constitutes a social labyrinth within which individuals and groups intersect. This web or network of social relationships is itself symptomatic of what Kracauer describes as the 'core principle' of Simmel's social theory, namely 'the fundamental interrelatedness [*Wesenszusammengehörigkeit*] of the most diverse phenomena'. This implies that

> All expressions of cultural life . . . stand in an inexpressible plurality
> of relationships to one another, none is capable of being extracted from
> the contexts in which they find themselves associated with others.[57]

Each individual element is 'enmeshed' within this 'context of diversity'. The 'liberation of things from their individual isolation' takes place either through tracing real relationships between social phenomena or through revealing possible relationships by recourse to analogies.[58]

Since there exists, in principle at least, no hierarchy of significance in forms of interaction, we might expect that he would be equally interested in the fortuitous and seemingly insignificant social phenomena. In the first vesion of his 'Sociology of the Senses' (1907),[59] Simmel argues that just as 'the science of organic life' now concerns itself with 'the smallest agents, the cells'[60] of human life, so too social science has recently come to concern itself with 'the beginnings of microscopic investigation'. It, too, originally started out from

> States and trade unions, priesthoods and forms of family structure, the nature of guilds and factories, class formation and the industrial division of labour – these and similar major organs and systems appear to constitute society and to form the sphere of science concerning it.[61]

Without denying the existence of these 'structures of a higher order', Simmel's interest lay not in these structured interactions but in 'countless others which, as it were, remain in a fluid, fleeting state but are no less agents of the connection of individuals to societal existence'.[62] The manner in which people look at one another, the fact that they write letters to one another, that they eat a midday meal together, that they are sympathetic or antithetical to one another, that they dress and adorn themselves for others are also momentary or persistent relations between people that go to make up society. Here Simmel's concern is quite explicitly with the 'fortuitous fragments' of social interaction:

> On every day, at every hour, such threads are spun, are allowed to fall, are taken up again, replaced by others, intertwined with others. Here lie the interactions – only accessible through psychological microscopy – between the atoms of society which bear the whole tenacity and elasticity, the whole colourfulness and unity of this so evident and so puzzling life of society.[63]

Simmel is convinced that their investigation produces a 'deeper and more accurate' understanding of society than does the study of society's major structures and institutions.

> We can no longer take to be unimportant consideration of the delicate, invisible threads that are woven between one person and another if we wish to grasp the web of society according to its productive, form-giving forces; hitherto, sociology has largely been concerned to describe

> this web only with regard to the finally created pattern of its highest
> manifest levels.[64]

For his sociology of modernity, Simmel required to examine 'the
delicate, invisible threads' which, as fleeting moments of interaction,
were themselves a feature of modernity. They also provide
fundamental insights into the workings of society. His brief sketch
for a sociology of the senses, for instance,

> rests upon the belief that the appropriate procedures, in sociology too,
> will draw from the reality of its object more deeply and accurately than
> the mere treatment of the major simply supra-individual total structures
> is capable of.[65]

With reference to a sociology of the senses, Simmel maintains that
'each sense, according to its distinctive features, brings typical
contributions to the construction of a societal existence, the nuances
of its impressions correspond to the unique aspects of the social
relationship'.[66] Access to such 'otherwise unrealisable sociological
depth [*Färbung*]' is only available by means of this distinctive
approach.

There exists another neglected dimension of Simmel's approach
which his 'Sociology of the Senses' merely touches upon, namely the
significance of a 'psychological microscopy' for the analysis of
modernity. Since he defines modernity as 'psychologism', as the
experiencing the world as an inner reality, Simmel focuses time and
time again upon the 'inner life' of human beings, upon the *psychology*
of modernity. This is an interesting emphasis given sociology's
attempts at the end of the nineteenth century to demarcate itself as
an independent discipline not merely from history, from philosophy,
but also from psychology. Simmel, who originally started out from
the *Völkerpsychologie* of Lazarus and Steinthal, retained a sensitivity
to psychological processes that proved essential to his analysis of the
modes of *experiencing* modernity. Simmel was not merely a master in
the sociology of fleeting encounters and interactions; he was also a
key figure in the development of a sociology of emotions and intimate
interaction – as Birgitta Nedelmann has persuasively argued[67] – and,
one must add, of a psychology of emotional life.

Perhaps we are now in a better position to answer the first question
posed: what is the justification for starting out from the 'fortuitous
fragment' of social reality? Is the 'fortuitous fragment', the snapshot,

the fleeting image of social reality merely a fragment? Simmel's 'psychological microscopy' is appropriate to a conception of the world which presupposes that 'we are all fragments', that the past 'comes down to us only as fragments', and that knowledge itself must necessarily be fragmentary. This could lead some of his students such as Ernst Bloch to see that in Simmel's work it is 'always merely the colourful, nervous, purely impressible margins of life that are painted'.[68] It led Kracauer to conclude that Simmel was 'a master in the . . . elaboration of fragmentary images of the world'.

Yet what was the aim of this 'elaboration' of the fortuitous fragments of social reality? From a certain perspective, these 'fragmentary images' are the key to the totality of social reality. That perspective is an aesthetic one. It is a mode of apprehending the world that Simmel developed in the mid-1890s which coincides with the start of his most typical sociological works. Its early formulation is to be found in the important essay 'Sociological Aesthetics' (1896):

> For us the essence of aesthetic observation and interpretation lies in the fact that the typical is to be found in what is unique, the law-like in what is fortuitous, the essence and significance of things in the superficial and transitory. It seems impossible from any phenomenon to escape this reduction to that which is significant and eternal. Even the lowest, intrinsically ugly phenomenon appears in a context of colours and forms, of feelings and experiences that bestow upon it a fascinating significance. We only need to involve ourselves deeply and lovingly enough in the most indifferent phenomenon – that in isolation is banal or repulsive – in order to be able to conceive of it too as a ray or symbol of the ultimate unity of all things, from which beauty and meaning flow and for which every philosophy, religion and moment of our most heightened emotional experience seeks out symbols. If we pursue this possibility of aesthetic preoccupation to its conclusion, we find that there no longer exists any distinction between the amount of beauty in things. Our world view becomes that of aesthetic pantheism. Every point conceals the possibility of being released into absolute aesthetic significance. To the adequately trained eye, the *total* beauty, the *total* meaning of the world as a whole radiates from every single point.[69]

If we accept that Simmel himself adopts an aesthetic perspective in the articulation of his social theory, then the justification for commencing with the social fragment is quite apparent since the fortuitous fragment is no longer merely a fragment: the 'unique' contains the 'typical', the fleeting fragment is the 'essence'. There

exists no ontological ordering of these fragments which permits the
observer to say that one is more significant than the other. Every
fragment, every social snapshot contains within itself the possibility
of revealing 'the total meaning of the world as a whole'. This notion
of the superficial fragment as providing the key to the fundamental
aspects of social reality is also to be found in Simmel's analysis of
the metropolis (1903) where he maintains that

> from each point on the surface of existence – however closely attached
> to the surface alone – one may drop a sounding into the depth of the
> psyche so that all the most banal externalities of life finally are
> connected with the ultimate decisions concerning the meaning and style
> of life.[70]

Once more it is clear that it is not merely that the fragmentary and
superficial can be the starting point of sociological reflection but that
its significance lies in its being 'connected' with the essential. Simmel
thus oscillates between asserting that the fragment is the totality and
that the fragment, by virtue of its connections with the essential,
provides the gateway, as it were, to the totality.

In the observation of human action, there exists, for Simmel, an
'infinitely varied mixture' between 'the same, steady recurrence of
a few basic themes [Grundtöne]' and the 'changing wealth of their
individual variations'. However varied the individual manifestation
and variations may be, from the standpoint of 'the most general
observation of life' they can be reduced to the basic 'dualism of
movements of thought and life'. In order to fully grasp the significance
of an epoch, we cannot search for laws and causal explanations:
'Rather, only in *symbols* and *examples* can this deep living opposition
in all that is human be grasped.'[71] If we generalize from this
conception of the basic oppositions in life to the social world as a whole,
then we have a key to the significance of fragments in Simmel's
approach to social reality. His essays are populated with examples
that are, at the same time, the instances of basic typical human
interactions. Simmel's *Philosophy of Money* itself can also be
characterized as a preoccupation with symbols of 'all that is human'.
Time and time again, Simmel refers to money as a symbol 'of the
completely dynamic character of the world', of 'the behaviour of
objects', of 'the relativistic character of existence', of human
relationships, of society itself in ceaseless interaction. This was quite
apparent to Simmel's contemporaries who saw money as 'a timelessly

valid symbol of the essential forms of motion themselves' (Köhler),[72] who saw Simmel as captivated by money's symbolism (Schmidt)[73], and who noted Simmel's preoccupation with money as a 'pure symbol, an abstract expression of abstract relationships' (Durkheim).[74]

But with regard to the profusion of examples that is so typical of Simmel's work, and especially of *The Philosophy of Money*, there is a danger that the wealth of examples become overpowering. This can lead to a situation which Adorno contrasts with Benjamin's approach when he argues that one should not pursue 'the innocuous illustration of concepts through colourful historical objects as Simmel did when he depicted his primitive metaphysics of form and life in the cup-handle, the actor, Venice'.[75] What Adorno specifically objects to in Simmel's approach to social reality is the manner in which the preoccupation with the fragment and the exemplary instance – shared by Benjamin as well – never leads to their historical concretion but to their reduction to the eternal realm, to 'simply interchangeable examples for ideas'.[76] In other words, Simmel's snapshots of social reality are consistently viewed *sub specie aeternitatis*.

However, the emphasis upon the example and the symbol reveals another dimension of Simmel's approach that is closely related to his conception of 'aesthetic observation and interpretation'. In *Der Impressionismus in Leben und Kunst* (1907), Hamann views Simmel as a master of symbolism:

> The *symbolism* of facts, i.e. wherever possible to speak of one fact as opposed to another merely on the basis of analogies, is quite in keeping with impressionistic thought. *Likenesses, symbols* replace ideas. The most significant work in this direction is Simmel's *Philosophy of Money*.[77]

The social fragment can thus function as a symbol of some wider totality, whereas a systematic, logical analysis of the fragment is rejected. Its historical origins are also seldom examined systematically. Indeed, some critics also saw that his very commitment to modernity prevented him from developing a consistent, rigorous analysis. For Troeltsch, Simmel 'together with modernity . . . transformed the self into . . . mere "life"', into 'a fleeting wave'. Instead of rigorous analytical concepts, 'the realm of ideas resembled a forest that had been felled, where only the stumps remained standing, with roots that were dying out, incapable ever again of being a forest, but rather, aesthetically overgrown with all kinds of ornament'.[78] The nuances of Troeltsch's sceptical image suggest that though the basis exists for an analysis of modern life, in Simmel's works it remains incomplete and fragmentary.

Nonetheless, to view the fragment as a symbol of a wider whole certainly does liberate the fragment from its isolation and locate it in a broader context. So, too, does the extensive use of analogies. But it is analogies rather than likenesses (*Gleichnisse*] that we find most often in Simmel's work. As Kracauer remarks, 'Simmel is incorrigible in his demonstration of analogies' in order to convince us of the often hidden connections between the most diverse social phenomena. More accurately than Hamann, Kracauer points both to the 'very infrequent number of likenesses' compared with analogies in Simmel's work and to the difference between the two: 'The analogy: a relationship between objects; the likeness: the presentation of relationships between subject and object'.[79] Whereas the former's value 'lies exclusively in its objective validity', the latter is 'a creation of fantasy'. But the problem with Simmel's extensive recourse to argument by analogy lies not merely in his lack of interest in the validity of his analogies – which, stimulating as they are, abound in his *Philosophy of Money* – but in their substitution for analytical accuracy. Where recourse to analogies becomes too excessive, the reader is likely to lose track of the central direction of a work, as Conrad Schmidt pointed out with reference to *The Philosophy of Money*:

> In the proliferate intertwining of analogies, that start out as astounding but then subsequently in this abundance become merely monotonous and depressing, one loses one's direction at every moment . . . the basic ideas, . . . when one has extracted them from the unique, disguised philosophical linguistic finery and the glittering decorations of analogies, seem too simple.[80]

Schmidt's negative judgement of the value of analogies is more sympathetically supported by Kracauer who argues that 'this wandering from relationship to relationship, this extension into the far and near, this intermeshing secures no resting place for the mind which seeks to grasp a totality: it loses itself in infinity.'[81]

Nonetheless, Kracauer elsewhere points to the basic significance of Simmel's predication and revelation of 'the *essential interrelatedness* of the most diverse phenomena' and his extensive use of analogies:

> The unmasking of the intertwining threads that exist between phenomena forms merely one of the (unending) tasks that Simmel develops out of his fundamental convictions. His other task must be

to conceive of what is diverse as a totality and somehow to master this totality and to experience and express its essence. From the principle that everything exists in relationship with everything else there follows directly the unity of the world. Each individual constellation possesses the characteristic that it is merely a fragment of the major world totality, without whose prior interpretation and encompassment one can merely bring to light, in a fragmentary manner, incomplete complexes.[82]

Kracauer goes on to argue that Simmel came closest to grasping this totality in his *Philosophy of Money*. There, Simmel's conviction that 'everything exists in relationship with everything else' is confirmed by his emphasis upon money as the symbol of exchange in society, indeed by his conviction that society is constituted by exchange relationships. Exchange as 'a sociological phenomenon *sui generis*' indeed embodies 'le transitoire, le fugitif, le contingent' as Baudelaire characterized modernity.

VI

Simmel's theory of modernity does not take the form of a historical analysis, but rather an account of the modes of experiencing the social reality of modernity. In this respect, Simmel shares a central preoccupation with Kracauer and Benjamin. Indeed, in Benjamin's case, the very project of retracing the 'prehistory of modernity' can only be understood as an attempt to recapture social experience lost in the very process of modernity itself. This subsequently made itself felt, in Benjamin's case, in the need for a materialist theory of experience, one which, although only sketched out, rested upon the distinction between individual lived experience (*Erlebnisse*) and concrete experience (*Erfahrung*). Simmel too seems to have conceived of a limited number of privileged forms of experiencing social reality.

It is no accident that the social experiences which provide the basis for Simmel's insights into modernity should coalesce around individual inner experiences (*Erlebnisse*). This is particularly true of the emphasis Simmel places upon inner nervosity provoked by metropolitan life and by alienating relationships in a mature money economy. In this respect, it was not difficult for his contemporaries to detect a social psychology of modernity in his writings or even, as Goldscheid intimated, a psychological counterpart to Marx's *Capital*. In another respect, this emphasis upon the inner life of the individual was quite in keeping with Simmel's intention to preserve and later – with the increasing acceptance of the inevitable widening division between subjective and objective culture – to reconstitute individuality. This is the critical intention that lies somewhat veiled in his sociology but is quite explicit in his later writings on the philosophy of life.

But in terms of our present interests, there is a more significant aspect of Simmel's emphasis upon individual inner experience. In one of his very few explicit references to the nature of modernity, he characterizes modernity as indeed this preoccupation with inner experience. The context is an essay on Rodin's sculpture ('Rodin' 1909; revised 1911)[83] as not merely the expression of modernity but also the resolution of its inner tensions. Rodin's sculpture is an artistic expression of 'the many sided, vibrant element of the modern soul'. Whereas ancient sculpture sought out 'the body's logic, Rodin seeks its psychology'. As we have already seen, for Simmel 'the essence of modernity' was 'psychologism, the experiencing [*das Erleben*] and interpretation of the world in terms of the reactions of our inner life and indeed as an inner world'.[84] Already implicit in Simmel's conception of modernity is the absence of concrete experience (*Erfahrung*) derived from interaction with and intervention in an external world. The latter has become 'an inner world'. In other words, *Erfahrung* has been reduced to *Erlebnis*. This important distinction is not made explicit by Simmel as it was later to be by Benjamin.

Rather, this definition of modernity sums up Simmel's treatment of it. Modernity consists in a particular mode of experiencing the world, one that is reduced not merely to our inner responses to it but also to its incorporation in our inner life. The external world becomes part of our inner world. In turn, the substantive element of the external world is reduced to a ceaseless flux. The fleeting, fragmentary and contradictory moments of our external life are all incorporated into our inner life. Viewed in this manner, modernity presents a distinctive problem for its analysts, one that we posed at the outset of this study: how is it possible to capture a fleeting, fragmentary and contradictory social reality that has been reduced to individual inner experience?

Simmel provides two not unrelated answers, one explicitly the other implicitly. The first response is to look for those forms of human expression which can capture the fleeting nature of inner experiences in order that we can recognize them and temporarily at least hold them constant. The form of human expression which best performs this task is, for Simmel, the work of art. This he makes quite explicit in his essay on Rodin. In the light of his definition of the essence of

modernity, Simmel views music – upon which he so seldom wrote
subsequent to his rejected dissertation on its origins – as 'the genuinely
modern art' since it is 'the most dynamic of all the arts'. Similarly,
modern art emphasizes colourfulness and facets of the object rather
than total structures in landscapes and in portraiture, 'modernism
emphasises the face' rather than the body since it more readily
illustrates 'human beings in the stream of their inner life'.[85]

Simmel's admiration for Rodin's sculpture stems both from its
embodiment of modernity and its resolution of modernity's
contradiction. Starting out from the assumption that art is 'an agent
or reflection of general culture', Simmel maintains that two modern
sculptors have given the plastic arts a new object (Meunier) and a
new form (Rodin). Meunier took 'the immediate experience' of
physical labour as action to be the subject of art and created an object
that viewed the heroic in the everyday and the universal. In so doing,
Meunier achieved in the aesthetic sphere what Maeterlinck's
philosophy of life saw as the feature of the individual, namely that
'our happiness, our value, our greatness does not live in the
extraordinary, in heroic breakthroughs, in prominent deeds and
experiences, but rather in everyday existence and each of its regular
nameless moments'.[86] In passing, we may note that this is not merely
another expression of Baudelaire's notion of modern heroism but also
the starting point for much of Simmel's sociology.

In contrast, Rodin provides modern sculpture with a new form or
style, 'that expresses the response of the modern soul to life'. Simmel's
account of the aim of Rodin's art illustrates his own conception of
art as a totality and even art as a model for his own social theory,
as when he maintains that,

> In contrast to mechanistic naturalism and to conventionalism, Rodin
> certainly seeks out the impression but . . . the impression of the supra-
> momentary, the timeless impression; not that of the particular side
> or individual moment of objects, but of the object as such . . . Just
> as the major achievement of Stefan George is to have given a
> monumental form to the lyrical expression of subjective experience,
> so too Rodin progresses along the path towards a new monumentality –
> that of becoming, of motion.[87]

What Rodin has achieved is discovery of 'the artistic timelessness of
pure movement', an obsession with movement as such that reflects
'the modern soul that is so much more unstable, in its attitudes and
self-created fates much more changeable' than in earlier times.

But the real achievement of Rodin's art lies not merely in its presentation of 'the modern *transmutabilita*', 'without a fixed decisive pole or resting point' but in his art being a resolution of the contradiction of modernity. At the very end of his essay on Rodin, Simmel states not merely his artistic ideal but also; implicitly, the aesthetic ideal of his social theory:

> If one . . . regards salvation from the trouble and whirl of life, the peace and conciliation beyond its movements and contradictions as the permanent goal of art, then one might think that artistic liberation from the disquiet and unbearableness of life is achieved not merely by the flight into its opposite, but also in fact by the most complete stylisation and increased purity of its own content . . . Rodin saves us precisely because he shows us the most perfect image of this life that germinates in the passion of movement . . . Insofar as he allows us to experience our deepest life once more in the sphere of art, he saves us from precisely that which we experience in the sphere of reality.[88]

In the dimension of social theory, the presentation of the restless motion of everyday modern life – its snapshots, as it were – takes the form of highlighting their eternal forms *sub specie aeternitatis*. This is, as it were, the ideal of Simmel's social theory that, like the perfect work of art, is so seldom realized.

Yet if this aesthetic ideal motivates much of Simmel's social theory, an almost contrary image illuminates the source of his insights. Although Simmel spent some considerable amount of time explicating and classifying the problem of sociology in his earlier works at least, we very seldom find any reference to the task or role of the sociologist. This may not be surprising if we consider that he was contemptuous of those narrow definitions and demarcations of disciplines which then, as now, predominated in the social sciences. But it might also suggest that, where Simmel seldom chose to identify himself as a 'sociologist', he was willing to describe himself as a philosopher. His major work in social theory prior to the *Soziologie* is undoubtedly *The Philosophy of Money*, that is, a 'philosophy' rather than a 'sociology' of money, however much it might contain an elaborate social theory. Hence, it is not surprising to find that Simmel provides us with clues as to his identification with philosophy in the broadest sense, as a mode of reflection upon reality. In one of his essays, Simmel combines this with reflections upon the experiential sources of such reflections, some of which unwittingly anticipate Benjamin's outline of a theory of experience of modernity. The essay also supplements the argument that Simmel may, in part, be regarded as a sociological *flâneur* which has been outlined elsewhere.

In his essay 'The Philosophy of Adventure' (1910, subsequently 'The Adventure' 1911)[89] Simmel seeks to explicate the features of an adventure as 'a *form* of *experience*'. Since he identifies himself as a philosopher and describes the philosopher as 'the intellectual adventurer' in the world who 'treats this unsoluble as if it were soluble',[90] we may justifiably take this account as a description of Simmel's own attitude. Combined with the earlier image of 'The Stranger' (1908) – which both Coser and Landmann take to be the key to Simmel's social experience as the basis for his social theory[91] – the notion of the adventure expresses the experience of the 'extraordinary'. As a 'wanderer' through the everyday world, Simmel is able to adopt 'a distinctly "objective" attitude' to social reality since he possesses that lack of attachment and the necessary distance of the wanderer.[92] The stranger is not a part of the everyday world in which he or she moves. Similarly, the most general feature of the form of the adventure is 'that it falls outside the context of life' in the sense of the continuity of everyday, routinized life. But just as the concept of the stranger only makes sense in terms of his or her location *within* a social environment, so the adventure is not merely 'a foreign body in our existence' but also 'a form of being inside' it.

Before analysing the experience of the adventure, Simmel briefly makes two analogies which, in their different ways, are significant for a theory of modernity. The first is the analogy with dreaming. Simmel maintains that

> for memory, the adventure easily acquires the nuance of dreaming. Everyone knows how quickly we forget dreams, because they too place themselves outside the meaningful context of the totality of life. What we characterise as 'dream-like' is nothing other than a remembrance which is connected with fewer strands than other experiences to the unified and continuous process of life . . . The more 'adventurous' an adventure is, that is, the more perfectly it accords with the concept, the more 'dream-like' it will be for our memory.[93]

This process may even take the form of being so dream-like that we conceive of the adventure as if it had been undertaken by someone else. It confronts us in our remembrance of it as something strange. As we shall see, the 'dream-like' nature of social phantasies is a central preoccupation of Benjamin's theory of experience. It is also highly relevant to Kracauer's deciphering of the hieroglyphics of society.

Simmel's second analogy refers to the circumscribed nature of the adventure that, more definitely than other experiences, has a demarcated beginning and end. Here Simmel detects the affinity between the adventurer and the artist, 'for it is indeed the nature of the work of art that it cuts out a piece from the endless continuous series of perception or experience, releases it from connections with all this sidedness and that sidedness and gives it an autonomous, determinate and cohesive form as if from an inner core'.[94] In other words, it extracts one part of human existence and creates a totality out of it that is experienced as 'a closed entity' in the same way as we experience an adventure. Both acquire a self-enclosed autonomy. This could also stand as an instance not merely of Simmel's conception of the work of art but also as a description of his own procedure especially in his essays and including 'The Adventure'.

Simmel shared this 'unique attitude to life' of the adventurer. The experience of the adventure in the social context constitutes an apparent break from the flatness of reified existence, from the indifference that he saw as so apparent in modern society. The adventure takes on a dynamic; it is filled with a different form of experiencing time. The isolated and fortuitous experience that often forms the content to experience also illuminates Simmel's method of social analysis in so far as it commences from 'the fortuitous fragment of reality'. The fortuitousness and uniqueness are heightened in experience. Again, anticipating another of Benjamin's motifs, that of the gambler, Simmel records the affinity between the adventurer and the gambler. The gambler 'is indeed at the mercy of the meaninglessness of coincidence' but seeks to invest it with meaning. The gambler sets out from the conviction 'that in the coincidence there resides a meaning, some kind of necessary – though not a necessity that accords with rational logic – significance'.[95] The game challenges the seriousness of everyday routine. Hence, what Simmel describes as the quickened time of the adventure also accords with the experience of time by the gambler:

> Its atmosphere is . . . unconditional presentness, the quickening of the process of life to a point that possesses neither past nor future and therefore contains life within itself with an intensity that, compared with the content of what has gone before, is often relatively indifferent.[96]

Here is yet another unwitting anticipation of Benjamin's notion of the shock experience (*Chockerlebnis*). The 'unconditional present-ness' of the game as such rather than the prospect of winning is what motivates the gambler. For the adventurer, it is this same 'intensity and tension' that fills out our experience of the isolated coincidence.

It is worth noting here that over a decade earlier, in his 'Sociological Aesthetics' (1896), Simmel refers explicitly to the shock experience in a context almost identical with Benjamin's subsequent treatment. There, Simmel argues that modern life itself 'makes us more and more sensitive to the shocks [*Chocs*] and turmoils which we confront in the immediate proximity and contact with people and things'.[97] This experience is given a much more specific location than merely 'modern life' in his *Philosophy of Money*.

Both the gambler and the adventurer seek out the tension of immediate presentness that resides in the game or the adventure. In this respect, the erotic adventure of a fleeting sexual relationship, is itself only a heightened form of the more general erotic pleasure derived from the adventure as such: 'the adventure is the exclave of the life-context, that which has been torn away [das *Abgerissene*]'. But the intensity and tension with which the immediate present of the adventure is experienced rests upon the fact that we cannot live in permanent tension; we cannot experience an endless adventure. Rather, 'from the most secure bourgeois activity to the most irrational adventure there exists a continuous series of manifestations of life . . . In that the adventure characterises the one extreme in this series, so necessarily does the other play a part in its character.'[98] In this way, the adventure is 'only one piece of existence amongst others', even though the radical nature and amount of tension experienced 'makes the mere lived experience [*Erlebnis*] into an adventure'. The adventure is abstracted from 'the fragmentary and varied quantity and circumstances' in which average everyday existence takes place.

But this placing of the adventure once more on the continuum of life experiences, suggests that, in the last resort, Simmel is not prepared to consider the radical nature of the disjunction between the adventure and everyday existence. The fleeting, transitory attraction of the adventure only exists in so far as it is removed from the everyday. That is, the contradiction between the two is removed by the elevation of the adventure into an autonomous sphere. It is not that the adventure, like the dream, radicalizes or even shatters the everyday mundane conceptions. Rather it stands 'over and above life'. Like art for Simmel it constitutes an image of life beyond all decisions. The adventure, like art, exists in a timeless realm:

> Precisely because the work of art and the adventure stand juxtaposed to life . . . the one and the other are analogous to the totality of a life itself, as it is presented in the brief outline and the condensation of the dream experience. Thereby, *the adventurer is also the most powerful example of the unhistorical person, of the contemporary essence. On the one hand, he is determined by no past . . . on the other, the future does not exist for him.* [My emphasis.][99]

The experience of modernity is precisely this immediate presentness. But since the adventurer has no historical boundaries, it is a motif that is also rendered eternal by Simmel.

It should come as no surprise, therefore, to discover that several decades later Benjamin associated the adventure with this lived experience in the nineteenth century. In a section of his Arcades Project on idling (*Müssiggang*), Benjamin comments that 'the intentional correlate of "lived experience" [*Erlebnis*] has not remained the same. In the nineteenth century, it was "the adventure". In our day it appears as "fate".'[100] In both cases, it centres around the notion of the 'total lived experience', broken away from any concrete historical experience. The implication of Benjamin's analysis is that any autonomy which the merely lived experience attains is a false one. It suggests the need to examine more closely those experiences which were significant for the development of Simmel's theory of modernity.

VII

In one of his incomplete sketches for his *Passagenarbeit*, Walter Benjamin points to the social experiences that inform Baudelaire's work, experiences which are the foundation for his reception of *modernité*. These social experiences, Benjamin argues, are

> nowhere derived from the production process – least of all in its most advanced form the industrial process – but all of them originated in it in extensive roundabout ways . . . The most important among them are the experiences of the neurasthenic, of the big-city dweller, and of the customer.[101]

Such experiences are also paramount in Simmel's treatment of modernity. But it is not merely that Simmel devotes some considerable attention to their analysis but also that his own reflections are largely derived from these same social experiences, though in a different context. A contemporary commentator characterized Simmel as an 'intellectual neurasthenic'.[102] His son Hans recalled his father saying that 'Berlin's development from a city to a metropolis in the years around and after the turn of the century coincides with my own strongest and extensive development'.[103] At the centre of much of Simmel's analysis in his *Philosophy of Money* stands the consumer of commodities and the exchange process. His other essays on fashion and style, for instance, also testify to his preoccupation, not with the production process and hardly at all ever with industrial production but rather with the forms of experiencing the indirect consequences of such a process.

Yet Simmel's presentation and reception of *modernité*, unlike Baudelaire's, is not a poetic one. Nor, on the other hand, can it be characterized as a rigorous historical analysis of modernity. Yet at the same time, Simmel's presentation of *modernité* does contain elements of both tendencies. His sociological impressionism and his aesthetic stance vis-à-vis his object of study brings him close to an artistic response to modern life.[104] As Hamann comments, 'impressionist thought is quite transformed into art'.[105] On the other hand, especially in his *Philosophy of Money*, Simmel does seek to provide not merely a description but also an explanation for the modernist way of life.

The social location of Simmel's reflections upon *modernité* constitute both the source of his insights and their limitation. If we commence our analysis of the social location of Simmel's sociology with its relationship to metropolitan life, then it will not be difficult to move on to the other two sources that Benjamin also gives for Baudelaire's inspiration. The experiences of the neurasthenic appear at the very start of Simmel's analysis of metropolitan life which, at the same time, also closes with an indication of the extent to which its features are related to the development of the money economy.

Simmel's attachment to Berlin and his location within it during the period of its most rapid expansion, as well as its significance for his own work, can be readily documented. Margarete Susman – one of his students – points to the fact that 'metropolitan, lively, restless Berlin on the corner of Leipziger – and Friedrichstrasse was decisive for his life and thought.[106] His friend Karl Joël argued that Simmel's

Philosophy of Money, which 'has overheard the innermost tone of modern
life', 'could only be written in these times and in Berlin'.[107] Simmel
himself maintained that the 'specific achievement, that I have in fact
brought to fruition in these decades, is indoubtedly bound up with
the Berlin milieu'.[108] But though such statements testify to the
significance of Berlin for Simmel's work, they do not begin to answer
either the question as to his precise location within it or how Simmel
himself conceived of it.

At a somewhat abstract level, we might view Simmel as a sociological
flâneur, but not one 'who goes botanizing on the asphalt'.[109] Rather,
Simmel's social vignettes are not always those of someone who wanders
through the whole class structure. Sometimes, as in his account of
urban transport or his outline of a sociology of the senses, Simmel
expresses the response of a member of the bourgeoisie towards the
working class. They are the observations of someone who stands
outside the lower social strata, even of someone who remains distanced
from many social contexts. And yet this very distance was also the
source of many of his insights into social situations.

In order to clarify this location, it is necessary to point out that,
even in his famous essay on metropolitan life, Simmel is unwittingly
describing a particular type of urban social environment – that of
capital cities. The social ecology of industrial cities is not of specific
interest to Simmel. On the other hand, the fact that capital cities,
as institutional and administrative centres, are often the location for
the cultural hegemony of the bourgeoisie and furnish a large middle
class population with a livelihood, is reflected in Simmel's examples
of urban social interaction. Yet neither is this specification of the class
structure of metropolitan centres the focus of Simmel's concern.
Though at the end of his life in Strasbourg, he felt cut off from the
Berlin milieu and its metropolitan life, this does not mean that
Simmel's relation to Berlin was that of the documentary reporter.
His social vignettes are not informed by a social documentary interest
in big city life. The 'snapshots' of social interaction and the fragments
of sociability that lie at the heart of his analysis are those of someone
who can retreat from the asphalt. Whereas for the *flâneur*, as Benjamin
puts it, 'the joy of watching is triumphant', for Simmel it is perhaps
the search for 'the transitory, fleeting beauty of our present life' – as
Baudelaire characterized Constantin Guy's aesthetic interest – that
is paramount. Simmel is a privileged observer within his social milieu
but he is also a sociologist who seeks to typify what he observes. The
typification exists not as critical social reportage, as in Kracauer, for

instance, but as the search for the essentiality of social situations and interactions. Even the notion of 'snapshots' viewed from the aspect of eternity – as Simmel entitled several of his essays – is misleading in this respect. There are no specific persons in Simmel's snapshots. Rather, there are fleeting images of human types, of types of sociability and interaction that are viewed *sub specie aeternitatis*. This search for the 'essence' of forms of social interaction leads Simmel firmly away from their 'historical' analysis. In the present context, we can plausibly argue that Simmel's approach to modernity results in him rendering it eternal. In contrast, as we shall see, Benjamin's conviction, even in his early *One-Way Street*, was that 'this burdened totality of modernity was in decline'.[110]

Thus, when Kracauer maintains that Simmel is 'a person of the multitude and a loner, an empathetic person, a sociable person who possesses, moreover, a knowledge of the entire situations in which he places himself',[111] such qualities can only be applied to a somewhat restricted social range of situations. Simmel does provide us with a masterly account of the consequences of urban life – in themselves based on a money economy – but it is a very distinctive one that does not encompass the 'entire situation' of urban life but highly selective aspects of it.

Nonetheless, the urban context is as central to Simmel's account of modernity as it is to those of Kracauer and Benjamin and as it was to Baudelaire. Just as Benjamin argues that 'the *flâneur* is the priest of the genius loci'[112] so too is Simmel's account of *modernité* located in specific spatial configurations. Simmel was the first sociologist to reveal explicitly the social significance of spatial contexts for human interaction. Spatial images of society were later to be crucial to Kracauer's own 'topography of social space' as well as Benjamin's analysis of the relation between the *flâneur* and the arcades, the bourgeois *intérieur* and the spatial location of commodities. But no other social theorist was so preoccupied with social distance, with detachment from reality, with 'the intersection of social circles' as was Simmel. In the analysis of modern society, all are located primarily within an urban context.

The metropolis is the focal point for the other social experiences that are the basis for the analysis of *modernité*. Even when we characterize Simmel's own approach to his subject matter as sociological impressionism, this too, according to Hamann, has its origins in city life. Benjamin, too, suggests that 'the technique of Impressionist painting, whereby the picture is garnered in a riot of dabs

of colour, would be a reflection of experiences with which the eyes
of a big-city dweller have become familiar'.[113] In Simmel's case, the
affinity might be with the myriad of social vignettes that populate his
works. The riot of social encounters and experiences in the metropolis
is also one of the sources of neurasthenia, a central consequence of
urban life. Simmel's analysis of the consumer is located within the
context of the metropolis, as are his related accounts of fashion, style
and trade exhibitions. The metropolis and modern urban life in general
are the location of the consequences of the modern money economy.
The last chapter of Simmel's *Philosophy of Money*, dealing as it does
with 'The Style of Life', not merely seeks to demonstrate that the
consequences of urban life result largely from the extension of the
money economy but also that we may view its most extreme
consequences within the metropolis. The three central experiences
of a dramatic increase in nervous life, the experience of the
metropolitan dweller, and the participant in a mature money economy
must now be examined in greater detail.

Neurasthenia

Almost as a paradigm for modernity, Simmel describes the inner core
of modernity amid 'the clamorous splendour of the scientific techno-
logical age'. The individual's inner security is replaced by 'a faint
sense of tension and vague longing', by a 'secret restlessness', by a
'helpless urgency' which 'originates in the bustle and excitement of
modern life'. This restlessness is manifested most obviously in urban
life:

> The lack of something definite at the centre of the soul impels us to
> search for monentary satisfaction in ever-new stimulations, sensations
> and external activities. Thus it is that we become entangled in the
> instability and helplessness that manifests itself as the tumult of the
> metropolis, as the mania for travelling, as the wild pursuit of
> competition and as the typically modern disloyalty with regard to taste,
> style, opinions and personal relationships.[114]

The extreme consequences that we find in urban life are the result
of the extension of the money economy. Not surprisingly, therefore,
Simmel sees this nervous tension as a feature of 'modern times,
particularly the most recent' which 'are permeated by a feeling of
tension, expectation and unreleased intense desires'.[115] The neurosis
which 'lies below the threshold of consciousness' originates in 'that

increasing distance from nature and that particularly abstract existence that urban life, based on the money economy, has forced upon us'.[116]

At the very outset of his essay on the metropolis, Simmel maintains that 'the psychological foundation of the metropolitan personality type is the *increase in nervous life*, which emerges out of the rapid and unbroken change in external and internal stimuli'.[117] Such 'psychological preconditions' for the modern nervous personality are created by the metropolis itself – 'with every crossing of the street, with the speed and diversity of economic professional, social life'. In its extreme form, this constant bombardment of the senses with new or ever changing impressions, produces the neurasthenic personality which, ultimately, can no longer cope with this jostling array of impressions and confrontations. This leads to attempts to create a distance between ourselves and our social and physical environment. Though Simmel views this distance as 'an emotional trait' that is peculiar to the modern period, its 'pathological deformation is so-called agoraphobia: the fear of coming into too close a contact with objects, a consequence of hyperaesthesia, for which every direct and energetic disturbance causes pain'.[118] This is the extreme form of the modern 'sense of being oppressed by the externalities of modern life' to which we become increasingly indifferent. Urban existence, as an extreme form of the objectification of social relationships brought about by the money economy, requires a distance between the individual and his social environment. It requires

> an inner barrier . . . between people, a barrier, however, that is indispensable for the modern form of life. For the jostling crowdedness and the motley disorder of metropolitan communication would simply be unbearable without such psychological distance. Since contemporary urban culture, with its commercial, professional and social intercourse, forces us to be physically close to an enormous number of people, sensitive and nervous modern people would sink completely into despair if the objectification of social relationships did not bring with it an inner boundary and reserve.[119]

This 'psychological distance' of which Simmel speaks here, can take the extreme form of agoraphobia and hyper-sensitivity. It can also take the form of total indifference, an indifference that is located in the blasé attitude to life. In his essay on the metropolis, Simmel maintains that

There is perhaps no psychological phenomenon that is so unreservedly associated with the metropolis as the blasé attitude. The blasé attitude results first from the rapidly changing and closely compressed contrasting stimulations of the nerves . . . A life in boundless pursuit of pleasure makes one blasé because it agitates the nerves to their strongest reactivity for such a long time that they finally cease to react at all. In the same way, through the rapidity and contradictoriness of their changes, more harmless impressions force such violent responses, tearing the nerves so brutally hither and thither that their last reserves of strength are spent . . . There thus emerges an incapacity to react to new sensations with the appropriate energy.[120]

However, Simmel goes on to suggest that 'this physiological source of the metropolitan blasé attitude' is closely bound up with one derived from the money economy. The levelling process operating in the latter – the reduction of everything to the common denominator of exchange value – also produces a personality type who

has completely lost the feeling for value differences. He experiences all things as being of an equally dull and grey hue, as not worth getting excited about . . . Whoever has become possessed by the fact that the same amount of money can procure all the possibilities that life has to offer must also become blasé. As a rule, the blasé attitude is rightly attributed to satiated enjoyment because too strong a stimulus destroys the nervous ability to respond to it.[121]

Yet it has an opposite source, derived not from 'the attraction of things' but from their mode of acquisition as when

the more the acquisition is carried out in a mechanical and indifferent way, the more the object appears to be colourless and without interest.[122]

This is especially true in the advanced money economy where almost everything can be acquired through financial transactions. Yet, paradoxically, the blasé response to this condition is for ever-new attractions, out of which

there emerges the craving today for excitement, for extreme impressions, for the greatest speed in its change . . . the modern preference for 'stimulation' as such in impressions, relationships and information – without thinking it important for us to find out why these stimulate us – also reveals the characteristic entanglement with means: one is satisfied with this preliminary stage of the genuine production of values.[123]

Stimulation itself becomes the cure for total indifference. In 'The Berlin Trade Exhibition' (1896), Simmel was already arguing that the 'over-excited and exhausted nerves'[124] of modern urbanites produced a thirst for yet more amusement, such as was afforded by the distractions of world exhibitions. With reference to big city life, Simmel maintains that individual self-preservation, in the context of urban life and commodity exchange, is purchased at the price of devaluing the objective world and devaluing individuals too. This need for self-preservation also affects the mode of interaction in city life. It manifests itself in an 'external reserve' towards others that has its origins not merely in indifference – as in the blasé attitude – but 'a slight aversion, a mutual strangeness and repulsion, which will break into hatred and struggle at the moment of a closer contact, however caused'.[125]

The neurotic forms of behaviour that Simmel outlines result largely from the oscillation between close confrontation with objects and people and an excessive distance from them. As Troeltsch pointed out, this oscillation is to be found within Simmel's own characterization of modernity. In *Der Krieg und die geistigen Entscheidungen* (1917), Simmel argues that

> There exists a deep inner connection between too close a captivation with things and too great a distance from them which, with a kind of fear of contact, places us in a vacuum. We knew for a long time that we were suffering equally from both of them.[126]

Troeltsch adds that 'this is stated with a degree of self-criticism'. In 1917 Simmel added that we 'were indeed ripe for the restoration of our health'.[127]

Even this brief outline of Simmel's preoccupation with the dramatic increase in nervous energy necessitated by urban life and a developed money economy dominated by exchange values should suggest that it is a central theme of his account of modernity. Troeltsch seems to suggest that Simmel himself was afflicted with this modern neurasthenia which he so often describes. Another astute contemporary described him as an 'intellectual neurasthenic'. Altmann, reviewing *The Philosophy of Money*, observes that 'Nervous to the fingertips, of the almost frightening sensibility of the neurasthenic, Simmel is one of the most ingenious interpreters of psychic emotions, incomparable in the gift to feel the most subtle vibrations of the soul.'[128] Simmel's friend Karl Joël also maintained that 'whoever saw and heard him only externally, would notice particularly strongly in him the fundamental symptoms of the times, a nervous restlessness'.[129] In other words, Simmel's own social experiences were the foundation for his account of modernity. He not only described the features of modernity that he saw in contemporary society, he also lived them out. 'The experience of the neurasthenic' is reflected in his writings as a preoccupation with what 'lies below the threshold of consciousness'. In a somewhat different context, Everett Hughes characterizes Simmel as 'the Freud of the study of society'.[130] Though such a description is in keeping with his sociological account of neurasthenia, it is clearly deficient in so far as Simmel was unconcerned with tracing symptoms back to their subconscious origins. Indeed, Simmel's procedure may be characterized as almost the converse: what lies below the threshold of consciousness is traced to the processes operating on the surface of society. Simmel's account of neurasthenia is in terms of its social preconditions in urban life and the developed money economy.

But we must guard against the assumption that this neurasthenia was always conceived negatively by Simmel and his contemporaries. As someone whose very approach to his subject-matter rested upon an aestheticization of reality, this hypersensitivity was essential to Simmel's *'Anschauungsweise'*. Its role in creativity is not dissimilar to that of Simmel's contemporary, Stefan George. In his study of European aestheticism, Wuthenow speaks of George's 'highly developed sensitivity and avowed nervousness' and asserts that 'the "neurasthenia" of modernism is positively applied as an expression of refinement, as the extension or sharpening of the capacity for apperception and as the expansion or deepening of the realm of experience'.[131] In Simmel's case, one may point to the emphasis upon the notion of distinction (*Vornehmheit*) or refinement and its association with creativity, which abounds in his work, at least from *The Philosophy of Money* onwards. At the biographical level, Simmel stood close to the George circle around the turn of the century, influenced their thought and even, according to some contemporary observers, imitated George's mode of dress. This circle of intellectuals and artists was very much distanced from the urban crowds. This was in contrast to Baudelaire, as Wuthenow points out, when he suggests that 'George held himself haughtily at a distance from the crowd to which Baudelaire avowedly offered himself.'[132] As we have already argued, Simmel's own interest in urban life is hardly that of the documentary reporter but that of someone who could retreat to his salon to prepare what von Wiese somewhat disparagingly termed 'the sociology of an aesthete'.[133] Furthermore, this heightened social distance would suggest that whereas, in Benjamin's terms, the first moment of *modernité* that is expressed in Baudelaire's work is still concerned with concrete experience, with *Erfahrung*, the second moment of *art nouveau* (*Jugendstil*) gains its inspiration from inner experiences (*Erlebnisse*) that are the product of a distance from social reality and a retreat into the *intérieur*. But in order to arrive at this inward retreat, we must first confront Simmel's account of the metropolis.

The Social Experience of the Metropolis

How does Simmel conceive of the metropolis? What are its features and what is it that interests Simmel about the metropolis? What features of modernity have their roots in urbanism? Is the metropolis actually their source or is it part of a wider whole such as the money economy? In order to answer these questions we must turn not merely to his essay on the metropolis but to some of his other writings.

Within the context of Simmel's sociology of space, the city as such is to be defined in terms of its sociological rather than its territorial boundaries. Though it is a distinctive social space that 'fundamentally acts upon social interactions within it', the city is 'not a spatial entity with sociological consequences, but a sociological entity that is formed spatially'.[134] The metropolis is not merely the focal point of social differentiation and complex social networks, but also the location of indefinite collectivities – crowds whose impulsiveness and enthusiasm rests in part upon the fact that 'they either find themselves out in the open or in a . . . very large space'.[135] This openness, that also manifests itself in the city as a transportation centre bringing together diverse social strata, contrasts sharply with the social distance signified by 'a concentrated minority' in the ghetto. This fixing of the spatial locations is also illustrated by Simmel in the concept of the rendezvous which 'characterises both meeting together itself as well as its location'. It is something individual and unique. Similarly, the individualization of place – in cities originally by name and then by number (a feature instanced both by Simmel and later by Benjamin for Paris) – contrasts with the continuous flow and levelling of social interaction in the city.

The big city provides the possibility for total indifference towards one's neighbours, not merely in the sense of those with whom one lives in close proximity but also those whom one confronts in everyday social contexts. Confronted with the crowd of potential interactions, the individual seeks some form of self-preservation that in city dwellers is associated with indifference. It also results from another feature that Benjamin chose to emphasize in his own analysis of urban life by quoting from Simmel:

> The person who is able to see but unable to hear is much more . . . troubled than the person who is able to hear but unable to see. Here is something . . . characteristic of the big city. The interpersonal relationships of people in big cities are characterised by a markedly greater emphasis on the use of the eyes than on that of the ears. This can be attributed chiefly to the institution of public conveyances. Before buses, railroads and trams became fully established during the nineteenth century, people were never put in the position of having to stare at one another for minutes or even hours on end without exchanging a word.[136]

Simmel also points to our sense of smell as a dissociating sense – having to confront the odour of other social groups (Simmel's questionable examples are 'the negro' in the US, 'Jews and manual workers').[137]

The social reserve prevalent in social interaction in big cities as a means of preserving social distance and maintaining the individual self intact threatened by the tumult of continuously changing stimuli, brings us back to the theme of the inner consequences of metropolitan life. But before returning to Simmel's 'Metropolis and Mental Life', a further example from his 'Sociology of Space' is instructive.

As an instance of the consequence of change of place and travel – both having increased with urbanization – Simmel points to an interesting social consequence that seems to operate in the opposite direction to the indifference and hostility to those we come into contact with in big cities:

> Acquaintance on a journey . . . often develops an intimacy and open-heartedness for which there exists really no inner reason. It seems to me that three elements are at work here: detachment from one's usual milieu, the communality of momentary impressions and encounters and consciousness of the succeeding and definite parting of the ways.[138]

Acquaintanceship on a journey, seduced by the feeling that one is under no obligation, and that one is confronted by a person from whom one will be shortly parted for ever and who is actually anonymous, often leads to quite remarkable confidences, to unlimited compliance compared with our impulse to express ourselves which we have learned to control in the light of experience of its consequences in our usual long-term relationships.[139]

A not dissimilar anonymity was to become much more commonplace in another social context that Simmel does not describe, namely psychoanalysis. Here, however, we have another instance of Simmel's unswerving interest in the vignettes of social interaction, and that even formed the starting point for much of the literature that was originally produced to distract travellers on long railway journeys in the nineteenth century. Of more general significance here, however, is the fact that Simmel was the first sociologist to explicitly emphasize the analysis of social space, an interest that was extended by Kracauer and Benjamin in their own analysis of modernity.

Yet if we return to Simmel's 'Metropolis and Mental Life' essay, we find that it is not merely the dramatic expansion of nervous life in the urban population, nor merely the sociological significance of the spatial organization of cities that interests Simmel. In that essay, the opening passage provides the context for a central theme of his work around the turn of the century. There, Simmel maintains that 'the deepest problems of modern life derive from the claim of the individual to preserve the autonomy and individuality of his existence in the face of overwhelming social forces, of historical heritage, of social culture, and of the technique of life'.[140] Sociology must seek to solve 'the equation which structures like the metropolis set up between the individual and the super-individual contents of life' and inquire 'how the personality accommodates itself in the adjustments of external forces'. This is predicated upon the assumption that 'the person resists being levelled down and worn out by a social-technological mechanism' such as the metropolis.

But this 'social-technological mechanism' is one that we have created but which, as a reified objective culture, stands over against our subjective culture as something alien. Elsewhere, Simmel asserts that

No one, in fact, will fail to concede that the style of modern life, precisely as a result of its mass character, its hasty variety, its equalisation, extending beyond all possible boundaries, of countless hitherto conserved entities has led to unheard of levelling of the personal form of life itself.[141]

But Simmel has already pointed to the opposite consequence, perhaps the result of this very levelling, namely the attempt to accentuate individuality and subjectivity. As compensation for this levelling process we find the 'exaggerated subjectivism of the period' to which Simmel so often refers.[142]

This extreme subjectivism as a response to the extreme objectification of culture reaches its apogee in the metropolis which is

> the genuine showplace of this culture which grows beyond all that is personal. Here, in buildings and educational institutions, in the wonders and comforts of space-conquering technology, in the formations of communal life and in the visible state institutions, there is offered such an overpowering wealth of crystallised, impersonalised mind, as it were, that the personality cannot maintain itself when confronted with it.[143]

This preponderance of the objective over the subjective in the metropolis has its deeper origins in the fact that the metropolis is the seat of the money economy. Indeed 'the money economy dominates the metropolis'. The extension of the money economy and the domination of the intellect ultimately coincide. The pure objectivity of the treatment of people and things leads to an indifference as to what is distinctive since money transactions are concerned only with exchange values. On the other hand, the heightening of this very intellectuality in metropolitan people acts as a form of self preservation since the reaction to the shocks and tempo of urban confrontations 'is shifted to that organ which is least sensitive and quite remote from the depth of the personality'.[144]

The subjective objectivity or 'dissociation' in dealings with other human beings in the urban context 'without which this mode of life could not at all be led', is in fact 'only one of its elementary forms of socialisation'. Like the developed money economy, it has a positive side, 'namely, it secures for the individual a kind and measure of personal freedom for which there exists no analogy under other circumstances'. Yet this very freedom, in turn, has an obverse potentiality.

> For the mutual reserve and indifference, the psychological conditions of life of broad sectors are never felt more strongly by the individual

with regard to their impact upon his independence than in the densest throng, because the bodily proximity and confined space makes the mental distance all the more readily visible. It is clearly merely the obverse of this freedom if, under particular circumstances, one nowhere feels so lonely and lost than in the metropolitan crowd. For here, as elsewhere, it is in no way necessary that human beings' freedom be reflected in their emotional life as a sense of well-being.[145]

The individual's struggle for self-assertion, when confronted with general indifference, may take the form of stimulating a sense of distinctiveness from one's fellow urbanites. This also takes excessive forms which

> ultimately entice one to adopt the most tendentious eccentricities, the specifically metropolitan excesses of aloofness, caprice and fastidiousness, whose significance no longer lies in the content of such behaviour but rather in its form of being different, of making oneself stand out and thus attracting attention.[146]

This is made all the more necessary in the light of 'the brevity and infrequency of meetings which are allotted to each individual compared with interaction in a small town' and which necessitate coming to the point as quickly as possible and making as striking an impression in the briefest possible time. The 'calculating exactness of practical life' – resulting from a money economy – also reinforces this tendency since

> The relationships and concerns of the typical metropolitan resident are so manifold and complex that, especially as a result of the agglomeration of so many persons with such differentiated interests, their relationships and activities intertwine with one another into a many-membered organism. In view of this fact, the lack of the most exact punctuality in promises and activities would cause the whole to break down into an inextricable chaos. If all the clocks in Berlin suddenly went wrong in different ways even only as much as an hour, its entire economic and commercial life would be derailed for some time.[147]

But this very diversity of interests that requires such exact co-ordination is itself the result of a further factor – the division of labour and social and functional differentiation.

For Simmel, cities are 'the seat of the most advanced economic division of labour'. To the division of labour in production is added the associated specialization in consumption – the 'differentiation, refinement and enrichment of the needs of the public – which is so apparent in the metropolitan context. It is 'the money economy which dominates the metropolis'. As a result of both, we are confronted with a monumental objective culture that threatens individual creativity and growth. We are faced, Simmel argues, by 'the atrophy of individual culture through the hypertrophy of objective culture' whose divergence is particularly apparent 'in the upper classes'. With the reintroduction of this theme we are once more confronted with the same problematic with which Simmel opened his analysis of the metropolitan life. It is a problematic which Simmel works through here in the context of the metropolitan psyche but which remains a permanent theme in his socio-cultural critique of modern society.

The individual is confronted with the domination of society, historical tradition, external culture and technology all of which threaten to overwhelm him. But there is something contradictory about this apposition. It contradicts, in part, Simmel's presupposition of the fundamental interrelatedness of all social phenomena in so far as we can conceive of this objective culture becoming so reified that it has no relationship whatsoever to individuals. In other words, some significant sectors of social phenomena become so congealed and solidified that they bear little relation to their creators, except as an overwhelming 'hypertrophy of objective culture'. Secondly, at the methodological level, social institutions and structures are not of particular interest to Simmel as a sociologist. Perhaps because they are not analysable by him from his particular perspective they become unnecessarily overpowering. They become, as it were, 'society' in the sense of that reified abstraction whose introduction into sociology Simmel so consistently opposed.

But is there a more specific social significance of this central theme in Simmel's work, one that is connected with his account of modernity? We have already seen that the response to this alienating objective culture on the part of its victims is a growing indifference to people and values, an increasingly blasé attitude towards the world and a retreat to the inner sphere. Indifference and a blasé attitude can be readily incorporated into a wider aestheticization of reality that seeks to emphasize the distance between the individual and the world. The retreat into inwardness (*Innerlichkeit*) and the *intérieur* is often taken to be a consistent feature of *Jugendstil*. The inward retreat, for certain strata of society, especially the *Kulturbürgertum* at the turn of the century, was readily combined with the beautification (*Verschönung*) of life from a subjective standpoint. Reserve and indifference as defence mechanisms in the metropolis are most likely to be used by those social strata who, from a relatively secure social position, can afford to adopt this response. This cloak of functional objectivity is adopted towards metropolitan man's 'merchant, his customer and with his servant, and frequently with the persons with whom he is thrown into obligatory association'.[148] Simmel's account of metropolitan life would appear to refer particularly to specific social strata.

There is another way in which Simmel's account of metropolitan life is significant for his work as a whole. It was suggested by one of his contemporaries that metropolitan life itself was the source of Simmel's methodology in its widest sense. Hamann, who made substantial use of Simmel's social analysis in *The Philosophy of Money*, argued that at least one current artistic tendency – impressionism, within which rubric Hamann also included many features of *Jugendstil* – also had its basis in the metropolis. Since it has been argued elsewhere that Simmel's own approach to his object of study in this period may be characterized as a form of 'sociological impressionism' in this same wider sense, it is important to see how the experiences that are the basis for Simmel's account of modernity also have their roots in an aestheticization of reality.

Hamann's neglected study, *Der Impressionismus in Leben und Kunst* (1907) somewhat unwittingly confronts the features of modernity. His account of the arts, literature and philosophy at the turn of the century centres around a conception of impressionism that fails to distinguish it from *Jugendstil*. Impressionism he views as grounded philosophically in psychologism and socially in subjectivism and individualism. A positive value is placed on the unsystematic, symbolism and imagery, such that

> One *thinks and speaks in images*. Simmel's psychology derives its attractiveness from the fact that, in a psychologically interesting manner, he does not break down the total individual experiences that motivate people into abstract analytical elements but represents them through vivid images.[149]

That is, rather than being impressed by the strength of Simmel's analysis, we are confronted with the 'rapid interpretation of the momentary' and 'the aestheticisation of thought'. The description of impressionism provided by Hamann – including as it does many undifferentiated elements of *Jugendstil* – can also be read as an account of modernity.

But of greater interest is Hamann's attempt at a sociological explanation for the location and population of impressionism. It is one which draws heavily, as he acknowledges, upon Simmel's work and especially his *Philosophy of Money*. Hamann maintains that

> the impressionistic style of life finds a favourable basis in the *metropolis*. The external circumstances of life in such a large city are well suited to explaining much of impressionistic life.[150]

The particular features of metropolitan life that Hamann sees as being responsible for the growth of the impressionist stance are those that Simmel had already outlined as characteristic of urban life. The potential social isolation and lack of bonds made possible by urban life provides 'a greater moral normative freedom'. 'The number and variation of relationships', 'this fleetingness and superficiality of interaction' leads to a new evaluation of the momentary, to the unbounded 'charm of the moment'. On the other hand, within the context of objectified relationships, 'precisely this spatial and temporal distance, unburdened by memories and freed from any definite obligation to future behaviour, allows a general amiability to develop'.[151] Since the metropolis is the meeting point 'of the most diverse social strata, occupations and characters', it is not merely a concentration of individuals but is 'the focal point in which all threads converge, as a metropole' which continually provides 'new impressions and diversions' in newspapers, diverse political parties and standpoints and the like. The plurality and wealth of possibilities for enjoyment of all kinds provides a kind of erotic search for 'the variation of attractions and the passive ease of pleasure in consumption'. The rapid tempo of life encourages a capacity to react quickly and decisively' to mere intimations, fragments of a phenomena'. This 'diversity of attractions, relationships and opinions' constitutes the metropolitan milieu.

Hamann goes on to argue that out of this milieu the social strata within which impressionism has the greatest scope for development is 'the commercial strata' with its liberalism, its lack of active contact with production and its desire for an object to which it is not bound. As mediators operating with the ultimate economic mediator – money – use-values are of only momentary interest. With nothing besides money as a 'permanent' possesion, 'an aestheticism, a superficial impression' predominates vis-à-vis life. In other words, it is a strata of society which even outside the confines of the metropolis within which it is usually located experiences its features most strongly. But Hamann's central thesis is stated more simply as follows: namely that

> impressionism as a style goes along with a centralising tendency, a developed money economy, the domination of capitalism and the commercial and financial strata who provide its distinctive tone. Modern impressionism as art and life is totally at home in metropolitan centres – Berlin, Vienna, Paris, London.[152]

Hamann maintains in this context, that the connection between the money economy, commerce and the metropolis 'has found an interesting and significant expression in a *Philosophy of Money* by Georg Simmel, in fact in a completely impressionistic philosophy'.[153] It is one that embodies all the features of impressionism as Hamann interprets it – so much so that he was able to rely heavily upon Simmel's own account to symbolize the impressionist tendency.

The metropolis may well be the focus of a new kind of sociability, 'a general amiability' (Hamann), but only for specific social strata. Both the representation of social relations in the metropolis and its conception as the convergence and intersection of diverse social strands, produce an image of the metropolis as a harmonious whole that may well exist in the experience of specific strata in this configuration but hardly reflects the nature of the metropolis at the turn of the century. Such an interpretation, which shuts out other social realities, is reinforced by a sociology which sees as the central feature of society sociation and its purely abstract for sociability. Arguing against rationalism's dismissal of sociability as 'empty idleness', Simmel pleads for sociability as not merely 'the *play form of association*' but as the pure form of sociation itself:

> The political, the economic, the purposive society of any sort is, to be sure, always 'society'. But only the sociable gathering is 'society' without qualifying adjectives, because it alone presents the pure, abstract play of form, all the specific contents of the one-sided and qualified societies being dissolved away.[154]

Earlier Simmel had declared that 'humanity has created sociation as its form of life – which was not, as it were, the only logical possibility'.[155] Similarly, by transforming and dissolving the everyday world of the metropolis into forms of sociability, and thereby into a permanent harmony, the sociologist engages in a form of forgetfulness that obscures or even ignores the other social realities of the metropolis.

In so far as such an intention finds echoes in some dimension of Simmel's sociology, it too results in an image of society that is surprisingly harmonious and ultimately not disturbing. The undifferentiated manner in which social relations intermesh and converge in the metropolis suggests an image that also applies to Simmel's notion of society itself, namely the labyrinth.

The image of the labyrinth symbolizes not merely the metropolis but also the whole of society. But this 'web of group affiliations' or 'intersections of social circles' that partly constitutes the social labyrinth does not reveal the workings of society except at the level of ceaseless everyday interactions. To take as a contrast a literary example by an author preoccupied by the metropolis, it is plausible to argue that Dickens's *Bleak House* especially, as well as several of his mature novels, revolves around a conception of society as a labyrinth whose connections are undisclosed at the outset. By the end of the novel, key characters have revealed how the most unlikely members of the class structure are actually related to one another. However intricate the labyrinth of social connections – and Dickens's conception of society develops into a remarkably complex one by the time he writes *Our Mutual Friend* – there is a principle of differentiation at work which enables central figures to reveal the hierarchy of society as well as merely its connecting elements. Yet precisely this is not Simmel's intention. The labyrinth of society is illuminated aesthetically and not politically. Social circles may well intersect but their contradictions are not exposed. In the aestheticized conception of social reality, either they do not exist or they can be rendered harmless.

But if the labyrinth is a central motif in Simmel's work, what is it that holds it together? Since a labyrinth is not a hierarchical symbol, what is it that renders hierarchical differentiation unimportant? If society is a closely-woven web, where is Simmel's spider? Simmel's contemporaries were certainly aware of this powerful image in his work. Kracauer saw Simmel's *Philosophy of Money* as revealing 'the interwoven nature of the assembled parts of the diversity of the world', as presenting 'a comprehensive picture of the interconnectedness and entanglement of phenomena'.[156] Rudolph Goldscheid, in the same context, spoke of the 'excessive cobweb-like nature of his presentation of real circumstances'.[157] Lukács, with reference to Simmel's sociology, argued that 'this web of interrelationships must remain a labyrinth and cannot be a system'.[158] Yet is this motif of the labyrinth confined to the metropolis? At the end of his essay on the metropolis, Simmel notes that the origins of its specific features lie in the money economy.

The World of Money and Commodities

Benjamin maintained that the third social experience which afforded
Baudelaire his insights into modernity was that of the consumer. In
Simmel's case, we must extend this experience more broadly to cover
experience of the money economy as a whole. For Simmel, the
prehistory of modernity lies in the development of the money economy.
He saw the latter, rather than capitalism, as responsible for the
transformation of social relations and for the origins of major features
of metropolitan life. But there is no concrete historical interpretation
of the advent of modernity in Simmel's work. The fact that everything
flows into everything else, that the world is in continual flux, suggests
that Simmel retained his early evolutionism derived from Spencer
and others but as an evolutionism without 'stages' or 'breaks'. For
Simmel reflections upon the consequences of the mature money
economy represents the core of his analysis of modernity.

Simmel commenced his sociological reflections from the
metaphysical principle of the fundamental interrelatedness of all
phenomena. The various groups in society, the diverse forms of social
relationships are connected with one another as in a labyrinth. At
the end of his *Philosophy of Money*, Simmel asserts another metaphysical
principle that not only are all phenomena interrelated, they are also
in perpetual flux:

> In reality itself things do not last for any length of time: through the
> restlessness with which they offer themselves at any moment to the
> application of a law, every form becomes immediately dissolved in the
> very moment when it emerges; it lives, as it were, only by being
> destroyed; every consolidation of form into lasting objects – no matter
> how short they last – is an incomplete interpretation that is unable to
> follow the motion of reality at its own pace.[159]

Such a principle not only incorporates a motif of modernity – the
fleetingness of phenomena and our experience of them, a motif that
is particularly apparent in different ways in both impressionism
and *Jugendstil* – but also reveals its inner intention. The 'fleeting
beauty' in the fragments of modern life are to be rendered eternal
through art. Simmel's adherence to this dialectic of the permanent
and the transitory also throws light upon his description of some
of his own essays – 'snapshots *sub specie aeternitatis*'. More generally,
Simmel also argues that 'the goal of our thoughts is to find what

is steadfast and reliable behind ephemeral appearances and the flux of events'.[160] In keeping with the contemporary aesthetic currents of the time with which Simmel's work can be identified, this expresses his own intentions, namely to capture the fleeting images of modernity but to translate them into universal 'forms'. This paradoxical project must be qualified since 'whereas timeless objects are valid in the form of permanency, their opposites are valid in the form of transition, of non-permanency'.[161] Phenomena may be analysed from either vantage point since

> Only because reality is in constant motion is there any sense in asserting its opposite: the ideal system of eternally valid lawfulness. Conversely, it is only because such lawfulness exists that we are able to comprehend and grasp that stream of existence which would otherwise disintegrate into chaos.[162]

Leaving aside here the important question as to whether Simmel ever looked for 'laws' of society, we need to ask what social phenomenon embodies both the interrelatedness of the motif of society as a labyrinth and the notion of the dialectic of flux and permanence in the world?

Simmel's answer is unambiguous. 'There is no more striking symbol of the completely dynamic character of the world than money . . . the vehicle for a movement in which everything else that is not in motion is completely extinguished. It is, as it were, an *actus purus*.'[163] Yet money is also capable of embodying the opposite tendency by representing not merely 'a single economic value' but also 'abstract economic value in general'. In other words,

> As a tangible item, money is the most ephemeral thing in the external-practical world; yet in its content it is the most stable, since it stands at the point of indifference and balance between all other phenomena in the world.[164]

Money not merely symbolizes movement within society conceived as a labyrinth; its function within exchange also creates the very connections that constitute the economic labyrinth. It is the spider that weaves society's web.

In a roundabout manner, the experience of the consumer is a prominent source of Simmel's insights into modernity. Simmel's notion of society itself seems at times to rest upon the process prior to consumption, namely exchange. As 'a sociological phenomenon *sui generis*', the significance of exchange for society lies in the following:

as the economic realisation of the relativity of things . . . exchange raises the specific object and its significance for the individual above its singularity, not into the sphere of abstraction, but into that of lively interaction which is the substance of economic value.[165]

For Simmel, 'the interaction between individuals is the starting point of all social formations' and its symbolic object par excellence is money since it 'represents pure interaction in its purest form; it makes comprehensible the most abstract concept; it is an individual thing whose essential significance is to reach beyond individualities . . . and which interweaves all singularities and, in this fashion, creates reality.'[166] Exchange

> is obviously one of the functions that creates an inner bond between people – a society in place of a mere collection of individuals . . . exchange is a form of socialisation. It is one of those relations through which a number of individuals become a social group, and 'society' is identical with the sum total of those relations.[167]

Thus, social interaction is the basis of society and, since exchange is 'the purest sociological occurrence, the most complete form of interaction', exchange is a crucial form of sociation.

Within this context of the centrality of exchange relations, what grounds are there for arguing that consumption itself is crucial for Simmel's analysis of modernity? Simmel's subjectivist theory of value is probably derived from Menger and Böhm-Bawerk. The economy is grounded in exchange not in production. Value and exchange 'are mutually conditioning' and the economy itself 'is a special case of the general form of exchange', since 'exchange is the source of economic values'. It is not surprising, therefore, that Simmel has no specifically social theory of production. Instead he speaks of 'the exchange with nature which we call production' and exchange itself as 'just as productive and value-creating as is production itself'. Since Simmel maintains that 'it is of great importance to reduce the economic process to what really happens in the mind of each economic subject', there exists no difference between exchange in a subsistence and a market economy, nor between the exchange of goods or land and the same 'subjective process of sacrifice and gain in the individual mind' occurs in both instances. Not surprisingly, it is the psychological consequences of money transactions that so preoccupy him in *The Philosophy of Money*.[168]

Simmel's analysis of the consequences of a mature money economy hovers between an assertion of the eternal nature of its contradictions and a critique of its reifying aspects. Thus, it is argued that money is

> the reification of the pure relationship between things as expressed in their economic motion. Money stands between the individual objects related to it, in a realm organised according to its own norms which is the objectification of the movements of balancing and exchange originally accomplished by the objects themselves.[169]

This spectral objectivity realized in money transactions as 'the reflection of exchange among people, the embodiment of a pure function' is challenged by Simmel on the grounds that 'in the last analysis, it is not objects but people who carry on these processes, and the relations between objects are really relations between people'.[170]

Within this reified world of monetary relationships – itself, for Simmel, part of a wider reified object culture – each individual's own opportunity for creativity and development becomes increasingly restricted. This theme, already encountered in Simmel's account of the metropolis, is given greater force by virtue of Simmel's attempt to seek out 'the concrete, effective causes' of this widening separation of subjective and objective culture in modern society.

Simmel's unequivocal answer as to the cause of this separation is surprising in the light of his much more thorough analysis of the money economy. The increasing expansion of objective culture of 'the fragmentary life-content of individuals' and the ever-widening gap between the two results from 'the division of labour within production as well as consumption'. In so far as the reification and fragmentation of individuals is a feature of modernity, the discussion of the division of labour as its root cause is significant for understanding Simmel's wider response to modernity. As we shall see, however, it is not the division of labour within production that Simmel follows up in his later writings but rather its effects upon consumption. It is, again, the *consequences* of an advanced division of labour for consumption and people's awareness of them that continued to interest Simmel. This is true of his earlier interesting account of the world of commodities at 'The Berlin Trade Exhibition' (1896) as well as his essays on 'Fashion' (1895, 1905 and 1911) and 'The Problem of Style' (1908). Even within the context of his discussion of the division of labour in *The Philosophy of Money* such a direction can already be discerned in the title of the chapter within which it is located – 'The Style of Life'.

With regard to the division of labour and specialization within production itself, Simmel does provide an account which at times echoes that of Marx, though with significantly different emphases. Simmel commences by arguing that in the modern production process – though this is hardly specified or differentiated even to the extent of Marx's account in *Capital* which was known to Simmel – 'the product is completed at the expense of the development of the producer' whose total personality 'often even becomes stunted because of the diversion of energies . . . indispensable for the harmonious growth of the self. In other cases, it develops as if cut off from the core of the personality.' Individual workers cannot recognize themselves in what they produce since the significance and meaning of the latter is solely derived 'from its relationship with products of a different origin', namely other commodities. What is produced is a fragment that lacks the concrete definition 'that can be easily perceived in a product of labour that is wholly the work of a *single* person'.[171] The relationship of workers to what they produce within an advanced division of labour is contrasted with the work of art which, for Simmel, is 'the most perfectly autonomous unity, a self-sufficient totality' that, because of its close connection with its producer, 'expresses a subjective spiritual unity'. This expressive function is totally lost in modern production, where it is increasingly plausible 'for the worker to consider his work and its result as purely objective and autonomous, because it no longer touches the roots of his whole life-system'.

This sense of alienation on the worker's part is reinforced by 'the separation of the worker from the means of production' since where the capitalist's function is 'to acquire, organise and allocate the means of production, these means acquire a very different objectivity for the worker than for those who work with their own materials'.[172] In turn this process is strengthened by 'the fact that, in addition to the means of production, work itself is separated from the worker' wherever 'labour power has become a commodity'. Under such circumstances, 'labour now shares the same character, mode of valuation and fate with all other commodities'.[173] But rather than engage in a historically specific analysis of the ramifications of this process, Simmel maintains that it is merely 'one side of the far-reaching process of differentiation by which specific contents of the personality are detached in order for them to confront the personality as objects with an independent character and dynamic'.[174] In other words, this historically specific process is to be understood within the context of a universal, unhistorical separation of subjective and objective culture.

This process of the separation of the worker from the means of production is even more apparent in the case of automatic machine production which is

the result of a highly advanced breakdown and specialisation of materials and energies, akin to the character of a highly developed state administration . . . In that the machine becomes a totality and carries out a growing proportion of the work itself, it confronts the worker as an autonomous power, just as he too is no longer an individual personality but merely someone who carries out an objectively prescribed task.[175]

But machine production is also imbued with other characteristics. Firstly, it is the embodiment of objectified knowledge (what Simmel terms 'the objective mind') that is far greater than that of the individual producer. Not only does the resulting product 'contain energies, qualities and additional potentialities that lie quite outside the grasp of the individual producer' but an advanced division of labour also

imbues the product with energies derived from a very large number of individuals . . . This accumulation of quality and excellence in the object that forms their synthesis is unlimited, whereas the growth of individuals, in any period of time, and by their very nature, has quite definite natural limits.[176]

According to Simmel, the perfection of the machine-made product, moreover, cannot match that produced by the single individual. Such judgements provide yet another indication of his adherence to the threatened notion of the individual producer – in this case, the artisan but more often than not the artist.

However, not merely the production process but also the product itself stands over against its producer as an alien object, since 'the product of labour in the capitalist era is an object with a decidedly autonomous character, with its own laws of motion and a character alien to the producing subject', and 'is most forcefully illustrated where the worker is compelled to buy his own product'.[177] But individual workers are also confronted with a greatly increased range of possible items of consumption. Here the process at work is one of levelling of quality and price:

The broadening of consumption . . . is dependent upon the growth of objective culture, since the more objective and impersonal an object

is the better it is suited to more people. Such consumable material . . .
cannot be designed for subjective differentiation of taste, while on the
other hand only the most extreme differentiation of production is able
to produce the objects cheaply and abundantly enough in order to
satisfy the demand for them.[178]

As 'a bridge between the objectivity of culture and the division of
labour', consumption too is transformed in this process, not merely
quantitatively but also qualitatively.

Here, Simmel contrasts custom production with mass consumption.
Whereas the former 'gave the consumer a personal relationship to
the commodity', in the latter case the commodity is something external
and autonomous to the consumer. Not only does the division of labour
destroy custom production, *'the subjective aura of the product* also
disappears in relation to the consumer because the commodity is now
produced independently of him [my emphasis]'.[179] Whereas the loss
of aura is a central theme of Benjamin's work on modernity, Simmel
emphasizes the objectification of consumption as part of 'the objectivity
of the style of life' itself in the modern period.[180] The individual
becomes increasingly estranged not merely from the wider cultural
milieux but also from 'the more intimate aspects of our daily life'.
Our earlier attachment to our immediate surroundings – even the
furniture which we grew up with – has broken down. Simmel discerns
three reasons for this. Firstly, 'the sheer quantity of very specifically
formed objects makes a close and, as it were, personal relationship
to each of them more difficult'.[181] This dramatic increase in the
quantity of 'concurrent differentiation' of commodities is dealt with
at the personal level in *The Philosophy of Money*, and in the public sphere
in his essay 'The Berlin Trade Exhibition'. The second factor
responsible for our estrangement from our objective culture –
'consecutive differentiation' or changes in fashion – is dealt with only
briefly in *The Philosophy of Money* but more fully in Simmel's reworked
essay 'Fashion'. The third factor, 'the plurality of styles' is also dealt
with at greater length in Simmel's essay 'The Problem of Style'. The
examination of these three factors will lead us on to a consideration
of how Simmel viewed the individual's response to this growing
objectification of modern culture.

Within the private sphere, the wealth of commodities with which
we encumber our lives brings about a 'sense of being oppressed by
the externalities of modern life' which 'confront us as autonomous
objects'. Housework now takes on the form of a 'ceremonial

fetishism' – though why this was not the case earlier cannot be traced
back to the paucity of utensils as Simmel does. The 'impersonal origin
and easy replaceability' of 'those numerous objects that swarm around
us', leads to a situation in which this clutter of commodities becomes
'an interconnected closed world that has increasingly fewer points at
which the subjective soul can interpose its will and feelings'.[182] This
process of estrangement is completed by the 'independent, impersonal
mobility' of commodities that reaches its apogee in the slot machine
and the five cents store.

In the public sphere, 'the universe of commodities' (Benjamin) is
revealed in world exhibitions. In 'The Berlin Trade Exhibition'
(1896)[183] Simmel highlights a number of important features of this
phantasmagoria of commodities. World exhibitions are, for Simmel,
a form of socializing as well as a form of bringing together the most
diverse range of commodities. Diverse commodities are exhibited in
the social context of amusement, a distinctive form of sociability
since

> The close proximity within which the most heterogeneous industrial
> products are confined produces a paralysis in the capacity for
> perception, a true hypnosis . . . in its fragmentation of weak
> impressions there remains in the memory the notion that one should
> be amused here.[184]

Any sensitive person 'will be overpowered and feel disorientated by
the mass effect of what is offered here'. Yet 'precisely this wealth and
colourfulness of over-hastened impressions is appropriate to over-
excited and exhausted nerves' need for stimulation'. Such exhibitions
represent a concentration of commodities produced from ever-
increasing specialization within production. On the other hand,

> it seems as if the modern person wishes to compensate for the one-
> sidedness and uniformity of what they produce within the division of
> labour by the increasing crowding together of heterogeneous
> impressions, by the increasingly hasty and colourful change in
> emotions. The differentiation of the active spheres of life evidently
> complement one another through the comprehensive diversity of their
> passive and receptive spheres.[185]

In other words, the tedium of the production process is compensated
for by the artificial stimulation and amusement of consumption. In
the case of world exhibitions, however, it is the totally 'passive' sphere

that is paramount since their visitors are there merely to observe and marvel, not to touch or purchase.

Simmel's other major interest in world exhibitions is in their aesthetic dimension. On the one hand, visitors must be impressed by the vastness of what is on offer. On the other, the fleeting life of the commodity is also reflected in their architecture. Thus, whereas the architecture reflects 'the conscious negation of the monumental style', 'the character of a creation for transitoriness' becomes the dominant impression. This transitory impression must still embody something of 'the eternity of forms' in order not to totally reveal the illusory nature of the seemingly permanent character of the contents of such exhibitions. But not merely the architecture itself but the whole layout of exhibitions does reveal an aesthetic dimension, an 'aesthetic super-additum', which aims 'to give new aesthetic significance through the arrangement of their coming together – just as the ordinary advertisement has advanced to the art of posters'. This 'aesthetic productivity' manifests itself in

> the increase in what one might term the shop-window quality of things that is evoked by exhibitions. Commodity production . . . must lead to a situation of giving things an enticing external appearance over and above their usefulness . . . one must attempt to excite the interest of the buyer by means of the external attraction of the object, even indeed by means of the form of its arrangement.[186]

What Simmel hints at here is the process by which the exchange value of commodities is not merely enhanced but also masked by their aesthetic appeal.

In contrast, 'consecutive differentiation' of commodities manifests itself most clearly in fashion. Whereas Simmel's fuller treatments of fashion as a social phenomenon emphasize its universal and almost eternal character arising out of the dual nature of humanity with regard to uniformity and differentiation, his brief discussion in *The Philosophy of Money* concentrates upon its most modern manifestations. In general, fashion is a social form which combines 'the attraction of differentiation and change with that of similarity and conformity' and which is usually located within social classes in order to express social differences. But the weakening of class barriers and increased upward mobility, together with 'the predominance of the third estate' have increased the pace of changes in fashion. Both the breadth and speed of the spread of fashions creates the illusion that fashion itself is 'an independent movement, an objective and autonomous force which follows its own course independently of the individual'. In other words, 'it becomes less dependent upon the individual and the individual becomes less dependent upon fashion. Both develop like separate evolutionary worlds.'[187] This assumption of the individual becoming less dependent upon fashion seems to contradict Simmel's earlier analysis of trade exhibitions and his subsequent discussion of the plurality of styles. More remarkably, the analysis of fashion both here and in its fuller treatment elsewhere, gives little importance to the very factors which Simmel had already highlighted in his essay on the Berlin trade exhibition, namely commodity production. Rather, fashion is related to the 'dualistic nature' of mankind, 'the antagonistic tendencies of life', the dual tendencies 'in the individual soul as well as in society', 'the psychological tendency towards imitation', and so on. Fashion itself is viewed as 'a universal phenomenon in the history of our race'. In other words, this treatment of fashion is symptomatic of Simmel's tendency to reduce modernity to eternity, to ultimately concern himself with a social analysis *sub specie aeternitatis*.[188]

Nonetheless, in its most extensive form (1911),[189] the essay on fashion does contain a number of specific references to modernity, however much its opening passages confirm Simmel's tendency to render modernity eternal. Within social life and 'its fragmentary reality', it is possible to see the whole history of society as a dialectic and ultimately a compromise between two tendencies: adherence to and absorption in a social group on the one hand, and individual differentiation and distinction from group members on the other. This is a duality that is 'revealed finally in biological forms as the opposition between inheritance and selectivity'.[190] The origins of the first 'social embodiment of these contradictions' lies in 'the psychological tendency towards *imitation*'. The second tendency towards 'individual differentiation' is embodied in a different kind of personality who, going beyond the given and the past, is orientated towards creating something for the future. Hence, 'the goal-orientated person is the counterpoint to the imitative person'. These two tendencies constitute 'the living preconditions for fashion as a permanent phenomenon in the history of our species'. In passing, Simmel notes that this wider contraction – expressed not merely in fashion but in the contrast between individualism and socialism – is embodied in 'social institutions as the – never permanent – reconciliation' of these two antagonistic tendencies.[191] Here, too, we may note that this is another reason why his social analysis does not concentrate upon fixed social institutions since for Simmel they too are always in a state of flux.

Fashion is a form of life that embodies 'the tendency to social equalisation' as well as social differentiation. This is revealed by the fact that, on the one hand, 'fashions are always class fashions', 'a product of class division' and, on the other, that fashions spread from one class to another, usually from above to below, in the course of their own dissemination and, finally, disintegration. Fashion can be 'ugly' and yet 'modern', as if we are 'aesthetically quite indifferent' to its content, as if fashion 'demonstrates its complete indifference to the actual norms of life'. In this sense, fashion is abstract:

> This abstraction of fashion, rooted in its deepest essence and as 'estranged from reality' bestows a certain aesthetic cachet of modernity itself upon quite non-aesthetic areas, also developed in historical phenomena.[192]

But, in contrast to its earlier, more personal origins, 'the invention of fashions in the present period is also increasingly incorporated into the objective work conditions of the economy. Hence,

> There not merely emerges an article somewhere that then becomes fashionable, rather articles are produced for the express purpose of being fashionable. At certain intervals of time, a new fashion is required *a priori* and now there exist creators and industries which exclusively carry out this task. The relationship between abstraction as such and objective-social organisation is revealed in the indifference of fashion as a form to any significance that lies in its specific content – and in its increasingly more determined transition to social-productive economic structures.[193]

It would be a short step to translate this analysis into an account of the relationship between fashion's embodiment of exchange value and the need to increase '*a priori*' the circulation of commodities. Fashion's abstraction, in Simmel's sense, is not too far removed from the abstractions of commodity exchange. This even becomes apparent when he notes that 'the domination of fashion' is most unbearable where it takes over those spheres of life – religion, the economy, politics – in which only objective decisions should be made. But this is not the direction of Simmel's analysis. It is, rather, to reiterate, once more, the 'aesthetic attraction' of fashion that is created by 'the distance from the significant content of things', even though this too might be translated into the categories of exchange and use-value. Indeed, it echoes Baudelaire's aesthetics of modernity.

In what other respects does Simmel's analysis of fashion relate to his theory of modernity? Simmel characterizes modernity here and elsewhere as increasingly fragmented social life and individuality, a fragmentation that requires some counterbalance. This is to be found in adherence to fashion which bestows upon individuals a certain supra-individuality. Hence

> For contemporary life with its individualistic fragmentation this element of homogeneity possessed by fashion is particularly important . . . Changes in fashion indicate the amount of deadening of nervous excitement; the more nervous an epoch is, the more rapidly will its fashions change, because the need for the attraction of differentiation, one of the essential agents of fashion, goes hand in hand with the languishing of nervous energies.[194]

This latter characteristic Simmel associates with higher social strata. The general feature of fashion outlined here is, of course, related to his account of the neurasthenia of modern life, as Simmel makes evident in his amplification of the origins and consequences of changes in fashion.

The dialectic of changes in fashion necessarily incorporates its logical contradiction – the expansion or extension of fashion must lead to its own destruction. The assimilation of fashion must reach a point at which it ceases to be a fashion. This dialectic is accelerated in the modern period:

> The fact that fashion takes on an unprecedented upper hand in contemporary culture – breaking into hitherto untouched areas, becoming more obsessive in existing ones, i.e. incessantly increasing the speed of changes in fashion – is merely the coalescing of a contemporary psychological trait. Our internal rhythm requires increasingly shorter pauses in the change of impressions; or, expressed differently, the accent of attraction is transferred to an increasing extent from its substantive centre to its starting and finishing points.[195]

This is indicated at the most seemingly insignificant level by the replacement of the cigar by the cigarette, by the passion for travel which breaks 'the life of the year' into ever-shorter periods. In turn, this implies that 'the specific "impatient" tempo of modern life signifies not merely the craving for the rapid in the qualitative content of life but also the strength of the formal pleasure of boundaries, of beginnings and ends, of coming and going'.[196]

Fashion is, then, part of the more general process of accentuation of time-consciousness in a distinctive sense. Our simultaneous pleasure in newness and oldness indicates that the question 'is not one of being or non-being, rather it is simultaneously being and non-being; it always stands on the water-shed of past and future and thus, as long as it exists on this level, *gives us such a strong sense of presentness as do few other phenomena* [my emphasis].'[197] This 'concentration of social consciousness' upon the transitory only serves to increase its attractiveness since, given the dialectic of fashion, at this very same point there 'already lies its seed of death'.[198] It follows from this that we only denote as fashion that which disappears as quickly as it emerged.

Here Simmel's analysis of fashion deals with a central feature of modernity: the dialectics of 'le transitoire', 'le fugitif':

> Amongst the reasons why fashion today so strongly dominates consciousness there belongs also the fact that major, permanent, unquestioned convictions increasingly lose their force. In this way, the fleeting and changeable elements of life gain that much more free space. *The break with the past . . . increasingly concentrates consciousness upon the present. This emphasis upon the present is clearly, at the same time, an emphasis upon change . . .* [My emphasis][199]

But if the domination of fashion consciousness and 'presentness' is a characteristic of the modern period, can we specify its location more precisely? Simmel provides one reason why some people are predisposed more than others to become fashion addicts. Since fashion consciousness relies upon a mixture of emotions of affirmation and envy, it is 'the genuine arena for individuals who are inwardly lacking in independence and needing support, yet whose awareness of self, at the same time, nonetheless requires a certain distinction, attention and particularity'.[200] In other words, such individuals need fashion as a means of expressing their own absent individuality. It is an important social medium through which people 'seek to preserve, all the more fully, inner freedom',[201] whilst providing a vehicle for the individual to indicate externally his or her position in relation to society as a whole. Through fashion, individuals also seek to counteract 'the superiority, autonomy and indifference of the cosmos' in which they live. This proves to be an illusion since 'in the last instance, they have gained no domination over things but rather only over their own falsified phantasy. Yet the sense of power that flows from this indicates its lack of foundation, its illusory nature in the rapidity with which such manifestations of fashion pass by.'[202]

Fashion is even more precisely located by Simmel both in relation to specific social strata and distinctive social milieu. Fashion is most closely associated not with upper or lower social strata, whose tempo of life is too slow, but with the middle classes with whose emergence has coincided a wider dissemination of fashion consciousness. It is also located in the metropolis which is a 'breeding ground for fashion', with its rapid changes in impressions and relationships, its levelling and simultaneous highlighting of individuality, its crowdedness and corresponding social distance and 'above all, the economic upward movement of low strata in the speed that they take on in the metropolis must favour the rapid change in fashion'.[203] Hence, fashion cannot be so expensive as it was earlier. It is therefore associated with the cheapening of what is produced and an even quicker change in fashion. Whereas those spheres of industry less subject to fashionable changes in their product can increasingly proceed with 'the rationalisation of production' relatively independently of the market, those concerned with production of a purely fashionable commodity experience an opposite tendency since 'the form of feverish change is here so fundamental that they exist as in a logical contradiction in relation to the developmental tendencies of the modern economy'.[204]

Yet this does not prevent the fashionable commodity itself from creating its own contradiction since 'compared with this feature [of 'feverish change'], however, fashion also reveals the highly remarkable characteristic that each individual fashion to a certain extent emerges *as if it wishes to live for eternity* [my emphasis]'.[205] As such, it embodies the transitory and the eternal. It is 'the eternal return' of the ever-same. Indeed, the circulation of fashion is like that of the commodity: ever-new but ever-same.

Fashion is, for Simmel, the symbol of consecutive differentiation and world exhibitions the epitome of concurrent differentiation of modern culture. The roots of both lie, in part, in 'the multitude of styles that confronts us when we view the objects that surround us'.[206] Not surprisingly, the whole of the last chapter of Simmel's *Philosophy of Money* is devoted to 'The Style of Life', to its seemingly surface, superficial manifestations that are, at the same time, the clue to its very essence.[207] The 'bewildering plurality of styles' had already been noted in his 'Sociological Aesthetics' (1896), as an instance of modern disloyalty to any one style.[208] In *The Philosophy of Money* this is explained as 'the result of the enlargement of our historical knowledge, which in turn is associated with modern man's penchant for change'. Indeed, the entire visible environment of our cultural life has disintegrated into a 'plurality of styles'. Given their independent objectivity, we are now confronted with 'these forms on the one side, and our subjectivity on the other'.

In his later reflections on 'The Problem of Style' (1908),[209] Simmel argues that, by virtue of the very plurality of styles, individuals seek to express their subjectivity in the 'unmistakeable, inimitable cachet' of the household objects they surround themselves with. Within the aesthetic sphere of the household in better-off strata – and the contemporary *Jugendstil* movement sought to stylize 'every pot and every chair' as Olbrich sarcastically put it – the stylized objects of the *intérieur* signify a balance between the expression of individuality and the indication of 'supra-individuality' since we share this style with many others. In this way,

> a supra-individual form and law is produced between the subjective personality and its human and objective environment; the stylised expression, form of life, taste – all these are limits, forms of distance in which the exaggerated subjectivism of the times find a counterbalance and a cloak.[210]

The 'background or basis of daily life' must be stylized since 'in their rooms, human beings are the main object, the focal point as it were'. In order for 'an organic and harmonious total feeling' to emerge, the *intérieur*, with its 'spatial confinement' in order that it 'does not mix with immediate life', must be given a focal point that can only be fulfilled by the stylized work of art and not by the 'necessary accessories' of everyday life. This modern thirst for stylization has its roots in the seemingly paradoxical attempt on the part of the individual to escape from the excessive subjectivism and individualism fostered in modern society:

> What impels modern people so strongly toward style is the unburdening and masking of the personality that is the essence of style. Subjectivism and individuality have accelerated almost to breaking point and in the stylised creations of form . . . there lies a tempering and toning down of this extreme individuality into something general and more universal.[211]

But we need to ask whether the modern individual actually escapes from the burden of the excessive subjectivism of the times by its sublimation in the stylized *intérieur*.

It is clear that in his essay on 'The Problem of Style', Simmel is largely concerned with style as manifested within the environment of the *intérieur*. The essay was written in a period in which the stylization of the *intérieur* in the *Jugendstil* movement had extended into the *extérieur*, into the whole of our physical environment. In the attempted realization of the 'total work of art', the whole of the social and physical environment was to be stylized in the interests of a 'beautification of life'. But this was only to be achieved within the boundaries of existing social antagonisms which meant, ultimately, either a retreat into a bourgeois *intérieur* or the attempt to render the public sphere into another *intérieur*.

The resolution of the contradictions of an excessive individualism and subjectivism is to be found within the individual sphere in Simmel's work. The essay on style is no exception and in no way contradicts the notion of the ossification of cultural development in the objective sphere. Indeed, the stylization of the *intérieur* as a relief from excessive subjectivism is matched by the proliferation of style in the *extérieur*, in objective culture, that Simmel was later to characterize as 'the *stylelessness* of our times'. This, in turn, is a consequence not merely of the expansion and rapid developments within our material culture but, at the individual level, is the result of the fact that 'personal values are sought in a dimension in which they in no way exist', namely in the search for cultural progress in technical progress. This accounts for 'the whole haste, extreme covetousness and addiction to enjoyment of the times'. In other words, individuals seek to realize their fundamental values in an objective culture that confronts them as something alien. Later, Simmel was to speak of this increasing separation of subjective and objective culture not merely in terms of a 'crisis of culture', or even a 'tragedy of culture', but as the 'pathology of culture'. Society as second nature had ceased to be historical: as a 'natural' state, it had ceased to be second nature at all.

VIII

The preceding analysis of Simmel's social theory of modernity sought to reconstruct both its methodological presuppositions and its main substantive features. There is little doubt that, starting out from the 'fortuitous fragments' of social reality, and 'the delicate invisible threads' in social relationships, Simmel attempted to distil from 'each of life's details . . . the totality of its meaning'. At the substantive level, Simmel's social theory of modernity quite explicitly concentrates upon the transformation of modern experience of time (as transitory) space (as fleeting) and causality (as fortuitous or arbitrary). All three arise out of a conception of modern experience of the immediate present as differentiated and discontinuous. Although the location of the discontinuity of modern experience is both the metropolis and the mature money economy, it is ultimately the development of the latter which accounts for the origins of the experience of modernity. The development of the mature (implicitly capitalist) money economy constitutes the historical origin of the experience of modernity. At the aesthetic level, money is also the *symbol* of modernity: the most 'striking symbol of the completely dynamic character of the world', 'the most ephemeral thing in the external-practical world', with 'its own emptiness and merely transitional character'. Its overwhelming power of differentiation reduces everything, including individuals themselves, to fragments. Its necessary objectification and quantification (including calculability) of everything that exists generates a world of 'spectral objectivity', a world in which everything exists upon the same level (and is therefore arbitrary) and in which total indifference predominates.

It is not merely that 'the objectivity of human interaction . . . finds its expression in purely monetary economic interests', nor merely that money is largely responsible for 'the objectivity of the life style' in the modern world. Money creates a quasi-natural universe on the basis of its measurement of everything 'with merciless objectivity'; it creates 'a web of objective and personal aspects of life . . . which is similar to the natural cosmos with its continuous cohesion and strict causality. This web is held together by the all-pervasive money value, just as nature is held together by the energy that gives life to everything.'[212] Money as the ultimate and pure means, the indifferent tool or instrument lies at the centre of this quasi-natural cosmos. It is indeed the expression of the unity of its diverse elements, the 'integrating force that supports and permeates every single element'. Simmel's search for the cause of this central role of money remains, however, a circular one which seldom escapes from the attributes of money's functions and capacities. In so far as this is the case, it places in question the notion that the money economy itself is the origin of modernity.

What specifically interests Simmel, however, is the inversion of the teleology of means and ends and the development of an account of the consequences of a mature money economy. This leads him to a theory of cultural alienation which culminates in the tragedy of culture, in the inevitable conflict and ever-widening gap between subjective and objective culture, in which individuals are locked within the experience of the eternal present of modernity. Money as the ultimate means expresses the preponderance of means over ends which 'finds its apotheosis in the fact that the peripheral in life, the things that lie outside its basic essence, have become masters of its centre and even of ourselves'. At the centre of the constant expansion of our objective culture (including both its material and ideational components) lies the production of technical means:

> what nature offers us by means of technology is now a mastery over the self-reliance and the spiritual centre of life through endless habits, endless distractions and endless superficial needs. Thus, the domination of the means has taken possession not only of specific ends but of the very centre of ends, of the point at which all purposes converge and from which they originate as final purposes. Man has thereby become estranged from himself; an insuperable barrier of media, technical inventions, abilities and enjoyments has been erected between him and his most distinctive and essential being.[213]

Simmel's response to this alienation of the individual was not to go in search of 'the laws of motion' of the society that produced this estrangement; nor was it to search for the internal contradictions within the existing socio-economic formation that might lead to its transcendence. Indeed, in so far as Simmel saw an alternative social formation such as socialism as a possibility, he maintained that it too would produce the same processes that generated estrangement and would probably accelerate their alienating consequences. This is despite the fact that Simmel was by no means so hostile to socialism as was Weber, having himself positively espoused a socialist standpoint in the first half of the 1890s.

But with a conception of modern society whose internal dynamic stood in danger of being reduced to the *inevitable* clash of objective and subjective culture, no alternative social formation could be conceived other than the one which already existed. And since a mature money economy, with all its concomitant objectifying, differentiating and levelling effects, was its defining characteristic, individuals remained caught within its web. They would have to find their own way out of its alienating consequences or remain incorporated within it and live out their lives within the alienating forms which it offered. As Böhringer has argued,

Money, Simmel stated, objectified the 'style of life', forces metropolitan people into 'objectivity', 'indifference', 'intellectuality', 'lack of character', 'lack of quality'. Money socializes human beings as strangers. Just like things, so money also transforms human beings into *res absolutae*, into objects. Simmel's student, Georg Lukács, correctly noticed that this objectification (in his words: reification and alienation) did not remain external, cannot, as Simmel maintained, be the 'gatekeeper of the innermost elements', but rather itself becomes internalized.[214]

Reconciliation with this objectified world is thus obtained through the internalization of its basic features. Just as money reconciles the irreconcilable, so we too can participate in the 'positive consequences of the negative trait of lack of character' of the modern world: 'the ease of intellectual understanding which exists even between people of the most divergent natures and positions', 'the trend towards conciliationess springing from indifference to the basic problems of our inner life' and adoption of 'the relativistic view of the world (which) seems to express the momentary relationship of adjustment on the part of our intellect'.

This reconciliation with the objectified world takes place within the context of our creation of distance from it. Just as money 'carries out the function of imposing a distance between ourselves and our purposes . . . more purely and completely' than other mediations, so too 'the individual mind can enrich the forms and contents of its own development only by distancing itself still further from that (objective) culture and developing its own at a much slower pace'.[215] We can, 'under favourable circumstances, secure an island of subjectivity, a secret, closed-off sphere of privacy', even though this is merely one instance of the deeper subjectivism of the modern times. It is, in fact, an instance of that which Simmel characterized as modernity – the experiencing of the external world as an inner world.

This world of modernity which Simmel so brilliantly describes is a world that is temporally located in the immediate present, indeed in an eternalized present. When Habermas defines what is modern as that which 'assists in the objective expression of a spontaneous, self-renewing presentness [*Aktualität*] of the spirit of the times',[216] he could have chosen no better instance than Simmel's analysis of the mature, modern money economy. Simmel's theory of cultural alienation signifies precisely this 'self renewing presentness'. The conflict between subjective and objective culture is self-renewing. The experience of objectification is broken off from past experience whilst the future holds in store merely the reproduction of this same conflict between subjective and objective culture. The experience of time in modernity is evocatively highlighted by Simmel in his description of the gambler's experience of time as 'unconditional presentness' and in his typification of the adventurer as 'the most powerful example of the unhistorical person, of the contemporary essence. On the one hand, he is determined by no past . . . on the other, the future does not exist for him.' Within the workings of the money economy and the circulation of commodities, this immediate presentness is constantly recreated in fashion which 'gives us such a strong sense of presentness as do few other phenomena' and which 'increasingly concentrates consciousness upon the present', even though 'each individual fashion . . . emerges as if it wishes to live for eternity'. That eternity, however, is filled with the endless reproduction of ever-new fashions.

That which is new, the immediately present, does not necessarily point towards a new future. Rather, as Habermas maintains, 'the cult of the new in fact signifies the glorification of an actuality that is born out of new, subjectively determined pasts. The new consciousness of time . . . not merely expresses the experience of a mobilized society, an accelerating history, a discontinuous everyday world. In the over-evaluation of the transitory, the fleeting and the ephemeral, in the celebration of the dynamic, there is expressed just as much the desire for an untarnished, still-intact present.[217] In Simmel's case, it might even be argued that the recognition of the present as transitory is countered by the search for the eternal forms that are present in the transitory itself. The ceaseless, transitory nature of the present can be analysed by Simmel because he views society itself as ceaseless social interaction. Its 'most complete form' is the exchange process itself.

Does Simmel's analysis of modernity therefore remain with the fleeting, the transitory, the emphemeral? Is the origin of the experience of modernity to be located in the mature money economy? Money's role in the exchange and circulation process certainly produces a world in permanet flux, fleeting and transitory; it is itself 'continuous self-alienation'. Further, 'as a tangible item money is the most ephemeral thing in the external-practical world'. On the other hand, 'in its content it is *the most stable*, since it stands at the point of indifference and balance between all other phenomena in the world [my emphasis]'.[218] If we search, in this context, for the source of the fleeting, fortuitous and arbitrary experiences created by the money economy, we return to the money economy itself. This apparent paradox arises out of the fact that the money economy – as the domination of exchange values – inverts the world of reality. As Scheible comments, 'the exchange principle, rendered universal, brings about a genuine reversal of the poles of the static and the dynamic. That which is apparently stable, use value, declines totally into the economic dynamic, whilst the dynamic principle, exchange, because of the universality in which it prevails, becomes the ultimate "stabilizing pole".'[219] In Simmel's words, 'all concrete things drive on in restless flight' towards their monetary evaluation and their devaluation. Their resting place is thus in what is most transitory.

There is little doubt that Simmel provides us with a remarkable account of the world of money exchange and, by implication, the world of commodity exchange and circulation. This is the location for the experiences of modernity. It is, for Simmel, also their source. But viewed as a closed universe of commodity exchange and circulation, it cannot illuminate anything other than the way in which such a world appears to us and is experienced by us. Simmel certainly recognized the subtleties of this world of commodity exchange. But it is necessary to ask whether a vision of society as rooted in the exchange and circulation processes (the world of ceaseless social interaction) is the adequate location of the origin of modernity or whether it is the sphere in which its manifestations appear to us.

If the experience of modernity lies in the immediate present that is always transitional, then in this context, it is a transition to the ever-same circulation of commodities (including money), to the eternal reproduction of the fleeting, the transitory and the fortuitous. Its analysis falls back upon the analysis of a form without a content. Indeed, since Simmel accepted the basic tenets of marginalist economics, he could not break out of the sphere of exchange and circulation into the sphere of production, into the origins of these processes. Despite this, the one social theorist whose work Simmel seeks to explicitly challenge in *The Philosophy of Money* – Marx – would probably have applauded and concurred with his description of the experience of modernity, of the way in which the world of commodity exchange appears to us. But Marx is a better guide out of the world of appearances generated by the exchange and circulation processes precisely because, like the classical political economists before him, he did not regard them as the end point of his analysis.

Marx does point out that the world of commodity exchange, the world of circulation of exchange values (including money as the universal equivalent) does appear to take on a formally independent existence. But the circulation process, for instance, cannot itself be a self-renewing process. It must be explained by something that exists outside itself. This is also true of money circulation which 'as the most superficial (in the sense of: driven out onto the surface) and the most abstract form of the entire production process, is in itself quite without content . . . simple money circulation . . . consists of an infinite number of indifferent and accidentally adjacent movements.'[220] In turn, this movement cannot be explained in terms of itself since 'the factors which affect the mass of commodities thrown into circulation . . . are all circumstances which lie *outside* simple money circulation itself. They are relations which express themselves in it; it provides the names for them as it were; but they are not to be explained by its own differentiation.'[221] Thus, although '(at first sight), circulation appears as a *simply infinite* process' and although it is 'the first totality among the economic categories',

> *circulation . . . does not carry within itself the principle of self-renewal. The moments of the latter are presupposed to it* not posited by it. Commodities constantly have to be thrown into it anew from the outside, like fuel into a fire . . . Circulation, therefore, which appears as that which is immediately present on the surface of bourgeois society, exists only so far as it is constantly mediated . . . Its immediate being is therefore pure semblance. *It is the phenomenon of a process taking place behind it.*[222]

For Marx that process is the production of commodities. The social relations necessary for the production of commodities, the relations between capital and labour, are what the exchange and circulation presupposes.

This kind of argument enables us to question whether Simmel accurately located the origins of the experience of modernity. If the world of exchange and commodity circulation is not an independent, self-renewing process, then its origins must be sought elsewhere. The contradictions between the money economy as it appears to us and the production of that which is exchanged and circulated within the mature money economy is sometimes hinted at by Simmel in his specific analyses (e.g. of world exhibitions). But ultimately, the major contradiction in his theory of cultural alienation remains the uneven development of subjective and objective culture. Since the objective culture is not seen as internally contradictory and transitory, then there can be no world confronting the individual other than the eternal present. Modernity is then itself an eternal present.

3

Siegfried Kracauer

'Exemplary Instances' of Modernity

The place which an epoch occupies in the historical process is determined more forcefully in the analysis of its insignificant superficial manifestations than from the judgments of the epoch upon itself.

Siegfried Kracauer

Spatial images are the dreams of society. Wherever the hieroglyphics of any spatial image is deciphered, there the basis of social reality presents itself.

Siegfried Kracauer

If the material base were in order, then one could live calmly in the superstructure.

Siegfried Kracauer

. . . a loner. A discontent, not a leader . . . A rag-picker early in the dawn, who with his stick spikes the snatches of speeches and scraps of conversation in order to throw them into his cart, sullenly and obstinately, a little tipsy, but not without now and then scornfully letting one or other of these discarded cotton rags – 'humanity', 'inwardness', 'depth' – flutter in the morning breeze. A rag-picker, early – in the dawn of the day of the revolution.

Walter Benjamin on Siegfried Kracauer

I

In the 'autobiographical statement' accompanying the posthumously published study, *History. The Last Things Before the Last* (1969), Siegfried Kracauer viewed his total life's work as attempts 'to bring out the significance of areas whose claim to be acknowledged in their own right has not yet been recognised'.[1] Kracauer himself included

amongst these attempts his *Die Angestellten* (1930)[2] and his study of
Jacques Offenbach and the Paris of his Times (1937).[3] One could easily
extend this list to include many of his articles from the Weimar period,
most of which were originally published in the *Frankfurter Zeitung*, of
which he was a prominent reviewer from 1920 to 1930 and Berlin
review editor from 1930 to 1933. All these studies

> so incoherent on the surface . . . have all served and continue to serve,
> a single purpose: the rehabilitation of objectives and modes of being
> which still lack a name and hence are overlooked or misjudged . . .
> a region of reality which despite all that has been written about them
> are still largely *terra incognita*.[4]

Kracauer returned time and time again to 'the exotic of the everyday
world', to the 'unknown areas' of social life. In such terms, for
instance, he described the world of white collar workers in Berlin in
1930 'whose life is more unknown than that of the primitive tribes
whose customs white collar workers marvel at in films'.[5] One of his
friends, Richard Plant, has described Kracauer's Weimar studies as
attempts 'to fill out totally unresearched areas, blank spots on the
sociological atlas: white collar workers, workers, the cinema, kitsch,
wishful dreams'.[6] Even this list does not do justice to the range of
his analysis of the seemingly superficial phenomena or 'refuse' of
modernity. Alongside his illumination of the labyrinth of metropolitan
life (largely in Berlin and Paris), he also followed Simmel in his grasp
of the 'fortuitous fragments of reality' which revealed the hidden secrets
of modernity. Indeed, it has been suggested that, along with Bloch
and Benjamin, 'Kracauer belonged . . . in the 1920s to the first authors
who sought to describe the achievements of modernity from the
standpoint of the . . . fundamental transformations in the structure
of everyday experience, especially the experience of time.'[7] One
might add here, in the light of his deciphering of the hieroglyphics
of social space, the experience of metropolitan space too. In more
general terms, Witte has described Kracauer's 'most important
contribution' as lying in the fact that 'his observation fell upon the
marginal zones of high culture and came to rest upon the media
of popular culture: the cinema, streets, sport, operetta, revues,
advertisements and the circus. The unifying feature from the early
to the late works is the intention of deciphering social tendencies
immediately out of ephemeral cultural phenomena.'[8] Such an
intention he shared with Ernst Bloch and Walter Benjamin, despite
their very different approaches to their material.

II

But when we turn to Kracauer's earliest writings, we find that his acute deciphering of the topography of modern metropolitan life, whose analysis is rooted in the material itself, is not yet in evidence. Nonetheless, many of these early and largely unpublished works do contain not only many echoes of, and confrontation with, earlier historical–philosophical theories of modernity but also announce several central themes that Kracauer was to subsequently treat in a much more concrete manner. In turn, however, these themes are not always announced in the titles of these early, often substantial works: 'On the Experience of the War' (published 1915),[9] 'Suffering from Knowledge and the Longing after the Deed' (1917),[10] 'On the Essence of the Personality' (c.1917),[11] 'On Expressionism. The Essence and Meaning of a Movement of our Times' (c.1918),[12] 'On the Ethics of Duty' (1918),[13] 'On Friendship' (published 1917/18).[14] Although a detailed analysis of the content of these and other wartime essays and monographs would lead us too far away from our present theme,[15] it is necessary to indicate some of their central and recurring orientations. A further, equally important reason for examining these central themes is that Kracauer himself came to confront some of them only a few years later in the course of turning away from his earlier position and orientating himself more decisively towards the material reality of an unrevealed everyday world.

Aside from his doctoral dissertation on wrought iron (1915)[16] – which marked the culmination of his studies as an architect (after turning down the possibility of writing his doctoral dissertation under Simmel) and the commencment of the unhappy years as a practising architect from 1915 to 1920 which are 'documented' as it were in his autobiographical novel *Ginster* (1928)[17] – Kracauer's first known publication is an article entitled 'On the Experience of the War' (1915). Here, in the context of an essay ostensibly devoted to explaining the meaning of the feeling 'love of the Fatherland', Kracauer already announced some themes that concerned him both during and after the war. As in this and other wartime works, Kracauer is preoccupied with the consequences of the growth of a material civilization emptied of meaning and the increasingly problematic individual whose inner core or essence remains either lost or unfilfilled. In a manner reminiscent of Simmel's wartime writings, with their emphasis on the tragic separation of an objective material culture from an unrealized subjective culture of the individual, Kracauer outlines the nature of this debilitating separation:

> During the last decade, Germany was caught up in an enormous material advance. But the inner element was not able to keep pace with this external flowering, indeed it was in many ways nipped in the bud . . . The life of the majority took place within stale social conventions and professional callings. As the sole supra-individual forms they secured a fixed goal and determined the possibilities for development. If one distanced oneself from their sphere, then one stepped into the empty space, otherwise there was little which bound people together and not merely bound them together but also stimulated their highest impulses . . . Above all else, the most important need of the soul, the religious, lay broken; there were no living, universally binding beliefs, that expressed our essence.[18]

In other words, human existence was played out within social forms, including the higher professional callings of 'the teacher, the artist and the politician' that were 'incapable of liberating essential inner needs'. As a result 'the inner life of human beings' consisted of 'empty, unbuilt-upon spaces'. In this context, Kracauer distinguishes two groups of human beings and their response to the war. The one group found in the war 'the liberation of their essence through an idea'. The other group 'whose core experience' is an aesthetic one could not so readily respond to the idea of the Fatherland since 'their thoughts, feelings and actions do not stand in unison with one another'. Thomas Mann, according to Kracauer, has revealed their 'deepest longing: the longing for a bourgeois existence [*die Bürgerlichkeit*]', a longing that arises from the fact that 'they find themselves outside the mass of people, they wish so much to be absorbed into the everyday world'. In their distance from the everyday mass of the population, they are burdened by the feeling of loneliness, so much so that they recognize that 'only the close community with other human beings, the same actions and life as theirs, can bring salvation'.[19]

That Kracauer himself, who already experienced the painful experience of the sensitive outsider, the nervous inwardness of Simmel's 'stranger', identified with this second group is borne out not only by his autobiographical novel, *Ginster*, but also by his longest unpublished monograph written in 1917: 'The Suffering from Knowledge and the Longing after the Deed'.[20] There Kracauer again takes up the disjunction between those who search for an ever-greater accumulation of knowledge about the world and those who are searching for action, for the deed: 'Action, powerful intervention, that is the slogan of the present times'. In the present age, people are suffering from too much knowledge that has been reduced to ideas. This applies not merely to science but also to 'the excessive knowledge of the soul'. Although there has been a dramatic increase in knowledge this has coincided with 'the absence of meaning in the world' – a viewpoint also consonant, of course, with Weber's most pessimistic visions of the present.

But what is wrong with this increasing knowledge of the world? What are its origins? For Kracauer they lie in science and capitalism:

> First of all, however, capitalism is fully in agreement with science with regard to the fact that, like the latter, it lays claim primarily to the intellectual capacities of human beings. Logical thinking, the endowment of similarity and devaluation of the most diverse things with reference to their money value and their utilisability, the calculation of reason that is accustomed to rapidly calculating large amounts – and it sees in the world only quantities that it must dispose of – all this rises up and its possession becomes appropriate for the world of a human being. The capitalist economic system offers these qualities many, secure ways of being sold, gives them goals and lets them be honoured and become universally applicable . . . Just like science, capitalism possesses a deep indifference to the 'what' of things . . .[21]

Not surprisingly in this context, Kracauer rejects any notion of progress in the material sense since it does nothing for the inner individual. But it is not merely capitalism and science that offer no way out of the loss of meaning in the world. Socialism too 'directs its gaze exclusively upon a specific action of human beings. It does not raise the question of existence.'[22]

As a result, modern human beings are caught up within a system which is incapable of realizing the potentiality of human individuality: 'the striving to realize oneself in the sense of the system becomes an end in itself and takes hold of the soul.'[23] Indeed, the human being 'is a cog in a powerful soulless machine which rests upon the interlocking of countless little wheels. The goal that is striven for vanishes from the inner gaze.'[24]

This endless striving for the deed, the act, without an ultimate goal finds its expression not merely in the capitalist system but also in the metaphysics of the times. Kracauer points to Bergson's metaphysics as reflecting the alienated existential condition he has described:

It may well be no coincidence that a doctrine which interprets life as an eternal striving and pressing from one new thing to another and takes everything permanent and unchanging from life and bans it to matter, a doctrine which places movement and not the goal [*das Wohin*] of this movement at the centre of its observations should find precisely at the present time extensive acceptance and, what is decisive, entry too into the soul.[25]

Here, in perhaps a more vivid way than 'the German Bergson' (Simmel), Kracauer highlights the theme of movement that is so central to the problematic of modernity.

In a similar vein, in his monograph on expressionism in the following year, Kracauer returns to the meaningless nature of the objective world. The world of reality possesses a degree of objectivity – secured by conventions – that the various individual subjective world lack. But 'the world of reality, in comparison with this subject-world, is a chaos. Unfettered by unified value principles, unformed and lacking in substance, it extends itself.'[26] Thus, in the development of our intellectual life today, one feature stands out: 'it is the discovery of the autonomous nature of reality for the purpose of its ever more perfect domination.' This reality is created in part by science, since 'the more science elevates itself into a power of life, all the more untouchable and objective the world becomes'. The economic development of capitalism follows the same path with its impersonal laws and the quantitative reduction of all values. Within this reified reality, human beings are bound together by interests, especially occupational interests, 'as one of the main forms of communal action and intellectual cohesion in the present period'.[27] However, what is almost totally lacking in any occupation 'is the existence of the human being, his or her complete essence'.

Whereas Weber could still identify some occupational callings as worthy ones, Kracauer's existential critique of the existing social order – based on the necessity of the fulfilment of a human essence in the personality – permits no such confidence. And whereas Simmel could see in the functionalization of occupational interaction the possibility at least of individuality being preserved elsewhere, this too is rejected by Kracauer. It is as if Kracauer had radicalized Simmel's theory of cultural alienation by infusing it with a quasi-religious existentialism – itself not totally absent from Simmel's own later works. The feelings and values of the individual can no longer be integrated into the social functions that are available. The modern individual, in his or her inner core at least, remains isolated. The only values that can be striven for are those of a lost humanity. But they can only exist in this objectified world as private residues (such as friendship). Such relics have nothing in common with that individualism which is compatible with capitalist strivings: 'the self-adjustment to the rigid reality and the superior totality has its counterpart in an unbounded, arbitrary individualism.'[28] In turn this results in a veritable anarchy of values and the reduction of the form of association of human beings to that of civilization. What is totally absent, and what Kracauer calls for, is a form of association based on community. This longing for community, for friendship, for the fulfilment of inner life, for the realization of the individual personality all remain longings that cannot be realized.

Kracauer's passionate image of the reified world of reality, that not unwittingly corresponds with his reading of Kierkegaard, incorporates several important themes. At first sight, it seems to have affinities with Weber's secularization thesis but, on closer inspection, Kracauer's thesis is nothing less than the disintegration of the world itself. More radically than Weber, and probably as a result of Kracauer's existential vision, he presents the thesis of the absence of meaning in the world. The individual personality can no longer identify with the world of reality: the identity of existence and meaning has been lost. In the social context, Kracauer's conception of reality is reminiscent of that of many romantic anti-capitalist visions, both conservative and radical (the early Lukács, for instance). The triumph of scientific and capitalist reason – and its philosophical underpinning in transcendental idealism – is, for Kracauer, an expression of the disjunction between knowledge and existence. The world as a coherent totality has been shattered. Only its individual fragments remain. And Kracauer himself is not yet in a position to engage in a reconstruction of this fractured world. Rather, the empty intellectual void is filled only with longings for something, often for religion.

This inner constellation is expressed by Kracauer most forcefully in his essay 'Those who Wait' (1922),[29] which starts out by identifying these people afflicted by 'a common fate':

> They mostly pass their days in the solitariness of big cities, these academics, businessmen, doctors, lawyers, students and intellectuals of all kinds; and since they sit in offices, deal with clients, engage in transactions, visit lecture theatres, they often forget, above the noise of bustling activity, their own inner existence.[30]

When, however, they return to the core of their being from the superficial surface of everyday existence they suffer from 'a deep sadness' of 'loss of a higher meaning in the world'. Instead they confront the 'empty space' of *inner* existence. This 'emptying of the intellectual space that surrounds us' can be traced back to the process of the 'sundering' of the self from its bond with God, with a 'community grounded in tradition, statutes, dogma'. The 'timeless rational self of the Enlightenment' is increasingly 'atomised' in 'the age of materialism and capitalism' which 'gradually robs [reality] of its substance' and 'leads ultimately to the chaos of the present time'.

Confronted with this situation, Kracauer detects a number of responses amongst his contemporaries. Some, faced with the lack of any relationship to the absolute fall into 'the trap of relativism which renders every element of the infinite diversity of intellectual phenomena' and the world itself of equal value. Kracauer places Simmel in this position, despite his attempt to escape this relativist position in his *Lebensphilosophie*. Others seek religious or emotional fulfilment in beliefs that are all too readily at hand. This may take the form of commitment to Rudolf Steiner's anthroposophy, to messianic communism (perhaps with Bloch in mind) or to a formal belief in community (the Stefan George circle). Those who choose to remain in the empty vacuum sometimes take up the position of the 'fundamental sceptic' (such as Max Weber). Yet others, and much more common, are those who find a way out of the present predicament by taking a short cut to any form of refuge and thereby indulging in the self-deception that a genuine escape has been found.

Finally, there are those who wait in a state of *'hesitant openness'*. For them, and for Kracauer who clearly identifies with this position, the goal is

> to shift the main burden from the theoretical self to the total human self and to turn away from the atomised, unreal world of formless forces and of things robbed of meaning back into the world of *reality* and the spheres which encompass it.[31]

This return to reality – however variously defined in succeeding decades – always implies 'its function as the symbol of a deficit and thereby, at the same time and however rudimentary, as the cipher of an eschatological hope'.[32] It implies a return to the concrete corporeal world of the everyday away from religion – which was Kracauer's earlier hope – and decisively turning away from any form of idealism, of pure thought. It is a return to the material world and constitutes the first step towards a critical materialism that Kracauer came to espouse.

In fact, at the time of writing this essay Kracauer was already confronting or had already confronted some of the approaches to this reality out of which he was to develop his own position.

III

When Kracauer decided, however programmatically, to turn to the reality of the everyday world which 'requires to be seen concretely' he did not embark upon this project theoretically empty-handed. If Kierkegaard's philosophy had been important for his early writings (and remained significant for *The Detective Novel*, 1922–5), the early post-war years also saw an interest in Lukács's work, especially his *Theory of the Novel* which Kracauer reviewed twice in 1921.[33] Its attraction lay in its congruence with Kracauer's own early philosophy. The novel, for Lukács, arose when 'meaning vanished from the world' and 'opened up the abyss between soul and form, the inner and the outer world'. As an 'expression of the transcendental homelessness' of the modern period, of 'the world disintegrated into a chaos', Lukács's characterization of the novel announced a central theme of Kracauer's work: the transcendental homelessness or later the ideological homelessness of humanity or specific social strata.

But if these and other writings were significant for the development of a philosophy of modern existence, they did not provide the key to Kracauer's approach to the material reality of the everyday world. That lay with his critical study of the works of Simmel, his confrontation with the phenomenological tradition as applied to sociology and, in the crucial period of transition in his work between 1924 and 1926, Marx and Marxism. As we shall see, Kracauer as an outsider never identified himself fully with these or any other theoretical traditions. And unfortunately all the material is not to hand with which we could fully assess Kracauer's relationship to Marx's work. He wrote only two detailed monographs on social theorists: one, which has disappeared, on Marx and another in Georg Simmel. His study on *Sociology as a Science* (1922) and his critical remarks on Scheler (1921) do provide us with firmer indications of his relationship to phenomenology.

In his monograph on *Georg Simmel: A Contribution to the Interpretation of the Intellectual Life of Our Times* (1919)[34] of which only the introductory chapter was published (1920),[35] Kracauer declares that 'the gateway to reality was first opened for us by Simmel'. What was it that Kracauer found attractive in Simmel's work? Simmel's sociology gave preference to 'the small detailed work', to 'psychological microscopy' in his analysis of social reality. He 'very early on proved himself to be a master in the . . . elaboration of fragmentary images of the world'.[36] These he detaches from the totality which is itself merely the totality of interconnected elements: 'Always when Simmel observes individual forms, he sets them apart from the macrocosm and detaches them from their interwovenness with phenomena; he treats them as independent entities, he disdains the incorporation of the individual microcosm in the global totality.'[37]

A further positive feature of Simmel's approach to reality is, for Kracauer, his rejection of abstract conceptualizations as the starting point for his analysis of reality:

he resists the systematic derivation of individual facts in a conceptually strict form from general higher concepts. All his intellectual developments *cling closely to the immediately experienced* – but not accessible to everyone – *living reality* . . . his whole thought is fundamentally only the grasping of the object by means of the perspective upon it. [My emphasis.][38]

In a different context and with different means, Kracauer too set himself the task of clinging closely to 'the immediately experienced . . . living reality'. As a journalist in the Weimar period, however, he had to render his own fragmentary images accessible to everyone.

Indeed, Kracauer's assessment of Simmel's work suggests a number of affinities between the two figures. Kracauer described Simmel as 'a guest, a wanderer' who possesses 'the capacity for association, the gift of seeing the connectedness and meaningful unification of arbitrary phenomena. Simmel is an eternal wanderer between things; an unlimited capacity for combination allows him to step out in any direction from any single point.'[39] This capacity was most forcefully expressed in 'the unifying core conception' of Simmel's *Philosophy of Money*: 'from any point of the totality one can arrive at any other, each phenomenon bears and supports the other, there is nothing absolute that exists unconnected to other phenomena and that possesses validity in and for itself.'[40]

This capacity for moving surreptitiously between phenomena is assisted by Simmel's 'very typical' attempt 'to preserve his incognito, often even nervously'. But the price that is paid for this eternal wandering 'is necessarily connected with something negative: with the thinker's lack of a central idea' since 'this wandering from relationship to relationship . . . secures no resting place for the mind which seeks to grasp a totality: it loses itself in infinity.'[41] And, in contradiction to Kracauer's earlier praise of Simmel's grasp of reality, he also maintains – and this must be read in the context of Kracauer's own view of the world in this period – that

> Simmel is full of interest in the world but he holds all that he has interpreted at that distance which is expressed in the concept of interest understood in its widest sense; i.e. he never engages his soul and he forgoes ultimate decisions. There is nothing more characteristic of his works . . . than that they so strongly arouse interest . . . Yet the reverse side of this is, in fact, that they only arouse interest. One does not feel pressured by them in a specific direction, they indicate no course in which our life should flow.[42]

This is, in part, because Simmel 'did not feel himself drawn into the flow of historical development'. In turn, this is reflected in his analysis of social forms since 'none . . . live in historical time. A thin air swirls around them; they do not appear in sequence; we know nothing of their historical milieu.'[43] Hence, 'one thing flows into another. Not for nothing is "nuance" a catchword of the times. Everything shimmers, everything flows, everything is ambiguous, everything converges in a shifting form. It is the realm of chaos in which we live.'[44] It is, in other words, an expression of the fleeting, transitory and fortuitous experience of modernity. For Kracauer, Simmel transposes 'everything that is interwoven in the past and future . . . into eternity, that is, into the sole form of existence in which it can exist as pure essentiality and can also be contemporary with us at any time'.[45] Later, in 1923, Kracauer was to maintain that Simmel's method is bound up with a search for the unity of life and form 'in the aesthetic realm' away from that of 'lived life'. And here Kracauer pointed to this hypostatization of the work of art in which 'its illusory reality becomes for him the substitute of the genuine reality of life'.[46]

In contrast, Kracauer goes in search of the immediate concrete reality of everyday life. To what extent is he aided in this task by his early interest in phenomenology, in a tradition which indeed now often identifies itself with the everyday world? In *Sociology as a Science*

(1922)[47] Kracauer's goal is nothing less than 'to unveil the structure of the . . . sphere of reality' which sociology deals with. In the course of this study, Kracauer seeks to demonstrate that all forms of idealist thought and formal philosophy are unable to grasp the concrete meaning that lies bracketed in reality. As in his early writings, Kracauer contrasts an earlier 'epoch filled with meaning' (a notion derived from Lukács) in which 'the whole world is covered by meaning' with the reality of the modern period in which

> the world is split into the diversity of what exists and the diversity of the human subject confronting it. This human subject, who was previously incorporated into the dance of forms filled by the world, is now left solitarily confronting the chaos as the sole agent of the mind, confronting the immeasurable realm of reality . . . [He is] thrown out into the cold infinity of empty space and empty time.[48]

Sociology, like history, 'finds itself confronted first with the immediately experienced reality, in fact the living reality of socialised human beings. This reality offers itself as a diversity of phenomena.'[49] Sociology's task is to 'deindividualise' the 'experienced facts' with which it is faced. Kracauer argues against the application of abstract categories as a means of ordering this reality and favours instead a phenomenology of 'intentional existence and events'. Sociology must give up its claim to universal and causally necessary knowledge of reality since, for Kracauer, this is only possible in 'an epoch filled with meaning'. Sociology must instead confront 'the disintegration of the world bound up with meaning'. An empirical sociology cannot perform the task of filling this world with meaning again: the 'empirical sociological procedure is naturally forbidden to oversee and transfix the flow of emergent reality. Swarming out from individual . . . points of diversity as it were, it can only always move on to individual points, it never extends itself to the whole constellation of reality.'[50] Sociology's role, for Kracauer, is a limited one. It is concerned with the 'intentional life manifestations of sociated human beings'. Its goal is the 'mastery of the immediately experienced social reality of life'. This cannot be achieved by abstract conceptualization. Rather, the starting point must be the object itself, whose empirical diversity provides no enclosed system of concepts.

But if Kracauer was sceptical of the larger claims of sociology, and although he appeared to be supporting a phenomenological procedure in sociology (adapted from Husserl), he was already also sceptical of the ontological claims made in some of Max Scheler's works. This is surprising given that Scheler was perhaps the most prominent phenomenologist who sought to apply his phenomenonological approach to sociology. Although later recognizing the value of Scheler's contribution (in his obituary of 1928),[51] Kracauer already criticized Scheler's *Vom Ewigen im Menschen* (1921) as exhibiting his eclecticism in a work which was 'an outflow of relativistic intellectuality' itself grounded 'in the intellectual situation of a period which only now begins to recognise all that is missing in it and now, more at its end than its beginning, shimmers in the thousand broken colours of the transition'.[52]

Kracauer's own 'transition' to the study of the immediate empirical reality of society, although already announced several times in these early works, is only decisively brought about in the period between 1924 and 1926. One indication of Kracauer's change of position is to be found in an ostensibly unexpected source: his review of Martin Buber's and Franz Rosenzweig's new German translation of the Old Testament which appeared in 1925.[53] The burden of Kracauer's critique of the Buber–Rosenzweig translation lies in his questioning the relevance of the translation to the profane society of today. A translation should serve to render a text contemporary. This Luther achieved in a period of revolutionary protest in which 'his translation became a means of struggle' and 'through its actualisation . . . the truth of the Bible was preserved'. The Buber–Rosenzweig translation 'advances the claim of thoroughly renewing the reality of the text'. Instead, 'the language is very largely *rendered archaic*' by reliance on the neo-romanticism of the late nineteenth century. In so doing, the text takes on 'a *reactionary* meaning. Insofar as it avoids profane language, it destroys the profane; insofar as it is elevated from the sphere of ordinary public life, it loses the pressing need with which it holds the truth.'[54] Indeed, it renders the profane unreal and becomes part of an ideology of reality that makes the actuality of today abstract. Kracauer's critique closes with the statement that 'the access to reality is now in the profane'.

This conclusion signifies a decisive break from Kracauer's early religious, metaphysical philosophy. Reality is no longer something totally lost. In an unpublished later piece on 'Two Types of Communication', Kracauer contrasts the terminology of theology and Marxism. He speaks of those people in their thirties who once took up the 'theological vocabulary' that seemed so appropriate to the early post war years. Now, however, 'they see through earlier held doctrines as ideologies. They know that ideologies are not only ideologies.'[55]

Later, in the years of inflation after the war, 'one spoke . . . of revolution. When didn't one do so then?' In the course of these discussions Kracauer opposes the thesis that

> first the circumstances must be changed and only then can human beings themselves change. A thoroughly Marxist characterisation. I didn't understand it. I advanced the contrary thesis that the change of circumstances is unavoidably dependent upon that of human beings . . . 'The way to salvation,' I said, 'leads only through the narrow gateway of inwardness.'[56]

Kracauer goes on to declare how he abandoned this view and took up a different position:

> Over the years I have increasingly come round to the view that at least nowadays the form of our economy determines the form of our existence. Politics, law, art and morality are as they are because capitalism is there. It is not from within that the outside world derives its character but rather the circumstances of society condition those of the individuals. For this reason, for precisely those who are concerned with the reintroduction of the contents intended by theology into reality there is only one way: to work for the transformation of the dominant social order. That is the small gateway through which they must pass.[57]

It follows from this that 'in our situation one must leave theology behind; in the interests of theology itself.'

But this does not mean, conversely, that Kracauer accepted 'the bare Marxism' of a rigid base-superstructure determination. This mechanistic Marxism ignores the fact that:

> theological language indicates contents which still remain contents when the economic situation from which they emerged has passed away. Each content is always connected with a specific situation, but it is often more than a mere reflection of it.[58]

One can bracket such contents but not treat them as if they were 'only reflections, empty ideologies'.

Further evidence for the materialist turn in Kracauer's development is to be found in his correspondence with Ernst Bloch, most probably instigated by Benjamin sending the latter Kracauer's Buber-Rosenzweig critique with which Bloch largely concurred.[59] This correspondence, dating from the summer of 1926, indicates Kracauer's confrontation with the writings of a number of Marxists and with some of Marx's own work. It concerns the renewal and actualization of Marxist theory. Here, Kracauer sees three possible paths towards such a project. The first, embodied in Lukács's work, and despite Kracauer's earlier appreciation of his *Theory of the Novel*, is firmly rejected as idealist. For Kracauer, Lukács

> has indeed attacked the empty and worn out idealism, but rather than transcending it, has lost himself once more in it. His concept of totality, though despairing of its own formality, has more affinities with Lask than with Marx. Instead of imbuing Marxism with realities, he turns to the spirit and metaphysics of an exhausted idealism, and, already on the way, allows the materialist categories to drop which were to have been interpreted. Rudas and Deborin, however dreadfully shallow they may be, are unknowingly correct on many points against Lukács. He sacrifices himself for nothing; he is philosophically – I don't like to say it in public – a reactionary. Just think, for instance, of his concept of the personality.[60]

Although not explicitly stated here, Kracauer's criticism is directed against Lukács's *History and Class Consciousness* and his contribution to the debate on the nature of Marxism in the early 1920s directed against the orthodox and mechanistic Marxism of Rudas, Deborin and others. As Jay has pointed out, Kracauer's response to the Hegelian Marxism of Lukács and the young Korsch (in his *Marxism and Philosophy*) placed him closer to Benjamin than to other unorthodox Marxist figures. According to Jay 'Bloch and Adorno, although not entirely in agreement with the Hegelianized Marxism posited by those works [of Lukács and Korsch], were far more favourable than Benjamin, Lowenthal or Kracauer.' Indeed 'his general attitude towards metaphysical speculation was such that Benjamin could call him an "enemy of philosophy" in 1923'.[61] However, although Jay's judgement is important with regard to Adorno, who was often critical of both Kracauer and Benjamin for not dissimilar reasons, it does not do justice to the very different positions of Bloch and Lukács at this time.

Having rejected Lukács's 'abstract intellectuality' as a foundation for 'the actuality of Marxism', Kracauer praises Bloch's position on the grounds that it wishes to present the materials of intellectual resources . . . in their immediate form, impregnated with the revolutionary energies that live within them. That this material totality may not be ignored, in this I agree with you (and certainly with Benjamin too) – against Lukács.[62]

Since Marxism, 'especially in the hands of official Soviet philosophers' has become 'no longer actual', it must be renewed by confronting its 'genuine truth contents' in order to make it 'a major revolutionary theory before which the European intelligentsia must shudder'. Kracauer now has praise for one of Bloch's main motives:

> the endeavour to bring together the individual truth contents that have been passed on in a theological form with Marxist revolutionary theory. These truth contents are presented by you with 'religious' means.[63]

But though affirming Bloch's position as a valuable one – and contrary to his earlier pronouncements on Bloch's work and upon 'messianic communism' – it does not fully accord with Kracauer's own intention.

Kracauer speaks of 'a third way towards the realization of revolutionary theory' in which

> one extracts the hidden elements of truth, which are encountered in theological language in naive ignorance of their diverse internal and external determinations, from out of their mythological masks and places them in their present position; this means, therefore, that one would find the actual and thus sole real form of these truth contents in Marxism; this would be possible by presupposing a materialist philosophy which accepted a progressive demythologisation of those categories that are hiding the truth, a real migration and transformation of these categories in the course of the historical process, until they withstand the spectacle of the simplest needs and the most superficial things; only then would they reach their destination.[64]

In other words, and following on from his Buber–Rosenzweig critique, Kracauer is convinced that '*one must confront theology in the profane*, whose holes and gaps have to be indicated into which the truth has sunk'.

In practical terms, this implies that the major truth contents which illuminate the concrete world we live in are indicated by Marxism. But this is a Marxism that must first be reconstructed and cannot be derived from an idealistic interpretation of its philosophy of history that may be ready to hand.

Its concept of the human being and of nature, its elimination of ethics, its fleeting dream-like glance at the anarchism of the fairy tale – these are all *signs which point to the truth in still uninhabited cellars and attics* . . . Perhaps you can now see that not out of any pragmatic grounds do I wish to extingish magic or remain oblivious of the totality. Rather, the magic should not come from candles or be merely an inner glow and *the notion of totality should not blind one to the instances of superficial life. To start out from the substantive and the superficial seems to me not to be banished from a genuine revolutionary theory.*[65]

In fact this theoretical reconstruction of Marxism is not a task to which Kracauer himself devoted much attention. Rather his 'theoretical' work is firmly rooted in the substantive 'surface' of the everyday world. 'Exemplary instances' of reality are Kracauer's starting point and even where he does theorize he usually relies upon 'short, aphoristic evocations to make a philosophically-laden point'.[66]

Nonetheless, Kracauer decisively established for himself a materialist philosophy of history within which he could operate as an 'eccentric realist' (Adorno).[67] When he saw Bloch's aim as that of 'unveiling as well as preserving' concrete fragments of social reality, he indicated his own goal as well as that of Benjamin. At no point did he abandon the view – in the subsequent Weimar years at least – that 'the way today only passes through a flat materialism, not over it'.

This did not mean that Kracauer created for himself a secure place within the Marxist tradition. Writing to Bloch he admitted that 'I am, in the last instance, an anarchist, though of course sceptical enough to hold anarchism as it exists to be a distortion of its intentions'. Indeed,

The dream, the ultimate definition of genuine anarchism is 'the association of free human beings' (Marx) . . . The question is, however, whether and how the approach to the reality intended by anarchism is possible. Here what inspires me . . . is an unbelief that is Kafka's too and it seems to me as if the truth in its reality always rests precisely on that spot over which we have just stepped.[68]

Although from different sources, Kracauer also shared this anarchism with Benjamin at least in his early years and possibly later.

What inspired Kracauer in Marx's writings in this period at least was largely the early works up to *The German Ideology*. From other sources, Kracauer also developed a particular interpretation of Marx. Again criticizing Lukács's Hegelian Marxism, Kracauer maintains that Lukács obscures Marx's crucial concepts since

Marx comes, more decisively than Lukács presents and perhaps knows, from the French Enlightenment and, in fact, from that branch of the Enlightenment which goes back to Locke and that is represented by the names Helvetius and Holbach. This means that decisive categories of Marxism such as the concept of the 'human being' or even 'morality' can be understood only if one builds a tunnel under the massive mountain of Hegel from Marx to Helvetius.[69]

No doubt, in part, with the aim of criticizing Lukacs's discussion of the human personality in the last chapter of *History and Class Consciousness*, Kracauer announced to Bloch in June 1926 that 'in roughly half a year's time, I intend to write a short monograph on the concept of the human being in Marx'. From other sources, we know that this was completed (under the title 'The Concept of the Human Being in Marx') but the original manuscript has thus far not been found. But in the light of Kracauer's earlier work and his correspondence with Bloch it is clear that he would have argued for the recognition of a 'genuine humanism' in Marx's work, based on a concept of the human person derived from the French Enlightenment, Kierkegaard and Marx. Implicit in this lineage is the emphasis upon the humanism of the French Enlightenment against the domination of abstract reason in German idealism. The 'demythologization' of the world brought about by the application of a particular form of reason in science and economic life must be continued by demythologizing the hypostatization of formal rationality itself.

III

The presentation of a world estranged by an empty rationality receives its first fullest expression in Kracauer's study, *The Detective Novel* (1922–5).[70] It constitutes his first attempt at the interpretation of the surface phenomena of bourgeois culture. Its philosophical orientation still places it largely within the context of his earlier writings though both the subject-matter itself and some of the themes relating forms of existence to social spaces already point forward to his later studies of the 'insignificant, superficial manifestations' of the modern life-world. Kracauer's study represents the fullest analysis of 'a distinctive genre which resolutely presents its own world with its own aesthetic means', a genre which fascinated his contemporaries such as Bloch and Benjamin. Its focus is necessarily upon the earlier form of detective novel exemplified by Conan Doyle's Sherlock Holmes stories or the detective novels of Gaboriau and Maurice Leblanc.

The study is divided into sections which suggest typifications of actors and scenes in the detective novel: 'Spheres', 'Psychology', 'Hotel Lobby', 'Detective', 'Police', 'Criminal', 'Conversion', 'Trial', and 'End'. Its tone is that of a philosophical (existential-phenomenological) morphology of the detective novel. It commences with a statement as to what Kracauer takes to be such novels' central idea:

> the idea of the thoroughly rationalised, civilised society which they comprehend with radical one-sidedness and in aesthetic refraction embody in a stylised manner. They are not connected with the naturalistic reflection of this reality itself which is termed civilisation, rather from the very outset with the inversion of the intellectualistic character of this reality. They hold a refracted mirror in front of that which is civilised out of which a caricature of its obverse essence stares back at it. The image which they offer is terrifying enough: it reveals a state of society in which the unbounded intellect has gained its ultimate victory, a merely more external juxtaposition and jumble of figures and things, that seem lurid and perplexing because it distorts into a caricature the artificially eliminated reality.[71]

Already in this presentation of the world of the detective novel, it is possible to see a central leitmotif from Kracauer's earlier work which is now given more concrete expression in its application to a seemingly superficial literary genre: the juxtaposition of a genuine community of total human beings who exist in a world which is endowed with meaning and an artificial society whose individual atoms circulate in the empty space of a reality that no longer has meaning. The genuine human community is rooted in Kierkegaard's notion of a religious community and Lukács's notion of an epoch filled with meaning. The empty reality of the civilized world is the product of a formal reason and is exemplified in German idealist philosophy. The genuine moral community constitutes the upper sphere of reality, the world of society constitutes the lower sphere.[72]

The detective novel deals with the world of the lower sphere with a 'civilised society that has been constructed to its ultimate point'. In the 'spheres of lower reality', 'clouded meaning loses itself in the labyrinth of distorted events, about whose distortion it no longer knows anything'. The detective novel 'without being a work of art', nonetheless shows 'a society without reality', shows 'its own face more clearly than it would itself be capable of'. Its 'stylisation of one-dimensional unreality' does not terminate in critique; rather it retains an aesthetic construction of a 'totality that is itself veiled to the agents of civilised society'. Indeed 'just as the detective reveals the buried secret that lies between people, so in the aesthetic medium the detective novel reveals the secret of the society rendered unreal and its substanceless marionettes'.[73] The agents of this society are 'fragmentary' individuals who no longer live in a moral universe of binding laws but 'move along the lines of legal rules' within a system governed by 'mere legality'. This universe of formally rational legality requires only 'illusory individuals' for its continued existence. Its rules 'create no atmosphere of communal life, rather they serve as a communication network between figures who merely still carry only the names of individuals and thereby lack precisely this communality'. These empty individuals 'spread themselves out in an unbounded spatial desert and are never together even when pressed in close proximity in the metropolis. Only the military roads of convention run indifferently from place to place.'[74]

The absolutisation of *ratio* driven to its extreme' presents the world of individuals as 'composed out of configurations of unconnected particles of the soul', in which 'an associative psychology predominates that grounds the totality in the parts'. As in other forms of literature for 'amusement', the individuals presented in the novels become mere repositories of bundles of emotions, they themselves are most often reduced to typifications. The world so created 'is like the facade of a tumbled down house which now only awakens the illusion of lived-in rooms'.[75] It is a 'herbarium of pure externalities'. In the detective novel its 'negative ontology' ensures that 'its actors are formula-like entities to which *ratio* possesses the key'. Its world of formal figures and 'conventional gestures' creates 'the possibility that correct behaviour hides illegal actions'.

In order to emphasize the purely formal nature of relationships in the world of the detective novel, Kracauer draws a striking comparison between the location of a religious community in 'the House of God' and a focus of action in the detective novel: 'the hotel lobby'. In both the church and the hotel lobby one enters as a guest. But in the hotel lobby 'the impersonal nothing which the manager represents here takes the place of the unknown person in whose name the church community comes together'. Whereas the latter constitutes a unified coming together of people, 'those dispersed in the lobby submit without question to the incognito of the host. They are simply people lacking a relationship to one another.' They meet in a vacuum which, although it constitutes a break from the everyday world, does not result in the creation of a community of people. In other words, this aesthetic distance from the everyday world does not lead to any positive relationship (as in the church), rather the identical situation of those within the hotel lobby establishes a relationship to nothing at all: 'one finds oneself in the lobby vis à vis de rien, it is a mere void'. The relationships there become those of a

> mere game, that elevates the unserious everyday world precisely to a serious one. Simmel's definition of society as a 'playform of sociation' can be taken in its own right, but it is incapable of extending itself beyond a mere description. It is the formal conformity of figures which present themselves in the hotel lobby and which signify an identity, that of depletion, not fulfilment.[76]

There one becomes a 'member of society in itself'. The triviality of conversation in the lobby is, as it were, 'merely the counterpart to prayer'. Even the fact that in both the hotel lobby and the church the preservation of quiet is required and secured indicates that both groups are in a similar situation, except that the bounded 'we-ness' of the religious community has its counterpart in the hotel lobby as 'the isolation of anonymous atoms'. The incognito of the latter 'no longer serves any other purpose than that of meaningless movement within the paths of convention'. The 'action' which takes place in the hotel lobby is that of 'a coming and going of unknown persons . . . for whom the offer of the superficial is an attraction, for whom contact with the aura of the exotic is pleasant'.

In the religious community the secret of existence, though it stands above all human laws, is nonetheless unveiled and revealed to its members in worship. Just as the whole human community is embodied in a transcendental manner in the religious community, so too

> the quite unsuspecting figures in the hotel lobby represent the whole of society . . . because the machinery of immanence still disguises itself. Instead of the secret extending itself beyond human beings, it inserts itself between the lava; instead of the secret penetrating through the shell of humanity, it is the veil that surrounds all that is human.[77]

Enclosed within this illusory world, the figures move around in it unaware of 'the hidden nature of the whole legal and illegal transactions' that are taking place.

F

The 'primal mist of the hotel vestibule' hides the reality of the unreal world. In the detective novel, it becomes clear that the revelation of reality takes place only through abstract reason, 'that *ratio*, as the constitutive principle of a world emptied of reality, dominates the scene in diverse roles'. Its representative is, of course, the detective: 'the detective roams in the empty space between the figures as the relaxed representative of *ratio* . . . he does not direct himself towards *ratio*, rather he is its personification.'[78] More than this, '*ratio*'s claim to autonomy makes the detective the counter-image of God himself', even though 'to be God is not his main occupation either' and even though 'this detective-God is nonetheless God in a world that God has deserted'. He seeks to unravel the mystery of that which he has not created by virtue of his intellect and he celebrates his communion, as it were, in the hotel lobby. As the representative of the absolute principle of intellect, the detective cannot assume the full drapery of a hero in the true sense since he cannot die. Instead, 'frustrated from one task to the other, he represents in fact the *progressus ad infinitum* of *ratio*, which leads to a solution of the tasks only in distorted infinity'. In other words, the detective is the agent of an objective process, 'a neutral entity', 'neither erotic nor unerotic', a 'pseudo *logos*'.

This central figure of the detective novel operates 'with and against, above and between the police and the criminal who, in the totality of the aesthetic structure, become the decisive forces of the thoroughly rationalised society'.[79] Grown out of 'societal necessities', the police, in contrast to the detective, serve an undisclosed master whose name remains 'covered in darkness'. They serve the principle of legality or, better still, they are the personification of what is formally legal, 'the agent of society in the narrowest sense of the word'. The police move in the public sphere of 'streets, hotels and halls' as well as in private spheres which have been rendered public. Their task is to ensure 'that this public life, which is still nothing definite, carries on in peace, security and order'. This order is merely an abstract statistical order that is not filled with meaning; it is rather a deceptive stability that has little to do with a moral order.

Similarly, the criminal, like the criminal act itself, is merely 'the negation of the legal', 'a disturber of the peace of society' in the sense which Kracauer gives this empty interaction of elements. The grounds for criminal acts are given only in terms of 'ideological substructures', as '*post festum* justifications'. The detective's triumph over the criminal represents 'the overcoming of panic which, in the detective novel, may rely upon a mysterious disposition of human beings. It is not the force of the event which takes one's breath away but the opacity of the causal chain which determines the fact.'[80]

As the personification of *ratio*, the detective neither identifies with the criminal nor with the police: 'rather, he unravels the puzzle largely in order to enjoy the process of unravelling'. Indeed, he may be quite indifferent to the legal or the illegal. He asserts his sovereignty over the police by virtue of his ironic stance. The police are allowed to follow through their false theories even though the detective knows them to be false.

But the decisive activity in the detective novel is, in fact, 'the process of unravelling the puzzle which the detective completes'. This 'activity' rather than 'act' of unravelling is conceived of in purely intellectual terms since the detective 'not merely lacks a soul, but even its appearance'. Formal reason solves the puzzle. It is the most appropriate instrument for performing this task in a world in which 'what occurs is isolated from the person' so that knowledge of it can be assembled 'as a conglomeration of factual scraps'. At the outset of the novel, such facts are kept at a minimum and they are surrounded by 'an impenetrable darkness'. Further, 'the material itself permits not the slightest clue for the ordering of its absence of context'. This indicates one of the basic principles of stylistic construction of the detective novel: the 'ungiveness of the given'. In other words, 'it groups the facts in such a way that their embodiment in a context seems impossible'. The chaos of sense impressions arises out of the fact that the diverse material that is present is robbed of its own form in order that formal reason may operate with it: 'this flight of the material before the context degrades it to mere material, that in itself possesses no order, but rather, in order to gain form, requires to be worked upon by the intellect.'[81]

The detective, as the personification of *ratio*, and by virtue of his possession of categories, can make 'the connection between the parts of the diversity; the unity of the immanent connection is achieved by the idea'. What this means, however, is that what is actually revealed itself remains within an immanent connection and has no meaning in itself. This is the only totality that exists.

In terms of the activities of the detective, the process of unveiling the 'real' connections often takes place by his assumption of disguises that preserve his incognito. The significance of this wandering through the various spheres of society lies in the fact that these spheres are not populated by unique individuals but rather they constitute an environment 'whose figures are at any time reproducible objects'.

In this respect, the detective is engaging in experiments with a reality whose content has been reduced to the status of discrete entities.

But unlike the positivist description of scientific experiments, here 'coincidence must come to the aid of the experiment in order that the process be completed. In the detective novel, the coincidence is not a psychological concept . . . but the distortion of a determination which operates as reality.'[82] Amongst the traces of disconnected materials 'the coincidence predominates in all the places where in this sphere one does not expect to find meaning. The coincidence is thus not introduced fortuitously, rather it fills out a gap in the sphere subjugated by *ratio*, which the latter does not fill.'[83] The detective novel in this way completes the emptying of reality by robbing decisive action of its meaning and imputing meaningful occurrence to the coincidence. In other words, the fortuitous, the contingent element of Baudelaire's definition of modernity here finds its fullest expression.

The rational process in the detective novel thus takes on the character of an end in itself. It does not bestow meaning to real events, it does not transcend the chaos of the immanent. The detective, 'torn away from the ground of existence' and embodying a formal rationality, exhausts himself in the method of detection itself. Even the secret which is revealed by the detective usually resides in 'some fact or other which in itself says nothing'.

It is not surprising, therefore, in a world robbed of meaning and robbed of genuine human emotion, that 'the feeling which the decisive action of the detective novel answers is simply that of tension. Tension produces the struggle between player and counter player, the tension of uncertainty as to how the secret will be revealed.'[84] But this tension is 'no meaningful feeling that was born out of existential tension but rather the reflex of the immanent–temporal course of what is given in the figure robbed of soul; more precisely, that form of soul, corresponding to the process of creation, in which its content disappears'.

What is, then, the finale of the detective novel? It is 'the undisputed victory of *ratio* – an end without tragedy, but heightened by that sentimentality which is an aesthetic constituent of Kitsch'. Kitsch brings about a reconciliation of that which has gone by without once touching reality. It cannot give a reality to that which it claims to give meaning to. In the detective novel,

Ratio . . . persuades the lost feelings that the production of the unquestionable immanent connection also indicates the end. The end, that is not one since it only brought unreality to an end, lures out the feeling, that is unreal and solutions, that are none, are brought in at the finale in order that heaven, which does not exist, may conquer the earth. In this way, Kitsch betrays that thought emptied of reality which dresses itself in the appearance of the highest sphere.[85]

Kracauer's concluding remarks should perhaps be seen in the light of his later assertion that 'no kitsch can be discovered that cannot be excelled by life itself'.[86]

The significance of Kracauer's first major venture into the analysis of the superficial phenomena of modernity lies in a number of directions. Kracauer's almost allegorical presentation of the contrasting worlds of the religious community (genuine human existence) and the world of the detective novel (reified unreal world of reason) allows him to extend both Lukács's images of 'transcendental homelessness' contrasted with 'epochs filled with meaning' and Weber's often ambiguous analysis of the fate of western rationality into a concrete sphere. In the development of these contrasting world views, it is reminiscent of the subsequent sociological analyses of Lucien Goldmann – who also started out from the early Lukács's writings – in his study of *Kant* and, most fully, in *The Hidden God*. Kracauer's delineation of a world in which God and human meaning are absent is indeed reminiscent of Goldmann's latter study. And although philosophical in orientation, it already presents a picture of a reified world more concretely than did Lukács earlier. It, too, is a critique of formal reason and idealist philosophy.

Looking forward to Kracauer's subsequent work, certain future strands are already in evidence. It already testifies to his thesis – made explicit in *The White Collar Workers* – that only from its extremes can reality be grasped. The image of the world robbed of meaning is certainly pursued to its fullest extent in the study of the detective novel. As others have pointed out, the focus of Kracauer's later social analysis is illuminated by the figure of the detective penetrating unknown spheres of social reality. Even in his last work on history, Kracauer describes his exile years in a manner reminiscent of his presentation of the detective. The exile 'has "ceased to belong"'. Where then does he live? In the near-vacuum of extra-territoriality . . . The exile's true mode of existence is that of a stranger . . . faced with the task . . . of penetrating . . . outward appearances.'[87] And in this context, his method is not that of a naive empiricism. Kracauer's critical perspective, though not yet fully developed in his detective study as a critical realism, already prompts him to commence with the unreality of reality and to go beyond the level of appearance. Like the detective, however, he can only penetrate the profane world of reality. And, like him, Kracauer is already fascinated by the fortuitous. Indeed, as Jay suggests, Kracauer's diverse projects all possess 'the common goal of redeeming contingency from oblivion'.[88] But in his later works, Kracauer's illumination of the mosaic of social reality and his penetration of the labyrinth of the material and social world lies in giving concrete meaning to what he observes and experiences. Rather than report upon reality, he goes in search of its hidden meaning.

IV

The detective, in the constant search for traces of meaning, 'will always have something to uncover' but his task will never come to an end. But the 'cleverly laid-out labyrinth' of the good detective novel is largely a formal intellectual creation. From the mid-1920s until his dismissal from the *feuilleton* section of the *Frankfurter Zeitung* in 1933, Kracauer produced a whole series of pieces for the newspaper which indicate his preoccupation with another, for him more real, labyrinth: that of the metropolis.[89] If the detective novel provides an 'exemplary instance' of a formal intellectual labyrinth, then, for Kracauer, the exemplary instance of society as a labyrinth is the city. What is it that Kracauer goes in search of? In the context of the 'unwinding of abstract formal relationships' in society, 'the exclusion of genuine cognitive contents from the societal constellation leads to their suppression. One does not wish to take notice of them, one passes over them. They alone, however, take into custody that which is human.'[90] It is these forgotten, lost, suppressed traces of humanity that Kracauer goes in search of. These fragments of lost experience are not ready to hand. They have to be sought after, to be reconstructed out of that which has been deconstructed.

In Kracauer's work, the images of the city are to be found in his brief essays. They are concerned largely with Paris – the city Benjamin later described as 'Capital of the Nineteenth Century' – and with Berlin, a 'new' city that was the focus of modernity in Weimar Germany. In their essayistic form, these brief pieces take on the character of fleeting phenomenological analyses. In both form and content, they very much represent fragments of modernity. As 'conscious constructions' of aspects of urban reality they are to be distinguished from the products of reportage which were popular in Weimar Germany as a result of the *neue Sachlichkeit* movement and from which Kracauer explicitly distanced himself. Inka Mülder well captures the essence of these fragmentary images which do not lay claim to a relationship with 'comprehensive theory'. In these images of the city

> there is, first of all, as a foundation, the experience of the city as a labyrinth of fragmentary signs concerning which the phenomenology of the superficial seeks an entry into the secret *genius loci*; and, at the same time, the presupposition of this experience: an astonishment that breaks through the accustomed perspective, liberates the object from out of the illusory self-evidentness of its conventional context in which the available view has been reified as 'from above'; finally, the deciphering of topographical ciphers . . .
>
> Kracauer's intention . . . in the metaphorical deciphering of superficial images is to release 'mute' and 'unconscious' phenomena from their natural-like reification, 'enlighten' them as historical, to leave them as alive.[91]

Before examining these images further and this description of them, it is important to note that they constitute a decisive break with Kracauer's earlier works, both in form and in intention. Much more directly than his earlier writings they are orientated towards the experience of the material, concrete object itself. More than most of Kracauer's earlier large monographs and, indeed, some of his later ones, these short essays capture the essence of modernity. Indeed, Mülder justifiably claims that 'a knowledge of these smaller studies is the prerequisite for any fundamental confrontation with Kracauer'.[92]

In one of these essays originally entitled 'Berlin Landscape',[93] Kracauer reveals one dimension of his interest in the urban labyrinth. He starts out by distinguishing between two types of image of the city. On the one hand, there are those that 'are consciously formed' and usually 'illuminated with a small star' in Baedeker's guide books. There are others – which Kracauer seeks out – 'which reveal themselves unintentionally'. These

> are not compositions . . . but rather *fortuitous creations* [*Geschöpfe des Zufalls*]. Wherever masses of stone and lines of streets are to be found together, whose elements emerge out of quite diversely orientated interests, there such an image of the city comes into existence that is

itself never the object of some interest or other. It is no more
constructed than is nature and is similar to a landscape in that it
unconsciously asserts itself. Unconcerned with how it looks, it continues
to glow through time. [My emphasis.][4]

Kracauer goes on to present the 'fairy tale-like adroitness' of an
inconspicuous square and intersection of streets with a railway bridge
across which pass trains from Charlottenburg station in Berlin
'emerging suddenly from behind a larger than life wall of tenements'.
It is quite explicitly the child's view of the city restored to its full
astonishment and awe, the view of 'heavy express trains rushing
towards famous cities such as Warsaw and Paris that are built up just
around the next corner'. It is an image that is present in several *neue
Sachlichkeit* and American realist paintings and films of the twenties
and thirties. Kracauer's landscape here is that of a 'raw Berlin.
Unintentionally, there is expressed in it . . . its contradictions, its
ruggedness, its openness, its simultaneity, its glamour. *Knowledge of
cities is bound up with the deciphering of their dream-like expressive images.*
[My emphasis.][95]
    These images of dimensions of cities are not therefore already
created for us. Kracauer, with his sociological and architectural
training, with his powerful visual sense, seeks out the fortuitous
fragments of urban life in order to reveal their hidden meaning and
thereby indicate some features of modernity in general. But Kracauer's
method cannot be reduced to that of mere representation of urban
images. It is a critical method prompted by what Schröter has termed
'the longing for the totality' in a social reality that has destroyed and
continues to destroy the unity of the object. Kracauer's images are
not mere 'reproductions' that 'merely take up what is given, as is
the case with the banal view' of things, thereby reproducing merely
a 'confused assortment of the fortuitous'.[96] What characterizes
Kracauer's approach is what Mülder terms 'experiential thought' or
what Schröter formulates as the confrontation of the following problem:
'Experience presupposes knowledge every bit as much as conversely
knowledge presupposes experience. Where both come as closely
together as possible material reality coheres into a meaningful
image.'[97] Zohlen maintains that Kracauer elevates his images above
mere description, a process indicated often in the title or opening
sentence of his text. 'It makes possible deconstruction instead of this
"reproduction": Kracauer destroys the confidence in the object
derived from the everyday viewpoint in that, by means of the text, he

constructs a different, new possibility of perception and interpretation.'[98] The confidence that the reader has in his or her
knowledge of the streets or social spaces which Kracauer illuminates
is shattered in such a way that the object appears unfamiliar to us.

Kracauer's increasingly critical materialist standpoint was developed
out of his growing confrontation with Marx's work and with his greater
engagement in Marxist circles, especially his sometimes uneasy
relationship with Bloch, Benjamin and Adorno. In so far as his writings
from around 1926 onwards take up a distinctive critique of ideology,
they also indicate a growing distance from Simmel's sociological work
and from a purely descriptive phenomenology. This is evident, as
we shall see, from his essays on 'The Mass Ornament' (1927) and
'Photography' (1927) and his confrontation with mass culture,
especially film (cf. 'Film and Society' 1927). It is no less apparent
from his analysis of the urban labyrinth.

Kracauer's early city images often deal with foreign cities and
towns – Marseilles, Positano – and, above all, Paris. Although not true
in every instance, the juxtaposition of Kracauer's images of Parisian
and Berlin city landscapes does suggest a more positive response to
Paris. In part, this rests on the juxtaposition of the historical with
the new, the dream with the nightmare, humanity with emptiness.
In one of these city images 'Parisian Observations' (1927)[99] –
typically a constellation, almost a montage, of vignettes of Parisian
life – Kracauer quite explicitly draws the contrast between Paris and
Berlin. Its first scene, already anticipating a distance from its object,
concerns Paris 'viewed from Berlin' in which Paris, to the German
from Berlin 'who comes with his problems packed up to Paris, believes
he has been transplanted in a huge *provincial town* . . . life and society
seem to him to be those of a hundred years ago.' He returns to Berlin
'with the awareness that here he once more breathes the raw reality,
as it is termed'. But Paris is a city with tradition which 'does not
preserve museum pieces but retains the handed-down possession as
something alive (if in Germany something has not crumbled which
remains standing in France, then this is only because it has never
existed for us; perhaps a society).' Paris's class-stratified society is
built upon 'the volcanic *lava*' of a seemingly timeless uprooted
peasantry and 'if one searches through its quarters and bars, one can
understand the occurrence of the French Revolution, whose traces
have been erased from the image of higher society'. Indeed, 'the
ordinary people in Paris give one more hope than the society
itself'.[100]

Just as Benjamin identified modernity in the juxtaposition of the city as antiquity and the masses as modernity, so Kracauer too locates ordinary people within Paris as rooted in a historical context. Paris 'carries the signs of age upon its brow. Out of the pores of its houses there spring up memories, and the rain constantly washes the monuments of the Madeleine so that they are white like snow. The white of age is the colour of the city. Beneath its veil, however, it lives protected and is fresh as on the first day.'[101] In 'Analysis of a City Plan' (1928),[102] Kracauer again draws the contrast between the old and the new in Paris, between the *faubourgs* and the centre. 'Several of the Parisian *faubourgs* are the huge asylum of ordinary people' whose form of communal life over centuries has taken on 'the form of an asylum, that is certainly not bourgeois but also neither is it proletarian in the sense of chimneys, barracks and chaussée. It is both impoverished and human at the same time. Their humanity does not rest solely in the fact that existence in the *faubourgs* contains the remnants of natural life which it fills. Rather, more decisive is that this filled existence stands as a symbol of debris.' Hence, 'not for nothing did the revolutions start out from the *faubourgs*. Happiness, sensuous glamour, was absent from them.' In contrast to this nether world, the upper world of the boulevards in the centre contains a very different crowd, unconcerned by purpose or time: 'it ripples timelessly.' Here, 'in the headquarters of nightlife the illumination is so shrill that one must close one's ears to it . . . Its adverts press down upon one without being decipherable. The red shimmer which they leave behind lies as a veil over thought.'[103]

Kracauer had earlier taken up a similar theme in 'Street People in Paris' (1927).[104] In its streets 'their flourishes the vegetation of common people. Whilst higher society disappears in the four walls of cars and homes, they grow everywhere out of the houses . . . Their humus is the pavement, the public sphere is their home. Though they may be composed of workers, tradespeople, conductors, they are not absorbed in statistics. This people has created the city landscape in which it can persist, an indestructible web of cells that is hardly harmed by the architectural perspective of the king and the enlightened haute bourgeoisie. The smallness of the cells corresponds to the smallness of human proportions and needs . . . The people are incalculable like its network of streets.' This culture however does not 'strive heavenwards', it disperses itself, 'its forms break off suddenly without forming a surface, its objects stand colourfully alongside one another'. This culture always prevents its being brought together into 'a readable pattern'. In contrast, 'bourgeois society seeks out security beyond the immediate moment and moves in a system of lines that are just as straight as the avenues (of course, the system has no durability). The image in which the common people represent themselves is an *improvised mosaic*. It leaves many cavities free.' Elsewhere, Kracauer declares that 'the value of cities is determined according to the number of places in which improvisation is permitted'.[105]

The implication of Kracauer's images of Paris is that its labyrinth is not merely spatial but temporal. It has a history that is decipherable, though this later became Benjamin's rather than Kracauer's task. Its common people who themselves constitute a labyrinth (again Benjamin later refers to the *flâneur* seeking his way through the labyrinth of the crowd) are located in this historical network. The crowd and the network of streets constitute a constellation whose elements 'are intermeshed with one another like the parts of a body'. In 'Memory of a Paris Street' (1930),[106] Kracauer refers to his goal – a street which he was obsessively drawn towards – as having been directed through 'a secret smuggler's path [which] led into the sphere of hours and decades, whose street system was presented in just as labyrinthine a manner as that of the city itself'. Kracauer's goal is not, like Proust's, merely 'a remembrance of things past' but an attempt at a remembrance of a history lost. This was still possible in Paris since there 'the present has the glimmer of the past. While one still walks through the living streets, they are already distant like memories in which reality mixes with the multistoreyed dream of that reality and refuse and constellations of stars meet one another.'[107] Indeed, Kracauer said of the labyrinth that 'those who dream know its order'.[108] The same is true of the deciphering of architecture too: 'The fragments of architecture are ciphered communications that only the initiated are able to decipher. Just like the lover to whom a half a word discloses the secret of the loved one, so he too draws them out of the avenues, the streets, the squares which do not at all immediately reveal themselves.'[109]

But although Paris too has its 'endless street',[110] none compare with those which Kracauer illuminates in the vanguard city of Berlin with its 'unhistorical nature' and 'the formless disquiet with which it is permeated'.[111] The time of its streets is an empty, unhistorical time. This Kracauer graphically presents in 'Street without Memory' (1932):[112] 'If some street blocks seem to be created for eternity, then the present-day Kurfürstendamm is the embodiment of empty flowing time in which nothing is allowed to last.' The 'eternal change' within its facades, the 'rootlessness' of its ever-changing shops and other enterprises 'effaces the memory of them'. Many of them 'no longer take the effort to create the feeling of a securely grounded concern, but rather from the very first awaken the impression of improvisation'. Where one concern replaces another – and here Kracauer has in mind a tearoom he used to frequent now replaced by a confectioner's shop – the former's reality

> is not merely superseded but so completely displaced as if it never even existed at all. Through its complete presentness it is plunged into a state of being forgotten from which no force can any longer rescue it; it then becomes *the fortuitous* over which the everyday world quickly closes once more. Elsewhere, what has passed remains fixed to the place which during its lifetime was its home; on the Kurfürstendamm it makes its exit without leaving behind any traces . . . the new enterprises are always absolutely new and those that have been displaced by them are totally extinguished. What once existed is on its way to being never seen again, and what has just been claimed is confiscated one hundred per cent by today. A frenzy predominates as it did in the colonies and gold rush towns even though veins of gold had hardly been detected in these zones. Many buildings have been shorn of the ornaments which formed a kind of bridge to yesterday. Now *the plundered facades stand uninterrupted in time and are the symbol of the unhistorical change that takes place behind them.* Only the marble staircases that glimmer through the doorway preserve memories: those of the pre-war world first class. [My emphasis.][113]

Here, most forcefully, Kracauer seeks to go beyond experience of the fortuitous in the empty time of modernity into the possibility of historical experience. Similarly, he seeks to reveal what lies beneath the surface of everyday reality, what lies behind the facades. Perhaps more clearly than in some of his earlier city images another dimension of his analysis makes itself evident. This, Zohlen argues, is 'the motif of the economy' which permeates the whole text:

> The house becomes delapidated because it is no longer economically viable. The enactment of the fetish 'nouveauté' is the frenzy of a gold-rush town (the vein of gold of the twenties was the consumer!). It is the enterprises containing fashion, luxury and saleable goods which emerge in the *spectre of reality*. In this motif, Kracauer creates the critical and debatable relationship between the natural scientific exact calculation of time and economic interests for which it is a cardinal precondition.[114]

The spectral objectivity presented here is that of 'the ever-same prevailing actuality or, more precisely, the frenzy of the fetish "nouveauté" as an unhistorical presentness'.[115]

In 'Repetition' (1932),[116] the personal experiential consequences of living in this unhistorical actuality are again located in Berlin as

> the place in which one quickly forgets; indeed, it appears as if this city has control of the magical means of eradicating all memories. It is present-day and, moreover, it makes it a point of honour of being absolutely present-day. Whoever stays for any length of time in Berlin hardly knows in the end where he actually came from. His existence is not like a line but a series of points; it is new every day like the newspapers that are thrown away when they have become old. I know of no other city that is capable of so promptly shaking off what has just occurred. In other places, too, images of squares, company names and enterprises unquestionably transform themselves; but only in Berlin are the transformations of the past so radically stripped from memory. Many experience precisely this life from headline to headline as exciting; partly because they profit from the fact that their earlier existence vanishes in its moment of disappearing, partly because they believe they are living twice as much when they live purely in the present.[117]

This moment of presentness itself, however, never remains present. It is always on the point of vanishing. Hence the endless search for the ever-new and the permanent transformation of consciousness of time in metropolitan existence which Simmel had already hinted at and which was to preoccupy Benjamin even more.

If the economy – in the later Weimar city images – and the fleeting nature of the unhistorical present are central motifs in Kracauer's, then there is another motif more closely related to personal experience: dread or angst. As in the abstract world of the detective, so in the metropolis stripped of its glamour, there is a permanent tension, a fear. Just as empty time is not filled with historical events but with the fortuitous, the coincidental, so empty space is filled with distraction. The 'profane' lighting surrounding the Kaiser-Wilhelm memorial church at night for instance – presented in 'Picture Postcard' (1930)[118] – gives it a 'glamour full of secrecy', which is in reality 'a reflection of the facades of light' that 'make night into day in order to banish the dread of the night from the working day of its visitor'. This facade of lights from illuminated monuments, neon signs and advertisements together constitutes 'an attack on tiredness which wishes to take over, on the emptiness which wishes to escape at any price. They roar, they pummel, they hammer with the brutality of the insane upon the crowd . . . a flashing protest against the darkness of our existence, a protest of the thirst for life.'[119]

Away from the centre of the city there are other indications of this sense of dread. 'The Underpass' (1932)[120] beneath a railway also bears this 'sense of dread' in which there is present 'the contrast between the enclosed, unshakeable construction system and the vanishing human jumble which produces the terror'. In the empty square too 'the force of the quadrant' without compassion entraps the solitary individual in its middle: 'the angst is stark naked.'[121]

This sense of terror reaches its peak in 'Screams on the Street' (1930).[122] Kracauer discerns in the 'friendly and clean' streets of west Berlin with their 'nice green trees before its houses' an inexplicable 'angst', an impression of 'panic-like horror'. The sense of angst which these streets evoke arises perhaps from the fact 'that these streets lose themselves in infinity; that buses roar through them, whose occupants during the journey to their distant destinations look down so indifferently upon the landscape of pavements, shop windows and balconies as if upon a river valley or a town in which they would never think of getting off; that a countless human crowd moves in them, constantly new people with unknown aims that intersect like the linear maze of a pattern sheet. In any case, it sometimes seems to me as if an explosive lies ready in all possible hidden places that, in the very next moment, can indeed blow up.'[123] Sometimes in these streets 'laden with an unbearable tension' there does erupt the noisy violence of 'a National Socialist gang', though this is not what Kracauer has in mind.

In contrast, there are 'whole city areas to which there clings the penetrating odour of political riots; Neukölln perhaps or Wedding. By their very nature, their streets are streets for parades.' But it is possible to grasp the nature of these streets from the very outset.

> In contrast to such spaces, there flows in these streets in the west a terror that is without an object. They are neither inhabited by the proletariat, nor are they witnesses to rebellion. Their populace do not belong together and the atmosphere in which communal actions emerge is completely lacking in them. Here no one expects anything from anyone else. Uncertain, they extend themselves, without content and empty.[124]

Indeed, it is as if the streets themselves 'cry out in their emptiness'.

In other words, what Kracauer is seeking out are the 'less obvious symptoms of the real state of affairs' that belong to 'the *nervousness in the everyday world*' and which is associated with social crisis. This crisis is not invisible even to the stranger to the city. 'Rather, its signals loom like the masts of a sunken ship up above the mirror-flat surface,' as he puts it in 'Beneath the Surface' (1931).[125]

Yet it is not merely in the streets themselves that Kracauer seeks out the traces of modernity. They are to be found too in the *intérieur* of public life. One instance, which as it were constitutes both an *extérieur* and *intérieur* and which was the central focus of Benjamin's unfinished project on modernity, is the arcade. It is the subject of Kracauer's 'Farewell to the Linden Arcade' (1930).[126] The Linden arcade, like 'all genuine bourgeois arcades', symbolized for Kracauer as a child the dark entry into a passage which opened up a world of fantasy. The arcade's main characteristic was that it constituted a 'passageway through bourgeois life, that which existed in front of its entries and that which lived above them. Everything, that was cut off from it because it was not worthy of representation or even ran counter to the official world view, nestled itself in the arcade.' Here, such objects acquired 'a kind of right of residence'. Here, those desires which 'appear in the waking dream' can be satisfied. The objects of those desires 'flourish as in a swamp': an anatomical museum exhibiting 'the excrescences and monstrosities' of the body, pornography 'at home in the twilight', as well as photographers, hairdressers, stamp collectors' shops, cafés and the like. In short, 'what linked the objects in the Linden arcade and caused them all to participate in the same function was their withdrawal from the bourgeois front'. Their goal was 'to organise an effective act of protest in the twilight of the passageway against the facade culture outside. They laid bare idealism and exposed its products as kitsch.' They constituted, as it were, 'a critique' of the bourgeois world. But as the product of a world that was itself drawing to an end, its contents became more rapidly obsolete so that they arouse no 'sensation' today. Instead, 'all the objects are stricken with muteness. Shyly, they crowd together behind the empty architecture which once upon a time held them completely neutral and later once more will hatch out who knows what – perhaps fascism or even nothing at all. What is the point still of an arcade in a society that is itself only an arcade?'

If the arcade is very much a bourgeois public *intérieur* whose function has long since disappeared, then in the same period in which Kracauer was writing there was one public *intérieur* – a proletarian *intérieur* – whose inmates were rapidly expanding as a result of the deepening economic crisis: the employment exchange. And if Kracauer's analysis of the Linden arcade is tinged with melancholy, this is certainly not the case with 'On Employment Exchanges' (1930).[127] More explicitly than elsewhere, it contains both elements of Kracauer's sociology of space as well as its links with a critique of ideology. It is also an arcade of a very different kind.

Just as in *White Collar Workers* Kracauer declares – in a specific sense – that 'reality is a construction', so here space is also viewed as a social construction:

> Each social strata has a space that is associated with it. Thus, that *Neue Sachlichkeit* study which one recognises from films belongs to the managing director . . . As the characteristic location of the small dependent existences who still very much like to associate themselves with the sunken middle class, more and more suburbs are formed. The few inhabitable cubic metres, which cannot even be enlarged by the radio, correspond precisely to the narrow living space of this strata. The typical space for the unemployed is more generously proportioned but as a result is the opposite of a home and certainly not a living space. It is the employment exchange. An arcade, through which the unemployed should once more attain a gainfully employed existence. Today, unfortunately, the arcade is heavily congested.[128]

The social space of the middle strata is more thoroughly examined in Kracauer's contemporary study of white collar workers. It is also the subject of a whole range of shorter 'constructions' of the interiors of 'distraction',[129] 'oases'[130] – including hotels[131] and cafes[132] – from everyday life and in 'Das Mittelgebirge' (1926)[133] the consequences of 'the narrowness of the illusory private sphere' which 'strengthens the urge to flee from their own four walls'.[134] In the hills around the major cities – and Kracauer probably took the area surrounding Frankfurt as his example – which as a result of the speed of traffic become 'smaller and smaller in the course of time', the middle strata take to their small cars, 'the major ornament of the *Mittelgebirge*', in search of a pastoral idyll.

For the unemployed, however, no such illusory retreat is possible. Their dream lies in the possibility of attaining employment again or even for the first time. And whereas the experience of unemployment lacks a reality in the wider society even where it is debated and presented, its actuality is ever-present in the one social space created for it: the employment exchange. Kracauer visited several in Berlin, not 'in order to indulge the enjoyment of the reporter' in discovering the unfamiliar, the exotic, but rather

> in order to ascertain what position the unemployed actually occupy in the system of our society. Neither the diverse commentaries on unemployment statistics nor the relevant parliamentary debates give any information on this. *They are ideologically permeated* and, in one sense or another, straighten out reality; whereas the space of the employment exchange is filled by reality itself. Each typical space is brought into being by typical social relationships that, without the distorting intervention of consciousness, express themselves in it. Everything that is disowned by consciousness, everything that would otherwise be intentionally overlooked, contributes to its construction. *Spatial images are the dreams of society. Wherever the hieroglyphics of any spatial image is deciphered, there the basis of social reality presents itself.* [My emphasis.][135]

Here Kracauer's intention is not to describe some surface phenomenon of society but to reveal a reality that is obscured in society at large and which is obscured also by those who constructed the social space. Indeed, seldom had any social theorist been so preoccupied with spatial images as was Kracauer. The ordered space might well be a dream for those who constructed it but an empty nightmare for those who occupy it. His mode of uncovering a hidden reality he termed a 'material dialectics' that remained firmly convinced of the importance of analysing concrete reality.

At first sight, Kracauer's preoccupation with spatial images as 'the dreams of society' seems to have affinities with Benjamin's uncovering of collective dreams. Indeed, Adorno, referring to this text, declared that 'With astonishment and, however, in agreement with you, I have noticed that you have accepted the Benjamin hypothesis of buildings as the dreams of the collectivity – yet without using the word collective which I too cannot stand. The piece is really very aggressive and hard-hitting.' Kracauer, however, argued that he was not working with Benjamin's hypothesis: 'Certain spatial images I did speak of as the dreams of society, because they present the existence of this society that is veiled by its consciousness.' In this respect what is common to both Benjamin and Kracauer lies 'only in the word dream'. Benjamin's 'interpretation of the city as a dream of the collectivity still seems to me to be romantic'.[136]

Whether this is true of Benjamin's conception remains to be seen. What certainly is true is that Kracauer's presentation of employment agencies is lacking in any form of romanticism. If reality is a construction for Kracauer, its theoretical or conscious construction obscures that reality. The social space of the employment agency is one that is buried away from 'normal places of work', often hidden behind other buildings that obscure it from view. It reflects the position of its occupants 'in the present production process. They are secreted from it as waste products, they are the left-overs that remain. Under the prevailing circumstances, the space accorded to them can hardly have any other visage than that of a junk room.' And in contrast to his earlier essay 'Those who Wait', Kracauer fills out concretely the empty act of waiting in the employment agency: 'just as waiting in the employment agency finds no fulfilment . . . so too the elementary existence here is not built in and embraced. It stares into emptiness without being taken up by consciousness.' Its empty space is filled with bare minimal furniture and sparse warnings such as 'Unemployed! Protect and Preserve Common Property', a 'common property that is not common enough to forfeit its private character'. Kracauer asks cryptically here

> What is the whole expenditure of grandiose vocabulary for? For a couple of miserable tables and benches that neither deserve the pretentious name of common property, nor do they require preservation or even any special protection. Thus society preserves and protects property; it fences it in, even there where its defence is not at all necessary, with linguistic trenches and ramparts. It probably does it unintentionally, and perhaps one of those affected hardly notices that it does it. But that is precisely the genius of the language; that it fulfils instructions that it has not been informed of, and erects bastions in the unconscious.[137]

Helms, commenting on such passages, maintains that as 'a better Marxist than many who lay claim to the title, he rigorously distinguished between the necessary false consciousness evoked through the relations of production and the ideologies produced for concrete purposes of domination'.[138] One can also add today that by commencing from the concrete reality of every day he came closer to indicating the effectiveness of false consciousness than those who start out from abstract ideological state apparatuses and the like.

As in his study of white collar workers and elsewhere, so here too Kracauer lays bare the empty justifications for the present state of affairs that seems so systematically arbitrary that they constitute 'anything other than pure arbitrariness'. It is individualistic justifications and notions of justice that predominate, that 'travel into the lower stratum like a streak of lightning out of the serene heaven of the upper strata'. Kracauer asserts the converse: 'Only with the mass itself can a sense of justice rise up that is really just.'[139]

Whether this was likely to take place or not was indirectly an underlying theme of Kracauer's preoccupation with the culture of the mass. His powerful optical sense and critical materialist position were not only increasingly evident in his images of the city. They also came to the fore in his exploration of the culture of the mass.

V

Kracauer's 'The Mass Ornament' (June 1927)[140] can be seen as a theoretical contribution in its own right that spans the themes of his earlier work and his later, more materialist essays. A closer observation of its themes suggests that it can also be viewed within the context of an increasing preoccupation with the means for distracting large sections of society from their real circumstances. Here belong the essays 'The Cult of Distraction' (March 1926),[141] 'They Sport' (January 1927),[142] 'Film and Society' (March 1927),[143] – later retitled and better known as 'The Little Shop Girls go to the Cinema' – and 'Photography' (October 1927),[144] as well as many other briefer reflections in the course of shorter film notices.

Its methodological preface expresses Kracauer's intention in his social images of the period:

> The place which an epoch occupies in the historical process is determined more forcefully from the analysis of its insignificant superficial manifestations that from the judgments of the epoch upon itself. As the expression of historical tendencies, the latter form no conclusive evidence for the total constitution of the period. The former preserve their unconsciousness as a result of an immediate access to the basic content of what exists. Conversely, their significance is linked with their knowledge. The basic content of an epoch and its unobserved impulses reciprocally illuminate one another.[145]

This insistence on the significance of the apparently superficial phenomena in society, Kracauer shares with Bloch and Benjamin. Kracauer himself examines how far in the surface phenomena 'the respectively included elements both emphasise their own value as well as accommodate a significant totality. The relationship between

richness and form in the small phenomenon is the index for order
or disorder in the totality.'[146]

The superficial, surface phenomenon which Kracauer takes as his
exemplary instance of 'the physiognomy of the period' is here
a 'product of American distraction factories': the Tiller Girls.
The 'geometric precision' of the Tiller Girls in revues in which
'they are no longer individual girls but indisoluble constellations of
girls whose movements are mathematical demonstrations' is also
reproduced on a large scale in huge stadiums in which the 'regularity'
of the 'pattern' of bodies constitutes an ornament which 'consists
of thousands of bodies, sexless bodies in bathing costumes'. The
decisive 'agent of the ornament is the *mass*', not people who are
part of a community, not individuals with distinctive personalities.
The elements of the mass ornament are mere 'building blocks'
assembled together in abstract configurations, elements without
history, without sex, without personalities, without human relationships. In contrast to the earlier ornamental configurations in ballets
and parades, which still contained elements of 'erotic life' and 'patriotic
feelings', the mass ornament is 'an end in itself' that moves in 'an
empty space, a linear system'. It does not require the conscious
participation of the masses who bring it into existence. It remains
so rigorously linear that it is similar to 'the *aerial pictures* of landscapes
and cities' in that 'it does not grow out of the inner elements of what
is given but appears above them'.

The mass ornament is thoroughly '*rational*', consisting of geometric
planes and circles. It is 'the aesthetic reflection of the rationality that
the dominant economic system strives for':

> Since the principle of the *capitalistic production process* does not solely
> emerge from nature, it must break up the natural organisms which
> for it are a means or points of resistance. The community of people
> and the personality disappear when calculability is demanded; only
> the human being as a small particle of the mass can smoothly climb
> to the top of the chart and serve machines. The system, indifferent
> to differences in form, leads to the effacement of national characteristics
> and to the fabrication of masses of workers who can be employed in
> an identical manner at all points of the earth. The capitalistic
> production process, like the mass ornament, is an end in itself.[147]

Kracauer's interpretation of capitalism at this point is reminiscent
of that fusion of Marx, Weber and Simmel which is exemplified in
Lukács's earlier discussion of reification. It is one which enables him

to draw the connection between capitalist organization and the 'organization' of the mass ornament, as when he maintains that

> The production process terminates publicly in the hidden sphere. Each person takes care of his position on the moving conveyor belt, carries out a partial function, without knowledge of the whole. Like the stadium pattern, the organisation stands over the masses, a monstrous figure . . . It is designed according to rational basic principles, from which the Taylor System merely extracts the ultimate consequences. The Tiller Girls' legs correspond to the hands in the factory.[148]

Looking back on the emergence of the Tiller Girls in 'Girls and Crisis' (1931),[149] Kracauer expanded more graphically on this convergence of the mass ornament and capitalism:

> When they formed an undulating snake, they radiantly illustrated the virtues of the conveyor belt; when they tapped their feet in fast tempo, it sounded like *business, business*; when they kicked their legs high with mathematical precision, they joyously affirmed the progress of rationalisation; and when they kept repeating the same movements without ever interrupting their routine, one envisaged an uninterrupted chain of motor cars gliding from the factories into the world, and believed that the blessing of prosperity had no end.[150]

And unlike many intellectuals who both condemn such manifestations of a mass culture and retreat into past, outmoded artistic forms, the mass's aesthetic appreciation of the ornamental movements of masses is *'legitimate'*.

It is not merely Weber's conception of capitalism, with its decisive emphasis on the organization of production, which Kracauer takes up but also his vision of the historical process as *'the process of demythologisation* which results in the radical destruction of constantly newly occupied positions of what is natural'. But unlike Weber, Kracauer's emphasis is upon the dialectics of enlightenment, thereby foreshadowing Adorno's and Horkheimer's own *Dialectics of Enlightenment* (1944), and upon the persistence of *'mythological* thought' that has been seemingly built over by a dominant 'rational' system. However, 'reason does not move in the circle of natural life. Its task is the establishment of truth in the world. Its realm has already been dreamed of in the genuine *fairy tales* that are not miraculous stories but suggest the wonderful arrival of justice.'

Within this broad historical process of demythologization, 'the capitalist epoch is one stage on the way to disenchantment'. What is decisive about the way of thinking embedded in its economic system is not so much its capacity to exploit nature but the fact that 'it makes itself ever more independent of natural conditions and thus creates a space for the intervention of reason'. Its rationality, deriving in part if not entirely from the reason embedded in fairy tales, is not, however, reason itself. In fact, 'the *ratio* of the capitalist economic system is not reason itself, but a reason rendered dreary', one that does not include human beings themselves. Kracauer's position here echoes that which he developed earlier in his analysis of the *ratio* of the detective novel. But he continues by criticizing his own earlier call for a community to replace a capitalist society that has destroyed human rationalism. Such calls for a return to community 'mistake the core defect of capitalism. It does not rationalise too much, but rather *too little*. The thought which it bears resists the completion of reason which speaks from the foundations of humanity.' This form of thought is trapped in its own abstraction – its most characteristic feature.

Yet the very abstract nature of present-day thought is itself '*equivocal*'. Viewed 'from the standpoint of mythological teachings . . . the process of abstraction . . . is a gain in rationality . . . From the perspective of reason the same process of abstraction appeared conditioned by nature; its loses itself in an empty formalism.' The problem arises, however, as to whether to succumb to this reason or opposite it: 'The more abstractness crystallises, becomes fixed, the greater the tendency of humanity to be left behind, untouched by reason' and therefore to become subjected to the forces of nature once more.

But it is not merely abstract *ratio* that is equivocal; 'the *mass ornament* is just as ambivalent as abstractness'. Not only is nature 'deprived of its substance' but 'the bearer of the ornament does not figure in it as a total personality'. Rather 'the human figure . . . has begun its *exodus* from the organic splendour . . .' and become anonymous. Thus 'only remnants of the human complex . . . enter into the mass ornament'. But 'if the mass ornament is viewed from the standpoint of reason then it reveals itself as a *mythological cult* that hides itself in an abstract guise'. This guise of rationality is, however, 'an illusion which the ornament assumes in contrast to the physical representation of concrete immediacy. In reality it is the crass manifestation of inferior nature. The more decisively capitalist ratio is cut off from reason and bypasses reason, vanishing into the emptiness of the abstract, the more this primitive nature can make itself felt.' Reason does not 'speak out' in the mass ornament; its 'patterns are *mute*'. It is merely the '*empty form* of the cult', an ultimate 'regression to mythology'.

The significance of the mass ornament has not been understood by privileged intellectuals who, unconscious of their own position in the economic system, remain 'untouched by the reality present in the stadium pattern'. The bearers of the mass ornament are, of course, 'swallowed up by the nature of the event', unaware of the relationship that the cult of 'physical culture' has with the *status quo*. Indeed,

> Physical training expropriates energies; production and mindless consumption of the ornamental figures divert from the transformation of the existing order. Reason is impeded when the masses into which it should penetrate yield to emotions provided by the godless mythological cult. Its social significance is not at all unlike that of the Roman *circus games* sponsored by those in power.[151]

This thesis, later elaborated in his planned research project on 'Mass and Propaganda' (1937) which was rejected by Adorno and Horkheimer, and actually realized in his study of Nazi films – *From Caligari to Hitler* (1947) – is commented upon by Witte in terms of its foresight into the subsequent use of the mass ornament:

> If the massive consumption of the ornamental figures distracts people from changing the current social system, it becomes understandable why, a short time later in 1933, the fascists were able to mobilise those energies which lay devoid of meaning, substance and interpretation, so that the masses could actually claim to see their own triumph of the will in that megalomaniacally contrived and hypertrophically staged spectacle in Nuremberg.[152]

Kracauer himself, at the time of writing in 1927, could only point to a whole range of 'hopeless attempts to reach the higher life from mass existence', to link humanity to nature in a romantic manner not via a rationality that has yet to be realized but by a 'retreat to mythological substance. Their fate is irreality.' For attempts to 'reconstruct a form of the state, a community, an artistic formulation without considering our historical place . . . cannot hold their own against the baseness of the mass ornament and having recourse to them is not an elevation above their empty and external triviality but *a flight from its reality*. The process leads directly through the mass ornament, not away from it. [My emphasis.]'[153]

For Kracauer, too, the way forward lay in rejecting any form of return to idealized communities of the past and any false reconciliations in the future. From around 1927 onwards, Kracauer concerned himself increasingly with the consequences of the formation of a seemingly homogeneous mass public, especially in metropolitan Berlin with its affinities to the abstract identity of individuals created in a system of commodity production. In particular, he analysed the apparently egalitarian need of cultural distraction within this mass urban public, the attendant changes in perception of reality that it created and the extent to which the real identity of the mass as wage earners was masked and obscured by such distractions.[154]

There exists, then, another context for understanding Kracauer's analysis of the mass ornament. As Holz has pointed out, 'the intention of understanding the emergence of masses, indeed the mass society itself as an ornamental phenomenon, is not merely a sociological metaphor, but reflects, in a thought-provoking manner, something of the nature of the ornament itself'.[155] Whereas the conscious architectural production of buildings for a mass urban public, spurred on by the rise of formalism and *neue Sachlichkeit* and evident in the writings of Loos and Courboisier, led to the negation and eradication of ornament, Kracauer could point to the continuation of the ornament, not in the facades of urban architecture nor even in their *intérieurs* but rather through the mass itself.[156] This juxtaposition of the city as 'decrepitude' and the mass as modernity in motion was later to constitute a central theme of Benjamin's study of Baudelaire. Kracauer, with his emphasis upon modernity as the actuality of present-day existence, could draw the connections between the mass ornament and the modern capitalist production process with greater immediacy. As Lethen has shown, Kracauer's analysis of the mass ornament could also find considerable resonance not merely in view of the popularity of the body culture in this period but also its cultural–philosophical celebration as drill for work discipline and the eradication of the erotic in the works of writers such as Fritz Giese.[157]

Yet Kracauer's interest in the social foundation of spatial configuration was not merely confined to the mass ornament. The transformation of the conception of time and space that is a constituent feature of modernity is examined by Kracauer with reference to photography and film. In his confrontation with these media, he again takes up a central problematic from the mass ornament, namely the disjunction between the natural reality and its human and technical presentation and obfuscation.

Photography,[158] emerging roughly parallel with historicism, 'offers a spatial continuum; historicism wishes to fill in the continuum of time'. Indeed, 'for historicism the problem is the photography of time. Its photography of time is comparable to a huge film which duplicates from all sides the facts that are embedded in it.' Like historicism which empties history from its images, so photography leaves behind images of the original that are 'opaque like the milk glass, through which a glimmer of light hardly penetrates'. Yet the appearance of the image seems otherwise. The film star in the illustrated magazine is presented in all her actuality, surrounded by all the ordered details of her life, 'a complete appearance'. No one could mistake her. Compare the photograph of someone's grandmother at the same age as the film star. Her mode of dress seems comical today, unlike that of the film star. Yet 'though the grandmother has disappeared, the crinoline nonetheless remains. The totality of what has been photographed is to be interpreted as the *general inventory* of nature that cannot be reducible any further, as the catalogue collection of a number of phenomena that offer themselves in space.'

In contrast, 'the *memory* takes in neither the total spatial appearance nor the total temporal course of a state of affairs. In comparison with photography, its images are full of gaps.' The memory leaps over places and time, it is selective as to that which means something to it. Hence, 'photography grasps what is given as a spatial (or temporal) continuum, the pictures in the memory preserve it insofar as it means something.' To the memory, therefore, photography appears to be 'a mixture that is composed in part of scraps'. Photography produces fragments of the totality of a human being whose 'ultimate image is . . . their own history'. Thus, 'beneath the photographs of a human being is their history, as if buried beneath a layer of snow'. In order for history to be represented 'the mere surface constellation which photography offers must be destroyed.'

Photography itself, however, cannot grasp history, it can only trap its elements since it is too much bound up with time: 'Photography's boundedness by time expresses precisely that of *fashion*. Since it has no other meaning than that of the contemporary human mask, what is modern is transparent and what is old is left behind.' The fashionable details remain in the old photographs; they create a 'spectral reality' that is 'unredeemed'. Expressed more dramatically, photography gathers fragments around what does not exist. As the grandmother stood before the lens, she entered for a second into the spatial continuum which the lens offered. What has been rendered eternal, however, is, instead of the grandmother, this perspective. It makes the observer of old photographs shiver. For they illustrate not the knowledge of the original but the spatial configuration of a moment in time; it is not the person who steps out of his photograph but the sum of that which can be stripped away from him.[159]

If this is the fate of the individual photograph, what are the implications for mass culture and its extensive reliance on the fragmentary image?

Writing in 1927, Kracauer maintains that the most significant development is the increasing popularity of illustrated newspapers and their extensive use of photography. It juxtaposes images alongside one another, each possessing an equal degree of relevance and actuality. The intention of the illustrated newspaper and magazine is 'the complete reproduction of the world that is accessible to the photographic apparatus; they register the spatial impression of persons, circumstances and events from all possible perspectives.' They offer a phenomenal weekly output of images to the reader. This seemingly positive advance, however, has serious negative implications:

> If they offer themselves as support for the memory, then the memory must determine their selection. Yet the flood of photos sweeps away its barriers. So powerful is the assault of collections of images, that it perhaps threatens with destruction decisive traits of present consciousness. Works of art also meet with this fate through their reproduction . . . In the illustrated magazines the public sees the world whose perception of it is hindered by the illustrated journals themselves.[160]

The contours of the 'history' of what the camera captures disappears in the spatial continuum in which it is presented. Thus, instead of being an aid to memory and to knowledge of reality they encourage its opposite. Indeed,

> Never before has an epoch known so little about itself with any certainty. In the hands of the dominant society, the organisation of the illustrated magazines is one of the most powerful means of striking against knowledge. The successful implementation of the strike is not merely served by the colourful arrangement of the pictures. Their *coexistence* systematically excludes the context which opens itself to consciousness.[161]

Its photos 'gobble up the world' and this is itself 'a sign of the *fear of death*. Through their sheer number, the photographs seek to ban the remembrance of death that is conjured up in every memory image. In the illustrated newspapers, the world is turned into a photographable present and *the photographed present is rendered completely eternal*. It seems to be snatched from death; in reality it surrenders itself to it. [My emphasis.]'[162]

The implication of Kracauer's central argument here is significant. It consists in the fact, which Mülder highlights, that 'transformations in the perception of reality themselves express transformations in perceivable reality'.[163] The natural fundament of practical material life emptied of meaning is a prerequisite for the capitalist production process. This 'same mere nature that appears on the photographs lives on in the reality of the society' produced by this process. It is 'the society reduced to mute nature'. Photography reproduces this natural-like state of total presentness in which history is absent: 'To the spatial inventory there corresponds the temporal one of historicism.' The transparencies of photography only capture the empty sequence of events: 'The naked self-advertisement of spatial and temporal objects belongs to a social order that organises itself according to economic laws of nature.'

Photography thus presents the world of reality as a fragmentary unordered chaos. But the confrontation with this demythologized and empty world reveals the possibility of its radical transformation. Second nature has emancipated itself from first nature but is unable to be realized as a unity other than as an estranged nature. Photography reproduces this estranged nature in its own configurations of natural elements in which it reveals a dead world that exists independently of human beings. Therein lies 'the gamble of history'. If we recognize 'the *provisional nature* of all given configurations, perhaps even an inkling of the correct order of the natural world', then the possibility of its transformation opens itself up before us. The monogram, the fragmentary memory of humanity reveals the possibility of another reality. So too does the film in transcending the 'relations between the natural elements'. It does so 'wherever it brings together fragments and extracts into alien structures'. Whereas the representation of images in the illustrated magazines is a chaos, this game which the film plays with dismembered nature reminds one of 'the *dream*, in which the fragments of daily life are rendered perplexing'. The film, then, constitutes a potential aesthetic deliverance of phenomena.[164]

The film's potential, however, must be seen in the context in which it is produced in a capitalist society, where it becomes a commodity like any other. In the context of a 'cult of distraction',[165] its images are offered for sale in picture palaces, in 'distraction palaces', where the chief characteristic of these mass theatres is 'the smart *splendour of the superficial*', 'places for the worship of pleasure'. Within these palaces the total programme on offer becomes 'the *total work of art of effects*'. Their public is '*the homogeneous, metropolitan public*'. What is offered is such continuous excitements of the senses 'that not even the smallest reflection can squeeze itself between them'. 'Reactionary tendencies reside within . . . their goal'; they create unities and resolutions of 'the unregulated chaos of our world' that no longer exist.

When Kracauer announces that 'films are the mirror of existing society', he does not have in mind the mere reproduction of the material reality of society. Indeed, as Schröter argues,

> What Kracauer did not find in the films of the Weimar period was the presentation of *social reality*, of class divisions and repression; the presentation of a *significant reality* . . . and the attentive, respectful confrontation with material reality. The untruthfulness of interpretation, the renunciation of interpretation, the ignoring of the contradictory individual elements in an interpretation – all these are aspects of one and the same defect, that Kracauer . . . characterised as the *obduracy* of society.[166]

In fact, contemporary German films sometimes present the converse of reality in so far as 'they colour the blackest settings red and paste over the red ones'. In doing so, however, 'they do not cease to mirror society. On the contrary, the more they incorrectly present the surface, the more correct they become, the more obviously the secret mechanism of society appears in them'.[167] Once more, Kracauer highlights the fact that his preoccupation with the superficial surface phenomena of society has as its aim the transcendence of the mere phenomenological description of such phenomena. It indicates his commitment to a critical realism.

On the other hand, this does not imply that he merely has in mind some naive presentation of the 'real circumstances' that lie beneath the surface. Rather, the surface phenomena are themselves permeated by those circumstances in a distorted manner. In particular, 'the ridiculous and unreal film fantasies are the daydreams of society, in which its genuine reality comes to the surface, in which its otherwise suppressed wishes take shape'.[168] This is true for a whole range of genre. Historical films 'which only illustrate the past' are basically 'attempts at creating delusion'. They often take up some historical period, especially the Middle Ages, that cannot be directly related to the present day. The more they approach the present day the less real are the circumstances which they present. More generally, a whole range of films contain a very 'limited number of typical motifs . . . they indicate how society wishes itself to be seen. The totality of film motifs is, at the same time, the sum of societal ideologies which, through the interpretation of these motifs, are demythologised.' Their presentation of social relations is one that is already filtered: avoidance of class distinctions, avoidance of reference to the working class except as 'funny lower railway officials and patriarchal craftsmen' and the like, and an emphasis on a lumpenproletariat 'that is politically helpless' all characterize the film presentation of the lower orders. As for poverty itself, 'society clothes the places of misery with romanticism in order to render them eternal'. Love, of course, conquers all 'especially if love is made financially secure'. War memories 'contradict decisively the assertion of the materialistic basic emotions of the present day world' and transpose them into heroic idealism. The exoticism of far-away places, travel and distant settings, 'distract from the mendacity of the societal status quo whose monotony is forgotten by means of the adventure of travel'. Indeed, travel itself 'is one of the greatest possibilities for society to hold itself in a permanent situation of absent-mindedness which preserves itself from a confrontation with itself . . . it leads to the splendours of the world in order that its ugliness goes unobserved (the increase in knowledge of the world which it brings serves the transfiguration of the existing system in which it is acquired).' Even the average documentary film cuts us off from life, 'it overwhelms the public with such a wealth of indifferent observations that it dulls our perception of the important ones'.[169] Indeed, it often merely creates confusion in the viewer's mind.

Though Kracauer did observe a positive potential in the film medium – especially in early Soviet films, for whose reception in Germany Kracauer was often largely responsible, and in some of Chaplin's early films – he never ceased to be critical of the average commercial film production as 'a commodity like other commodities . . . produced not in the interests of art or the enlightenment of the masses but for the purposes of utility', that is, to create a profit.[170] Elsewhere, in 'Misery and Distraction' (1931),[171] he maintained that the average film production 'makes out of the misery of the public the virtue of distraction and totally forgets in doing so the public's need for enlightenment'.

The film critic – and Kracauer was one of the most prominent in Weimar Germany – should also play a role in this process of enlightenment. Indeed, 'the good film critic is only conceivable as a critic of society. His mission is to unveil the social conceptions and ideologies hidden in the average film and, by means of this unmasking, to break the influence of the films themselves wherever it is necessary.'[172] In other words, as Mülder explains, for Kracauer 'political praxis – including the praxis of the critic of society – in accordance with his more anarchistic rather than marxist influenced conception, has to be carried out basically as destruction, as the destruction of the false abstract constellation of the dominant social system and its ideological formations. The anticipation of the future is retained in art as the sphere of play.'[173] Such a conception is also contained in Benjamin's notion of 'The Destructive Character'. The centrality of art as anticipation of the possible, of the future is shared – in their often very different ways – by Simmel, Benjamin, Bloch and Adorno.

VI

Kracauer's preoccupation with the changing modes of experience of modernity that is evident in his study of metropolitan life, the new media of film and radio and the emergence of the mass ornament, all presuppose a particular stance on the part of the writer himself. By the end of the 1920s, Kracauer was no longer the person waiting or even merely the *flâneur* in Paris (he had already declared that this role was not possible in Berlin) and elsewhere. It is true that he remained an outsider in his lack of attachment to the social and intellectual status quo, as he so graphically describes in his autobiographical *Ginster*. Through his analyses of metropolitan life and culture, Kracauer expressed an increasing critical engagement with the modernity of Weimar Germany. This did not mean that this manifested itself in orthodox engagement in political party activity. But, as Benjamin in 1930 titled one of his two reviews of *White Collar Workers*, this study above all indicated that 'an outsider makes himself known'.[174] This 'discontent' – as Benjamin termed him – was now concretely engaged in unveiling dimensions of the reality of Weimar Germany. Indeed, as Benjamin put it,

> This much is . . . certain: that this man no longer plays along with things. That he rejects putting on a mask for the carnival which the

surrounding world sets up – he has even left his sociologist's doctoral hood at home – and that he boorishly jostles with the crowd, in order here and there to lift up a particularly saucy mask.[175]

As far as Kracauer himself was concerned, the demythologization of the world could not take place within the context of an empty 'formality'. However impressed he was with Mannheim's *Ideology and Utopia*, for example, he failed to see any concrete 'sociological diagnosis of the times' outlined in it. Such formal diagnoses as Mannheim offered were 'lacking on content', their theoretical claim could not be fulfilled. In fact, such analyses contain the danger that 'the avant-garde of the intelligentsia' can 'vanish in syntheses which indeed ultimately can serve the existing society'.[176]

Kracauer's criticism of the contemporary intelligentsia did not cease with its academic variant. In 'On the Writer' (1931),[177] he juxtaposes the changing position of the writer and the journalist – roles in which Kracauer himself was intimately engaged. Their typical features are to be analysed 'not like a phenomenologist who encounters their essential determinations in an empty space, but rather as a practician who gives shape to experiences'. At first sight, it seems as if the writer creates something for eternity whereas the journalist creates for the moment since the latter, in Peter Suhrkamp's words, 'wishes to change what is to be changed'. But in the present economic crisis, the roles seem to be reversed out of economic necessity: 'the possibility of free journalistic expression of opinion within the bourgeois press is today almost more restricted than at the time of imperial military power'. The press that is so dependent upon capital increasingly compels the genuine journalist to neutralize any report, he is forced 'to observe events as a spectator'. Conversely, 'the new type of writer' – Kracauer has in mind Döblin, Tretjakov and others – is actively engaged in the process of changing society, even 'in the direction of a classless society' and no longer in the direction of 'the idealist absolutes' of eternity, no longer orientated towards contemplation but towards engagement. Unlike the Soviet model of collective transformation – which increasingly interested Kracauer – the context of the contemporary writer in Germany is that of 'individual isolation. Only as an individual (or at best in conjunction with like-minded) up to now can he destroy false consciousness, prepare a correct one and fulfil all other decisive functions to which he is obliged in contemporary society.'[178]

In more general but similar terms, Kracauer addresses himself to socialist intellectuals in 'A Minimal Demand upon Intellectuals'

(1931).[179] His simple advice is: 'Intellectuals, apply your intelligence!'
For intellectuals who accept the basic premises of dialectical
materialism, and for whom thought is as important a realm as action
in the transformation of existing reality, participation in this
transformation should commence from 'the situation . . . in which
intellectuals actually find themselves'. This implies that 'one does not
hunt after utopias, but starts out from the concrete situation, at first
less in the direction of the actions of intellectuals than in the
unrestricted use of their intellect. The intellect too is a productive force
and, according to historical materialism, productive forces lead into
the classless society.' Returning to a familiar theme, Kracauer declares
that 'the intellect is nothing other than the instrument of the destruction
of all mythical things around and in us . . . Its mission is the *dismantling
of natural forces.*' This implies that the intellect 'is directed towards a
destructive procedure. It must indeed unmask ideologies' and not assert
abstract socialist ideals which 'easily degenerate into sabotaging
socialism'. The starting point of this destructive procedure on the part
of intellectuals must always be that of the situation of its agents. Its
goal is 'the concretions of the intellect'.[180]

But Kracauer's radical demands upon intellectuals should not
detract from the fact that – like Benjamin too – he was deeply sceptical
of the position of the left intelligentsia as well. In *White Collar Workers*,
he suggests that they often fail to recognize their own position in society
and do not take account of the concrete changes taking place within
it: 'The intellectuals are either themselves white collar workers, or
they are free and then for them the everyday world of the white collar
workers is usually uninteresting. Radical intellectuals, too, do not easily
get behind the exotic of the everyday world.'[181] More pointedly,
Kracauer criticizes the 'young radical intelligentsia' especially in
Berlin, that all too easily takes up protests against capitalism, but
usually only in relation to 'extreme instances: the war, crass
miscarriages of justice, the May unrest, etc., *without appreciating normal
existence in its imperceptible dreadfulness* [my emphasis]'[182] – a criticism
to be found also in Bloch's work and reminiscent of Benjamin's critique
of the ultra-left as 'left of everything possible'.

Kracauer's emphasis upon the concrete actuality of everyday
existence thus increasingly takes on a political significance. To ignore
its contours is to engage in a form of displacement of political interest.
Kracauer castigates those who ignore 'the construction of this existence
itself' since their rebellion grasps merely its symptoms. In other words,
this rebellion

castigates blatant instances of corruption and forgets in so doing *the consequence of minor events out of which our normal social life is composed* and as whose result these instances of corruption are to be first understood. The radicalism of these radicals would carry more weight if it really penetrated the structure of reality instead of meeting its instructions from the *bel étage* above. How is the everyday world to change when those who were called upon to transform it also fail to give any attention to it? [My emphasis.] [183]

This, then, is a crucial dimension of the political context within which Kracauer's analysis of white collar workers in Berlin takes place.

The methodological context within which *White Collar Workers* is conceived is more difficult to reconstruct. Kracauer's contemporary correspondence with Adorno on his methodology does not necessarily fully illuminate Kracauer's methodological stance. Adorno 'described the methodological approach of his study as hovering somewhere between Benjamin's and Lukács', using the strengths of one to counter the weaknesses of the other'.[184] Kracauer, in reply, distanced his approach from that of contemporary orthodox Marxism – the 'last offshoot of totality philosophy' and termed it a 'material dialectics'. In particular, Kracauer considered his work

> methodologically very important insofar as it constitutes a new form of presentation, one which does not juggle between general theory and special practice, but presents its own special way of observation. It is, if you will, an example of materialist dialectics. Analogous cases are the analyses of situations by Marx and Lenin, which are excluded by Marxism as we know it today.[185]

This somewhat extravagant claim also fails to locate precisely Kracauer's methodological approach.

On the other hand, to claim, as Jay does, that 'the book pioneered a technique the Lynds were developing in America at approximately the same time in their study of Middletown, a technique known as participant observation',[186] is even further from the mark. Jay is here following Adorno who also maintained that its 'method shares something with that which in the United States is termed the procedure of the participant observer, like that of the Lynds in Middletown'.[187] Although it is based on interviews with white collar workers, it does not possess that degree of orthodoxy which would enable us to subsume it under sociology. Indeed, at the time of its publication, the book went largely unnoticed in sociological circles. In this context,

Benjamin's second review of the book is pertinent. Benjamin suggests that there was a time when the book would have been titled ' "Towards a Sociology of White Collar Workers". Indeed, it would not have been written at all.' Sociology steps back in terror from 'presenting in a politically clear manner, political phenomena, in order instead to swathe it in a web of academic empty phrases' and 'the euphemistic whispering of sociology'.[188] Bloch, too, in his review, saw the book's methodology as having little in common with academic scientific method which 'does indeed look into the machinery but with an inadequate language and above all it does not commence with the everyday world, which alone is real, but makes "facts" out of it, methodically pure, so that it can then more easily apply its customary concepts and "laws" '.[189]

Nor can Kracauer's methodology in his *White Collar Workers: Out of the Newest Germany* be subsumed under the then fashionable reportage. Again, Bloch maintained that 'mere reportage no longer helps; where everything becomes so construed and artificial as in present day life, naive recording is not appropriate, the overlit foreground merely envelops once more the true background.'[190] Kracauer himself singles out reportage as a totally inadequate mode of procedure. He maintains that reportage has become in Germany 'the most favoured of all modes of presentation . . . the reproduction of what is observed is the cry of the day.' It arises out of

> A hunger for immediacy that without doubt is the result of under-nourishment by German idealism. The abstract nature of idealistic thought . . . is countered by reportage as the self-advertisement of concrete existence. But in so doing existence is not captured in such a way that one possesses it once more at best in a report.[191]

The social reality which Kracauer seeks to capture is much more elusive:

> A hundred reports from a factory do not lend themselves to being added up to the reality of the factory, but rather remain for all eternity a hundred views of the factory. Reality is a construction. Of course life must be observed for it to come into being. But in no way is it embodied in the more or less arbitrary series of observations of reportage. Rather, it is embodied solely in the mosaic that is assembled together from out of the individual observations on the basis of knowledge of its content. Reportage photographs life; such a mosaic would be its image.[192]

Reportage itself remains an assemblage of abstract contents unless it is given a form that is derived from insights into the structure of social reality itself.

On the other hand, this does not imply that Kracauer has a ready-made theory to hand and then goes in search of empirical instances that confirm it. 'Quotations, conversations and observations' of the white collar workers' milieu in Berlin constitute 'the foundation of the study'. But, *they are not to count as examples of some particular theory, but rather as exemplary instances of reality* [my emphasis]'.[193] They, and the work as a whole, are not an exemplary instance of a theory but of reality itself. For Adorno this implied that 'dialectical thought was never in accordance with his nature'. He proceeded by 'precisely locating the particular in favour of its use as an instance for general states of affairs'. The 'need for strict mediation in the object itself' was left out of account. Interestingly enough, this critique of Kracauer's approach is almost identical with Adorno's critique of Benjamin's first draft of his Baudelaire study.

Many contemporaries and subsequent commentators have pointed to the structure of Kracauer's study as akin to that of a novel, as a form of literary montage. Indeed, it has been suggested that Kracauer's study not only has affinities with Tretjakov's notion of 'operative literature' but is 'unquestionably the most successful attempt by a left liberal bourgeois author to approach the methods of marxist operative literature'.[194] Leaving Helms's epithets aside, the author does suggest a plausible affinity between Kracauer's project and that of Tretjakov, especially in the latter's conception of the function of montage as 'a method by which facts are so entwined (set against one another, compared with one another) that they begin to exude the social energy and the truth that resides within them'.[195] The plausibility of this comparison is strengthened by Kracauer's interest in Tretjakov's work as instanced by the number of reviews Kracauer devoted to it. One of its central themes, with which Kracauer concurred, was a new relationship to praxis for the writer: '*one describes reality instead of coming upon the traces of its errors of construction*, one abandons oneself to the aesthetic and thereby misses the opportunity of mobilising the forces directed towards action, one engages in metaphysics where one should be immersed in the economy.'[196] This later review (from 1932) expresses Kracauer's intention in his study of white collar workers: not that of a mere description but, given that reality is a construction, the search for 'the traces of its errors of construction' in order to intervene in that reality. Yet as Kracauer states in its preface, it is 'a diagnosis' that consciously renounces making 'recommendations for improvement'.

Its starting point is that of the situation of white collar employees in Berlin and their forms of consciousness. Berlin is where 'the situation of white collar workers [is] presented at its most extreme. Only from its extremes can reality be opened up.' This also means, for Kracauer, concentration upon the situation of white collar workers in large-scale organizations since they are 'the model of the future'. It is a picture, a mosaic of their existence that is directly 'out of the newest Germany'. It is also an entry into an 'unknown area' – the title of the first chapter – a 'small expedition . . . that is perhaps more adventurous than a film journey to Africa. For in that it goes in search of white collar workers it leads at the same time into the inner reaches of the modern metropolis.'[197] In particular, its location is contemporary Berlin as

> the city of decidedly white collar culture; that is, a culture made by white collar strata for white collar strata, and taken by most white collar workers to be a culture. Only in Berlin, where the bonds of origin and native soil are so repressed that the weekend can be the epitome of fashion, can the reality of white collar workers be comprehended. It is also a good part of the reality of Berlin itself.[198]

And it is in Berlin that 'the decisive practical and ideological confrontations take place'. But what lies behind this manifestly visible but largely unexplored culture? And why take up this culture in the first place?

In his perceptive analysis of Kracauer's work as a whole, Schröter provides a number of reasons why this theme was so appropriate for Kracauer. This stratum was of interest to Kracauer since its actual position in society was ignored, either being incorporated into the old middle class or absorbed without question into the proletariat. Secondly, since Kracauer had already introduced the process of rationalization in 'The Mass Ornament', he discovered a group who were both a product, in part, of this rationalization, and its victim. Kracauer could examine concretely its consequences for this stratum. The systematic reproduction and maintenance of the false consciousness of this group provided Kracauer with a concrete instance of a group without a concrete ideology. The theme announced in 'Those Who Wait' and earlier in Kracauer's use of Lukács's term of 'transcendental homelessness' was now to be made specific in the analysis of a group who were 'ideological homeless'. Finally, in terms of his cultural analysis, the white collar workers were crucial to the thesis of distraction. As he states in his study of them and in relation to the ideological situation in society, 'muteness above produces confusion below'. As Schröter comments: 'The reflex of confusion is the flight into distraction – a concept that Kracauer by now developed into a *terminus technicus* for those who knew him. The white collar workers are the agents or consumers of all the phenomena around whose analysis Kracauer's work in these years gravitated.'[199] More specifically, the original thesis on mass culture could be followed up in that of a concrete group. In this respect, and unlike many subsequent theories of mass culture, Kracauer's analysis moved in the direction of concretion away from abstract conceptions of the mass. Again, unlike much subsequent sociology which treats the world outside the workplace as an epiphenomenon, Kracauer was one of the first to highlight the dialectical relationship between work and 'leisure', between rationalization of the production process and the rationalization of 'free time' in 'pleasure barracks' and the like.

The substantive context for Kracauer's analysis of this 'unknown area' lies in the rationalization of production and distribution after the instigation of the Dawes Plan in 1924 in Germany, with its attendant dramatic increase in large scale organization, the sharp increase in the number of white collar workers in commerce, banking, transport and industry, and the increasing proportion of women in the white collar sector. In part, these processes were already documented by the white collar unions and by economists such as Lederer and Marschak. Indeed, the latter had earlier documented the emergence of a 'new middle class'.[200] By 1930, however, Lederer was speaking of the 'objective fact' that 'the white collar workers share the fate of the proletariat'.[201] Kracauer was sceptical of their status as a 'new middle class' and maintained that 'the proletarianisation of white collar workers cannot be doubted'. What interested Kracauer, however, was not so much this thesis as its non-recognition by white collar workers themselves. By means of his examination of 'the illegal grammar of everyday language', interviews, observations and the like, Kracauer went in search of the modes of experiencing the reality of white collar workers' existence in Berlin.

Kracauer's mode of procedure at first sight seems to be the presentation of a montage of themes, scenes and experiences that are themselves self-contained. The unnumbered 'chapters' and their titles suggest such a procedure. 'Unknown Area', 'Selection', 'Short Pause for Air', 'Organisation within Organisation', 'Oh, how soon . . .',

'Repair Workshop', 'Small Herbarium', 'Unconstrained with Style', 'Amongst Neighbours', 'Asylum for the Homeless', 'Viewed from Above', and 'Dear Ladies and Gentlemen Colleagues!' They are, however, 'arranged in the sense of a continuous, reciprocal commentary and interpretation' upon the material which they contain. But more than this, Mülder argues, 'a total picture emerges without what binds them together being merely asserted as the subjective position of the author or being rendered independent as the systematic connection of concepts over against the material. The reader must actively participate in the "construction of reality" whilst at the same time having "room for one's own position".'[202] Such a procedure is thus far removed from both mere reportage and an orthodox sociological presentation of empirical data.

The illusory world of the white collar worker commences at the moment of selection for a post. A position is gained on the basis of the employer regarding the employee as being 'nice and friendly', as creating a 'good impression', as being attractive, even as the head of one personnel department put it, on the basis of possessing a 'morally-rosy skin colour'. Kracauer comments 'A morally-rosy skin colour – this conceptual combination at a single stroke makes the everyday world transparent which is filled out with shop-window decorations, white collar employees and illustrated newspapers . . . They wish to cover life with a veneer that masks the by no means rosy reality.'[203] At the other extreme is the selection on the basis of spurious occupational psychology techniques which supposedly place 'the right person in the right position'. White collar employees must adapt to this rosy veneer:

> The rush to the many beauty salons also springs from anxiety about existence, the use of cosmetic products is not always a luxury. Out of anxiety of being removed from use through being an old commodity, women *and* men dye their hair, and forty-year-olds engage in sport in order to remain slim. 'How Can I Be Beautiful?' asks the title of a journal recently thrown on the market, to which the newspaper advertisement adds, that it shows the means 'by which one looks attractive for the moment and permanently'. Fashion and the economy work hand in hand.[204]

In the following chapter, 'A Short Pause for Air', and after an insight into the giddy, glossy world of necessary self-presentation, Kracauer looks at the reality of the employees' work situation.

That reality is one of rationalization of the work process in every sphere, except perhaps in the director's office where 'no noise permeates the room, the writing desk is sparsely covered with papers. This tree-top silence seems to predominate everywhere in the upper spheres.' In the lower spheres, however, the introduction of office machinery requires endless routine and concentration which contrasts sharply with the ideology of the realization of the personality through work. The increasing specialization, mechanization and routinization reduces job satisfaction into an inner sphere for the supporters of such a system. Kracauer illustrates this with reference to the growing area of occupational psychology which even then was insisting on the 'happiness of monotony' on the possibility of the workers having their minds free for themselves, perhaps even – Kracauer adds – to 'think in peace upon their class ideals'.

The subordination of the white collar employee in the work process is not confined to its mechanization and routinization. The hierarchical organization of the various sections also increases real subordination. Within the organization as a whole, abstract relationships predominate between its various departments and sub-departments. Knowledge of what is happening in the lower spheres is mediated by the departmental head. Even the directors of the sections are dependent upon those above. The hierarchy of dependency extends to the very top at which 'the peak of the hierarchy is lost in the dark heaven of finance capital'. The abstract relations of functional dependency serve to obscure the real relations in the organization and society as a whole. A further abstraction is, of course, the chances for promotion which remain minimal for the majority of employees, especially where the leading positions are all filled from outside the organization.

Indeed, the process we now term the process of deskilling, Kracauer highlights at the peak of the rationalization process as demotion and, at an increasingly younger age, dismissal. Hence the emphasis on staying young and the corresponding anxiety of older employees. Not surprisingly, therefore, youth 'is the fetish of illustrated newspapers and their public', a veritable 'flight from death'.

Kracauer goes on to show that white collar employees in Berlin and other large cities lead an existence that becomes increasingly similar. The media also have their stereotypes or 'normal types' of secretary, shop assistant and so on. In 'A Small Herbarium', Kracauer shows how this superficial identical existence hides the varied origin of members of this stratum, from the working class, the sunken bourgeoisie and even a white-collar bohemia.

But just as the apparent homogeneity of this stratum of the workforce hides important differences, so too the rationalization of the white collar employees' labour process is not an automatic process. The disruption which accompanies it, the discontent, the anxiety has to be smoothed over for the process to be successful. And this is secured not merely by means of co-operation of the trades unions or illusory forms of consultation committees. Equally important is the concrete ideology of community, often secured through paternalistic organization of welfare and sports facilities. More concretely, large organizations seek to secure the isolation of 'the diverse categories of personnel' and especially the separation of white collar employees from manual workers. In part, this is facilitated by individual wage agreements and the like which can create the illusion amongst white collar employees that they are a different category of labour power. But 'if each must thus stand for him or herself, then the community is an illusion'. The communal facilities – welfare, sport, housing, etc. – 'indeed hold the individuals in a state of dependency but only in order not to awaken the spirit of the collectivity'. Rationalization thus creates 'a neo patriarchalism' whose major interest is diversion from all forms of collective activity on the part of employees. At the personal level, this illusory communality manifests itself as 'the mistaken identity of joviality with a purely human communality'.

Are white collar employees' interests identical with those strata above them or below them? When they are 'amongst neighbours' with whom do they identify? Kracauer argues that 'on the basis of a monthly salary, so-called intellectual labour and several other similar immaterial characteristics', the white collar employee still lays claim to a bourgeois existence and even though 'the position of these strata has changed in the economic process, their middle class view of life has remained. They foster a false consciousness. They wish to preserve distinctions whose recognition obscures their situation; they indulge in an individualism that could only be sanctioned if they could still decide their own fate as individuals.'[205] At the pinnacle of these distinctive strata is the state official within the public sector, in the private sector it is the bank official. At the lower reaches of these strata are many who have risen from the working class. They are the ones who are most often caught within contradictory loyalties.

Many of the contradictions of these strata are resolved by a displacement of interest from work into leisure, into the 'pleasure barracks', into the 'asylum for the homeless'. In contrast to the manual working class who still have an ideological roof over their heads, although 'today full of holes', 'the mass of white collar employees is distinguished from the worker-proletariat by the fact that it is intellectually homeless'. Instead, this mass 'live at present without a doctrine that they can look up to, without a goal that they can ascertain. In short, it lives in fear of looking up and asking its way to the very end.' The aspiration to higher strata is not for its content but for the glamour. They do not look for the political or other meeting but for distraction. A stenotypist declares that ' "the young girls come mostly from a poorer milieu and are attracted by the glamour". In a highly remarkable way she justified the fact that the young girls in general avoid serious conversations. "Serious conversations", she said, "only distract and divert from the environment which one wishes to enjoy". If a serious conversation is credited with distracting effects, then distraction is an inexorably serious matter.'[206] The consequence of this search for the glamour of distraction is often that their expenditure on distraction is often greater than on day to day living expenses, in part in order to maintain their distinctive 'cultural' values vis à vis the class below them.

In the large department store, for instance, the employees can participate in the consumer wonderland, within 'the cheerful rooms flooded with light' and within them 'the higher strata'. And here,

> The comforting influence, that the flood of light exercises not merely on the desire to purchase but also on the personnel, may at most exist in the fact that the personnel are sufficiently bewitched by it that it can drive away the pain of the small, unlit apartment. The light deceives more than it enlightens, and perhaps the wealth of light, which more recently flows over our cities, serves not least to increase the darkness. But do not the higher strata beckon? It has become apparent that they beckon non-committally from afar. The glamour that has been dispensed should indeed chain the white collar masses to society, but only to raise them just so far as they remain all the more securely caught in the position that has been ascribed to them.[207]

Unable to move upwards, they seek diversion in amusement, in distraction, though depending upon their position in the white collar hierarchy they do so to a varying extent.

And just as the work process is rationalized so too are the 'pleasure barracks', the large bars and the like. Kracauer describes one of these large drinking places – 'Haus Vaterland' – whose 'core forms a kind of enormous hotel lobby', one which takes to excess the *Neue Sachlichkeit* style, for *only the most modern is good enough for our masses*. The secret of *Neue Sachlichkeit* cannot be anywhere more decisively unmasked than here. In fact, behind the pseudo-strictness of the lobby architecture Grinzing's grin exudes itself [*grinst Grinzing hervor* – not merely a play on words but a reference to the already outmoded kitsch symbol of the wine village of Grinzing in the northern suburbs of Vienna]. Just another step into the depths and one lingers in the midst of the most sumptuous sentimentality. This, however, is the most characteristic feature of *Neue Sachlichkeit*, namely, that it is a facade that hides nothing behind it, that it does not release any depth but rather it merely feigns to do so. [My emphasis.][208]

Each bar is decorated in the style of a distant place. This form of distraction is connected with the monotony in the workplace. The exotic world that is stimulated here is that of 'the panoramas of the nineteenth century', a paradise lost and not one to be aimed for. Kracauer emphasizes the significance of such spatial and ideological distraction:

> The more the monotony of the work day predominates, the more must leisure time be distanced from it as much as possible; presupposing of course that attention should be distracted from the backgrounds of the production process. The precise counter-attack against the office machine, however, is the richly coloured world. Not the world as it is, but as it appears in the pop tunes. A world that even in its most obscure niches is cleansed of the dust of the everyday world as if with a vacuum cleaner. The geography of the asylum for the homeless is born out of the hit tune.[209]

The short pause between the walls of such 'pleasure barracks' can be seen as 'a group outing for white collar workers in paradise' with its attendant glamour, but when the barman turns out the lights 'the eight hour day shines freely in yet once again'.

This general process of distraction is, of course, as Kracauer has shown elsewhere, reinforced in the average film production, illustrated newspapers and magazines, with their hypnotizing images: 'The flight of images is the flight from revolution and death'. As counterpart to the 'magic of images' that assails the mass from outside is sport, 'the whole body culture' which distracts from within as it were. In contrast to those who maintain that sport 'destroys complexes', Kracauer maintains that 'the expansion of sport does not destroy complexes but is, amongst other things, a phenomenon of repression on a large scale; it does not support the transformation of social relations but is as a whole a major means of depoliticisation.' Only a few years later, the body culture was to be utilized to its full effect. Critical questions were already banned.

Yet viewed from above – and this is where Kracauer also places the majority of the intelligentsia – this distraction and repression is necessary since the economic system can no longer rely for its justification on 'the belief in a pre-established harmony', no matter how often it is stated. It is better that whole strata shall 'float emptily without a world view', despite the call for moral principles and a community of interests.

Kracauer concludes his analysis by a brief examination of the possibilities for transformation of the white collar employees' position via the unions which represent them. Here Kracauer is equally critical of the strategy of compensating for the deleterious influence of mechanization by offering workers other intellectual or 'cultural goods' as if they are medicines that are effective against rationalization. Such a strategy 'is itself still an expression of the reification against whose effects it is directed'. The same is true of the unions' belief in sport as a similar counter-strategy. More seriously, the abstract incorporation of members into a collectivity whose goals are no longer questioned ignores the interests and everyday activity of the members themselves: 'The doctrinaire conviction with which the white collar unions often fail to confront the human reality, indirectly confirms the fact that the collectivity as such is an erroneous construction. The point is not that institutions be changed but rather that human beings change the institutions.'[210]

To the very last, Kracauer insists on the significance of the reality of human everyday existence. The whole book, according to Benjamin, is 'a confrontation with a piece of the everyday world, a built up "here", a lived out "now"'. In this way, it is able to grasp the nature of the emergence of a false consciousness that does not consist of a fixed, ready-made constellation. Rather, 'the products of false consciousness are like picture puzzles in which what is essential merely peeps through from out of the clouds, the foliage and the shadows'. And in contrast to the 'radical fashionable products' of reportage and the like, Kracauer's work is 'a milestone of the way to the politicisation of the intelligentsia', on the way to 'the politicisation of his own class. This indirect effect is the only one which a literary revolutionary from the bourgeois class can serve today.'[211]

Kracauer's own engagement in the problems which he raises in this study are continued in his subsequent confrontations with employers' ideology ('The Intellectual Decision of the Employers', 1930),[212] with the right wing intellectuals around the journal *Die Tat* ('Revolt of the Middle Classes', 1931)[213] and the like. The examination of the relationship between white collar employees and the mass culture was continued in a number of essays including 'Girls at Work' (1932)[214] in which Kracauer points to the necessity for examining 'the reality of the proletariat', a task which had occurred to him as he was writing his study of white collar workers. He remarks pointedly that 'the proletariat is even more unknown and even more difficult to get to know than the lower white collar strata that border them. For on the one hand, its life is carried on under quite different conditions as that of the bourgeoisie and its followers, and is thus only insufficiently to be grasped with imported bourgeois concepts and methods, and on the other its reality is so covered over with the rhetoric of political struggle that one must seek out and extract this reality very laboriously from under this cover.'[215] It is worth noting here that, although Kracauer did not carry out such an investigation, his suggested methodological orientation remained fixed upon the object itself and not some readily available method that could be applied abstractly to it.

Under very different and difficult circumstances than that of a by now renowned journalist and social critic, Kracauer returned to the theme of the mass, the mass ornament and false consciousness during his first exile in Paris. In December 1936 he completed an exposé for the now also exiled and dispersed Frankfurt Institute for Social Research on 'Mass and Propaganda'[216] – a research project which he hoped the Institute would finance.

The study was to commence with an analysis of the post-war crisis and its social consequences in Germany, for the proletariat, the proletarianized middle class and the unemployed. The ideological consequences of the crisis would look at 'the collapse of the bourgeois hierarchy of values', 'the intellectual homelessness of the masses' who 'ideologically live in a vacuum', the middle class caught up in their contradictions, and the contradictory ideological position of the unemployed. A third section on 'the decisive stage of the crisis' was to conclude with the dilemma: 'the masses should be reintegrated under the maintenance of the capitalist system and are however incapable of being reintegrated. Only an illusory solution is possible. Fascism is an illusory solution'. A further section would look at the commencement of the fascist illusory solution which exists in the fact that 'fascism not only does not dispense with the mass (which was

impossible anyway) but, on the contrary, decisively underlines
their character as a mass and, further, through appropriate
measures seeks to awaken the impression that the mass is in
fact reintegrated' – in fact via a combination of terror and
propaganda.

A fifth major section would look at 'the role of propaganda
in fascism'. The mass character of the mass is hypostatized in
propaganda by three means. Firstly, by forcing the mass 'to see
itself everywhere (mass meetings, mass processions, etc.). The mass
is thus ever-present and often in the aesthetically seductive form
of an ornament or an effective image'. Secondly, 'with the assistance
of radio, the living room is transformed into a public place . . .
Fascist propaganda grants to the individual only the sphere of
"inwardness" and seeks in general to transform it as a constituent
element of the mass. Finally, an attempt is made to 'extract all mythical
forces from out of the mass'. Fascist propaganda goes on to create
a cult of the masses. Here Kracauer wished to look at the historical
relationship between fascist propaganda and Charlatanism – 'for
instance the continuous awakening of fantastic hopes, etc.'. Its ultimate
aim is the 'pseudo reintegration' of 'the artificially prepared masses'.
It achieves this by the fact that 'it allows the masses to march and
to be uninterruptedly occupied everywhere, so that in the masses the
conviction must emerge that they already embody as a mass some
function or other'.

Other features of Kracauer's proposed study are that it presupposes
'that the illusory fascist solution is a means for preserving the
endangered capitalist economy', that the 'American achievements in
the spheres of advertising and propaganda' should also be closely
studied and that one should clearly distinguish between fascist and
communist propaganda.

This study, which announces in part the advent of modernity's
nightmare – the 'ever-present' mass ornament brought to total
mobilization, was heavily criticized by Adorno and Horkheimer and
was finally withdrawn by Kracauer who complained in disgust to
Adorno that 'you have not really edited my manuscript, but used it
as the basis of a new work'.[217]

But at the same time as Kracauer had been preparing the outline
of this project, he successfully completed a study which appeared in
French, German and English, one which directly relates to the
historical origins of modernity and which bears comparison with
Benjamin's study of Baudelaire.

V

In November 1934, Kracauer wrote to Löwenthal that he was
commencing a new work 'which perhaps has an international chance:
a biography from the time of the Second Empire, with a lot about
society in it'.[218] Early in 1937, *Jacques Offenbach and the Paris of his Time*
appeared in German (in Amsterdam) and shortly after in French and
English. Work on this study thus coincides with Benjamin's exposé
of his Arcades Project of 1935. Indeed, Benjamin wrote to Scholem
in August 1935, that as well as Bloch writing on a similar theme
('Hieroglyphics of the Nineteenth Century') in Paris, there was also
'Kracauer writing a book on Offenbach and there I must also remain
silent about my reflections. All this is not easy and could be more
satisfactory.'[219]

In the preface to his Offenbach study – unaccountably omitted from
the English translation – Kracauer announced that it was not intended
to be a biography in any orthodox sense. Thus, it 'does not belong
alongside those biographies whose main theme is limited to the
presentation of the life of its hero. Such biographies are like
photographic portraits, that in their portrayed form appear in front
of a faded background . . . It is not a private biography of Jacques
Offenbach. It is a *societal biography*.' It is concerned with 'the figure
Offenbach which society allows to emerge, which he moves in and
from which he is moved'. Not the music of Offenbach is its central
theme but rather 'the social function of Offenbach'.[220]

Kracauer's emphatic distance from orthodox biographical studies
must be understood in the context of his earlier attack upon the
increasingly popular biographical genre in Weimar Germany. His
analysis of 'the relations between society and Offenbach' has a critical
intention that is directed against the literary genre which he criticized
in 'The Biography as neo-bourgeois Art Form' (1930).[221] In the post-
war period, 'the confidence in the objective significance of some kind
of individual reference system' disappeared for ever. The absence of
this 'secure network of co-ordinates' has led to a crisis in the novel
which hitherto operated within this framework. An alternative, though
equally problematic, element was discovered in history which 'emerges
as a continent out of the sea of formlessness, of that which has not
been given a form'. The biography seems secure, based as it is on
a documentary facticity. Indeed, 'the moral of biography is that in
the chaos of contemporary artistic exercises it represents the only

apparently necessary prose form' – that of 'the stabilised *bourgeoisie*'. But 'the biography as a form of neo-bourgeois literature is a sign of *flight*; more precisely, of evasion', an evasion of 'the signs of fracture in our social construction'. Its flight is back into 'the bourgeois hinterland . . . rather than stepping out of it'. The biographical form is, however, more than a 'mere flight'; it is covered over with the motive of *preservation*'. Yet the preservation of the individual hero can only take place in the imaginary museum of historicism:

> If there exists a confirmation of the end of individualism, it is to be revealed in the museum of great individuals that present-day literature gives prominence to . . . It requires a picture gallery to be constructed in which the memory can ignore the fact that each picture is of identical value . . . the glamour of the farewell rests upon its community.[222]

Even the hinterland, the backcloth, disappears and the reader is left with the mythical great individual again.

In this context, Kracauer's 'societal biography', with its conscious anti-subjectivism, takes on an ideological–critical function. The society which it presents is that of France 'in the nineteenth century with its monarchies and dictatorship, its world exhibitions and revolutions'. The history of this society not merely has a documentary significance, but also a contemporary one:

> This society is not merely the immediate predecessor of the modern one because the birth of the world economy and the bourgeois republic take place within it; it is also its predecessor insofar as it announces in the most diverse spheres motifs that still continue to assert themselves today . . . It may undoubtedly be possible that the incomparably complex thought and conduct of the present time is in no small part to be derived from the models which came into existence during the nineteenth century in France.[223]

More correctly, Kracauer located his theme in Paris: 'the Paris of the nineteenth century is in fact the only city whose history is European history'. And mirroring even more closely Benjamin's theme in the Arcades Project, Kracauer declares that *'in the light of the events of our present time, no one will fail to recognise that precisely the phantasmagoria of the Second Empire possesses actuality* [my emphasis]'.[224]

But whereas Benjamin took Baudelaire as his key figure of the time, Kracauer chose Offenbach and his operettas – 'the most representative expression of the imperial era' which not merely 'mirror its epoch' but 'help to explode' it. In other words, Offenbach is chosen because he is located 'at the centre of his times'. Kracauer provides two other reasons for choosing Offenbach as his theme. He expresses a 'major sensitivity against the structure of the society which surrounds him'. His rise to fame coincides with the emergence of the preconditions for the production of operettas: of a state of dictatorship, 'of the domination of finance capital, of the breakthrough of the international economy, of the boulevard and the myriad Bohemia that lives on it'. The operetta, bound as it is to the Second Empire, also dies with it. Nonetheless, while it lasted, Offenbach not merely mirrored the society which brought the operetta into existence – and Kracauer maintains that in his work one can 'read off the most minute social changes as on a precision instrument' – but he was 'a mocker'. His satirical songs do not ridicule 'sacred institutions, official positions and functions' but only 'such things . . . that hide their appearance in sacredness'. In so doing, Offenbach reverses the accepted image of the world: what is below finds itself above, what is in a higher sphere is ridiculed as small. In this very way of focusing upon Offenbach, Kracauer hints at a theme announced in the first chapter of his study of the detective novel: the transformation of spheres of existence. But there is a new theme not present in the early work: the search for the utopian element in Offenbach's satirical operettas, glimpses of the apparent paradise.

As many commentators have pointed out, Kracauer's societal biography of Offenbach and, in particular, his presentation of the world of the operetta hardly ever concerns itself with the music itself. Rather, attention is largely confined to the librettos (especially those of Halévy). The strength of Kracauer's study must lie elsewhere, in the presentation of the material that constitutes the basis for the operetta's world. Its virtue does not especially reside in a new form of biography. Here, Adorno correctly remarks that 'distanced from Offenbach's material, the presentation indeed comes close to precisely that individualising novelistic biography which Kracauer so emphatically opposes'.[225]

The material for Offenbach's operettas was already present before they reached the height of popularity during Louis Napoleon's dictatorship. Indeed, Kracauer dates Offenbach's success more precisely in the following passage:

> The rise of Offenbach and the beginning of the evolution of his *genre*, the operetta, had coincided with the World Exhibition of 1855. With

the World Exhibition of 1867, in which the Second Empire appeared
in all its glory for the last time before it collapsed, the decline of the
Offenbachiade began. Its heyday lay between these two events, both of
which encouraged the international spirit. The operetta's zenith was
inescapable from Louis Napoleon's dictatorship, and when the
dictatorship collapsed the operetta's day was over.[226]

The lyrical presentation of this world of the Second Empire rested
upon a series of features of Parisian society that had already emerged
during Offenbach's early years in the city. Paris already had an
abundant and exotic street life in its older quarters, with its assortment
of beggars, dandies, prostitutes and bohemian street festivities
especially during the Paris carnival and small theatres in which the
cancan was already being performed in the 1830s, as well as the
fashionable elegance of the still existent salons and the glamour of
the new boulevards. In the salons of the society of Louis Philippe,
music was important in order 'to compensate for the emptiness and
meaninglessness of the atmosphere . . . of the Golden Mean'. As a
young musician, Offenbach 'the very personification of sociability',
'lived in the instant, reacting delicately to social changes and constantly
adapting himself to them', especially 'the Paris of the Boulevards' –
'the home of the homeless'. The 'little world of the Boulevards' was
populated by journalists who proliferated after Girardin's initiation
of the commercialization of the press in 1836. The journalists 'released
from the restraint of all sorts of traditional beliefs . . . became
Bohemians. But the money on which they depended for their livelihood
sharpened their acumen, and they very clearly perceived that many
things that were held up to honour were hollow shams and many
exalted ideals merely clues to economic interests. They consequently
became sceptics. The reverse side of the medal was that they allowed
themselves to be bought.'[227] On the boulevards, the journalists met
'the dandies and the *jeunesse dorée*, whose mental outlook corresponded
closely to their own'. And 'on the Boulevards, the dandies lived, so
to speak, extraterritorially' when they were not in their clubs, 'the
refuges of the homeless', and the location of their passion for gambling.
When not there, the *boulevardiers* would be in 'places of entertainment,
cafés and restaurants [that] . . . appear to be built entirely of gilt
and mirrors' along the Boulevard des Italiens. The dandy confined
himself to this world since, as Alfred de Musset announced, ' "It is
only a few steps from one end to the other, nevertheless they contain
the whole world." . . . He added contemptuously that beyond them

barbarism began.' That barbarism, of course, manifested itself in the life of the common people, castigated by the bourgeoisie for 'selfish pleasure-seeking'. Yet this miniature world of the boulevardiers

> had its roots in economic developments, which included the commer-cialisation of sex and of newspaper production, and super-imposed on the economic factors was their deliberate shutting out of the outside world, with all its pregnant social developments. The Boulevards constituted a little world, but an artificial one, surrounded by invisible barriers.[228]

Its myopic and artificial world produced a wit that 'became more and more refined. It indulged in subtle allusions, extravagant arabesques.' In the arts, it was technique which was all important.

The early 1840s ushered in a period of financial speculation which 'became the religion of the state, with the Bourse as its temple'. It was also the heyday of the *flâneur*, 'the aimless saunterer who sought to conceal the gaping void around him and within him by imbibing a thousand casual impressions . . . For the *flâneur* the sights of the city were like his dreams to a hashish smoker.' If Kracauer characterizes the *flâneur's* gaze as an aimless one – in contrast to Benjamin's more precise characterization – then this was true of entertainment too: 'the object of all forms of entertainment was entertainment only. The sole object was to kill time, not to give it a meaning.' In this context, Offenbach's dream of founding 'a mutual insurance society for the combating of boredom' takes on an added meaning since, Kracauer argues, 'it was out of this dream that he created the operetta'. Its music rapidly moved from the salons to the dance-hall, the theatre and the boulevard.

If, by the later 1840s, 'the salon was advancing into the street, and the street was pushing its way into the salon', this process drew to an abrupt halt in 1848. And like the *boulevardiers*, Offenbach withdrew when 'the invisible barriers that protected the Boulevards collapsed' and 'the revolution drove his public away'. Its aftermath, the dictator-ship of Louis Napoleon, required distraction from the real world. 'Joy and glamour' was Napoleon's motto. They were to accompany dictatorship and terror, the abolition of universal suffrage and the freedom of the press but, with the assistance of the Saint Simonists, to usher in a period of economic prosperity. This was Offenbach's operetta world. The operetta itself would never have been born had the society of the time not itself been operetta-like; had it not been living in a dream world, obstinately refusing to wake up and face reality.

At the beginning of the Second Empire the bourgeoisie were so effectively isolated that scarcely a breath of air from the outside world came to ruffle its composure. The dictatorship forbade all expressions of opinion and stifled all political life . . . the bourgeoisie withdrew more and more into private life; and private life was just as empty as public life.[229]

But 'the operetta-like qualities of Second Empire society could scarcely have flourished so exuberantly had not relatively wide sections of the population been assured of material prosperity', even though it was manifested more in speculation and finance than sound industrial development. Furthermore, this operetta-like world was an urban one and 'only in Paris were there present all the elements, material and verbal, that made the operetta possible'.

The structure of the city of Paris was itself being transformed by Haussmann for a variety of reasons, including making insurrection more difficult. There was to be a new Paris and alongside it, new fortunes to be made, though since 'the regime was based on a flight from reality, there was a visible diminution in the capacity for distinguishing real and fictitious values'. With the ban on politics, 'the theatre was becoming more and more the centre of life' for its growing number of adherents. The retreat into a dream world was crowned with the first World Exhibition of 1855 (where Offenbach also had a successful theatre) which provided an international public for Paris and for operettas. Offenbach's operetta genre 'corresponded exactly with the foreigners' secret wishes'; his music 'like Charlie Chaplin's films, were an international phenomenon in an age of international development, in which great hopes were entertained of permanent reconciliation between the peoples'. Offenbach's first major public success, *Ba-ta-clan*, a *chinoiserie musicale*, possessed 'the indiscriminate quality of a dream, a higgledy-piggledy of memories and wish-pictures'. The restrictions imposed on theatres with regard to what they could perform, the length of performance and the limited number of artists permitted (four in this instance) forced Offenbach to produce 'ideas and tunes that are as genuine as hard cash'. There was, then, something forced about the excitement and newness of cultural production, about the disorientation of this modernity. Indeed, those in power 'felt instinctively that only noise and excitement could prevent social antagonisms coming to the surface with disastrous consequences. The rebuilding of Paris, the frantic tearing down of old building and the setting up of new, were part of it all, just as were the innumerable *mésalliances* that now took place' at the personal level.[230]

Yet the operettas of Offenbach were not merely distracting spectacles. 'Orpheus' (1858) 'made a mock of all the glamour that surrounded the apparatus of power' and even the resuscitated cancan, 'in which the untamed passions of the people mingled with the unrest of nobles and bourgeoisie' for all its 'glamorous frenzy' appropriate to Imperial policy, contained the danger that it could lead 'straight to dionysian orgies which could only end in self-destruction'.

For Kracauer, the dream world of reality and the operetta were driven on by the phantasmagoria of money: as 'the magic wand' promising the effortless acquisition of boundless delights', in the form of reckless, manipulated stock exchange speculation. In Offenbach's early operettas 'winning tickets in lotteries and sudden and dramatic changes of fortune are part of the stock-in-trade'. Despite frequent financial disasters a kind of delirium set in and speculation became identified with voluptuousness.

By the early 1860s a central element of the public for the operetta had become a less exclusive Bohemia who lived as outsiders, outside the salons and bourgeois society. This status 'on the one hand drove them to mock at the dictatorship and on the other drew the sting from their mockery and made it harmless'. Their home was the new boulevards, less exclusive, more cosmopolitan, less dandified. A further significant group – also frequently typified in the operettas – whose ranks were swelled by the rise in speculation was that of the courtesans, who 'in an era of feverish speculation . . . constituted the most sought-after commodity on the love-market' and who 'often acted as agents for brokers and financiers, working on a commission basis among their clientèle. This fusion of the *demi-monde* and the *grande-monde* was facilitated by 'the enormous quantities of cosmetics' and the fashion for crinolines which made it more difficult to distinguish these two worlds. Kracauer commented cryptically that 'the more joy and glamour the Empire radiated the wider became the circumference of the crinoline. It did not begin to diminish till 1866.' The social life of 'the interlocking circles of foreigners, the world of fashion and the aristocracy' was endlessly displayed whilst at the same time, with increasing economic development, there were underlying democratizing influences at work, at least on the boulevards. This liberal democratic atmosphere was present in Offenbach's *La Vie Parisienne* (1866), whose location is 'contemporary, cosmopolitan Paris, which is a centre of world economy and world entertainment', a fusion of Bohemia and 'the social turmoil produced by Liberal capitalism'. The operetta-like world again presented the facade of the World Exhibition in the following year in 1867, but this already foreshadowed the end of the operetta itself, decisively killed off in the war of 1870–1 and the Paris Commune. In the 1870s Offenbach continued with pantomimes but, with reality now far in advance of the outmoded artistic form, what became important in them was the staging, the scenery. The operetta had become decor.

As 'a socially-conditioned phenomenon', the *Offenbachiade* was 'bound to fade away' after 1867. Kracauer's assessment of its significance and decline is worth stating in detail. The operetta

> had originated in an epoch in which social reality had been banished by the Emperor's orders, and for many years it had flourished in the gap that was left. Thoroughly ambiguous as it was, it had fulfilled a revolutionary function under the dictatorship, that of scourging corruption and authoritarianism, and holding up the principle of freedom. To be sure, its satire had been clothed in a garment of frivolity and concealed in an atmosphere of intoxication . . . But the frivolity went deeper than the world of fashionable Bohemia could see.

> At a time when the bourgeoisie were politically stagnant and the Left was impotent, Offenbach's operettas had been the most definite form of laughter, which shattered the compulsory silence and lured the public towards opposition, while seeming only to amuse them.[231]

The paradox of the operetta's relationship to reality only became apparent, however, when it became more critical and threatening since

> The more the unreality of the Imperial structure was revealed, the more manifest the reality of the *Offenbachiade* became, but the more superfluous it became as a political instrument. For with the decay of the dictatorship and the growth of the Left opposition, social forces, whose place had been taken by Offenbach's operettas, once more came into play. The isolated social stratum in which it had prospered broke up into its component parts, and reality drove the operetta away.[232]

In Kracauer's analysis it is often not so much the critical function of the operetta which is paramount but rather its accord with social circumstances, with the operetta world, with 'Boulevard Europe'.

As a result, as Adorno pointed out, Kracauer's method 'is not so much critical analysis as the construction of a pre-established harmony between society and author . . . The thesis of the pre-established harmony relates basically to the Second Empire.'[233] Although Kracauer is 'a materialist who is more dialectical than he presents himself', he passes over the opportunity of relating the operetta to the phantasmagoria of the commodity form. Indeed this is all the more remarkable in the light of his assertion of the relationship between the operetta and the circulation of money. Adorno suggests an alternative social analysis which could also form the starting point for the study of Offenbach's music. Kracauer saw clearly the relationship between Offenbach and journalism and the 'fleeting nature of his mode of procedure'. But precisely here is the location of his technique definable: that of the sketch which was first installed as a musical form by Offenbach. It brings together 'that extreme promptness and readiness to react to the moment which lends it its permanency with the ephemeral lack of substance and, at the same time, rigidity in the cliché which in fact transforms it into a commodity'. The later operettas owe their 'demonic or magical aura' to the fetish character of their commodity. The origin of kitsch can thus be revealed in such sketches, in this 'musical journalism'.

What this implies for Kracauer's analysis is, as Nagler has recently argued in one of the very few appreciations of Kracauer's study,[234] that 'conditioned by the absent socio-economic level of investigation, there runs through Kracauer's reconstruction of the Second Empire the danger of reproducing the surface of life itself'. The emphasis on 'the physiognomical experience' of reality led Kracauer away from fully grasping the importance of 'Marx's analysis of the commodity form for the deciphering of mystifications'. Thus, although 'Kracauer speaks of the ''new force'' of industry which, by means of unfettered production renders the social superstructure into capital . . . he is not able to explain why, since the birth of the culture industry, including, of course, the *Offenbachiade*, the production of cultural commodities tends toward the stripping away of the aura of the work of art by means of its huge production.'[235] The obvious contrast here is, of course, with Benjamin's Baudelaire analysis which is 'much more materialistic because he seeks to explain the social phenomena of the Second Empire . . . with the aid of exchange value analogies'. Whether the dialectic of use and exchange value is able to penetrate more deeply the phantasmagoria of modernity than is Kracauer's 'physiognomical concept of experience' must be assessed in the examination of

Benjamin's prehistory of modernity. Within the confines merely of
the study of Offenbach, Kracauer's analysis still remains today, as
Nagler pointed out, the only serious attempt to grasp the significance
of his operetta production.

VI

Kracauer's early writings evince a constant theme, that of the shattered
nature of the world as a totality, of a world emptied of meaning in
which individuals are left to confront the fragments of everyday
existence cut off from any higher meaning or significance. This is
true of his wartime work as well as his treatise on *The Detective Novel*.
The vision of the world is akin to that of Lukács in his *The Theory
of the Novel*, in which the individual confronts the 'objectivations of
transcendental homelessness – the homelessness of an action in the
human order of social relations, the homelessness of a soul in the ideal
order of a supra-personal system of values'. This world of the 'simply
existent' is 'the world of convention', 'a world that does not offer itself
either as meaning to the aim-seeking subject or as matter, in sensuous
immediacy, to the active subject. It is a second nature, and, like nature
(first nature), it is determinable only as the embodiment of recognised
but senseless necessities and therefore it is incomprehensible,
unknowable in its real substance.'[236] But whereas Lukács portrays
this world in the context of the classical novel, Kracauer delineated its
features in the 'trivial' genre of the detective story.

The contrast with Lukács goes further than this. Whereas Lukács
did subsequently seek out the totality of social existence in *History and
Class Consciousness*, indeed in 'an almost exclusively sociological
homogenisation of the (historical) process' (Bloch),[237] Kracauer
turned towards the concretion of the fragment, not towards the
perspective 'from above' but from below. This became the hallmark
of Kracauer's analysis of the refuse and insignificant corners of
modernity: 'his sensibility for the fortuitous, for the insignificant'
(Bloch). Indeed, Bloch's judgement of Kracauer's work underscores
this point:

His articles in the *Frankfurter Zeitung* are exceptionally good, they have
nothing at all to do with mere journalistics and review-writing. His
study of white collar workers is outstanding, his works on film . . .
are likewise without equal, they serve as models, precisely with regard

to his treatment of the small form, with his sense for the insignificant
and his rejection of the high tone.[238]

This should not lead one to conclude that the sensibility for the
insignificant and the unacknowledged implies that Kracauer's object
is itself merely the trivial and the fortuitous. Sometimes his analysis
of the everyday world suggests that even in a world robbed of higher
meaning, this 'higher sphere' has been displaced and is now located
in the seemingly trivial itself. In other words, it leads a hidden existence
in the superficial phenomena of the everyday world.

Although it often seems as if Kracauer, especially in his earlier
writings down to the mid-1920s, has accepted Weber's thesis of the
'disenchantment of the world', leaving a world emptied of any further
meaning beyond the rationally instrumental, closer examination of
his texts suggests that Kracauer adheres to a somewhat different thesis,
namely that the 'profane' has been invested, as it were, with the
'sacred', that ideal categories are now located in the superficial. In
itself, this does not necessarily negate the thesis of the rationalization
of life, though, going beyond Weber, Kracauer locates its origins more
firmly in the domination of technology and mechanization under
capitalism. In 'The Journey and the Dance' (1925),[239] for instance,
Kracauer indicates how the 'spatio-temporal passions' for the 'profane
activities' of travelling and dancing in the Weimar period have
acquired 'a *theological* significance'. Travel in modern bourgeois society
is not directed towards a particular place 'but simply a new place'.
The exotic place has lost its aura, the exotic itself has become relativized
and 'banned from reality'. Travel is now reduced to the 'pure
experience of space', just as dancing has become 'a scanning of time',
the 'representation of mere rhythm'. Experience of space and time
is reduced to that of mere events. The mechanization of time and
space, the Taylorization and rationalization of human existence places
individuals in a paradoxical position: 'They wish to experience the
infinite and are points in space, they wish to relate to eternity and
are entangled in flowing time. Access to the spheres they desire is
closed off.' The result is that human beings 'today find the substitute
for these spheres in travel and dance', they are invested with the
infinite and the eternal. The latter are located in the 'flat everyday
world' of the 'here and now'. The longing for an escape from the
everyday is forced into mundane spheres that appear to be broken
off from everyday existence but which are nonetheless intimately bound
up with it. Sometimes, these apparently autonomous spheres are

invested with a 'fantastic ideology' as in the case of the ideology of
modern sport – 'They Sport' (1927)[240] or the 'subservient oases' from
the growing economic and social crises – all attempts to escape from
a confrontation with the present. All are false attempts to redeem what
is lost.

If Kracauer's earlier Weimar essays locate the eternal and the
immutable in the fleeting and the transitory in the context of a social
analysis that sometimes goes no further than an attack upon
mechanization, then from the mid-twenties onwards a sharper focus
can be detected. Kracauer is not guilty of applauding the modernity
of the vanguard city of Berlin. The artistic symbolism of the modernist
movement, of art deco and Bauhaus, is not to be wondered at but
to be deciphered in its social context. In the contrast between Paris
and Berlin, Kracauer highlights a theme that was to be central to
Benjamin's prehistory of modernity – the experience of the new as
the loss of history, of the past, of memory. Berlin as the city without
a past and as the representative of the extremes of social reality in
the late Weimar period became Kracauer's focus for deciphering the
fragments of the reality of modernity sometimes, as in his essay on
employment exchanges, with a biting irony. There, 'human entrails
are hung out in the back courts of society like pieces of washing'.[241]

Kracauer goes quite explicitly in search of the discarded remnants
of modernity that can no longer be invested with the glamour of the
new. Such fragments are, as it were, part of the lost history of
modernity, of the absolutely new just as are the brighter fragments
of the new announced in the neon signs whose significance also remains
to be deciphered.[242] Yet it is not that the meaning of the fragment
resides in some far-away or lost totality, but rather that the
physiognomy of the fragment itself retains its own meaning that has
been covered over and obscured from view. Each of Kracauer's
analyses is a 'confrontation with a piece of the everyday world, a built-
up Here, a live-out Now'. Benjamin's assessment of Kracauer's *White
Collar Workers*[243] is valid for the majority of his later Weimar pieces.
They are the work, no longer of a person waiting, but of a 'discontent',
of one of those 'who prefers to pass anonymously and silently through
existence', but who, nonetheless, sometimes announces himself as an
outsider. And as a journalist, Kracauer did not rest content with mere
reportage, with mere portraiture since 'to this author unmasking is
a passion. And not as an orthodox Marxist, and even less as a practical
agitator does he penetrate dialectically into the existence of white-collar
workers but because to penetrate dialectically means to unmask.'[244]

Committed to 'the politicisation of one's own class' which is 'the only [indirect influence] which a literary revolutionary from the bourgeois class can today offer', Kracauer moved through the extremes of late Weimar Germany not merely as a journalist, or even – in the light of his earlier work – as a detective, but as a 'ragpicker'. Benjamin's characterization of Kracauer as a ragpicker was, as the status of this motif of the 'chiffonier' in his own work indicates, anything but pejorative.[245] It is indeed the ragpicker who redeems the scraps, the refuse of modernity from oblivion. The most vacuous fragments, those which represent 'an epoch's judgment upon itself', are left to flutter in the morning breeze. It is the ragpicker who makes use of the scraps, the fragments, since he is aware of their history. The fragments can be used again, they can be reassembled in a context that render their mosaic intelligible.

4

Walter Benjamin

The Prehistory of Modernity

Le monde domine par ses fantasmagories, c'est . . . la modernité.

Walter Benjamin

That which is modern stands in opposition to the ancient, the new in opposition to the ever-same. (Modernity: the masses; antiquity: the city of Paris.)

Walter Benjamin

Balzac was the first to speak of the ruins of the bourgeoisie. But it was Surrealism which first allowed its gaze to roam freely over it. The development of the forces of production had turned the wish symbols of the previous century into rubble, even before the monuments which represented them had crumbled.

Walter Benjamin

Benjamin wishes to wake the world from its dream.

Siegfried Kracauer

I

The fact that Benjamin's later work is motivated by the quite explicit intention of developing a theory of modernity might suggest that his account of modernity is readily to hand. Certainly, compared to Simmel and Kracauer, Benjamin very deliberately goes in search of a theory of modernity. But not merely is it the case that a major component of that theory remains 'a torso' which needs to be reassembled – as Witte suggests in relation to Benjamin's study of Baudelaire[1] – but also the whole project of a theory of modernity contained in the much more widely conceived Arcades Project (*Die*

187

Passagenarbeit – the fullest indication of the extent of this project on the prehistory of modernity, that originally commenced with the Parisian arcades of the early nineteenth century, is assembled in the notes that have now been published as *Das Passagen-Werk*) which extends from Benjamin's earliest notes in 1926 down to the theses on the philosophy of history outlined shortly before his suicide in 1940, must also be reconstructed. And even when this much is conceded, one cannot merely have recourse to a single conception of the whole project. For over a decade, Benjamin's plans for his Arcades Project took shape within the context of his philosophical, literary, political and personal concerns and changed at crucial moments in the light of them, to such an extent that the plans themselves must also be constructed. To trace their formulation, change and development is also to reconstruct the traces of their connections with his other projects.

Indeed, in a critical assessment of Benjamin's work, Adorno declared with respect to the Arcades Project that 'in fact, the whole is hardly capable of being reconstructed'.[2] On the other hand, Adorno's conviction rests upon an interpretation of Benjamin's work which comes very close to seeing in the Arcades Project merely a collection of surrealistically assembled fragments. For Adorno, Benjamin's intention was

> to abandon all apparent construction and to leave its significance to emerge solely out of the shock-like montage of the material. Philosophy was not merely to have recourse to surrealism but was itself to become surrealistic . . . To crown his anti-subjectivism, the major study was to consist only of quotations . . . The fragmentary philosophy remained a fragment, victim perhaps of a method about which it remained undecided as to whether it could be incorporated into the medium of thought at all.[3]

Certainly Adorno is correct to point to the major impact which surrealism – especially Aragon's *Le Paysan de Paris* and, to a lesser extent, Breton's *Nadja* – had upon the early delineation of the Arcades Project in the 1920s. The earliest notes, written between mid-1927 and early 1930 at the latest, do contain indications of the kind of commitment to surrealist method which Adorno points to. They are formulated most clearly in the following note:

> The method of this study: literary montage. I have nothing to say. Only to show. I will not appropriate any intellectual formulations, not

steal anything valuable. But the rags, the refuse: I will not describe but rather exhibit them.[4]

Yet these same early notes towards the Arcades Project also contain what was to become a crucial demarcation from Aragon's position in *Le Paysan de Paris*:

> Whereas Aragon stands firmly in the realms of the dream, here the constellation of awakening is to be found. Whereas in Aragon's case an impressionistic element remains – 'mythology' – . . . the aim here is the destruction of 'mythology' in the historical realm. Of course, this can only take place by means of the awakening of a still unconscious knowledge of what has taken place.[5]

However, this dissolution of the mythology of modernity in a historical context could not be carried out merely by a collector of crucial elements and refuse – however much the collector does point to *one* dimension of Benjamin's method. The prehistory of modernity could only be undertaken by someone with a clear topographical knowledge of the layers of phenomenal reality that were to be excavated. The distinctive form of historial archaeology which Benjamin practised presupposed a knowledge of the relevant topography of modernity before one could begin to excavate and remember ('Ausgraben und Erinnern') the past which had been lost.[6] It might require reducing the world to rubble, a crucial task of 'the destructive character' ('Der destruktive Charakter' 1931)[7] where the world and its 'wish symbols' had not already crumbled. But, 'he reduces what exists to ruins, not in order to create ruins, but in order to find the way that leads through them'.[8]

Benjamin did indeed seek a way through the rubble of the social reality of modernity at its inception. Like the collector, he sought to redeem a reality that had been lost. But the fragments, which his dialectical images both captured and pierced through with 'ultra violet rays', were to be presented in such a way that they were no longer mere fragments. At no point in the development of the *Passagenarbeit* were these fragments to consist solely of an assembled montage of quotations. The montage principle was never conceived as an end in itself. In the early 1930s already after his critique of surrealism – which he viewed as 'The last snapshot of the European Intelligentisia'[9] – Benjamin recognized that the montage principle could enable the Marxist method to achieve an 'increased vividness' within its presentation of history. The aim was thus 'to build up the major constructions out of the smallest clearly and precisely manufactured building blocks. Indeed, to discover in the analysis of the smallest individual elements the crystal of the totality of what exists.'[10]

Benjamin shared the ascription of such a significance to the fragment, although in a different manner, with Simmel and Kracauer. When he later came to see his *Passagenarbeit* as orientated around the central motif of commodity fetishism, he did not approach its analysis in any abstract manner or elevate it to a guiding principle in the philosophy of history as was the tendency in both Lukács's and even Adorno's later critique of capitalism. The fragment remains the gateway to the totality rather than the latter shedding light upon the former. Further, given that Benjamin's aim was the analysis of modernity and that he largely accepted Baudelaire's delineation of it as 'le transitoire, le fugitif, le contingent', even the historical construction of modernity in Paris in the mid-nineteenth century could not itself be grasped as a totality, only in dialectical images. This was true for mid-nineteenth century Paris and for that movement which half a century later sought the totality within the aesthetic realm: the 'total work of art' of *Jugendstil*. This too remained for a decade an essential if incomplete element of Benjamin's analysis of modernity.

Yet at his death, the only fragment to be published which *directly* relates to the Arcades Project was the essay 'On Some Motifs in Baudelaire'.[11] This published essay cannot stand as a testimony to 14 years of work on the Arcades Project. Although the largest section of Benjamin's 'Notes and Materials' to *Das Passagen-Werk* (which, as published, remains the fullest though possibly incomplete source for an understanding of the whole Arcades Project)[12] is indeed a section on Baudelaire (189 pages), it must be set in the context of the notes as a whole which, aside from other outlines, constitute a total of 911 pages. If Benjamin's planned Baudelaire book remains a torso, then this is all the more true of the whole Arcades Project itself. But since the latter contains the most elaborated sketch of Benjamin's social theory of modernity, then it is necessary to attempt that reconstruction which Adorno declared to be hardly possible.

II

Benjamin's intention to develop a 'prehistory of modernity' extends back to his visit to Paris in March 1926 with Franz Hessel and their joint unfulfilled resolve to write an article, if not a brief study, on the Paris arcades.[13] In the same year, Benjamin was working on *One-Way Street*, described by Adorno as 'the first of Benjamin's writings in the context of his planned prehistory of modernity',[14] in which he was already convinced that 'this culpable totality of modernity was in decline, whether from forces within itself or through forces that burst in upon it from outside'.[15] Indeed, *One-Way Street* has also been characterized as 'the physiognomical archive of the *Passagenarbeit*' and was later viewed by Bloch as 'philosophy in revue form', as 'typical of the surrealistic form of thought'.[16] In terms of Benjamin's biography, it marked a crucial turning point. When in May 1926 Benjamin referred to its original title *Closed-Off Street (Strasse Gesperrt!)*, he unwittingly pointed to the fact that as far as his personal career was concerned it marked the point of no return. In the same year, Horkheimer rejected Benjamin's plan to try for a second time to secure a *Habilitation* after his *Origins of German Tragedy* had already been rejected in Frankfurt.[17] Had he been at last successful in Frankfurt, this could have opened up an academic career for Benjamin.

Instead, Benjamin's intellectual project turned increasingly away from the strictly academic sphere. When he completed *One-Way Street* in September 1926, he had already embarked on a number of projects which gradually took shape as the Arcades Project. One of the pieces in *One-Way Street*, the 'Kaiser Panorama', had been started in 1923 under the title 'Journey through the German Inflation', the first of his writings to concentrate explicitly on the contemporary social and political scene. In the summer of 1925, he had received a contract for the translation of Proust's *Sodome et Gomorrhe*. In the previous year, he had begun to express an interest in communism. When in Paris with Hessel in 1926 he wrote to his friend Scholem that his 'small Parisian library consists primarily of several communist things'.[18]

This interest in Marxism – which temporally coincides with Kracauer's turn to Marx and Marxism – was, of course, greatly advanced by Benjamin's visit to Moscow from early December 1926 to late January 1927 stimulated in large part by his affair with Asja Lacis, a 'Russian revolutionary from Riga', whom he had met in May 1924 in Capri.[19] Whilst in Moscow, Benjamin seriously considered joining the KPD on his return to Germany and questioned whether his 'illegal incognito amongst bourgeois authors has any sense'.[20] Upon his return to Berlin, he intended writing about his 'totally unique experience' in Moscow as well as continuing his Parisian project. Indeed, in February 1927 he wrote to Kracauer that he could see 'how much I have instinctively come close to a characteristic of your Parisian sketches, which have in fact greatly impressed me. I might say that my Parisian ''observations'' are essentially identical with yours.'[21] The reference is to Kracauer's 'Parisian Observations' published in the *Frankfurter Zeitung*.[22] In turn, Kracauer's review of *One-Way Street* indicated how clearly, perhaps even more so than any of his contemporaries, he had grasped Benjamin's own intentions, possibly because they were so close to Kracauer's own. This is true of Kracauer's recognition of the monadological procedure in *The Origins of German Tragedy* as 'the opposite position to a philosophical system that wishes to secure the world in universal concepts; the counter position to abstract generalisation as such'.[23] It is equally true of his recognition of *One-Way Street* as being 'rich in explosive materials', in 'small material particles' that, in contrast to Benjamin's earlier work are now located in 'his distinctive *materialism*'.[24] As we shall see, Kracauer very early acknowledged the significance of Benjamin's illumination of the material fragments of everyday existence that were to become the 'dialectical images' of modernity.

When Scholem recalls that Benjamin already read sketches of his Arcades Project to him in August 1927, what he has in mind is probably the brief piece simply entitled 'Arcades' written by both Benjamin and Hessel – the first completed three-page sketch on this theme[25] – or possibly passages from the early notes to the Arcades Project commenced in mid-1927 and continued until early 1930 at the latest.[26] These earliest notes already announce a number of significant themes that were to preoccupy Benjamin for over a decade. Thematically and methodologically, Benjamin already pointed to 'architecture as the most important evidence of latent ''mythology''. And the most important architecture of the nineteenth century is the arcade – the attempt to awaken from a dream as the best example of dialectical upheaval. The difficult nature of this dialectical technique.'[27] Benjamin already conceived of the city of Paris as a labyrinth and the arcade as a labyrinth containing the 'primeval landscape of consumption' through which the 'dreaming collectivity' would pass.[28] Beneath the city streets lay a further labyrinth of catacombs and the metro, the mythical entrance to the underworld that linked the modernity of the life at street level with an antiquity that lay below it, an antiquity that revealed itself in architectural symbols. In this sense, too, the metropolis 'realised the dreamed-of architecture of the ancients: the labyrinth'.[29] This dialectic of antiquity and modernity and the recognition that antiquity exists *within* modernity itself already gives his conception of modernity one of its distinctive features. Even before Benjamin embarked more seriously upon the study of Nietzsche he pointed to the 'definition of "modernity" as the new in the context of what has always already been in existence'.[30] His intention was 'to render areas primal', to hack his way through 'the depths of the primeval forest' of illusions, myth and symbols with 'the polished axe of reason' in order to arrive at the 'origin' (*Ursprung*) of modernity.[31] Benjamin's concept of origin had already been applied and developed in his *Origins of German Tragedy*. As we shall see, it took on a new significance in his 'prehistory of the nineteenth century' which these notes already announced.

Indeed, these earliest notes already indicate a concern with 'the mythical topography of Paris' that was aided by his reading of Aragon's *Le Paysan de Paris* but a concern that was already moving beyond the mere analysis of myth to the history of modernity itself, to the history of the dreaming collectivity. Benjamin's distinctive form of history required not the historian in any orthodox sense but the archaeologist, the collector, the *flâneur*, all of whom are announced in these early notes along with the gambler and the counterfeiter. The search for the 'prehistory' was a search for the shock of recognition of the time of the present [*Jetztzeit*] – in a specific sense – that lay encapsulated in 'dialectical images' of modernity as 'the time of Hell'.

A path through the mythical images of Paris had already been forged by the surrealist movement in France. Benjamin confessed to Hofmannsthal in June 1927 he 'saw in it individual phenomena . . . at work that I am concerned with', in contrast to his sense of 'total isolation amongst the people of my generation in Germany'.[32] In January 1928, Benjamin was able to give his project a provisional title 'Paris Arcades. A dialectical fairy-tale', and to announce to Scholem – extremely optimistically – that it would be 'a work of a few weeks'.[33] This location of the project also coincides with his first systematic reading of one of Marx's works – *The Class Struggles in France*.

In these early stages, Benjamin still saw his Paris project in the context of his earlier work as when writing to Hofmannsthal in February 1928 he suggests that he should not see *One-Way Street* as 'a compromise with the "historical current"' . . . Precisely in its eccentric elements, the book is if not a trophy then indeed a document of an inner struggle out of which the object can be expressed in the words: *to grasp actuality as the reverse of the eternal in history* and to take the impression from this covered side of the coin. For the rest, the book is greatly indebted to Paris, the first attempt at my confrontation with this city. I am continuing it in a second work that is called "Parisian Arcades". [My emphasis.]'[34] In the following month, Benjamin confessed to Scholem that this latter project 'might turn out to be more wide-ranging than I thought it to be' and that its tone 'in a feeble manner' is set by the 'Stamp Shop' section of *One-Way Street*.[35] Later that same month, Benjamin suggests that he is coming to see where the main accent of his project must be: the philosophical analysis of fashion and the significance of 'this natural and totally irrational standard of time of the course of history'.[36]

In April 1928, Benjamin complains to Scholem 'how slowly and against what resistance the work gains a structure'. Once it is completed, however, he 'will . . . have put to the test how far one can be "concrete" in historical–philosophical contexts'.[37] Although now working 'further and almost exclusively on the "Parisian Arcades",' Benjamin was troubled by his aim which was 'not merely to call up experiences but to preserve several decisive moments of awareness of historical consciousness in an unexpected light'.[38] But it 'takes on the appearance of an increasingly puzzling, urgent thing and howls like a small beast in the night when I have not succoured it in the daytime in the most remote sources'.[39]

The Arcades Project also took on the form of a reason – perhaps a deliberate one – for not visiting Palestine at Scholem's request which had been projected for 1929. Writing to Scholem in August 1928, Benjamin gave as reasons for his rejection of Scholem's offer the completion of his Arcades Project and visiting Asja Lacis in Berlin in the autumn.[40] The visit to Palestine did not take place and was not to take place in the future, even as a place of refuge a decade later. Instead, along with many other writings – and Benjamin in 1929 wrote more than in any previous and subsequent year in part in order to pay back money to his estranged wife Dora[41] – he pressed ahead with the Arcades Project, though often still without a central focus.

Perhaps part of the anxiety associated with giving the project a coherent form lay in Benjamin's ambiguous and increasingly critical relationship to the surrealism movement, especially since Aragon's *Le Paysan de Paris* had given it an initial impulse. Not surprisingly, therefore, Benjamin complained to Scholem in October 1928 of the difficulty of extricating himself from 'an all too explicit affinity with the *mouvement surréaliste* that could be fatal for me'.[42] Instead the project may become '*the testimony* of surrealism', but only at the price of 'the manuscript acquiring a similarly pathetic time span as in the work on tragedy'[43] (which was drafted in 1916 and written in 1925).

Nonetheless, in the following year Benjamin did in fact publish his reckoning with surrealism – subtitled 'The Last Snapshot of the European Intelligentsia' – and saw it as 'an opaque screen before the Arcades Project'.[44] The project itself had become 'a neckbreaking, breathtaking undertaking' that still had affinities with 'the extreme concretion' of *One-Way Street*.[45] In the same month (March 1929), Benjamin cryptically informed Kracauer: 'I am in the arcades – "it feels as if it were in a dream", "as if it were a piece of myself"'.[46] In the summer of 1929, Benjamin completed another essay later to bear directly on the Arcades Project and more especially his work on Baudelaire. At the time, however, he saw his essay on Proust – with its emphasis on the significance of remembrance – as juxtaposed to the essay on surrealism. Indeed, '"Surrealism" is a counterpiece to it, which contains some prolegomena to the Arcades Project.'[47]

Almost as an echo of his original projected project with Hessel, Benjamin in the autumn of 1929 produced a small piece from out of the context of the Arcades Project on the occasion of a review of Hessel's book on Berlin (*Spazieren in Berlin*) under the title 'The Return of the Flâneur'.[48] Benjamin praised Hessel's attempt to do for Berlin what had already been done for Paris, namely to 'put together such an Egyptian dream book of those who are awakening'.[49] At the turn of the year, Benjamin himself was in Paris working on the Arcades Project amongst other things. He saw the need for a 'theory of historical knowledge' in this project and the study of 'certain aspects of Hegel' and 'certain parts of "Capital"'.[50] In his brief 'Paris Diary' (December 1929 to February 1930), Benjamin, like Kracauer earlier, contrasts Berlin and Paris, the latter with its streets as a 'lived out interior'.[51] Several months later Benjamin published his two highly favourable reviews of Kracauer's *White Collar Workers*, in one of which he sketched out the role of the collector of insignificant fragments of conversation and social reality as that of the 'ragpicker' – a central typification of Benjamin's own procedure too.[52] There Benjamin also criticized the fashionable Berlin political radicalism which, for all its ideological posturing, failed to 'really penetrate . . . the structure of reality' at the level of its everyday manifestations which, unlike Kracauer's work, it chose to ignore.

Benjamin's Arcades Project continued to live a somewhat subterranean existence in the early 1930s alongside his other literary activities. It does surface, as in earlier years, in some of his essays and other projects. Only late in 1934 did Benjamin announce to Horkheimer that he had worked out a plan for the Arcades Project, though even then he did not supply any details. However, in the context of the ever-deepening economic and political crisis in Germany, Benjamin's exile existence from 1932 onwards on Ibiza and then in Paris and the basic struggle to secure a minimum economic existence (in part through the writings of articles and reviews, whose placement became increasingly difficult in the shrinking market for critical German thought), he did continue to produce fragments associated with the Arcades Project up to the first major outline of it in May 1935. In February 1931 he announced to Scholem that he was still working on his (never completed) 'major essay on *Jugendstil* whose directions of thought in part already lie in the sphere of the Arcades Project'.[53] And lest it be thought that Benjamin's interests lay in the past, he replied to Scholem's critical comments on his political position (which Scholem regretted was becoming increasingly materialist and Marxist) with the question: 'Where does my production basis lie? It lies . . . in Berlin W., if you like W.W. The most developed civilization and the "most modern" culture belong not merely to my private comforts, but they are, in part, precisely the means for my production.'[54] Benjamin's 'small writing factory' did not lie in the east, with an artificial identification with proletarian groupings that had become fashionable within some Berlin radical literary circles. Benjamin's independent critical position was located outside the orthodoxy of political parties. Its anarchist element was to be found in 'The Destructive Character' (1931) – 'a kind of portrait sketch' – and other pieces of this period.[55] The summer and autumn of 1931 saw Benjamin becoming increasingly pessimistic of the political situation in Germany (in July he thought that civil war would break out no later than the autumn). That autumn Benjamin also reflected pessimistically to Scholem on the prospects for his Arcades Project: 'The indications for the Arcades Project are indeed painful – you have recognized that the study of photography ['A Short History of Photography' (1931)] emerges out of prolegomena to it; but what else will it indeed amount to other than prolegomena and paralipomena; I could only conceive of bringing the project to fruition if my work were placed on a secure footing for two years, since for months now it has never had even so many weeks.'[56] Indeed, Benjamin felt increasingly constrained to present his work 'in small pieces: a form to which firstly the materially endangered, precarious character of my productions, secondly the regard for its practical marketability draw me time and time again'.[57] Writing from Nice in July 1932, Benjamin regrets the fact that indeed many, or some, of my studies have become victories on a small scale, but . . . defeats on a large scale. I will not speak of the plans that have had to remain unfulfilled and untouched, but indeed at this point nonetheless enumerate the four books which actually indicate the location of ruins or catastrophies, whose limits I cannot envisage when I allow myself to cast my eye over the next two years. They are the 'Parisian Arcades', the 'Collected Essays on Literature', the 'Letters' [*Deutsche Menschen* (1935)] and a highly significant book on hashish.[58]

In fact, in his lifetime, only *Deutsche Menschen* appeared as a book.[59] By the autumn of 1932, Benjamin was working on sketches for his physiognomy and topography of his own childhood in Berlin at the turn of the century – 'Berliner Kindheit um 1900' – which, at a personal level as the excavation of 'the most recent past', relate directly to the Arcades Project.[60] These sketches 'in no way narrate chronologically but rather represent individual expeditions into the depths of remembrance'.[61] In the summer of the following year he was working 'intensively' once more on these sketches. Part of their methodological foundation is to be found in the published fragment 'Excavate and Remember' (1932).[62] By the end of 1933, and having moved to Paris, Benjamin was contracted to *Le Monde* to produce 'an article on the prefect of the Seine, Haussmann, who rebuilt Paris under Napoleon III'.[63] In January 1934 this project was still seen in terms of 'a comprehensive article' that would 'give a critical presentation of Haussmann's Parisian activities' on the basis of 'interesting materials already collected in earlier years'.[64] Though this project came to nothing in the sense that it did not appear in *Le Monde* – and in March 1934 Benjamin informed Brecht that he had decided not to publish it there, even though his 'material for this work is . . . fully complete'[65] – it undoubtedly forms the basis for part of the later Arcades sketches. Nonetheless, by the spring of 1934, Benjamin was not merely 'once more very busy' with the Arcades Project but also it had begun to achieve a concrete conception. He informed Scholem in March 1934 that 'at the moment, the Arcades Project is the *tertius gaudens* between myself and fate. I have not only been able to greatly advance the studies recently, but also – for the first time again after a long period – have been able to form an image of the kind of application of it. It goes without saying that this image deviates greatly from the first, original one.'[66] At night-time, he was preoccupied with other images: 'At present, when my fantasy is preoccupied in the daytime with the most degrading problems, I experience more and more regularly at night-time emancipation from them in dreams which almost always have a political object. I have very much wished to be able to be in a position to relate them to you. They represent an illustrated atlas of the secret history of National Socialism.'[67] However, not merely Benjamin's dreams were increasingly politicized. His association with Brecht – and he spent a good part of 1934 with Brecht in Svendborg – caused concern amongst his friends, especially Scholem but also, later, Adorno.[68] In this period, Benjamin declared not only that his 'communism . . . is nothing and absolutely nothing other than the expression of certain experiences, that I have made in my reasoning and in my existence'[69] but also that any alternatives which Scholem might offer 'do not possess for me a shadow of life force'.[70]

Benjamin's political interests are reflected in the completion of his essay 'The Author as Producer' in May 1934[71] and his proposed article on 'the cultural scientific and cultural political inventory of "Neue Zeit"' – the powerful Kautsky and Mehring journal of the turn of the century – for the *Zeitschrift für Sozialforschung*[72] (which subsequently took shape as the essay on Fuchs). More significantly, in the autumn of 1934 Benjamin announced to Horkheimer that 'as a result of the collapse of the last possibilities for journalistic work . . . in the course of this summer . . . nothing more would stand in the way of taking up that major book which rests on years of study on Paris and whose plan I have occasionally spoken to you about'.[73] By December he could already declare that 'I have begun to go over my studies on the "Arcades" precisely and systematically'.[74] In the following year the Institut für Sozialforschung in exile in Geneva requested – 'out of politeness I might say' (Benjamin) – 'an exposé of the "Arcades"'. This outline, 'Paris – The Capital of the Nineteenth Century', was important to Benjamin since not only could he declare that when working on it 'I was really and for the first time for many years alone with my studies on the Arcades' but also that 'it transpired that with this exposé . . . the project advanced to a new stage, primarily that it began to approach – from afar – a book'.[75] However, not being master of his conditions of work in the poverty of his Parisian exile, and mindful of the earlier lack of interest on the part of the Frankfurt Institute, Benjamin confided to Scholem in May 1935 that 'the prospects of positively interesting the Institute in Geneva, for instance, in this book are minimal. It will not permit concessions from any quarter and if I know anything at all about it, then it is that no school will rush to claim it for themselves.'[76]

Nonetheless, Benjamin for the first time felt himself in a position to be able to outline the Arcades Project in a more systematic manner. In some respects, it had close affinities with the early study on *The Origins of German Tragedy*. Both centre around 'an overarching concept . . . Where it was earlier the concept of tragedy [*Trauerspiel*], so here it will be that of the fetish character of the commodity. If the baroque book mobilised its own theory of knowledge, so the same will be the case to at least the same extent for the Arcades . . . Finally, the title "Parisian Arcades" had disappeared and the outline is called, "Paris, the capital of the nineteenth century" and secretly I call it "Paris, capitale du XIXe siècle". In so doing, a further analogy is indicated: just as the Tragedy book emerged out of the seventeenth century in Germany, so this one will emerge out of the nineteenth in France.'[77] There existed a decisive contrast between the two projects in so far as 'the whole mass of thoughts, originally metaphysically motivated, has come up against a total constellation in which the world of dialectical images is secured against all objections which metaphysics provokes'. This reliance upon 'dialectical images' might, in turn, provoke an attack on the part of orthodox Marxism 'against the project's method . . . I believe, on the contrary, that I have a secure position with it *à la longue* within Marxist discussion, even if only because the decisive question of the historical image is dealt with here for the first time in all its ramifications . . . For me, what is at stake . . . is above all the "prehistory of the nineteenth century".'[78]

The exposé of 1935[79] outlined a limited number of crucial themes in the form of dialectical images, together with their sometimes contrarily juxtaposed personifications: the arcades (Fourier), the panoramas (Daguerre), world exhibitions (Grandville), the *intérieur* (Louis-Philippe), the streets of Paris (Baudelaire) and the barricades (Haussmann). For Benjamin, the exposé signified the culmination of the development of the project that had begun with 'Aragon – the *Paysan de Paris*, of which I could never read more than two to three sides in the evening in bed . . . the first notes on the Arcades stem from this period. Then came the Berlin years, in which the best part of my friendship with Hessel nurtured itself in many conversations from the Arcades project. From this period, there emerged the – today no longer operable – subtitle "A dialectical fairy-tale". This subtitle signified the rhapsodical character of the presentation . . . This epoch was, however, also that of an unconcerned archaic, naturalistically biased philosophizing'.[80] This came to an end as a result of intensive discussions with the Adornos, Asja Lacis and Horkheimer. There then followed 'the dramatic confrontation with Brecht and thereby the high-point of all the problems for this project'.[81] Despite Benjamin's reference to the decisive influence with Adorno, the latter responded to Benjamin's exposé with a highly critical attack on the undialectical nature of his presentation and the dubious nature of many of his concepts such as that of the dreaming collectivity and 'the collective unconsciousness'.[82] In contrast, Horkheimer responded to the exposé with enthusiasm: 'Your project promises to be quite outstanding. The method of grasping the epoch from the small symptoms of the surface seems this time to demonstrate their full force. You are making a further step beyond previous materialistic explanations of aesthetic phenomena . . . You take up the economic element not so much in the form of the total production process and its tendencies as in specific individual aspects of it.'[83] However, it was not this project which Horkheimer commissioned for the Institute but an article on Eduard Fuchs – an opportunity which Benjamin used in order to introduce part of his critique of historicism that was to form the introductory chapter to the original Arcades Project exposé and, much later, the projected book on Baudelaire.

This historical interest should not be taken to indicate that Benjamin saw his projects as 'merely historical'. With reference to the Arcades Project, Benjamin wrote to Scholem in August 1935 that, 'I believe that its conception, however personal it is in its origins, has as its object the decisive historical interests of our generation'.[84] Such historical interests had to be asserted against Benjamin's own earlier position, as for instance in his enthusiasm for surrealism: 'The project represents both the philosophical utilization of surrealism – and thereby its transcendence – as well as the attempt to secure the image of history in the most unlikely locations of existence, as it were, in its refuse.'[85]

In the autumn, Benjamin was working on the essay devoted to the present, 'The Work of Art in the Age of its Technical Reproducibility' – whose final version was completed in April 1939 – which he saw as constituting 'a kind of counterpiece' to the Arcades Project.[86] In other respects the essay was bound up with the Arcades Project – in so far as it 'locates the present standpoint whose reality and problematics are to be decisive for the retrospective of the nineteenth century'.[87] Yet again, Benjamin insists upon the relationship between present concerns and the past. With reference to a possible criticism of the Arcades Project book, Benjamin suggests that 'if a reproach against the book is that it deals with the fate of art in the nineteenth century, then this fate only has something to say to us precisely because it is contained in the ticking of a clock whose hourly chime first pierces *our* ears'.[88] In other words, 'these reflections anchor the history of art in the nineteenth century in the knowledge of the present situation that we experience'.[89] Thus, whilst 'in terms of content, it is unconnected with the major book [the Arcades Project] . . . methodologically, however, it is intimately connected'.[90]

1936 saw Benjamin still struggling to give a total conception to the Arcades Project, whilst at the same time still collecting new material for it (in January in the Cabinet des Etampes he came across Charles Meryon's Paris engravings, which 'belong to the most remarkable folios that have ever brought a city to life').[91] The first months of 1937 found Benjamin totally preoccupied with finishing his essay on 'Eduard Fuchs, Collector and Historian', which was completed in April.[92] Its significance for Benjamin lay in the fact that 'the first quarter of it . . . contains a number of important reflections on dialectical materialism which are provisionally in tune with my book'.[93] However, as Fuld has argued,[94] many other aspects of Benjamin's project can be traced to his confrontation with Fuchs's work: the reflection on the history of reproduction techniques at the outset of the essay on the work of art and reflections on fashion which found their way into the first Baudelaire draft, 'Zentralpark', and elsewhere.

One theme which emerges directly out of the Fuchs essay and which is central to the Arcades Project is 'the confrontation of the bourgeois and materialist presentations of history – as a foreword to my book'.[95] Another area that Benjamin began to take up at this time was 'the significance of psychoanalysis for the subject of materialistic interpretation of history', though his plan to write on Jung and Klages in this context foundered on internal disputes within the Frankfurt Institute now in exile in New York.[96] Instead, and this is decisive for the later drafts of the Arcades Project, Benjamin turned to 'a work on Baudelaire', without, however, giving up entirely the intention of examining the archaic images of Jung's psychology (as an expression of Fascist ideology) since 'the confrontation of the dialectical image with the archaic image still constitutes one of the decisive philosophical tasks of the "Arcades".'[97] Indeed, in July 1937 Benjamin was still intent on combining the attack on Jung with the Arcades Project: 'It is my wish to secure systematically certain basic elements of the "Paris Arcades" by means of a critique of Jung's doctrines, especially those of the archaic images and the collective unconscious. Alongside its internal methodological significance it also possesses a public, political one.'[98]

The start of 1938 saw Benjamin working through the secondary literature on Baudelaire. At the turn of the previous year, he had discovered a text which shifted the later focus of his Arcades Project, namely Blanqui's prison manuscript *L'éternité par les astres*,[99] a work which, for Benjamin, 'will decisively influence the Project'. Blanqui's study portrays 'in the form of a natural order the complement to the social order . . . It portrays . . . the most terrible judgment upon a society that casts this image of the cosmos as its projection into the heavens. The study, in its theme of the eternal return, possesses the most remarkable affinity to Nietzsche; a more hidden and deeper one to Baudelaire in which in several remarkable passages it sounds almost identical.'[100] By April 1938, however, it was with Baudelaire that Benjamin was fully occupied. His intention was 'to reveal Baudelaire as he is embedded in the nineteenth century', but to create a view of him that is suddenly new as when one removes a stone in the forest revealing the impression which it had made. His conception of the Baudelaire study 'converges in the most fundamental motifs of the "Arcades"'.[101] Indeed there is a 'tendency for "Baudelaire" to develop into its miniature model'. For this reason, it is important to examine its outline in some detail.

This was sketched out to Horkheimer in April 1938 as a study with three sections.

> Their projected titles are: Idea and Image; antiquity and modernity; the new and the ever-same. The first part will indicate the decisive significance of allegory in the 'Fleurs du Mal'. It represents the construction of the allegorical interpretation in Baudelaire . . . An introduction provides the methodological relationship of the study to dialectical materialism in the form of a confrontation of 'redemption' with the common 'apology'.
>
> The second part develops as the form aspect of the allegorical interpretation, that of automatic dissolving by means of which antiquity came to the fore. This process determines both the poetical 'Tableaux parisiens' and the prosaic. In this transposition of Paris, the masses intervene in a decisive manner. The masses stand like a veil before the flaneur: they are the newest means of intoxication of those rendered lonely. – Secondly, the masses dissolve all traces of individuals: they are the newest asylum of the hunted. – Finally, the masses are, in the labyrinth of the city, the newest and least researched labyrinth. Through them hitherto unknown subterranean features are imprinted

in the image of the city. – To open these aspects of Paris is the task confronting the poet . . . In Baudelaire's sense, nothing comes closer to the task of the ancient hero in his own century than that of giving him his modern form.

The third section deals with the commodity as the fulfilment of the allegorical viewpoint in Baudelaire. It transpires that the new, which explodes the experience of the ever-same, under whose spell the spleen of the poet is trapped, is nothing other than the commodity's halo. Here, two digressions have their place. The one examines to what extent *Jugendstil* appears prefigured in Baudelaire's conception of the new; the other is concerned with the prostitute as the commodity which most totally fulfils the allegorical viewpoint. The distraction of the allegorical illusion is to be found in this fulfilment . . .

Whereas in the first section the figure of Baudelaire emerges in monographical isolation, in the second section his most important virtual and real confrontations – those with Poe, with Meryon and with Victor Hugo – stand in the foreground. The third section deals with the historical configuration in which the 'Fleurs du Mal', through the idée fixe of the new and the ever-same, confront Blanqui's 'Éternité par les astres' and Nietzsche's 'Will to Power (the eternal return)'.[102]

This outline of Benjamin's proposed Baudelaire project indicates the extent to which 'the fundamental categories of the "Arcades" which accord with the definition of the fetish character of the commodity, are fully in play in "Baudelaire"'.[103] The relation between the two projects was now conceived to be so close – 'the Baudelaire essay was originally planned as a chapter of the "Arcades", namely as the penultimate one' – that Benjamin suggested to Horkheimer that the work on Baudelaire should now form part of 'a Baudelaire *book*'. He justified this on the grounds that 'if there is a subject, besides the original outline, which offers an optimal chance to the fundamental conceptions of the "Arcades", then it is that of Baudelaire'.[104] The whole book was to be given the title: 'Charles Baudelaire – A Lyrical Poet in the Age of High Capitalism'.[105]

In the months that followed the despatch of the original extended outline to Horkheimer in April 1938, Benjamin continued to work on the conception of the whole study as well as write the central section which has appeared in translation as 'The Paris of the Second Empire in Baudelaire'.[106] The first and last sections were only sketched out – 'the first the presentation of allegory in Baudelaire as a problem, the third its social dissolution' – in contrast to 'the two fundamental sections of the second part – the theory of the flaneur and the theory of modernity'.[107] It was not merely that the Baudelaire essay could constitute 'a very precise miniature model of the Arcades Project', but also that 'several of the fundamental categories of the Arcades are here developed for the first time . . . primarily those of the new and the recurrent ever-same. Further, motifs enter for the first time in the study into relationship with one another . . . allegory, *Jugendstil* and aura'.[108] The third section of the Baudelaire study 'will possess an independent circle of motifs. The basic theme of the old "Arcades" project – the new and the ever-same – first comes into its own there; it appears in the conception of Baudelaire's activity and right up to the basic determining *nouveauté*.[109] Thus, this final section of the plan was to be the real location of the convergence of the basic themes of the Arcades Project with the Baudelaire study – 'the new and the ever-same, fashion, the eternal return, the stars, *Jugendstil*'.

Benjamin's optimistic vision of having at long last and after almost fifteen years since its inception brought 'the "flaneur" safely under cover from the world apocalypse (the frailty of a manuscript!)'[110] was countered by Adorno's profound disappointment upon reading the Baudelaire draft. Adorno saw it as constituting 'not so much a model of the Arcades . . . as a prelude' to them. He questioned whether the approach which Benjamin had applied to his earlier essays on Proust and Surrealism was appropriate to this project: 'Panorama and "trace", flaneur and arcades, modernity and the ever-same *without* theoretical interpretation – is this a "substance" that can patiently await interpretation without being consumed by its own aura?'[111] Further, Adorno argued that Benjamin's 'dialectic lacks one thing: mediation'. For this reason, Adorno saw it as being 'methodologically unfortunate to give conspicuous individual features from the realm of the superstructure a "materialistic" turn by relating them immediately and perhaps even causally to corresponding features of the infrastructure. The materialistic determination of cultural traits is only possible if mediated by the *total process*.'[112] Indeed, Adorno saw this first draft of the Baudelaire essay as highly untheoretical: 'a wide-eyed presentation of mere facts . . . at the crossroads of magic and positivism'.[113]

In his reply in December 1938, Benjamin made few concessions to Adorno's critique which, he suggested, arose partly because 'the missing theoretical transparency' to which Adorno referred was the result of the fact that Benjamin had chosen to work on the second part of the Baudelaire study without developing the first and the methodological aspects of the whole construction. Adorno's denigration of the study's identification with philological empiricism, Benjamin counters with the historical critique of the philological procedure which 'is an old concern of mine'. More fully, Benjamin declares that 'the appearance of closed facticity which attaches to a philological investigation and places the investigator under its spell, fades to the extent that the object is construed in an historical perspective. The base lines of this construction converge in our own historical experience. Thus the object constitutes itself as a monad. In the monad everything that used to lie in mythical rigidity as a textual reference comes alive.'[114] Certainly, Adorno was unreceptive to the monadological procedure in this context. In general, it is also possible that Adorno read the second part of the Baudelaire study as a draft for the whole book.

The manuscript's rejection for publication combined with other personal factors to produce in Benjamin 'an alienation from the present object of my work' by February 1939.[115] Nonetheless, he was still resolved to proceed with the whole book and did concede to Scholem that some of Adorno's reservations 'are, in part, justifiable'.[116] Despite this he informed Adorno in the same month that, after going over the criticisms again, he saw the basic elements of the 'Arcades' project 'intact and undamaged'.[117] As a result, Benjamin decided to rework the section of the *flâneur* in the context of the world of commodities and the role of 'idling in bourgeois society' within which he could locate Baudelaire as 'the most profound practician of idling'.[118] This new outline of his Baudelaire study – of which this was part – was to be distinguished from the earlier draft in so far as 'the confrontation of illusion and reality has gained primacy at every level'.[119] In particular, Benjamin was now – in March 1939 – concerned 'to place one of the fundamental conceptions of the "Arcades", the culture of the commodity-producing society as a phantasmagoria, at its core'.[120]

By June, the *flâneur* chapter was being thoroughly reworked and improved by the integration of 'decisive motifs of the study of reproduction ['The Work of Art in an Age of Mechanical Reproduction'] and the story-teller ['The Story-teller']',[121] and by its division into three sections: the arcades, the crowd, the social type.

By August 1939, the revised version of the Baudelaire essay was completed. It was the only piece directly related to the Arcades Project to be published during Benjamin's lifetime, under the title 'Some Motifs in Baudelaire'.[122] It does indicate that Benjamin in fact took account of some of Adorno's criticisms, though he persisted in retaining, for example, quotations from Engels and Simmel of which Adorno had been highly sceptical.

At the same time, however, Benjamin produced a second version of his 1935 exposé of the Arcades Project, this time in French. Aside from its modifications by virtue of an introduction, an extension of some of the sections (e.g. the *intérieur* now included its destruction in *Jugendstil*) and a conclusion which took account of his discovery of Blanqui's *L'éternité par les astres*, it does indicate a more dialectical conception of the development of the prehistory of modernity. However, at the same time its conclusion signifies 'a deep resignation' (Witte).[123] But the 1939 exposé is significant in another respect, namely that even at this late date, preoccupied with his Baudelaire study, Benjamin nonetheless thought it worthwhile to extend and modify his outline of the much broader Arcades Project itself. And this is despite the fact that it remained merely an outline.

Rather than take up other projects after completion of the published Baudelaire essay, Benjamin chose to continue working on Baudelaire. This was to have included the development of a theory of experience – the elements of which, he confided to Adorno, were to be derived from memories of his own childhood – and the expansion of his theory of auratic experience – the 'forgotten human dimension'[124] overlaid with forgetfulness and reification. In particular, in the late spring of 1940, under increasingly precarious circumstances in Paris, Benjamin was working on his 'Theses on the Philosophy of History' which 'indeed represent, for their part, a certain secret fund of my reflections on the continuation of "Baudelaire"'.[125] They represent the development of the ideas in the early part of the 'Fuchs' essay as well as 'serving as the theoretical armature for the second essay on Baudelaire'.[126] More significantly, however, they constitute the outline of the historical–philosophical introduction to the Baudelaire study and the Arcades Project.

In this sense, the outline of Benjamin's Arcades Project had turned full circle. At the very end of his life he had completed the aphorisms to the introduction to this project. He had started out with a notion of modernity as the period of hell. The 'Theses on the Philosophy of History' are very much concerned with this period and with the illusions of progress. They relate very closely to some of the reflections in 'Zentralpark', a somewhat earlier and fundamental collection of notes on the Arcades Project. There, Benjamin announced that 'the concept of progress is to be grounded in the idea of the catastrophe. The fact that it goes "on and on", *is* the catastrophe . . . Strindberg's reflection: hell is not that which lies in wait for us – but rather *this life here.*'[127] On 16th September 1940 in the Spanish border town of

Port Bou, fleeing from possible apprehension by the Gestapo, Benjamin took his own life.

III

The preceding outline of the stages in the development of Benjamin's Arcades Project suggests that there can be no ready-made starting point, no single framework of the whole from which we can reconstruct his methodology. What does exist is a whole series of reflections on how to proceed with a social theory of modernity, with a prehistory of modernity, that are scattered in a variety of published essays and aphorisms and a much wider complex of notes that make up the now published constellation of the Arcades Project – *Das Passagen-Werk*. The methodological introduction to the Arcades Project and to the projected Baudelaire book was never written. What exist are reflections in 'Zentralpark', 'Theses on the Concept of History', the early sections of the essay on Fuchs, and the like, that were to form the basis for such an introduction. In other words, unlike *The Origins of German Tragedy*, with which Benjamin occasionally compared his Arcades Project, there exists for the latter nothing that can compare with the 'Epistemo-Critical Prologue' to that earlier study of German tragedy. Any reconstruction of Benjamin's methodology must therefore commence from the existing disparate and fragmentary sources. In a double sense, therefore, the methodological issues involved in a social theory of modernity that commences from fragments of modernity must themselves commence from the fragmentary insights into his method that Benjamin left behind. A theory of modernity that was to be constructed on the basis of 'dialectical images' of modernity often contained insights into its own methodological starting point that themselves remain illuminating largely as fragmentary images.

In order to examine the important dimensions of Benjamin's methodological problems and their solutions that confronted his prehistory of modernity, it is necessary at the outset to indicate some features of his object of investigation. In his earliest notes to the Arcades Project, Benjamin introduces his 'definition of "modernity" as the new in the context of what has always been there'.[128] Modernity is here already identified with the discontinuity of experience in the sense that reflection upon the present has been broken off from that which already existed. The 'context' which explains this newness has been lost or is in danger of being lost. The announcement of that which is new is the prelude to Benjamin's analysis of *nouveauté* in its various forms, and especially in its most pronounced forms such as fashion – the absolutely new. In his later study of Baudelaire, fashion is juxtaposed with death (which is natural), with mortification, in the manner of a modern allegory.

Even in these early notes to the Arcades Project,[129] a dialectical image of the new and the primal or mythical is very much in evidence. So too is the juxtaposition of modernity with antiquity which is one of the central keys to Benjamin's analysis of modernity. The world of myth permeates the modern world of newness in such a way that, along with the surrealists, one can speak of the creation of modern myths of urban life. But to accept this as a real world is to accept the mythical world of symbols as a dream world. Myth permeates modernity and lulls the world to sleep.

Benjamin's early notes on the Arcades Project sought to give a location for the modern myths of modernity in the Parisian arcades of the nineteenth century. The Parisian arcade and the city of Paris itself constituted the key to the 'mythological topography of Paris' that had already been uncovered and presented surrealistically by Aragon in his *Le Paysan de Paris* (1926). But to view Paris as a 'mythe moderne' (Caillois)[130] was to place it further away from our own experience. Benjamin wished already to go beyond the experience of modernity in the present to its 'origins' in the nineteenth century. His intention was therefore not to celebrate the mythology of present modernity, nor the 'wish symbols' of the nineteenth century, but to render them transparent. Though the myth, like the dream, cannot become a permanent landscape, it was the starting point for Benjamin's early analysis of modernity. He pointed to 'architecture as the most important evidence of latent "mythology". And the most important architecture of the nineteenth century is the arcade.'[131] It constituted the gateway to the 'primal landscape of consumption',[132] to the labyrinth of secret dreams. Yet the arcade itself represented, as it were, a labyrinth within the larger, even more opaque landscape of the metropolis:

The most hidden aspect of the great cities: this historical object of the new metropolis with its uniform streets and incalculable rows of houses has realised the architecture dreamed of by the ancients: the labyrinth. Man of the crowd. The drive which makes the major cities into labyrinths. Completion in the covered passageways of the arcades.[133]

Benjamin even conceived of further labyrinths within the arcades themselves, of 'catacombs in the arcade'. The recognition of antiquity *within* modernity suggests already that Aragon's surrealist presentation of 'a mythology of modernity' was transposed into a 'prehistory of modernity'.

If Aragon's surrealism celebrated the dream world of modernity, then Benjamin wished to waken the world from its dream – an intention which Kracauer already detected in Benjamin's *One-Way Street*. In order to do that he had to go in search of the source of this dream world. Aragon's 'intoxicating reveries about a sort of secret life of the city' (Breton) certainly impressed Benjamin, and especially the conception of the city as a constellation of symbols. Aragon maintained that

> Wherever the living pursue particularly ambiguous activities, the inanimate may sometime assume the reflection of their most secret motives: and thus our cities are peopled with unrecognised sphinxes which will never stop the passing dreamer and ask him mortal questions unless he first projects his meditation, his absence of mind, towards them.[134]

This 'forest of symbols' (Baudelaire) is at its densest in 'those sunless corridors', 'these human aquariums', 'the voluptuous labyrinths' known as arcades, which

> deserve . . . to be regarded as the secret repositories of several modern myths: it is only today, when the pickaxe menaces them, that they have at last become the true sanctuaries of a cult of the ephemeral, the ghostly landscape of damnable pleasures and professions. Places that were incomprehensible yesterday, and that tomorrow will never be known.[135]

Aragon's starting point was the then already threatened Passage de l'Opéra whose demolition was to divert 'a good part of the human river which forces incredible floods of dreamers and dawdlers' back into the major boulevards, especially into Boulevard Haussmann and the dream world of the *grande magasins*.[136]

Benjamin, however, chose not to remain 'in the realms of the dream' but to create 'the constellations of awakening' through 'the destruction of "mythology" in the historical realm'. Even in his earliest reflections on the arcades, Benjamin recognized that the phantasmagoria of the dream world of commodities (already announced in several *Denkbilder* to be found in *One-Way Street*) required the unlocking of the key to the mystery of the commodity. The world of the circulation of the commodity is precisely the announcement of the new as the ever-same. The dream world of the nineteenth century presents itself as a mortified world of things, a world of reifications that are cut off from their origins. Benjamin's task was to go in search of the secrets of these often ephemeral things that were left behind by that century. The conception of the 'dreaming collectivity' in the nineteenth century, enclosed in the fantasy world of commodity fetishism and false consciousness, requires an equally important notion, that of the awakening from the dream. This is only possible if the world of phenomenal reality which leaves behind only traces of its origin is both destructured and restructured. At the phenomenal level, we are confronted only with a multitude of largely inexplicable picture puzzles, images whose dialectical key has been lost. As Benjamin puts it, 'The products of false consciousness are like picture puzzles, in which that which is important merely peeps out from behind the clouds, the foliage and the shadows'.[137] Benjamin's analysis of modernity does not commence with a ready-given object whose transparency permits it to be immediately investigated.

The image of the picture puzzle which encapsulates the product of false consciousness is closely related to another key image in Benjamin's analysis of modernity, that of the labyrinth.[138] At the outset of the Arcades Project, he chose to live periodically at the centre of the labyrinth about which he was writing – the labyrinth of the city of Paris. Later, after the Nazi seizure of power in Germany, he was forced to live there, reconstructing, deciphering and traversing the labyrinth of the dream world of the previous century. No image is more strongly associated with Benjamin's analysis of the topography of Paris than that of the labyrinth. At its centre stood the arcade, the primal, even auratic, threshold to the dream world of the nineteenth century. Its entrance was a threshold to the waking dream. This feature it shared with other entrances such as those to the metro and the railway station. But if the arcade was the crucial architectural trace of lost fantasies, it was located within the larger labyrinth of the city itself, through which one of Benjamin's key social types – the *flâneur* – could also indulge his desire for *flâneries*. Or the *flâneur* could lose himself in the eternally moving newest and animate labyrinth that was located on the streets themselves: the crowd. There exists a further labyrinth – if the arcade and the city are the first two spatial labyrinths – with which Benjamin constantly juxtaposed modernity: the labyrinth of the nether world, of the mythical, ancient world beneath the city. Its threshold lay at the entrance to the metro, to the catacombs and the old river bed of the Seine.

These three spatial, labyrinthine layers of reality, the arcade, the city and the underworld, were to be excavated by the archaeologist of modernity, excavated in order that the traces and signs of another reality could be both recalled and redeemed. The excavation was to reveal primal layers of experience, to cut a path through yet another labyrinth, as it were, that of human consciousness, of remembrance. The meaning of the primal forest of signs was to be brought to light. In a similar manner, the place which Baudelaire occupied in nineteenth century Paris was to be turned over like a firmly embedded stone in the forest and its impression exposed to daylight. A similar, more political concern and one which relates to the animate labyrinth of the masses who are juxtaposed to the ancient city is dramatically stated in an appreciation of James Ensor's etching 'The Cathedral', depicting a myriad of people assembled before the crumbling, porous stone of a cathedral. Beneath its stone is 'the exposed, the discovered mass . . . Very few already knew how things looked beneath this stone before which the masses worshipped. One of these was Ensor . . . he saw the countless contortions of those who queue before the gates of hell. Not the face, but the entrails of the ruling class.'[139]

Once more we are confronted with the problem that the key to modernity does not lie with that which is immediately given to us. The key, to follow Benjamin's metaphor, lies beneath the stones and remains to be uncovered. An understanding of modernity cannot be derived merely from everyday knowledge, from that to which concrete historical experience [*Erfahrung*] has been reduced: individual lived experience [*Erlebnis*]. Its 'secret', its past, remains hidden from us. These layers of reality await the archaeologist of the past, the present and the future. What immediately appears to us cannot be the end point of investigation since Benjamin is convinced 'that "the object in itself" is not "in truth"'.[140] His method is governed by the fact that 'its point of departure is the object riddled with error, with *doxa* [conjecture]'. Hence,

Historical knowledge of the truth is only possible as the transcendence of illusion. But this transcendence should not signify the evaporation, the actualisation of the object but rather, for its part, take on the configuration of a *rapid* image. The rapid, small image in contrast to scientific leisureliness. This configuration of a rapid image coincides with rendering oneself sceptical [*Agnoszierung*] of the 'now' in things.[141]

For Socrates, this *agnoia* was the methodical starting point of true knowledge, the prelude to the removal of our illusions or erroneous knowledge. This stripping away of illusion takes place for Benjamin in the rapid dialectical images of reality. These dialectical images are constructs that are to reveal the prehistory of modernity.

Whilst it is true that Benjamin is concerned with the fragments of modernity, with 'the rags, the scraps' of modernity that are the starting point for his prehistory of modernity, some are clearly more significant than others. The 'rapid image' is filled out into the dialectical image. Amongst the most important as the key to modernity is the dialectic of the new and the ever-same, which recurs in the juxtapositions of the new and the old, fashion and death, modernity and antiquity, modernity and myth, fashion and the commodity. In the analysis of Paris, we have the dialectic of the masses (as modern) and the city (as ancient). In Benjamin's later search for a materialist theory of experience, we have the juxtaposition of individual lived experience (*Erlebnis*) and concrete experience (*Erfahrung*), of dreaming and awakening. In the context of the universe of commodities, we have the dialectic of the frozen world of commodities (e.g. world exhibitions) and the social forces that lie hidden beneath them. At the level of the philosophy of history, we have history as an empty continuum of time and the real movement of history.

Against this background of the problematic confronting Benjamin, it is now possible to examine in greater detail some of the dimensions of his methodology. The fragment, the dialectical image, the concept of a prehistory of modernity and the critique of historicism, the dream and the process of awakening and remembrance, the archaeologist and excavation, the collector and the *flâneur* are all central to Benjamin's approach in the Arcades Project. Not all of these ideas and processes have their origin in the Arcades Project itself. Some are to be found exemplified in his earlier works, others exemplify Benjamin's methodological presuppositions. Yet again, there are others such as the three figures of the archaeologist, the collector and the *flâneur* which as social typifications indicate processes that are central to the destruction and construction, the preservation and even redemption of the spatial, social and imaginative labyrinths that the critic confronts.

If one of the central features of modernity is the discontinuous nature of modern experience and if another, according to Marx, is the reified nature of the world which we experience, then the world which we confront is one in which the totality has been lost, in which things exist either in rigid isolation or are deceptively connected with one another in a levelled continuum. Benjamin's physiognomy of objects seeks to do justice to the displaced world of things by setting them in a new context, by destroying the world of false images of these things. In order to do this, his starting point is the fragment and cannot be the totality.

Benjamin's activities in this regard for the fragment were recognized by those who also had similar intentions. Kracauer, for instance, saw in Benjamin's early works precisely this aim, as when he comments that 'Benjamin himself terms his approach monadological. It is the counterposition to a philosophical system that seeks to preserve the world in general concepts; the counterposition to abstract generalisation as such.'[142] Benjamin's 'distinctive concern is to demonstrate that what is large is small, what is small is large' in the process of 'uncovering those hidden places and nodal points of the course of history' that lie 'behind the back of things' but which nonetheless 'break into our dream-world'.[143] Benjamin digs around in this 'discontinuous structure of the world' in order to reveal from 'behind the piles of refuse . . . small material particles that indicate what is essential'.[144] Such a procedure arises out of 'his conviction of the lack of content of the immediately existent which he considers muddled . . . He records neither the impression of some form or other, nor does he open the door at all to the dominant abstract thought. His real material is that which has gone by; knowledge grows for him out of the ruins.' His aim is thus not the 'redemption of the living world' but the redemption of 'fragments of the past'. In the context of the Arcades Project, those fragments lay in the Paris of the nineteenth century. They too, like the fragments which Kracauer detected in *One-Way Street*, were 'rich in explosive materials'.[145]

This is also Bloch's judgement upon Benjamin's 'sensitivity for individual details and for the so often overlooked significance of the incidental in the observations of small, neglected elements, expressed quite unpathetically, of the corner stones that builders have thrown away and that exist everywhere . . . A feeling for the incidental: Benjamin possessed that which Lukács so totally lacked, he possessed a unique vision for precisely the significant detail, for that which lay alongside things, for the fresh elements that from here force themselves into thought and into the world, for the unusual and unschematic disconnected individual entity that did not fit into the refuse and which thereby deserved a quite special resonating attention. For such a detail . . . Benjamin possessed an unequalled micrological–philological sensitivity.'[146] This philological sensitivity for the superficial fragment requires that its significance be read correctly. Bloch suggests that Benjamin proceeds 'as if the world were a text, as if it described the course of things'. Its signs must be read in such a way that 'the "text"-structure emerges . . . in that the objective hieroglyphics of the object is thereby made evident to us'.[147]

There is indeed an insistence upon the significance of the fragment and a mistrust of systems that extends in Benjamin's work from his early publications down to the later reflections on the Arcades Project. As such, it signifies the rejection of Lukács's principle of 'the domination of the totality over the individual elements' and an attempt to do justice to the uniqueness of the individual element in its extreme form. Such a position is evident in the densely argued prologue to *The Origins of German Tragedy* where, in the context of a theory of concepts and ideas, whose aim is 'the salvation of phenomena and the representation of ideas', Benjamin declares that 'the empirical . . . can be all the more profoundly understood the more clearly it is seen as an extreme. The concept has its roots in the extreme'[148] – a presupposition of Kracauer's *Die Angestellten* too – and that 'the value of fragments of thought is all the greater the less their direct relationship to the underlying idea, and the brilliance of the representation depends as much on this value as the brilliance of the mosaic does on the quality of the glass paste'.[149] What is decisive is, then, the mode of presentation of the fragment, perhaps within a mosaic since 'mosaics preserve their majesty despite their fragmentation into capricious particles'.[150] Again, echoing Kracauer, Benjamin's search is 'for that which is exemplary, even if this exemplary character can be admitted only in respect of the merest fragment'.[151] The avowedly aesthetic significance of the fragment and its redemption does not derive from a method based either on induction, which fails 'to arrange and order' the fragments or upon deduction which projects them 'into a pseudo-logical continuum'. Neither method is true to the object with which it is confronted.

The uniqueness of the individual fragment is of central importance in aesthetics. Here, too, Benjamin asserts its significance, sometimes suggesting that the fragment is indeed a miniature of the totality as in the case of the work of art:

> Love for the object holds on to the radical uniqueness of the work of art and takes as its starting point the creative point of indifference where insight into the nature of the 'beautiful' or 'art' is confined to and

permeates the totally unique and individual work. It enters into its inner nature as into that of a monad, which . . . has no window, but which embodies in itself the miniature of the whole.[152]

Yet, as Kracauer pointed out, this monadological procedure was not confined to the investigation of the work of art but also to ideas and to any fragment of reality. It might also refer to the construction of human experience out of remembrance where, in a context in which the totality itself has been lost, one has 'to make do with what is resurrected only today, isolated pieces of interior that have broken away and yet contain the whole within them, while the whole, standing out there before one, has lost its details without trace'.[153] Such a procedure was also necessary in the construction of the lost collective experience of modernity that was to be reassembled as a mosaic of fragments. One of Benjamin's intentions within the Arcades Project was

> to carry the montage principle over into history. That is, to build up the large structures out of the smallest, precisely fashioned structural elements. Indeed to detect the crystal of the total event in the analysis of the small individual moment.[154]

Benjamin will thus make use of 'the trivia, the refuse' of history by extracting it from the 'encrusted surface' of reality.

The starting point of Benjamin's 'micrological and fragmentary method' lay, as Adorno remarked, in 'his basic proposition: the smallest cell of observed reality outweighs the remainder of the whole world'.[155] Yet the complexity of Benjamin's Arcades Project – nothing less than the prehistory of modernity – required a methodology that could not be summed up in a *single* method. When Adorno criticized Benjamin's approach to the Arcades Project as undialectical, as not having as its aim the Hegelian–Marxist totality, his criticism presupposed that there existed a ready to hand dialectical method. In so doing, Adorno overlooked Benjamin's heretical insight that

> every stage of the dialectical process . . . no matter how determined by every preceding stage, realizes a completely new trend, which demands a completely new treatment. The dialectical method distinguishes itself, therefore, by developing new methods as it moves into new contents. Only from the outside does the work of art have one, and *only* one form; only from without does a dialectical treatise have one, and *only* one method.[156]

Applied to Benjamin's Arcade Project, this means that his early method of 'literary montage', the assemblage of 'the trivia, the refuse' in a mosaic or a new constellation is only one element of this methodology. Even a narrow interpretation of his emphasis upon fragments would be forced to explicate the nature of Benjamin's treatment of those fragments.

In order to realize their significance, the fragments that are collected must be wrested for their usual context. They must be assembled anew alongside other fragments. Their uniqueness must be recognized and redeemed. This can only take place when we recognize the fragment as itself a distinctive whole riddled with its own tensions. If it is a historical fragment it must be snatched from the false context of the historical continuum in which it is embedded and placed in our present. This wresting of the fragment from its encrusted context requires a destructive intention in so far as the false continuum is reduced to rubble. Its significance is realized at that moment in which we confront it with surprise, with shock. At the very outset of *One-Way Street*, Benjamin gives an intimation of this process with reference to 'significant literary work' which 'must nurture the inconspicuous forms that better fit its influence in active communities than does the pretentious, universal gesture of the book – in leaflets, brochures, articles and placards. Only this prompt language shows itself actively equal to the moment'.[157] Benjamin's later methodological reflections on the Arcades Project gave this process a new context: that of expressing the prehistory of modernity in dialectical images that lay embedded in the buried fragments of the nineteenth century. He also retained his earlier 'monadological' procedure in his attempt to do justice to the objects that he investigated in nineteenth century Paris. But now it too was to be given a more conscious place within a 'materialist historiography' that he saw as being grounded in 'historical materialism'.

Thus, in order to realize the full significance of the fragments of modernity which Benjamin sought to reconstitute and in order to create the dialectical images of the prehistory of modernity, the origin (*Ursprung*) of modernity out of the monadological structure of the historical objects excavated from the past, Benjamin was compelled to reduce the continuum of the past, with its attendant driving forces of historicism and the notion of progress, to rubble. His aim was 'the actualisation' of the prehistory of modernity.

This destruction of the continuum of historical time was necessary in order to gain access to the real object of Benjamin's endeavour: the creation of the dialectical image of modernity. This 'destructive or critical moment in materialist historiography' lay in 'that blasting apart of historical continuity which allows the historical object to constitute itself'. In this sense, 'materialist historiography . . . does not pluck . . . [its objects] from the process of history, but rather blasts them out of it.'[158] The historical objects themselves were to be brought to life as dialectical images. In the context of his prehistory of modernity, focused as it was upon Paris as the capital of the nineteenth century, the historical objects were to be reassembled in a new constellation, in a 'panorama of dialectical images', in order to 'save-up the full power of the panorama'. As Buck-Morss has argued, 'Benjamin's images functioned like switches, arresting the fleeting phenomena and starting thought in motion, or, alternatively, shocking thought to a standstill and setting the reified objects in motion by causing them to lose their second-nature familiarity.'[159] However, in order that they might be constructed, Benjamin had to rescue them from their embeddedness within the historical continuum.

This historical continuum within which Benjamin's object is originally located is itself 'riddled with error'. The 'expressive character of the earliest industrial products, the earliest industrial structures, the earliest machines, as well as the earliest department stores, advertisements, etc.'[160] must itself be released from 'fields, where until now only delusion ran rampant', by attempting to 'clear the entire ground and rid it of the underbush of delusion and myth. Such is the goal here for the nineteenth century.'[161] Just as one of Benjamin's early guides into this task, the historian of architecture Siegfried Giedion, had taught him how 'we can read the basic features of today's architecture out of buildings around 1850, so would we read today's life, today's forms out of the life and the apparently secondary, lost forms of that era'.[162] Similarly, in the attempt to rid the study of historical phenomena of its illusions, Benjamin was aided by his own confrontation with the work of Eduard Fuchs, 'collector and historian'. These reflections were continued in the constellation of notes entitled 'Zentralpark' and in the 'Theses on the Concept of History'.

Drawing on his own earlier reflections on attempts to recover the 'origin' of historical objects, Benjamin maintains that

the price of any dialectical account of history is abandonment of the contemplative approach characteristic of historicism. The historical materialist must sacrifice the epic dimension of history. The past for him becomes the subject of a construction whose locus is not empty time, but the particular epoch, the particular life, the particular work. He breaks the epoch away from its reified *historical continuity*, and the life from the epoch, and the work from the life's work. But the result of his construction is that *in* the work the life's work, *in* the life's work the epoch, and *in* the epoch the course of history are suspended and preserved.[163]

Benjamin's task is nothing less than that of releasing 'the enormous energy of history that lies bonded in the "Once upon a time" of classical historical narrative. The history which shows things "as they really were" was the strongest narcotic of the century'[164] that lies behind us.

Instead of historicism's 'eternal image of the past', Benjamin wishes 'to set to work an engagement with history original to every new present'. Historical understanding in his sense thus has nothing in common with empathetic understanding (as favoured by Dilthey and others) but rather is conceived 'as an after-life of that which is understood, whose pulse can still be felt in the present'. The origin of the process of empathy is 'the indolence of the heart, *acedia*, which despairs of grasping and holding the genuine historical image as it flares up briefly'.[165] Indeed, 'if one asks with whom the adherents of historicism actually emphathize [then] the answer is inevitable: with the victor. And all rulers are the heirs of those who conquered before them. Hence, empathy with the victor invariably benefits the rulers.'[166] This is most evident in cultural history which displays its 'spoils' as 'cultural treaures'. It cannot recognize that this culture

owes its existence not just to the efforts of the great geniuses who fashioned it, but also in greater or lesser degree to the anonymous drudgery of their contemporaries. There is no cultural document that is not at the same time a record of barbarism. No history of culture has yet done justice to this fundamental fact, nor can well hope to do so.[167]

Thus, although cultural history might 'increase the burden of the treasures that are piled up on humanity's back . . . it does not give mankind the strength to shake them off, so as to get its hands on them'.[168] Instead, it adheres to a fetishistic, reified conception of culture whose history is 'nothing but the residue of memorable things and events that never broke the surface of human consciousness because they were never truly, that is politically, experienced'.[169] The past, unremembered, remains shut off from present experience and remains 'a tangle of purely factual details' instead of comprising 'the numbered group of threads that represents the weft of the past as it feeds into the warp of the present'.[170] Benjamin's conception of the subject matter of history thus 'offers not vague analogies to the present, but constitutes the precise dialectical problem that the present is called upon to resolve'. Elsewhere, emphasizing the present as his starting point, Benjamin asserts that 'every image of the past that is not recognised by the present as one of its own concerns threatens to disappear irretrievably'[171] – perhaps into historicism's imaginary museum.

The conception of history as that which takes place in an empty homogenous time continuum requires that this very emptiness be filled with something. Universal history in which historicism culminates, 'musters a mass of data to fill the homogenous empty time', to create 'the homogeneous course of history'. Benjamin maintained that this temporal space could also perhaps more dangerously, be filled by the notion of historical progress which was conceived as automatic and inevitable, especially within the Second International. Hence, he argued that 'the concept of the historical progress of mankind cannot be sundered from the concept of its progression through a homogeneous, empty time'.[172] The same is true of 'the concept of "period of decline"' since it and progress are merely 'two sides of one and the same thing'.[173]

By contrast, Benjamin's destructive historical task asserted that 'history is the subject of a structure whose site is not homogeneous, empty time, but time filled by the presence of the now [*Jetztzeit*]'.[174] It is 'a tiger's leap into the past' that arrests the illusion of continuous flow of events, that breaks the historical continuum in order to create the dialectical image of the past. This historical project, central to the prehistory of modernity,

> is based on a constructive principle. Thinking involves not only the flow of thoughts, but their arrest as well. Where thinking suddenly stops in a configuration pregnant with tensions, it gives that configuration a shock, by which it crystallizes in a monad. A historical materialist approaches a historical subject, only where he encounters it as a monad.[175]

Such a historian seeks to grasp 'the constellation which his own era has formed with a definite earlier one. Thus he establishes a conception of the present as the "time of the now" which is shot through with chips of Messianic time.'[176] Less theologically, 'the materialist presentation of history leads the past to place the present in a critical condition'.[177]

Benjamin's dialectical images of modernity possess 'a historical indexicality, but not in the sense that they belong to a specific time, . . . [rather] primarily that they only come to legibility at a specific time.'[178] Nor does this mean simply that the past throws light on the present or vice-versa:

> rather, an image is that in which the past and the present moment flash into a constellation. In other words: image is dialectic at a standstill. For while the relation of the present to the past is a purely temporal, continuous one, that of the past to the moment is dialectical: not of a temporal, but of an imagistic nature. Only dialectical images are genuinely historical, i.e., not archaic images.[179]

Such images illuminate at the moment of recognition, at the moment of 'committing the whole of life to its ultimate dialectical breaking point – waking' (as in Proust's 'representation of the space of someone waking').[180] The dialectical images of modernity can only be constructed at that point in which we awaken from the dreams of the nineteenth century. Benjamin described the Arcades Project as dealing with 'waking from the nineteenth century', which of course necessitates that 'the historian takes on the task of dream interpretation'.[181]

The 'construction' of dialectical images as 'that form of the historical object which . . . exhibits a true synthesis . . . the primal phenomenon of history' itself 'presupposes "destruction"'.[182] What is destructed is the continuum of history; what is constructed is 'the monadological structure' of the historical object which 'becomes evident precisely in the form of the historical argument which makes up the inside (and, as it were, the bowels) of the historical object, and into which all the forces and interests of history enter on a reduced scale'. In this way, 'the historical object, by virtue of its monadological structure, discovers within itself its own fore-history and after-history'.[183]

In this manner, the dialectical image reveals the tensions of both the past and present of the historical object. In other words, 'every historical state of affairs presented dialectically polarizes and becomes a forcefield in which the conflict between fore- and after-history plays itself out. It becomes that field as it is penetrated by actuality.'[184] Indeed, it signifies the point of highest tension:

When thinking reaches a standstill in a constellation saturated with tensions, the dialectical image appears. This image is the caesura in the moment of thought. Its locus is of course not arbitrary. In short, it is to be found wherever the tension between dialectical oppositions is greatest.[185]

In the context of Benjamin's prehistory of modernity it is to be found in the tension between antiquity and modernity, or, at the level of experience, at the threshold between dreaming and awakening.

The fact that Benjamin is intent upon the destruction of the continuum of historical time should indicate that he is not concerned with the emergence (*Entstehung*) of modernity out of the nineteenth century but rather with its origin (*Ursprung*) within it. In the context of the Arcades Project, he is to pursue

the origins of the forms and changes in the Paris arcades from their beginning to their decline, and grasp them through the economic facts. These facts, seen from the point of view of causation, that is as causes, wouldn't be primal events; they only become that insofar as, in their own progress – unfolding might be a better word – they allow the whole series of the arcades' concrete historical forms to emerge, *like a leaf unfolding all the wealth of the empirical world of plants.* [My emphasis.][186]

Each significant monad therefore can reveal the origin of the whole.

This primal element in the prehistory of the nineteenth century that is located in the monads or dialectical images drawn from Paris in the mid-nineteenth century is to be found no longer 'as it once was, concealed through the tradition of church and family', but is to be derived from the surface phenomena of that era that coalesce in distinctive images released from their often mythical or archaic presentation. Benjamin's aim is nothing less than the illumination of the

'prehistory of the nineteenth century' – this would have no interest if we understood it to mean that prehistoric forms are to be rediscovered among the stocks of the nineteenth century. The concept of a prehistory of the nineteenth century has meaning only where it is to be presented as the original form of that prehistory, that is as a form in which all of prehistory groups itself anew in images peculiar to the last century.[187]

Such dialectical images are no longer merely 'poetic', 'rhapsodic' or even 'surrealistic'. Rather, as Tiedemann suggests, their '*differentia specifica* . . . consists in their orientation towards objectivity: they are images of a concrete, historical nature: reified life, the commodity character of the world.'[188] Their starting point is often the mythical, dream world of the nineteenth century. The notion of the eternal return, for instance, to be found in the works of Baudelaire, Blanqui and Nietzsche is such a mythical starting point. Indeed, 'the "eternal recurrence" is the *fundamental* form of prehistorical, mythical consciousness. (It is in fact precisely a mythical one because it is unreflected).'[189] More than this, it accords with Benjamin's early definitions of modernity as 'the new in the context of what has always already existed'. This newness is itself 'the quintessence of false consciousness, of which fashion is the tireless agent. This illusion of novelty is reflected, like one mirror in another, in the illusion of infinite sameness.'[190] It culminates in one of Benjamin's most powerful conceptions of modernity itself, modernity as

> the period of hell. The punishment of hell are in each case the newest thing that exists in this sphere. The concern is not with the fact that 'again and again the same' occurs (*a fortiori* the eternal return is not what is meant here) but rather with the fact that the face of the world, the excessively large head, precisely in that which is the newest, never changes, that this 'newest element' always remains the same in all branches. This constitutes the eternity of hell and the sadist's search for what is new. To determine the totality of features in which this 'modernity' reveals itself, means to describe hell.[191]

That description is to be drawn from the nineteenth century but 'only where the nineteenth century is presented as the original form of prehistory, thus as a form in which the *whole* of prehistory is so renewed that certain of its older features become recognised merely as ancestors of those newest features'.[192]

In other words, the origin of modernity, quite literally, its original leap into existence, lies embedded in the nineteenth century as 'the immediately actual existence [*Jetztsein*] of immediately actual time [*Jetztzeit*]'.[193] The goal of Benjamin's prehistory of modernity is 'a growing concentration (integration) of reality . . . in which all that is past (for its time) can retain a higher level of immediacy than in the moment of its existence'. In turn, this can only be attained from the standpoint of the interests of the present since 'the dialectical penetration and rendering contemporary of past situations is the test of the truth of present action'.[194] This greater immediacy of the past and its concretion is only possible by freezing the dialectical motion of reality: 'dialectics at a standstill – that is the quintescence of method.' Benjamin goes in search of dialectical images of modernity that high-light the 'higher level of immediacy' of the past within our present. In this respect, 'the true method of rendering things present is to conceive of them in our space (and not ourselves in theirs)'. In other words, 'we do not place ourselves in them: they step into our lives'.[195] The dialectical images of modernity that make this possible can only be attained once the illusions in which they are embedded are dissolved.

The manner in which Benjamin goes about this task and the wider prehistory of modernity is illustrated by his recourse to three figures whose activities are constitutive for his methodology: the archaeologist, the collector and the *flâneur*. It has in fact been suggested by Sagnol – drawing on the work of Foucault – that Benjamin's Arcades Project is nothing less than an 'archaeology of modernity' or of Paris as the capital of the nineteenth century. Sagnol links this archaeology with Benjamin's earlier monadological procedure (already evident in his study of German tragedy) by suggesting that the arcades are crucial instances of nineteenth century monads – 'a world in miniature', a microcosm from which we can regain all the 'phantasmagorias' of the nineteenth century. Indeed, Sagnol links the two procedures in his characterization of Benjamin's method as an 'archaeomonadology'. Certainly the monadological procedure was recognized by Kracauer and others. More significantly, however, one of Benjamin's 'thought images' entitled 'Excavate and Remember', does indicate the relevance of the method of the archaeologist for stripping away the layers of historical refuse that conceal the primal origin of modernity.

Benjamin starts out from the fact that

> the memory is not an instrument for the reconnaissance of what is past but rather its medium. It is the medium of that which has been lived out just as the soil is the medium in which old cities lie buried. Whoever seeks to gaze more closely at one's own buried past must proceed like a man who excavates. Above all, he must not shy away from coming back time and time again to one and the same object – scatter it just as one scatters earth, root it up just as one roots up the soil . . . Indeed, the images which are extracted from all earlier constellations stand as valuables in the frugal chambers of our later insight – like torsos in the collector's gallery. And certainly it's useful to proceed with excavations according to plans.[196]

For a satisfactory construction of the past, 'real remembrances' must proceed 'epically and rhapsodically' and, 'just like a good archaeological report, must not only indicate the strata from which the object that has been discovered emanates, but also and above all those others which earlier had to be penetrated'.[197]

Such an account suggests, however, that Benjamin is an archaeologist of a special kind, concerned not merely with uncovering the various layers of what lies in ruins beneath the soil but also with uncovering the layers of meaning that remain embedded in human consciousness. The topography which Benjamin goes in search of – and he devoted considerable time and attention to the topography of Paris – requires not merely deciphering the signs and traces of the past but also of dreams and fantasies since 'the dream – that is the earth in which the finds will be made which provide evidence of the prehistory of the nineteenth century'.[198] The strata which the archaeologist must uncover and investigate not only lie beneath the ground but exist also above ground. They exist in architecture, in the street and in the *intérieur*.

In his own attempts at reconstituting his past in *A Berlin Childhood Around 1900 (Berliner Kindheit um Neunzehnhundert)* and in 'A Berlin Chronicle' ('Berliner Chronik'), Benjamin sought to reconstruct his childhood through the labyrinth of remembrance. There, 'the cautious probing of the spade in the dark loam' and the need for remembrance to 'assay its spade in ever-new places, and in the old ones delve to ever-deeper layers'[199] could sometimes prove unsuccessful. The uncovered fragment might not reveal the whole especially where earlier excavations had taken place and where it confronted Benjamin 'quite uselessly, similar to one of those Mexican temples that were excavated much too early and inexpertly, their frescoes having been long effaced by rain by the time the excavation of the ceremonial implements and papyri, which might have thrown some light on these images, could at last seriously begin'.[200] Even, in a different context, when he discovered Baudelaire's 'fresco of modernity', its after-history required skillful clearing away before it could reveal its secrets.

However, in the Arcades Project, it is not usually individual dreams that Benjamin seeks to excavate but those of the dreaming collectivity. They are often to be found in distinctive architectural configurations that still retain the traces of mythology. These are 'the dream houses of the collectivity: arcades, winter gardens, panoramas, factories, waxworks, railway stations'[201] and the like. Such remains, such monuments are all located within one of the central labyrinths of modernity – the city. The city is the crucial showplace of modernity and is crucial to Benjamin's Arcades

Project since, as Stüssi has argued, his pathways to remembrance leads

'downwards', they lead into the past, into the depths of the earth. For Benjamin, the past never lies merely 'behind' – it has not been disposed of – but rather 'below' in the depths. In the present it lies subliminally contemporaneous . . . the city still stands in whose ground its own past lies hidden. The present-day city transforms itself in the light of remembrance into an excavated one that bears testimony of the time of the past. Archaeology takes place on the showplace of modernity.[202]

The city as labyrinth is intimately bound up with remembrance of the lost past. As Szondi remarked, 'the labyrinth is thus in space that which in time is remembrance, which seeks in what has passed the trace of the future'.[203] Benjamin, like Kracauer earlier, sought to read the hieroglyphics of the spatial and social configurations of the city's landscape in order to discover its past. More specifically, Benjamin intended constructing a topography of Paris, not merely of its monuments and ruins but of its mythology. In a broader sense, he attempted a topography of the ideological landscape of Paris as capital of the nineteenth century.

In so doing, the archaeologist was to uncover not merely the contours of lost dreams and the wish-symbols of the nineteenth century but also the individual fragments and traces of a culture that could no longer be immediately recalled. The injunction to examine carefully the layers of reality through which the archaeologist has passed in order to reach the goal indicates a regard for the reconstitution of the history of the processes through which the traces that one eventually discovers have been lost. This is in keeping with his concern for the 'after history' of the fragment. It also suggests a need to view things in a new light, to place things in a new context. The fragments that are excavated must be assembled within a new constellation. In so doing, the mode of procedure goes beyond the typification of the excavator and moves over to that of the collector.

When Benjamin maintained that 'the true method of making things contemporaneous is to conceive of them . . . within our space', he added, 'this the collector does'.[204] The whole of the notes and fragments now assembled as *Das Passagen-Werk* are testimony to Benjamin's activity as a collector. They are instances of practical remembrance on the part of someone seeking to construct the prehistory of modernity. Indeed, 'collecting is a form of practical

J

remembrance and, amongst the profane manifestations of "closeness", the most valid one'.[205] In the act of collecting itself, what is decisive is 'that the object is wrested from all original functions in order that it can be placed in the closest conceivable relationship to that with which it has closest affinity. This is the diametrical opposite to utilization and is subsumed under the remarkable category of completion'.[206] Only then does the object, the fragment, come into its own. The collector, stripping each individual object from any property or status of mere possession, places the object in a historical system or constellation created by himself so that it is elevated 'into an encyclopaedia of all scientific knowledge of the age, the landscape, the industry, the owner from which it originated. Unlike the allegorist, the collector actually shows how seemingly disparate things are connected 'the collector . . . unifies those things which belong to one another'.[207] The activity of collecting itself 'is a primal phenomenon of study: the student collects knowledge'[208] and its 'most hidden motif . . .: it takes up the battle against distraction'.[209]

Yet, as Benjamin concedes in his appreciation of the work of Eduard Fuchs, 'the figure of the collector, which improves on closer acquaintance, has not often been given its due'.[210] This Benjamin sought to do not merely in his essay on Fuchs but also in his own procedure in the Arcades Project and elsewhere. The collector's desire to wrench objects from their false context was evident in *One-Way Street*. It manifested itself even earlier in Benjamin's delineation of the task of the literacy critic which was 'to wrest the elements of a work from their false context and to reconstruct them in a new one in such a way that the original, hidden truth of the work is revealed'.[211] Furthermore, Benjamin was already convinced that the 'false context' of a work arose 'not primarily in its structure but rather in its being handed down, in the manner in which it was received and absorbed in a tradition'.

This critique of the tradition through which an object has passed was not merely the task of the literary critic. It was also necessary within the context of any attempt to establish a critical Marxist historiography. Benjamin saw the critical hermeneutic intention as largely absent from many Marxist investigations. Indeed, 'it is an illusion of vulgar Marxism that the social function of a material or intellectual product can be determined without reference to the circumstances and the bearers of its tradition'. Yet, the tradition through which we have received any object or work 'bears historical scars which must be of interest to critical observers'.[212]

The task of the critic and that of the collector therefore retains the destructive element of Benjamin's methodology, especially since in the context of established traditions, 'the concepts of those who dominate have always become the mirror (of a kaleidoscope), thanks to which the image of an "order" came into existence. The kaleidoscope must be smashed.'[213] The collector, having rescued his objects from their original functions was to bring them into a real context with other similar objects. In this respect, the collector is devoted to the montage principle, reassembling 'the refuse of history' into a new configuration. This montage of reality emerged 'out of apparently quite distant incidental elements and equally the opposite of montage: separation, divorce of qualities and objects of these qualities that in the accepted realm of experience apparently live very close to one another'.[214]

Yet in so far as Benjamin's orientation is towards 'the refuse of history', his method has affinities not with the collector of fine works but with 'the refuse collector [*der Lumpensammler*]', with Baudelaire's *chiffonier* as Wohlfarth has decisively demonstrated.[215] And this is, of course, the aim which Benjamin quite positively ascribed to Kracauer. As Wohlfarth comments, the refuse collector 'dreams . . . of a world in which "things are freed from the compulsion of being useful". In this respect, he is to be distinguished once more from the great collector for whom it is a matter of investments and prestige' and, on other grounds, from 'a militant Brechtian utilitarianism'.[216]

The collector's activity therefore encapsulates both a negative moment – the destruction of the original context – and a positive one: the setting of the object in a new order of things. Benjamin emphasizes that this latter aspect is something extraordinary:

> To the collector, the world is present and indeed ordered in each of his objects. Ordered, however, according to a surprising – indeed, to the profane, unintelligible – configuration. The latter stands in relation to the commonly accepted ordering and schematization of things roughly as their order in a conversational lexicon stands to a natural one . . . All of this, the 'objective' data as well as all other, for the true collector turns . . . into a whole magical encyclopaedia, into an ordering of the world whose outline is the *fate* of his object.[217]

This manner of observing what has been collected, the recognition of a different rhythm of things, a quickened tempo of things in their new configuration, the transformation of our perception of the configuration by the addition of each new piece is Benjamin's aim in the Arcades Project. In precisely this manner, one observes the Parisian arcades as if they were possessions in the hand of a collector (Thus, one might say, the collector basically lives out a piece of dream-life. For in the dream too, the rhythm of perception and experience is so transformed, that everything – even the apparently most neutral element – thrusts itself towards us, affects us. In order to understand the arcades in their fundament, we sink them into the deepest layer of dreaming, we speak of them as if they thrust themselves towards us.)[218]

The collectors are certainly present in the arcades, they are 'people with a tactile instinct'. Yet the nineteenth century was, for Benjamin, a period of 'the primacy of the optical' sense. In a cryptical contrast, Benjamin notes: 'flaneur optical, collector tactile'.[219]

If the labyrinth of the city signifies the location of modernity, its showplace so to speak, then the figure who traverses its web is neither the archaeologist nor the collector. The figure with whom the arcade, as the repository of the dream world of the nineteenth century, is most often identified by Benjamin is the ambiguous one of the *flâneur*. It is the *flâneur* who passes through the labyrinthine world of the arcade, who seeks a way through the labyrinth of the city and through its 'newest labyrinth', the masses. Indeed, Bloch described the Arcades Project itself as a 'documentarium', a collection of seemingly miscellaneous documents that were 'viewed by a philosophical, metaphysical flaneur who passed by them'.[220]

This ambiguous dimension of the *flâneur* is evident in Benjamin's work in a variety of ways. Baudelaire's insights into modernity, for instance, often expressed allegorically, were the result of

the gaze of the alienated person. It is the gaze of the *flâneur*, whose way of living still bestowed a conciliatory gleam over the growing destitution of human beings in the metropolis. The *flâneur* still stood at the threshold, of the metropolis as of the bourgeois class. Neither of them had yet overwhelmed him. In neither of them was he at home. He sought his asylum in the crowd . . . The crowd was the veil from behind which the familiar city as phantasmagoria beckoned to the *flâneur*.[221]

The art of being a *flâneur* could also degenerate into that of the mere idler, the aimless stroller. The writer, too, could become deeply implicated in that which he or she observed. It was 'as *flâneurs* [that] the intelligentsia came into the market-place. As they thought, to observe it – but in reality it was already to find a buyer.'[222]

On the other hand, the *flâneur* who goes 'botanizing on the asphalt' could also illuminate the city's landscale, as surrealists such as Aragon and Breton had done, and produce not merely harmless physiognomies but insights into the secret topography of Paris that proved to be the starting point for Benjamin's own Arcades Project. Benjamin's 'endless *flâneries*' around the city of Paris had been guided by his friend Franz Hessel. Hessel himself described the 'suspicious role of the spectator' in his own *flâneries* through Berlin in *Spazieren in Berlin* (1929).[223] There he declared his aim: 'I wish to linger by the first glance. I wish to gain or to find again the first glance upon the city in which I live.'[224] Benjamin sought to do the same for his own childhood in the Berlin metropolis. Yet the art of doing so he discovered in Paris:

> Not to find one's way in a city may well be uninteresting and banal. It requires ignorance – nothing more. But to lose oneself in a city – as one loses oneself in a forest – that calls for quite a different schooling. Then, signboards and street names, passers-by, roofs, kiosks, or bars must speak to the wanderer like a cracking twig under his feet in the forest, like the startling call of a bittern in the distance, like the sudden stillness of a clearing with a lily standing erect at its centre. Paris taught me this art of straying; it fulfilled a dream that had shown its first traces in the labyrinths on the blotting pages of my school exercise books.[225]

That schooling of which Benjamin speaks here is intimately bound up with the art of the *flâneur*.

It is the *flâneur* who seeks a way through the labyrinths of the arcade, the city and the crowd: 'The city is the realization of humanity's ancient dream of the labyrinth. Without knowing it, the flaneur goes in search of this reality.'[226] And it was Paris that created the *flâneur*; 'it opened itself to him as a landscape, it closed around him as a room.'[227] The *flâneur* has a distinctive response to the metropolis: 'to the flaneur, his city . . . is no longer home. It presents for him a showplace' within which he can exercise 'the perfected art of the flaneur' – 'knowledge of living. The primal image of living is the matrix or the casing.'[228] This 'subterranean motif' is essential for one who wishes to create a 'prehistory' of the nineteenth century that is located in the city of Paris, a city in which 'the Parisians turn the street into an *intérieur*'.[229]

It is also the *flâneur* who provides the images that are the starting point for dialectical images. Indeed, the *flâneur* seeks out 'images wherever they are housed. The flaneur is the priest of the *genius loci*. This inconspicuous passer-by with the dignity of the priest and the

sense for clues of a detective.'[230] This is the art which Benjamin
detected in Hessel's work in which the *flâneur* not merely remembers
like a child but also insists upon his topographical knowledge: 'thus
the flaneur remembers like a child, thus he insists firmly like the sage
upon his wisdom.' He creates a topographical 'index' for his city,
an 'Egyptian book of dreams of those who are awakening'.[231] This
implies that the 'category of illustrative seeing [is] fundamental for
the flaneur. He writes . . . his day-dreams as text to the images.'[232]
Given the ambiguous position of the *flâneur*, that text might be the
harmless physiognomies of the early part of the nineteenth century,
the stories of Poe, the poems of Baudelaire, Engels's description of
London, the reportage of the journalist or the dialectical images of
modernity of Benjamin.

IV

Benjamin's intention in his prehistory of modernity of reading the
reality of the nineteenth century like a text that speaks to us in the
twentieth should not be taken to imply that merely a restricted
hermeneutic interest lay behind this project. That reality of the
nineteenth century was presented to itself as a phantasmagoria, as
a dream world, as a world of illusions, a mythical world. It was a
particular form of 'reason' that would 'clear the entire ground and
rid it of the underbrush of delusion and myth. Such is the goal here
for the nineteenth century.'[233] The recognition and then destruction
of the dream world was undertaken with the purpose of our awakening
through remembrance of the hidden past. Benjamin was impressed
by one of the young Marx's aims of 'waking the world . . . from its
dream about itself'. Like Marx, Benjamin came to realize that this
was no easy task for even the most critical method. Benjamin's starting
point had been the 'profane illumination' of surrealism which
confronted 'the world distorted in the state of resemblance, a world
in which the true surrealist face of existence breaks through'[234] and
which, in the work of Aragon, Breton and others, had also taken the
city of Paris as its location. For them 'no face is surrealistic in the
same degree as the true face of a city.' But Benjamin's prehistory
of modernity that also took Paris as its focal point, was both historical
and critical and not prepared to celebrate the myths of modernity but
to undermine them. In other words, he sought to reveal the dreams
of the collectivity wherever they were housed – in the arcades and other

'dream houses' – through the process of awakening. As a historical project, this meant the unification of awakening and remembrance: 'indeed, awakening is the exemplary instance of remembering: the instance in which it is our fortune for us to recall the most immediate, most banal, most nearby things. What Proust meant by the experimental rearrangement of furniture in the half sleep of early morning, what Bloch recognised as the darkness of the lived-out moment, is nothing other than what is to be secured here and collectively, at the level of the historical.'[235]

Benjamin therefore investigates 'the phenomenal forms of the dreaming collectivity of the nineteenth century'. This ' "critique" ' of the nineteenth century' commences not with that century's "mechanism and maschinism" but with its narcotic historicism, its craving for masks, in which in fact a signal of the historical existence was hidden that surrealism was the first to pick up. The present investigation is thus concerned with the deciphering of this signal.'[236] What was masked were the material relations under capitalism. For Benjamin, 'capitalism was a natural phenomenon with which a new dreaming sleep came over Europe and within it a reactivation of mythical forces'.[237] Capitalism's objects, its technology and, above all, its commodities and social relations were rapidly enveloped in illusions. Whether in the public or private spheres, individuals were surrounded with mythical, illusory phenomena, to the point at which 'collective consciousness sinks into an ever-deeper sleep'. To restore what has passed and a historical consciousness of what is now occurring, requires the process of awakening. It requires 'the new dialectical method of historiography (which) presents itself as the art of experiencing the present as the waking world, to which each dream, which we term that which has existed, actually relates'.[238]

This was to be achieved by 'the dialetical penetration and the rendering contemporaneous of past constellations'. These past configurations lay in the primal landscape of the arcades, in the phantasmagorias of the panoramas, in the materials of construction themselves (iron and glass), in monuments to transitory ends (railway stations and the like) in the whole world of the commodity (world exhibitions, department stores, fashions) down to the most trivial objects that filled the *intérieur* of the nineteenth century. Above all they lay in the city of Paris around the middle of that century. The whole of 'the explosive material that lies in what has passed'[239] in that city and in that century is to be brought to the point of being set alight.

This could only take place on the basis of illuminating knowledge of that past and that city which would enable those interested to penetrate the series of labyrinths that both contained. Benjamin points metaphorically to two aids to this task. There exists, he argues, 'an ultraviolet and an ultra-red knowledge of this city, neither of which allow themselves to be confined to the book form: the photo and the city plan, – the most accurate knowledge of the individual element and of the totality'.[240] The deciphering of the 'secret signs' of the dream world of the nineteenth century and its objects was to culminate in the rapid dialectical image. In other words, 'it is not the succession from one piece of knowledge to another that is decisive, but rather the leap into each individual element of knowledge itself'.[241] In contrast, the ultra-red knowledge of Paris is perhaps to be gained by the archaeologist who proceeds from a plan. In this respect, what Benjamin intended was nothing less than a new topography of Paris in the nineteenth century, the excavation of the site of the prehistory of modernity.

The archaeologist of modernity was to investigate the labyrinths of modernity within the Parisian arcades (even the 'catacombs in the arcade'), within the city itself and beneath the city in its underworld of real catacombs. The construction of a topography of the city was essential to his task of producing the dialectical image of antiquity within modernity. The labyrinths of the great modern cities, their most hidden aspect, represented the realization of the labyrinth of antiquity. This was one of the key features of modernity itself. If Paris in the nineteenth century was *the* city of arcades that housed the 'mythology of modernity' whose secrets the surrealists had penetrated, then so too, in his projected study of Baudelaire, Benjamin announced that he would deal with 'Paris as *the* city of modernity', as the location for Baudelaire's own 'fresco of modernity'. That study was to develop 'the sublating process by means of which antiquity comes to light in modernity, modernity comes to light in antiquity'.

In his earliest notes to the Arcades Project, Benjamin's intention was to seek out the 'mythological topography of Paris', as Aragon had done earlier on a more limited scale for the arcades with their 'whole fauna of human fantasies, their marine vegetation'. But more than this, he recognized the 'affinity between myth and topography, between Pausanias and Aragon (Balzac to be included)'.[242] Paris had been rendered not merely mythical but also ancient. This had been achieved a century before Aragon by Balzac, whose *Comedie humaine* represented 'something like an epic record of tradition'[243] and who had secured 'a mythical constitution for his world only through its distinctive topographical contours'. For Balzac,

Paris is the soil of his mythology, Paris with its two or three great bankers (Nucingen, etc.), with the doctors who appear time and time again, with its enterprising merchant (César Birotteau), with its four or five great courtesans, its usurer (Gobseck), its several military officers and bankers. Above all, however, it is always the same streets and nooks, chambers and corners from which the figures of this circle appear. This means nothing else than that topography is the contour of any mythical sphere of tradition, indeed that it can be its key, as it was for Pausanias in Greece, as the history, situation and distribution of Parisian arcades will be the underworld, sunk in Paris, for this century.[244]

This reference to Pausanias suggests an ancient model for the kind of topography of Paris in the nineteenth century that Benjamin had in mind.

This ancient model is significant in that 'Pausanias wrote his topography of Greece in the second century A.D. as the places of worship and many of the other monuments began to fall into ruin'. Balzac, Aragon and now Benjamin too all gazed upon 'the ruins of the bourgeoisie', in a context in which 'with the upheaval of the market economy, we begin to recognise the monuments of the bourgeoisie as ruins even before they have crumbled'; in which 'the development of the forces of production had turned the wish symbols of the previous century into rubble'.[245]

Pausanias's *Guide to Greece*[246] exhibits a distinctive approach to his subject matter – the ruins of ancient Greece and their mythologies – that is highlighted by Frazer's delineation of Pausanias's work as that of one who

interested himself neither in the natural beauties of Greece nor in the ordinary life of his contemporaries. For all the notice he takes of the one or the other, *Greece might almost have been a wilderness and its cities uninhabited or populated only at rare intervals by a motley throng who suddenly appeared as if by magic* . . . and then melted away as mysteriously as they had come, leaving the deserted streets and temples to echo only to the footstep of *some solitary traveller who explored with awe and wonder the monuments of a vanished race.* [My emphasis.][247]

His topography is that of someone who 'loves to notice the things, whether worshipped or not, which were treasured as relics of a mythical or legendary past'.[248]

Benjamin, too, examines the Parisian arcades as primeval landscapes, the city as 'a wilderness', uninhabited except for mythical entities as in Meryon's remarkable illustrations of the city. In his study of Baudelaire, Benjamin takes such an image of the city with its decrepitude as antiquity. In contrast, modernity is Pausanias's 'motley throng', the masses. Indeed, for Baudelaire, 'Paris stands as the true indicator of antiquity, in contrast to its masses as the true indicator of modernity'. Within the latter, the man in the crowd experiences the shock of sudden confrontation. Pausanias's 'solitary traveller' is perhaps the *flâneur* in the metropolis in search of the lost aura of civilization's monuments. Pausanias himself could wander around the monuments of ancient Greece amongst the dead ruins and the rubble that still retained a connection with a mythical past. Indeed, his reconstruction of such mythologies often commenced with a deserted ruin. Benjamin saw the threshold of mythology in the modern city in a similar manner:

> In ancient Greece, one was shown places from which the descent into the underworld was made. Our waken existence, too, is a land in which at hidden places the descent to the underworld commences, fully insignificant places where dreams come into their own . . . The labyrinth of buildings in the city resembles consciousness in broad daylight: the arcades (they are the galleries which lead into its past existence) terminate in the daytime unnoticed in the street. But at night time, beneath the dark masses of buildings their dense darkness exhudes menacingly and the late passer-by hastens past them.[249]

Benjamin saw architecture as embodying the latent mythology of modernity, and embodied in 'the large and small labyrinth' of the metropolis and the arcade. Beneath them there lay 'another system of galleries that extend underground through Paris: the Metro, where in the evening the lights glow red that show the way into the Hades of names'.[250] Yet another lay in the catacombs beneath the city and in the old bed of the river Seine. All represented the labyrinth of antiquity and mythology. All of these topographical layers of the city required excavation. In general terms, Benjamin saw his aim as being 'to build up the city topographically, ten times and a hundred times over out of its arcades and its gates; its cemeteries and brothels, its railway stations . . .'[251] More specifically, part of the planned Baudelaire book was to be devoted to 'Paris as *the* city of modernity . . . it brings the decrepitude of the city into the open, insofar as it regards this city as decor. The poet Baudelaire moves around in it as a play-actor.'[252] This powerful image of the city as decor was realized perhaps in Meryon's etchings of Paris: 'Meryon's Parisian streets are shafts high above which the clouds pass by.'[253] A not dissimilar image of the city was evoked by Pausanias centuries earlier: the city of empty, often ruined, buildings that still held the key to antiquity. This was also Benjamin's assumption. But for him the city was simultaneously the key to modernity as well.

Indeed, 'the ultimate and innermost affinity of modernity and antiquity reveals itself in their transitoriness', which in Baudelaire's work is reflected in 'the frailty and decrepitude of a major city'.[254] Above all, Benjamin detected in the *correspondences* and allegories of Baudelaire's poetry, drawing their inspiration from mid-nineteenth century Paris, precisely the relationship between antiquity and modernity. He judged 'the correspondence between antiquity and modernity' to be 'the sole constructive historical conception in Baudelaire. Through its frozen armature any dialectical conception was excluded.'[255] The decrepitude of the city of Paris manifested itself in its drabness: 'the new drabness of Paris . . . just like the drabness of men's attire, constitutes an essential element in the image of modernity.'[256] At the same time, however, this modernity evoked its opposite. It arose out of the fact that 'Baudelaire never felt at home in Paris. Spleen lays down centuries between the present and the just lived through moment. Spleen it is which produces the inexhaustible "antiquity". And, in fact, for Baudelaire modernity is nothing other than the "newest antiquity".'[257] Baudelaire, whose fund of images were derived from modern life, drew the connection between antiquity and modernity in the form of an allegory. This allegory 'holds fast to the ruins. It offers the image of frozen unrest.'[258] This emancipation from antiquity lay in the allegory. A real emancipation was impossible since modernity was so closely bound to modernity. In this sense, modernity is both 'anticlassical and classical. Anticlassical: as opposition to classical. Classical: as the heroic achievement of time which stamps its impression.'[259] Yet the allegorical treatment of antiquity is also forced into its opposite: 'the experience of allegory which holds fast to the ruins, is really that of the eternally transitory.'[260] In this respect, 'the image of frozen unrest that allegory represents is ultimately a historical one'.[261] Modernity's constant assertion of the ever-new cannot prevent its collapse into the ever-same. It too will decay, its monuments will fall into ruin, even when the monuments of modernity least expect it. Modernity, Benjamin asserts, 'possesses antiquity like a nightmare that creeps over it in slumber'.[262]

Such reflections lead Benjamin to conclude that 'it is very important that in Baudelaire modernity appears not merely as the hallmark of an epoch but as an energy by means of which modernity is immediately related to antiquity. Amongst all the situations in which modernity makes its appearance, its relationship to antiquity is an outstanding one.'[263] This is as true of Baudelaire's attempt to capture the heroism of modern life in all its forms as it is to the fleeting beauty of modernity in the great cities. For the former, 'nothing comes closer to Baudelaire's intention than in his century to give the role of the ancient hero a modern form'.[264] For the latter, it is expressed in modernity's 'opposition to antiquity, the new in opposition to the ever-same (Modernity: the masses; antiquity: the city of Paris)'.[265]

Yet however significant the figure of Baudelaire and his work were in providing a focus for Benjamin's Arcades Project, they by no means exhaust either the scope of his project or contain the fullness of his dialectical images of modernity. The archaeologist of modernity might take inspiration from Baudelaire's own topographical work, the collector might examine the refuse assembled by Baudelaire's *chiffonier* and the *flâneur* might recognize himself in Baudelaire's portrait. Yet the notes which constitute the Arcades Project are testimony to a wider conception of the prehistory of modernity that was even to be extended down to the turn of the century. Benjamin's researches extend beyond Baudelaire and beyond the mythological topography of Paris to dialectical images housed within the city and within the nineteenth century itself: the arcades, the street, the city itself, and its monuments; the masses, as crowds, as consumers, as revolutionary masses; the commodity in the arcade, in the department store, in the world exhibition; the commodity's ever-new face as revealed in fashion and advertising; images in panoramas, in photography, in mirrors, in lithography; in lighting, the interior and its various traces; individual types such as the *flâneur*, the idler, the gambler, the prostitute; individual figures such as Fourier, Saint-Simon, Hugo and Marx as well as Baudelaire; changes in historical experience and historical movements; dimensions of modern experience; the changing role of art and the artist. Even this does not exhaust the themes which Benjamin's notes suggest he intended treating. At certain stages in his Arcades Project, Benjamin did see many of them coalescing in his treatment of Baudelaire. But the project of a prehistory of modernity and its dialectical images has a wider scope, perhaps one that was too wide to encompass within a single work. Nonetheless, it is possible to illuminate some of the dialectical images of modernity that this wider project contained.

The labyrinth of city streets, the city's architectural monuments, the masses who populate the city and the whole world of commodities and its illusions as well as the illusory retreat from that world in the *intérieur* and the illusions of historical tradition house the most important of these images. To traverse these labyrinths is to become aware not merely of the dream world of the nineteenth century but of the changes in perception and experience that were their counterpart. For their part, these labyrinths were to be illuminated not merely through the topographical vision derived from the ultra-red knowledge of the city plan but also through the shocking image derived from the ultra-violet knowledge of the photo. Benjamin likened the activity of the materialist historian assembling images of the past to someone operating a camera who is interested not merely in the inverted reality of the actual photographic image of bourgeois society – that is as that society wishes to see itself – but in what the camera actually produces, namely negatives in which what is light is dark and vice-versa. Such a person can choose a close-up of the fragment or a 'larger or smaller extract' from the whole, 'a harsh political or a filtered historical lighting' for the images. Such images or fragments affirm the discontinuity of the past that is handed down to us, the fragments of the oppressed that are repressed by the oppressor in order that history may appear 'as the continuum of events' whilst hiding the fact that 'the continuity of tradition is illusory'. This implies nothing less than the fact that 'the conception of discontinuity is the foundation of genuine tradition'.[266]

The significance of Benjamin's metaphor of the camera and its images does not lie in its being an isolated reflection on his method. The Arcades Project was explicitly concerned with the production of images of modernity in the nineteenth century, not merely in art forms such as Baudelaire's poetry but also in the concrete sense of changes in images of the city brought about by their architectural transformations – and here the construction of the arcades, Haussmann's rebuilding of the centre of Paris and the Paris Commune's destruction of some of the city's monuments is of prime significance. Further, Benjamin was concerned with the transformation of perception and experience in the artistic realm. This included the decline of what he termed auratic experience primarily though not exclusively of art works. It also consisted of a concrete examination of the production of images themselves – in photography, in lithography, in mirrors, in forms of lighting and in building materials such as iron and glass. For Benjamin, technology were never reducible to 'the mastery of nature'. New techniques transformed the objects of perception themselves and human beings' relations with them. The study of all these things was an essential prerequisite for the investigation of the often mythical dream world of the nineteenth century. And out of those images, those fragments of the past, could step the future. Benjamin suggests for instance that we search the early photographs of individual subjects 'for the tiny spark of contingency, of the Here and Now, with which reality has so to speak seared the subject, to find the inconspicuous spot where in the immediacy of that long-forgotten moment the future subsists so eloquently that we, looking back, may rediscover it'. Photography reveals the secrets of motion by telling us 'what happens during the fraction of a second when a person *steps out*'.[267] Each fleeting moment could now be made to endure. In fact, 'a touch of the finger now sufficed to fix an event for an unlimited period of time. The camera gave the moment a posthumous shock, as it were.'[268] Baudelaire's response to the early daguerreotype, for instance, was that it was 'startling and cruel'. The shock element was indeed crucial to Benjamin's account of the trans-formation of modern experience. But photography could also reveal something else, namely, 'the physiognomical aspects of visual worlds which dwell in the smallest things, meaningful yet covert enough to find a hiding place in waking dreams, but which, enlarged and capable of formulation, make the difference between technology and magic visible as a thoroughly historical variable'.[269]

The 'smallest things' that one usually passes by are precisely what interest Benjamin. Enlarged, they take on a new significance. Benjamin praised Atget's photographs of Paris which never took as their subject-matter 'great sights and the so-called landmarks' but seemingly insignificant aspects of the city's streets. Atget's streets, like those of Pausanias, are almost always empty; 'the city in these pictures looks cleared out, like a lodging that has not yet found a new tenant.' Such photography's virtue lies in the fact that 'it gives free play to the politically educated eye, under whose gaze all intimacies are sacrificed to the illumination of detail'.[270] Benjamin's own 'politically educated eye' had earlier cast its gaze over his native Berlin after his visit to Moscow in the winter of 1926–7. His image of Berlin was one shared, at times, by Kracauer: a city not merely 'cleared out' but cleaned too. As Benjamin expressed it: 'For someone returning home from Russia the city seems freshly washed. There is no dirt, but no snow, either. The streets seem in reality as desolately clean and swept as in the drawings of Grosz . . . Berlin is a deserted city . . . Princely solitude, princely desolation hang over the streets of Berlin. Not only in the West End . . . they are like a freshly swept, empty racecourse on which a field of six-day cyclists hastens comfortlessly on.'[271] Like Kracauer, too, Benjamin turned to Paris as a city that retained for him an image of the human labyrinth which constitutes the city. The 'most vivid and hidden intertwinings' of people he discovered – so Benjamin informs us in 'A Berlin Chronicle' – in Paris

> where the walls and quays, the places to pause, the collections and the rubbish, the railings and the squares, the arcades and the kiosks, teach a language so singular that our relations to people attain, in the solitude encompassing us in our immersion in that world of things, the depth of a sleep in which the dream image waits to show the people their true faces.[272]

The illumination of Paris in the Arcades Project had moved, however, at least by 1935, into a less rhapsodical phase, impelled by an explicit concern for social history, Marxism and 'new and radical sociological perspectives'.

The materialist physiognomy of Paris was to proceed from the topographical layers of illusion to reveal the true face of the city and of modernity in images. Nineteenth century Paris was, for Benjamin, the location of modernity and its images. And its centre were the arcades, the collective 'dream houses' that included the panoramas and the dual aspects of the streets: as the symbol of modernity in Haussmann's destruction of old Paris and as 'the home of the collectivity' of the masses whose own symbol was, at times, the barricade. The threat of 'social movement' and social movements that was expressed not merely in the barricades strengthen a process already under way: the more rigid separation of public and private spheres and a retreat into the *intérieur*. Benjamin sought out the traces of the latter. Yet the city was not merely a particular location but also the site of countless social activities. In particular, the masses could constitute the dark side of modernity (as in Baudelaire's image of the 'sickly population'); they could, as crowds, form a veil through which the *flâneur* and the idler passed; they could, at times, constitute a revolutionary movement; and they could, as consumers, constitute a most advantageous mass to those concerned with the circulation and exchange of commodities. Finally, especially from the mid-1930s onwards, Benjamin constantly asserted that the central key to modernity lay in the fetish character of the commodity, indeed, as in 1938, that 'the fundamental categories' of the Arcades Project would 'be in agreement with the determination of the fetish character of the commodity'.[273] The commodity itself had already revealed its secret life in the arcade. It was to take on a more public role in the department stores and in world exhibitions. Its endless transformations were made possible by its ever-new face, enhanced by fashion and advertising. As a key to the experience of modernity, Benjamin hoped to link this ever-new face with the frozen historical world of the recurrence of the ever-same. Some of the consequences for modern experience were outlined in 'Some Motif's in Baudelaire' under the rubric of the shock of the ever-new.

The notion of the secret life of the commodity had first been revealed to Benjamin in Aragon's account of the Passage de L'Opéra in which the arcade, which was then falling into disuse and had already taken on the mystique of the archaic, contained a whole dream world of a past age. Benjamin sought to go beyond the mythology of Aragon's treatment of the arcade through the investigation of its historical and sociological foundations in the early nineteenth century. Benjamin quotes a contemporary Parisian guidebook which describes the arcades as

a new contrivance of industrial luxury, . . . glass-covered, marble-floored passages through entire blocks of houses, whose proprietors have joined forces in the venture. On both sides of these passages, which obtain their light from above, there are arrayed the most elegant shops, so that such an arcade is a city, indeed a world in miniature.[274]

The preconditions for their emergence in Paris in their heyday during the third and fourth decades of the nineteenth century were, Benjamin argued, 'the boom in the textile trade' and 'the beginnings of construction in iron' which was 'made use of for arcades, exhibition halls, railway stations – buildings which served transitory purposes'. The arcades were also 'the setting for the first gas-lighting' as well as indicative of the increased use of glass as roofing material. Economically they might be viewed as 'the temples of commodity capital', the forerunners of the early department stores (which also often displayed their wares beneath an elaborate glass canopy). Metaphorically, Benjamin described them as 'constructions or passages which have no outside – like the dream'.[275] Their capacity to function as dream worlds was enhanced by the arcade's affinity to 'the church nave with side-chapels'.[276] The passer-by and the *flâneur* could enter their quiet refuge from the streets dominated by traffic into an environment in which one of the two components of the street-trade and traffic – fell away. This suggests that 'what is really at work in the arcades is not, as in other iron constructions, the illumination of the inner space but rather the subduing of the external space'.[277] This paradoxical relationship between *intérieur* and *extérieur* constituted the 'complete ambiguity of arcades: street and house'.[278] This 'ambiguity of *space*' within the arcade was enhanced by 'its wealth of mirrors which extended spaces as if magically and made more difficult orientation, whilst at the same time giving them the ambiguous twinkle of nirvana'.[279] For all these reasons, 'something sacred remains, a remainder of the nave of this series of commodities which is the arcade'.[280]

The arcade symbolized a storehouse of latent mythology, a more secret labyrinth within that of the city. Its entrance was a threshold to the dream world, originally to the 'fairy grottos' of the Second Empire and in their decline to the 'primal landscape of consumption'. The arcade was, then, an interior landscape that even in its period of decline still clung to its secret dream world. They opened up for Benjamin not the mythology of modernity but its prehistory:

> Just as Miocene or Eocene rocks carry in places the impression of monsters from these earth periods, so the arcades lie today in major cities like caverns with the fossils of a subterranean monster: the consumers from the pre-imperialist era of capitalism, Europe's last dynosaur. On the walls of these caves there grows as immemorial flora the commodity and, like the tissue of an ulcer, it enters into the most irregular connections.[281]

In this primal landscape of consumption, 'the commodity hangs and forces itself unrestrained like images out of the wildest dream'.[282] This juxtaposition of disconnected exchange values that is the early trace of commodity fetishism has a different significance for Benjamin. The disorder is embedded in the dream world of the nineteenth century whose microcosm is the arcade. The 'landscape of an arcade' consists of an 'organic and inorganic world'. Amongst the former are 'the female fauna of arcades: whores, *grisettes*, old witch-like saleswomen, female second-hand dealers, *gantieres, demoiselles* – the latter was the name for female-attired arsonists around 1830.'[283] Amongst the inorganic world are 'souvenirs. The "souvenir" is the form of the commodity in the arcades.'[284]

The heyday of the arcades was, however, a short one. Benjamin started out from Aragon's surrealistic image of them at their point of disappearance. Their decline had been underway for decades. Benjamin gave as reasons for 'the decline of arcades: broadened pavements, electric lighting, the ban on prostitutes, the fresh air cult'.[285] The *flâneur* stepped onto the boulevards after Haussmann's reconstruction of the centre of the city. As significant was, however, the changes in lighting in the arcades since,

> As long as gas and even oil lamps were burning in them, they were fairytale palaces. But if we wish to think of the high-point of their magic then we imagine the Passage des Panoramas around 1870 when on the one side glass lights hung and on the other there still flickered the oil lamps. The decline began with electric illumination. But basically it was not really a decline, rather more accurately an abrupt transformation.[286]

There followed 'the epoch of forms and signs' and their names remained a filter of our knowledge of their past. The centre of commodity display moved elsewhere. This transformation signified for the arcades that 'at a single blow they were the hollow form from which the image of "modernity" was cast. Here, the century smugly reflected its absolutely newest past.'[287] The absolutely new had fallen into decay and the glitter of the commodity shone elsewhere.

Yet the arcade was not the only repository of the dream world of the nineteenth century that Benjamin sought to illuminate. They were housed, for instance, in the early dioramas and panoramas (sometimes located within arcades themselves) whose preparation 'reached its peak just at the moment when the arcades began to appear. Tireless efforts had been made to render the dioramas, by means of technical artifice, the *locus* of a perfect imitation of nature.'[288] Yet while they 'strove to produce life-like transformations in the Nature portrayed in them, they foreshadowed, via photography, the moving-picture and the talking-picture'.[289] The dioramas and panoramas portrayed towns and cities from far away, landscapes, classical events, decisive battles and the like. They also gave the spectator a view of his or her own city so that 'in the dioramas, the town was transformed into landscape, just as it was later in a subtler way for the *flâneurs*'.[290] Hence, 'the interest in the panorama is in seeing the true city – the city indoors. The true is that which stands in the windowless indoors.'[291] This is also the case for the arcade. The panorama's effect, however, was produced by standing high up on a circular platform in an enclosed building in which 'the painting ran along a cylindrical wall, roughly a hundred meters long and twenty meters high'.[292] The development of lighting techniques enabled the configuration of images to change, from diorama to nocturama and the like.

The phantasmagoria of the city as interior landscape was paralleled by the emergence of a 'panorama literature', and anthologies of 'individual sketches which, as it were, reproduce the plastic foreground of those panoramas with their anecdotal form and the extensive background of the panoramas with their store of information . . . They were the salon attire of a literature which fundamentally was designed to be sold in the streets.'[293] The world of bizarre-figures displayed in these physiologies 'had one thing in common: they were harmless and of perfect bonhomie.' The menacing dimensions of the crowd in the city's landscape could be transformed in this harmless view of the world.

Yet it was not merely the landscape of the city and its population that could be rendered harmless. The same could happen to history too, trapped in its own dream house: the museum. The thirst for the past could be controlled in the museum so that 'the inside of the museum appears . . . as an *intérieur* elevated into a mighty person'.[294] As to its contents, 'there exist relations between the department store and the museum, between which the bazaar creates a mediating link. The massing of art works in the museum approaches that of commodities which, where they offer themselves to the passer-by in masses, awaken the notion in him or her that in them too a portion must fall.'[295]

Yet if the entrance to such structures as museums, arcades, panoramas, railway stations represented the threshold to the dream world of the nineteenth century, to the labyrinth of dreams, they all existed within the context of a more diffuse labyrinth of the street. Like the ambiguous dream-houses themselves, the streets of Paris also exhibited a dual significance. They too could appear, at times, to be monuments to the bourgeoise. This was true, above all, from mid-century onwards, of Haussmann's 'urbanistic ideal . . . one of views in perspective down long street-vistas . . . The institutions of the worldly and spiritual rule of the bourgeoisie, set in the frame of the boulevards, were to find their apotheosis. Before their completion, boulevards were covered over with tarpaulins, and unveiled like monuments.'[296] This was, however, only one side of Haussmann's attempt 'to ennoble technical exigencies with artistic aims'. His other, 'real aim . . . was the securing of the city against civil war. He wished to make the erection of barricades in Paris impossible for all time . . . The breadth of the streets was to make the erection of barricades impossible, and new streets were to provide the shortest route between the barracks and the working-class areas.'[297] The open perspective of the new boulevards suggests that the streets were to be cleared of all except admirers, spectators and, with the inclusion of the *grand magasins* in the contours of the boulevards, above all, consumers. All this was accomplished on the basis of a limited technology. Haussmann 'revolutionized the physiognomy of the city with the most modest means imaginable: spades, pickaxes, crowbars, and the like. What measure of destruction had been caused by even these limited instruments! And along with the growth of the big cities there developed the means of razing them to the ground. What visions of the future are evoked by this!'[298] During the Spanish Civil War, a note by Benjamin reads: 'As the Spanish war shows, Haussmann's activity is today set to work by totally different means.'[299]

There is another dimension of Haussmann's rebuilding of Paris which is implicit in the possibility of the grand boulevards becoming a new *intérieur* for the bourgeoisie. One of Haussmann's contemporaries saw only one method by which that same bourgeoisie dealt with the housing question: 'That method is called "Haussmann".' By this Engels meant

> the practice, which has now become general, of making breaches in the working-class quarters of our big cities, particularly in those which are centrally situated, irrespective of whether this practice is occasioned by considerations of public health and beautification or by the demand for big centrally located business premises or by traffic requirements, such as the laying down of railways, streets, etc. No matter how different the reasons may be, the result is everywhere the same: the most scandalous alleys and lanes disappear to the accompaniment of lavish self-glorification by the bourgeoisie on account of this tremendous success, but – they appear again at once somewhere else, and often in the immediate neighbourhood.[300]

That process was to be accelerated after the Paris Commune in Paris itself. Whereas, on occasion, Haussmann himself 'expressed his hatred for the rootless population of the great city . . . this population kept increasing as a result of his works. The increase of rents drove the proletariat into the outskirts. The Paris *quartiers* thereby lost their characteristic physiognomy. The red belt appeared.'[301]

Similarly, to many Parisians, Haussmann 'had alienated their city from them. They no longer felt at home in it. They began to become conscious of the inhuman character of the great city.'[302] Some, like the artist Meryon, were able to capture the earlier Paris before it crumbled under the instruments of the *artiste démolisseur*. Baudelaire praised Meryon's engraving of Paris that 'brought out the ancient face of the city without abandoning one cobblestone. It was this view of the matter that Baudelaire had unceasingly pursued in the idea of modernity' and which he found in Meryon's work, in the 'interpretation of classical antiquity and modernity'.[303] Meryon's engravings were to have appeared with texts by Baudelaire. What does exist, however, is Baudelaire's appreciation of Meryon's work, in which

> Seldom have we seen the natural solemnity of a great city depicted with more poetic power: the majesty of the piles of stone; those spires pointing their fingers to the sky; the obelisks of industry vomiting a legion of smoke against the heavens; the enormous scaffolds of the monuments under repair, pressing the spider-web-like and paradoxical beauty of their structure against the monuments' solid bodies; the steamy sky, pregnant with rage and heavy with rancour; and the wide vistas whose poetry resides in the dramas with which one endows them in one's imagination – none of the complex elements that compose the painful and glorious decor of civilization have been forgotten.[304]

Yet, as Benjamin points out, Baudelaire's image of modernity and its affinities with antiquity, with eternity, could not survive. Even the fate of that which Benjamin took to be the secret subject of Baudelaire's poetry, the city of Paris, has been transformed:

> To be sure, Paris is still standing and the great tendencies of social development are still the same. But the more constant they have remained, the more obsolete has everything that was in the sign of the 'truly new' been rendered by the experience of them. Modernity has changed most of all, and the antiquity that it was supposed to contain really presents the picture of the obsolete.[305]

A measure of how fragile the modernity of Haussmann's boulevards was is the Paris Commune whose 'burning of Paris was a fitting conclusion to Haussmann's work of destruction'.[306]

Yet the Commune itself did not survive to erect its own monuments. During the period of the Paris Commune, however, 'the barricade was resurrected . . . It was stronger and safer than ever. It extended across the great boulevards, often reached first-storey level, and shielded the trenches situated behind it.'[307] At such points in history, the anonymous masses took on a definite form and entered the public sphere not as an anonymous mass but as a revolutionary, proletarian movement. Thus they constituted the not always dormant threat to the Parisian bourgeoisie in the nineteenth century, as the events of 1830, 1848 and 1870–1 testify. In response to this threat, the mass's *intérieur*, the streets themselves, were transformed by Haussmann only to be transformed, however temporarily, by the masses themselves during the Commune into barricades. The masses symbolized one of the essential features of metropolitan modernity: the fact that the phantasmagoria of the bourgeois world could be more transitory than had been dreamed of; the possibility that the nightmare of Marx's image of transformation in which 'all that is solid melts into air' could come to pass.

One way of dispelling this nightmare was to prevent the proletariat from entering the public sphere at all, whether in the guise of a formal political party or, more informally, as organized labour. For 'the private citizen', however, another strategy for relieving the burden of this nightmare lay in the retreat into the *intérieur*. This presupposed that the living-space be distinguished from the place of work. When this occurred that living space

> constituted itself as the interior. The office was its complement. The private citizen who in the office took reality into account, required of the interior that it should support him in his illusions. This necessity was all the more pressing since he had no intention of adding social preoccupations to his business ones. In the creation of his private environment he suppressed them both. From this sprang the phantasmagorias of the interior. This represented the universe for the private citizen. In it he assembled the distant in space and in time. His drawing-room was a box in the world theatre.[308]

This *intérieur* was populated with a whole array of objects, from furniture down to everyday utensils. Benjamin's aim was 'to decipher the contures of the banal as a picture puzzle'. They too are a part of the dream world of the nineteenth century: 'Picture puzzles as the schemata of the world of dreams has long been discovered by psychoanalysis. We, however, are not so much on the track of such certainties of the soul as on the track of things. We seek the totem-tree of objects in the thicket of prehistory. The highest, the ultimate mask of this totem-tree is kitsch.'[309] It too, however, provided no security against the transitory nature of modernity or against the waking dreams of the exterior.

As an inward retreat, it too was populated with a labyrinth of dreams and mystery. Rather than the *intérieur* being a retreat from the world of dreams outside, it was more true that 'the *intérieur* of this period is itself a stimulus to intoxication and the dream'.[310] To live within it was to be trapped 'within a spider's web, that dispersed the events of the world, hung up like the dried out bodies of insects'.[311] Hence, the *intérieur* did not recommend itself as a way out of the layers of dream world that enveloped it. Instead, it provided the casing for a reified world of individual lived-out experience (*Erlebnis*) that could blossom out in all its variegated forms. It supported the inwardness which Adorno claimed was 'the historical prison of the prehistorical human essence'.[312]

The inner space of the *intérieur* was filled out with furniture that retained the character of fortification, embattlements against the outside world, against its transitory nature. Its complementary aspects lay in the masking and encasing of the dwelling's contents. For the former, 'the styles' drive to enmask, that extends throughout the nineteenth century, is a consequence of the fact that the relations of domination become insecure. The bourgeois power holders often no longer have the power at the place at which they live (pensioner) and no longer in direct unmediated forms. The style of their homes is their false immediacy. Economic alibi in space. *Intérieur* alibi in time.'[313] The masks in which the interior was clothed were directed towards the dream world, indeed 'furnished for the dream. The change of styles, the Gothic, Persian, Renaissance etc. that meant: over the interior of the bourgeois dining room there was placed a festival hall from Cesar Borgia, out of the boudoir of the housewife there arose a gothic chapel, over the study of the master of the house there played iridescently the apartment of a Persian sheik.'[314] Such costumes hid what lay beneath them: 'they exchange glances of agreement with nothingness, with the trivial and the banal. Such nihilism is the innermost core of bourgeois cosiness.'[315] In his notes, Benjamin also cited Simmel on the plurality of styles at the turn of the century.

Benjamin recognized that the related strategy of encasing the contents of the interior was a complex one, extending even to the living space itself. Within the notion of the dwelling itself

on the one hand, the primal – perhaps eternal – must be recognized, the reflection of human being's stay in the womb; and . . . on the other side, disregarding this prehistorical motif, dwelling in its most extreme form as a state of existence of the nineteenth century must be grasped. The primal form of all dwelling is existence not in the house but in the casing. The nineteenth century, like no other, was addicted to the home. It conceived of the home as human beings' casing and embedded them with all their accessories so deeply into it that one could liken it to the inside of a compass box where the instrument, with all its replacement parts lies in deep, most often purple, velvet recesses.[316]

The bourgeoisie's compensation for 'the inconsequential nature of private life in the big city' was sought for 'within its four walls. Even if a bourgeois is unable to give his earthly being permanence, it seems to be a matter of honour with him to preserve the traces of his articles and requisites of daily use in perpetuity.'[317] The bourgeoisie found a casing for everything:

> for slippers and pocket watches, thermometers and egg-cups, cutlery and umbrellas . . . It prefers velvet and plush covers which preserve the impression of every touch. For the Makart style, the style of the end of the Second Empire, a dwelling becomes a kind of casing. This style views it as a kind of case for a person and embeds him in it together with all his appurtenances, tending his traces as nature tends dead fauna embedded in granite.[318]

Yet this casing never proved to be as secure as granite. By the turn of the century, it received its first major shock: '*Jugendstil* fundamentally shattered the nature of casing. Today it has died out and the dwelling has been reduced: for the living by the hotel room, for the dead by the crematorium.'[319] (Benjamin spent the majority of his exile existence in hotel rooms, whilst Kracauer's early architectural commissions were for post-First World War cemeteries.)

The casings themselves had served to hide the traces of the transitory, symptomatic of an unconscious recognition of their purpose. For instance, 'dwelling as the transitional – in the concept of the "lived out life", for example – gives an inkling of the hasty actuality which is hidden in this process. It lies in the fact of moulding a casing for ourselves.'[320] In the recesses of the *intérieur* the bourgeoisie could, for a while, create the illusion of their heroism by surrounding themselves with the costumes of greatness. The *intérieur*'s physiognomy was perhaps best seen in the dwelling of the great collectors of the nineteenth century in which the interior provided the casing for a museum.

But Benjamin detected a further dimension to the significance of the traces of living:

> Coverings and antimacassars, boxes and casings, were devised in abundance, in which the traces of everyday objects were moulded. The resident's own traces were also moulded in the interior. The detective story appeared, which investigated these traces . . . The criminals of the first detective novels were neither gentlemen nor apaches, but middle-class private citizens.[321]

This literary genre, which succeeded the harmless physiologies, 'concerned itself with the disquieting and threatening aspects of urban life'. One of these was the absence of traces of individuals in the metropolis, especially within the masses. Individuals sought asylum not in the *intérieur* but in the crowd, where 'the masses appear as the asylum that shields an asocial person from his persecutors. Of all the menacing aspects of the masses, this one became apparent first. It is at the origin of the detective story.'[322]

If the city is indeed 'the realisation of the ancient human dream of the labyrinth', then the mass, as a crowd, 'is . . . in the labyrinth of the city the newest and least researched labyrinth'.[323] The masses constituted an essential element of one of Baudelaire's recurring images of the city, whose other half was the city of Paris: 'For Baudelaire, Paris stands as a testimony of antiquity in contrast to its masses as testimony of modernity.'[324] Thus, though the streets could be viewed as a deserted labyrinth of buildings, they were not always merely an empty decor. Rather, the streets 'are the home of the collectivity. The collectivity is an eternally unquiet, eternally moving entity that lives, experiences, recognizes and feels between the walls of houses just as much as individuals in the security of their four walls.'[325] For them, even the arcades acquired a new significance. For the collectivity 'the arcade was the Salon. More than in any other location, the street indicated itself in it as the furnished, lived-out *intérieur* of the masses.'[326]

On the streets, this permanently moving and changing collectivity could appear as the crowd whose physiognomy fascinated nineteenth century commentators and writers, before becoming the threatening masses towards the end of the century and the subject of social psychological investigations. The crowd constitutes itself in a peculiar manner:

> A street, a conflagration, or a traffic accident assemble people who are not defined along class lines. They present themselves as concrete

gatherings, but socially they remain abstract – namely, in their isolated private interests . . . In many cases, such gatherings have only a statistical existence. This existence conceals the really monstrous thing about them: the concentration of private persons as such by the accident of their private interests. But if these concentrations become evident – and the totalitarian states see to it by making the concentration of their clients permanent and obligatory for all their purposes – their hybrid character clearly manifests itself, and particularly to those involved.[327]

Engels, whom Benjamin quotes elsewhere in this connection on 'the brutal indifference' of the crowd in the great cities concludes that 'one shrinks before the consequences of our social state as they manifest themselves here undisguised, and can only wonder that the whole crazy fabric still hangs together'.[328]

This unpleasant aspect of metropolitan existence, which Simmel also later recognized, could be countered for a while by the physiologies of the earlier part of the nineteenth century. They sought – as in Britain in Dickens's *Sketches by Boz* – 'to give people a friendly picture of one another. Thus the physiologies helped fashion the phantasmagoria of Parisian life in their own way. But their method could not get them very far. People knew one another as debtors and creditors, salesmen and customers, employers and employees, and above all as competitors. In the long run it did not seem very likely that they could be made to believe their associates were harmless oddballs.'[329] In so far as the crowd became class-specific, 'this dispersed the illusion of the mass by means of the reality of class'.[330] But the experience of the *flâneur* who produced the early physiologies ensured that such a realization would not transpire since 'the "crowd" is the veil that hides the "mass" from the *flâneur*'.[331] A note in 'Zentralpark' announces Benjamin's largely unfulfilled intention of dealing with 'the concept of the multitude and the relation between "crowd" and "mass"'.[332]

What is more fully worked out, however, is the relationship between the *flâneur* and the crowd. The *flâneur* could wander through Victor Hugo's 'teeming city, city full of dreams' only so long as the crowd did not take on a definite shape – as a social class, for instance – and only as long as the street could still be conceived as an *intérieur* (as it was most obviously in the arcades). The full, concrete horror of the city's 'human turmoil' did not strike the *flâneur* since

For the *flâneur* there is a veil over this picture. This veil is the mass; it billows in 'the twisting folds of the old metropolises'. Because of it, horrors have an enchanting effect upon him. Only when this veil tears and reveals to the *flâneur* 'one of the populous squares . . . which are empty during street fighting' does he, too, get an unobstructed view of the big city.[333]

This naked image of the city was, however, seldom revealed to the *flâneur*. Instead, in Baudelaire's work, the *flâneur* was one of the guises of the modern hero set against the landscape of the city. Another was dandyism – 'the last shimmer of the heroic in times of decadence'.[334] Along with the apache and the ragpicker, however, they were merely roles to be played in the face of modernity: 'For the modern hero is no hero; he acts heroes. Heroic modernism turns out to be a tragedy in which the hero's part is available.'[335]

The true *flâneur* was a transitory phenomenon threatened by the masses and the commoditization of production. His heroic stance, his idling stroll may have been 'a demonstration against the division of labour' but it had to confront 'the obsession of Taylor, of his collaborators and successors . . . the "war against *flânerie*" (Georges Friedmann). The *flâneur*'s attitude 'did not prevail; Taylor, who popularised the watchword "Down with dawdling!" carried the day.'[336] Changes in the nature of city life and the needs of commodity production and circulation deprived the *flâneur* of his milieu. He could no longer relate to his ancient garb: 'In the *flâneur*, one might say, the idler returns just as Socrates left him as discussant on the Athenian marketplace. Only Socrates exists no more and thus he remains unspoken to. And the slave labour, too, has ceased which guaranteed him his idling.'[337] It became more difficult for the *flâneur* to retain the conception that 'the product of idling is more valuable than that of work'. The *flâneur*'s composure gave way to the manic behaviour of Poe's 'Man of the Crowd'.

In the metropolitan crowd, the experience of shock is paramount, as Simmel had earlier recognized in his correlation of urbanism and the dramatic increase in nervousness. The minute mechanical movements and their rapidity and sudden consequences – striking a match, the photographer's 'snapping' where complemented by 'optic ones such as are supplied by the advertising pages of a newspaper or the traffic of a big city. Moving through this traffic involves the individual in a series of shocks and collisions. At dangerous crossings, nervous impulses flow through him in rapid succession, like the energy from a battery.' Baudelaire referred to this sudden immersion in a crowd as being as if 'into a reservoir of electric energy. Circumscribing the experience of shock, he calls this man "a *kaleidescope* equipped with consciousness".[338] In the century that has succeeded Baudelaire, the shocks of the new have become more refined and more frequent.

If the *flâneur*'s 'leisurely appearance as a personality' constituted for a brief period a 'protest against the division of labour which makes people into specialists' and 'against their industriousness',[339] then his abandonment and ultimate submersion in the crowd suggested that he had already succumbed to the world of commodities, either as a commodity himself or as a consumer. Benjamin detected this transformation of the *flâneur* with the development of mass consumerism and with it the transformation of the mass itself as commodities and as consumers. He argued that

> The crowd is not only the newest asylum of outlaws; it is also the latest narcotic for those abandoned. The *flâneur* is someone abandoned in the crowd. In this he shares the situation of the commodity. He is now aware of this special situation; but this does not diminish its effect on him and it permeates him blissfully like a narcotic that can compensate him for many humiliations.[340]

This is because 'the concentration of customers which makes the market which in turn makes the commodity into a commodity, enhances its attractiveness to the average buyer'. Ultimately, Benjamin saw the final apotheosis of the *flâneur* in the commodity advertising itself: 'The sandwichman is the last incarnation of the flaneur';[341] 'The true *flâneur salarié* (Henri Beraud) is the sandwichman'.[342]

More usually, however, Benjamin conceives of the *flâneur* as 'the spectator of the market'. As a writer in search of a market, the mass ceases to be an anonymous mass, it becomes a public. As a consumer, the *flâneur* negates his own existence; he becomes one of the crowd – of consumers. Benjamin saw the *flâneur*'s existence and habitat as fundamentally threatened by mass consumption:

> If the arcade is the classical form of the *intérieur*, which is how the *flâneur* sees the street, the department store is the form of the *intérieur's* decay. The bazaar is the last hangout of the *flâneur*. If in the beginning the street had become an *intérieur* for him, now this *intérieur* turned into a street, and he roamed through the labyrinth of merchandise as he had once roamed through the labyrinth of the city.[343]

But if mass consumption threatened the *flâneur*, then it transformed, equally, the shifting configuration of the mass itself.

If the mass was not welcomed in its threatening guise as a social movement and especially as a revolutionary movement, the same cannot be said of its configuration as a mass of consumers. It could willingly participate in the labyrinthine world of commodity exchange and circulation as a mass of consumers. This new constellation was indeed accentuated by the development of department stores – in Paris, the *grand magasins de nouveautés* – 'when for the first time in history, with the foundation of department stores, consumers begin to feel themselves as a mass'.[344] Like the arcades before them, the early department stores with their open floors, enabled the consumer to view the whole with a single glance. Architecturally, they sometimes borrowed elements of style from the oriental bazaar, perhaps to encourage a feeling of exoticism (and eroticism). Economically, they introduced a new principle of marketing: a large turnover and a smaller return on each individual item that was more than compensated by the mass sales. Benjamin summarized their characteristic as being that 'the customers feel themselves to be a mass; they are confronted with the stock of commodities; they pay fixed prices; they can "exchange".'[345]

But although the active participation of the mass as consumers was welcomed by those who introduced these new developments, their participation was encouraged on the basis of consumers' diminishing 'knowledge' and increased 'taste'. On the other hand,

> As a consequence of the manufacture of products as commodities for the market, people become less and less aware of the conditions of their production . . . The consumer . . . is not usually knowledgeable when he appears as a buyer . . . mass production, which aims at turning out inexpensive commodities must be bent upon disguising bad quality. In most cases it is actually in its interest that the buyer have little expertise. The more industry progresses, the more perfect are the imitations which it throws on the market.[346]

On the other hand, just as the expertness of the customer declines with mass production and mass marketing,

> the importance of his taste increases – both for him and for the manufacturer. For the consumer it has the value of a more or less elaborate masking of his lack of expertness. Its value to the manufacturer is a fresh stimulus to consumption.[347]

An active interest in the latest taste was therefore paid for by a more passive and diminishing knowledge of what it was that was being consumed.

This passivity existed not merely with regard to the fantasy world of the commodity in the arcade and the brightly lit department store (both could link the commodity with private dreams), but in the public sphere it reached its apogee in the second half of the nineteenth century in the world exhibitions – 'the places of pilgrimage to the fetish commodity' – to which the masses were invited as spectators. Indeed, 'the world exhibitions were the high school in which the masses, dragged away from consumption, learned to empathize with exchange value: "Look at everything, touch nothing." '[348] Their goal, as far as the masses were concerned, was distraction:

> The world exhibitions glorified the exchange-value of commodities. They created a framework in which their use-value receded into the background. They opened up a phantasmagoria into which people entered in order to be distracted. The entertainment industry made that easier for them by lifting them to the level of the commodity. They yielded to its manipulations while enjoying their alienation from themselves and from others.[349]

They formed the model, perhaps, for other temples for spectators: 'the exhibitions of industry as the secret construction schema of museums – art: industrial products projected into the past'.[350] That the world exhibitions were only for the anonymous masses is suggested by the fact that during the second world exhibition in Paris in 1855, worker delegations were excluded on the ground that they might create organizational possibilities for the workers.[351] Instead, the phantasmagoria of dead commodities in exotic settings continued to reign supreme within 'the universe of commodities'.

Those who go in search of the marketplace, the world of commodity exchange and the public face of the commodity in the world exhibition seek out the newness of the commodity. The ever-new face of the commodity that is created in new fashions and in advertising hides the ever-same reproduction of exchange values. This vital characteristic of modernity – the dialectic of the new and the ever-same – which Benjamin investigated earlier as the dialectic of modernity and antiquity, of the masses and the city, is examined now in the context of fashion and the life of the commodity. This was vital to Benjamin's Arcades Project since he maintained that its fundamental categories converged in 'the fetish character of the commodity'. The key to the dream world of the nineteenth century and to the central experiences of modernity were to be located in the commodity form which enveloped the environment in its spell. Benjamin cited Marx's claim that value in a commodity-producing capitalist society transforms every product of labour into a social hieroglyphic. In his own way, Benjamin sought to decipher the meaning of this hieroglyphic often in the least obvious places. The deciphering of the phantasmagoria of the nineteenth century was to bring his contemporaries to the point of awakening. The study of modernity was to be grounded in its prehistory in Baudelaire's nineteenth century Paris. There and elsewhere,

> it is precisely the modern which always conjures up prehistory. That happens here through the ambiguity which is peculiar to the social relations and events of this epoch. Ambiguity is the figurative appearance of the dialectic, the law of the dialectic at a standstill. This standstill is Utopia, and the dialectical image therefore a dream image. The commodity clearly provides such an image: as fetish.[352]

The image of the commodity was to be captured in the dialectic motion of the new and the ever-same.

The commodity makes its appearance on the market as something new. Baudelaire gave to modernity its strongest association with that which is absolutely new, a kind of heroic newness. Modernity shared this feature with an important dimension of the commodity:

> Newness is a quality which does not depend on the use-value of the commodity. It is the source of the illusion which belongs inalienably to the images which the collective unconscious engenders. It is the quintessence of false consciousness of which fashion is the tireless agent. This illusion of newness is reflected, like one mirror in another, in the illusion of the eternal ever-same.[353]

In the Paris of the mid-nineteenth century, the *flâneur* sought out the crowd 'in which he quelled his thirst for the new'.[354] His affinity with the newness of the commodity was even closer in that 'as long as the *flâneur* exhibited himself on the market, his *flânerie* reflected the fluctuations of the commodity'. In the end, his activity was graphically presented by the satirist Grandville as the 'adventure of the promenading commodity'.[355]

Yet this constant search for newness by the *flâneur* and the collectivity had important implications for the perception of time and space. On the one hand, 'the dreaming collectivity knows no history. To it, the course of events flows onwards as the ever same thing and the ever newest. The sensation of the newest, the most modern is, in fact, just as much the dream form of events as the eternal return of everything the same.' On the other hand, 'the perception of space that corresponds to this perception of time is the pervading and masked transparency of the world of the *flâneur*'.[356] The ever-new appearance of commodities as sensational and our shock-like perception of them serves only to dull the senses. We are compelled to seek out new ones in order to heighten the sensation once more – as Simmel had already maintained at the turn of the century.

Like Simmel earlier, Benjamin sought to analyse fashion in this light as 'the eternal return of the new' and also asks whether 'despite this, does there exist precisely in fashion the motif of redemption?'[357] Certainly, knowledge of fashion might take on the form of 'extraordinary anticipation' in the sense that 'each season brings in its newest creations some kind of secret flag signals of coming things. Whoever understands how to read them, already knows not only about new currents in art, but also about new legal statutes, wars and revolutions. – Undoubtedly, here lies the greatest attraction of fashion, but also the difficulty of making it fruitful.'[358] In this sense, the preoccupation with fashion in this century that could not deal with its natural future – death – becomes intelligible. Fashion endlessly mocks death, especially in its association with life, with women. Similarly, it is not surprising that in a century without expansive fantasies, 'the whole dream energy of a society had fled with renewed vehemence into the most inpenetrable, silent misty realm of fashion'.[359]

Again like Simmel, whose article on fashion he cited in his notes, Benjamin saw this eternal return of the same that manifests itself in fashion as having its origins in the 'dialectic of commodity production: the newness of the product (as stimulus to demand) acquires a hitherto unknown significance; the eternally ever-same appears obvious for the first time in mass production'.[360] Mass production produces the mass article whose resisting counterpart is the speciality which retains a faint aura of originality. In turn, the sale of mass articles and a mass of commodities required the development of ever-new fashions, new tastes and new forms of advertising. In 1861, Wilkie Collins's 'The Woman in White' was advertised on the first lithograph poster in London. By the end of the century art itself had taken to the walls in the *art nouveau* posters advertising commodities in an environment of pre-established harmony. Their ambiguity became evident. On the one hand, one might see that 'the advert is the ruse by which industry forces itself upon the dream'.[361] On the other, Benjamin asks of these posters of the turn of the century: 'did there not exist in these posters a likeness for things which in this earthly life none had yet experienced. A likeness for the everyday world of Utopia?'[362]

In such ways, Benjamin illuminated that which is often insufficiently recognized in the notion of the universalization of commodity production and exchange, namely that the masks which the commodity adopts extend into all spheres of life. One of Benjamin's important theses in relation to Baudelaire's work is that the latter's extensive use of allegory – which he shared with the baroque tragedies that Benjamin had studied earlier – reflects Baudelaire's attempt 'to trace the experience of the commodity back to the allegorical'.[363] Indeed, he argues, 'the specific devaluation of the world of things that is embodied in the commodity is the crucial aspects of Baudelaire's allegorical intention'.[364] The devaluation of the human environment by the commodity-based economy is not merely the source of Baudelaire's inspiration. It also calls forth a heroic, allegorical response to this devaluation and destruction that, unlike earlier allegories, does not have recourse to a lost world but is embedded in the present one from which there is no escape. Baudelaire's response involves confronting the commodity, as it were, head on. Yet, 'the recklessness of his attempt was exceeded by the recklessness of reality'.[365] Benjamin attempted, through his analysis of Baudelaire's work, to trace

> the remodelling of allegory in the commodity economy . . . Baudelaire's project was to bring out in the commodity its own aura. In an heroic manner, he sought to humanise the commodity. This attempt had its counterpart in the contemporary bourgeois one of humanising the commodity in a sentimental manner: like human beings, to give the commodity a house.[366]

An implication of this wider process was, of course, that people's objective environment took on increasingly 'the expression of the commodity'.[367] Yet, at the same time, the advert, for example, was to dissolve 'the commodity character of things. The deceptive obfuscation of the world of the commodity struggles against its distortion in the allegorical. The commodity seeks to look itself in the face. It celebrated its human manifestation in the whore.'

Again, like Simmel earlier, Benjamin took up 'the dialectical function of money in prostitution. It purchases desire and becomes, at the same time, the expression of shame . . . Certainly the whore's love is saleable. Not, however, the shame of her customers. It searches for a hiding-place for this quarter of an hour and finds the most genial one: in money.'[368] In the modern form 'which prostitution in major cities has acquired, the woman appears not merely as a commodity but in the most emphatic sense as a mass article'.[369] In its professional form, prostitution itself appears as wage-labour. But Benjamin seldom drew more radical conclusions from the portion of women as symbols and objects of sexual desire within the phantasmagoria of commodities and the world of unfulfilled desires, except in the context of his analysis of Baudelaire's images. The accent lay, in Baudelaire's case, upon male impotence. Baudelaire's images of women prefigure the erotical images of the art nouveau movement.[370]

Benjamin was more original in his analysis of the extension of the commodity form to the work of art. Its consequences, in terms of the reproducibility of the art work as a mass article, the disappearance of its aura and the reduction of the artist to a producer of commodities for a market, sealed off that retreat from modernity which, at times, had been suggested by Simmel. Ironically, however, the investigation of the author as producer was one of the few occasions upon which Benjamin looked in any depth upon the production process itself. Like Simmel before him, Benjamin came to it in a roundabout way through the analysis of consumption. It remained, as it were, the dark side of the commodity.

In his earlier work, especially 'The Work of Art in the Age of Mechanical Reproduction', Benjamin had already examined the social factors responsible for the decline in auratic experience. As Wolin explains, 'Benjamin defines the aura as "the unique phenomenon of a distance, however close (an object) may be". The aura testifies to the *authority* of art in its cultic form, its condition of inimitable uniqueness, a singularity in time and space which is the hallmark of its authenticity. "The uniqueness of a work of art", Benjamin observes, "is inseverable from its being embedded in the fabric of tradition".'[371] The increase in the technical means of reproduction means that the work of art's auratic value is displaced by its 'exhibition value' – especially within the *intérieur*. This is related to 'the desire of the contemporary masses to bring things "closer" spatially and humanly . . . Every day the urge grows stronger to get hold of an object at very close range by way of its likeness, its reproduction.'[372] This process signalizes, at the same time, the decline of the 'pathos of distance' which was asserted by both Nietzsche and Simmel.[373]

Later, Benjamin locates the decline of auratic experience more firmly within the sphere of commodity production: 'Within mass production there is an element of quite special significance for the decline of aura: that is the massive reproduction of images.'[374] Elsewhere, he saw two factors responsible. 'Mass production is the economic, the class struggle is the social major cause for the decline of aura.'[375] Of even greater significance for his attempt to outline the transformation in experience brought about by the commmodity was 'the threat to aura from the shock experience'.[376] The shock of the new replaces the aura surrounding the work of art embedded in tradition. Baudelaire, responding to the search for a market for his poetry sought to preserve both.

Baudelaire sought to make a heroic stand within the showplace of modernity, indeed 'to live at the heart of unreality (of illusion). Associated with this is that Baudelaire did not know nostalgia.'[377] There was no past that could be restored, no future that could be conceived as anything different from the present. Baudelaire adopted a heroicly defiant stance in relation to the world of the masses and the mass commodity. His image of life corresponded to this world of ever-same, new commodities; that of 'frozen unrest . . . that knows no development'.[378] It was an image of the world of commodity production – as in 'rêve parisien' – in which 'the forces of production appear at a standstill'. In turn, this 'phantasmagoria . . . recalls the world exhibitions, in which the bourgeosie acclaims the order of property and production of its ''halt awhile, you are so beautiful'''.[379] It accords with Nietzsche's doctrine of the eternal return in which he conceives of 'the major thought as Medusa head: all features of the world become rigid, a frozen death struggle.'[380] The very doctrine of the eternal return itself 'turns historical events themselves into the mass article'.[381] All the stranger, therefore, that this society should adhere to the notion of progress. As Benjamin asks: 'What does it mean – a world that sinks into rigor mortis, speaks of progress?'[382]

Such a world can do so because it reproduces the ever-new, the · continuous shock of the new. This exists primarily in the exchange and circulation of the commodity. The world of things becomes the world of commodities:

> The thing first exercises its effect of alienating people from one another as a commodity. It exercises it through its price. Insight into the exchange value of the commodity, into its substratum of equality – therein lies what is decisive. (The absolute qualitative identity of time,

in which work runs that produces exchange value, is the grey background out of which the screaming colours of sensation stand out in relief.)[383]

This ever-new world of modernity, originating in the world of commodities, but manifested elsewhere in the smallest and least significant places (the ever-same elevates the insignificant fragment into significance), transforms human experience of the world of nature, of things and of people.

In his revised version of the essay on Baudelaire – 'Some Motifs in Baudelaire' – Benjamin examined some dimensions of the transformation of human experience, indeed, in a specific sense, 'the increasing atrophy of experience'. Again, these insights were placed in the service of the illumination of Baudelaire's work. In particular, however, Benjamin sought to investigate an important dimension of the experience of modernity: the radical discontinuity of experience that is implicit in the fleeting, transitory and the fortuitous and is manifested as the shock or sensation of the ever-new. In a sense, therefore, his prehistory of modernity was to embody reflections on the social origins of the transformation of the structure of experience.

Benjamin's argument rests upon a distinctive conception of experience as being embedded in tradition and therefore connected with historical memory. For him, 'experience is indeed a matter of tradition, in collective existence as well as private life. It is less the product of facts firmly anchored in memory than of a convergence in memory of accumulated and frequently unconscious data.'[384] The latter is the product of the fusion of 'voluntary and involuntary recollection' that is rooted in concrete lived experience in which 'certain contents of the individual past combine with material of the collective past'.[385] Benjamin had earlier outlined such a conception of experience in relation to historical modes of communication in 'The Storyteller'. There, he distinguished between the activity of the storyteller and new forms of communication such as the modern novel or the provision of journalistic information. For the storyteller, 'it is not the object of the story to convey a happening *per se*, which is the purpose of information; rather it embeds it in the life of the storyteller in order to pass it on as experience to those listening.'[386] The story is the symbol of collectively secured experience. Hence, 'the replacement of the older narration by information, of information by sensation, reflects the increasing atrophy of experience'.[387] To take but one instance, that of journalistic information, its intention is 'to isolate what happens from the realm in which it could affect the experience of the reader. The principles of journalistic information (freshness of the news, brevity, comprehensibility and, above all, lack of connection between individual news items) contribute'[388] to this process. The individual, 'increasingly unable to assimilate the data of the world around him by way of experience' is forced either to take information abstracted from concrete experience as a substitute or to seek out other ways to experience that possess 'an issueless private character'. At the turn of the century and later, the search was underway for the inner '"true" experience as opposed to the kind that manifests itself in the standardized, denatured life of the civilised masses'.[389] It is a central motif of the whole *Jugendstil* movement that also informs Simmel's notion of modernity as the experience of the world as an inner world. It is summed up in the search for the inner, individually, lived-out experience (*das Erlebnis*). Collectively secured experience was being replaced by individually lived-out experience. Auratic experience was being replaced by the search for traces.

Possibly in response to Adorno's criticisms of the notion of the 'dreaming collectivity', Benjamin subsequently took up the issue of the dream in greater detail by drawing, however briefly, upon the work of Bergson, Freud and Theodor Reik. In particular, the notion of the constant bombardment of the mind by stimuli – and here Benjamin drew upon his earlier analysis of metropolitan experience and crowd (Simmel's examples figured here) – requires some organ that can take over these shocks and absorb or modify them. For Freud that organ was consciousness. Where it failed to register these shocks, the more likely were they to produce a traumatic effect. However, the shock could be constitutive for concrete experience as in the threshold to the arcades for instance or it might prevent the development of that concrete experience, as in adaptation to machine production.

Benjamin maintained, as had Simmel earlier, that the metropolis and the crowd were a central location for negative shock experience. Where consciousness is effectively alert as a screen against the bombardment of stimuli and impressions

the less do these impressions enter experience [*Erfahrung*], tending to remain in the sphere of a certain hour in one's life [*Erlebnis*]. Perhaps the special achievement of shock defence may be seen in its function of assigning to an incident a precise point in time in consciousness at the cost of the integrity of its contents. This would be a peak achievement of the intellect; it would turn the incident into a moment that has been lived [*Erlebnis*].[390]

Benjamin went on to extend this analysis of shock experience beyond the crowd and the metropolis – focal points of Baudelaire's own experience – to changes in the labour process. He thus extended his analysis of the experience of commodity exchange into that of commodity production, by drawing on Marx's account of machine production with its attendant reflex training for the worker, the worker's adaptation to the machine as an automat and the denial of the worker's previous experience of production. He drew an analogue here with the gambler whose activity exists within the time of experiencelessness (the gambler can always start afresh) and the worker within capitalist production, which recognizes only one conception of time, that of additional, equal units, i.e. empty, homogeneous time. More specifically, Benjamin asserts that

> The manipulation of the worker at the machine has no connection with the preceding operation for the very reason that it is its exact repetition. Since each operation at the machine is just as screened off from the preceding operation as a *coup* in a game of chance is from the one that preceded it, the drudgery of the labourer is, in its own way, a counterpart to the drudgery of the gambler. The work of both is equally devoid of substance.[391]

The restoration of creative work activity is a prerequisite for the development of concrete experience. Only in this sense does Benjamin's projected conclusion to one of his Arcades Project exposés hold true: 'Concrete experience [*Erfahrung*] is the product of labour. Individual lived experience [*Erlebnis*] is the phantasmagoria of the idler.'[392]

This empty, homogeneous time experience broken by negative shock experiences is complemented by the individual lived experience [*Erlebnis*] that is free of content and the past and therefore without any relation to real historical experience. The discontinuous experience of time, however, grasped in Baudelaire's *correspondences*, which 'may be described as an experience which seeks to establish itself in crisis-proof form',[393] does shatter the empty continuum of chronology. They constitute 'the data of remembrance – not historical data, but data of prehistory'.[394] Benjamin's own dialectical images sought to break into 'the time of the now' [*Jetztzeit*]. As has been pointed out in this context, 'the metaphorical reference to the flow of time has no place in this conception; instead of which, Benjamin speaks of a "field of force" and, even earlier in *One-Way Street*, of the work of art as a "centre of force"'.[395] The dialectical images of the prehistory of modernity were intended to illuminate this 'now time', not simply as a present time but that time in which the boundary between past and future had momentarily been breached. The historian who proceeds in this way is a kind of retrospective prophet who has more to say to us than those who keep in step with the present.

V

Benjamin's intended prehistory of modernity, located largely in Paris as capital of the nineteenth century, was to be secured in central dialectical images of antiquity and modernity, the city and the mass and the new and the ever-same. It commenced from the dream world of the nineteenth century whose sway over us had in many ways remained. Even experience of the world of modern technology could reveal correspondences between itself and the archaic symbol world of mythology. Benjamin's intention was to break through the phantasmagoria of modernity at its inception. Even the forms of heroism in modern life were to be exposed as forms of modern melancholy and boredom – the latter being conceived 'as index for participation in the dream of the collectivity'.[396] Boredom with the experience of modernity may be 'the threshold to great deeds', but they, in turn, are only likely to call forth forms of modern heroism. In the last chapter on his 'The Salon of 1846', for instance, entitled 'On the Heroism of Modern Life', Baudelaire pointed not merely to dandyism as a form of heroic resistance to boredom but also to the ultimate form of resistance, as it were, '*modern* suicides'.[397] In this way, Benjamin comments, 'suicide appears as the quintessence of modernity'.[398] Several decades after Baudelaire's death, the sociologist Emile Durkheim felt compelled to assess the role of 'the different currents of collective sadness' and 'collective melancholy' in causing the 'morbid effervescence' of suicide.[399]

As the individual's ultimate negation of the future, modern suicide is merely one of the extreme manifestations of the absence of the future in modernity. Just as 'the dreaming collectivity knows no history', so equally it cannot conceive of its future. Herein lie 'the social grounds for impotence: the fantasy of the bourgeois class ceased to concern itself with the future of the forces of production that it had unleashed (comparison between its classical utopias and those of the mid-nineteenth century). In that period, the distinctive ''cosiness'' goes together with this well-founded waning of social fantasy'.[400] What is left is 'the disordered mass of dead knowledge'[401] over which the brooder is left to puzzle and the labyrinths of modernity.

The most significant of the modern labyrinths was located in the world of commodity exchange and circulation which reproduced the ever-same as the ever-new. And 'in order to grasp the significance of *nouveauté*, one must return to the novelty in everyday life. Why does each person inform the other about the newest things? Probably in order to triumph over death. Thus, only if there is nothing really new.'[402] The elaboration of such experience into the doctrine of the eternal return was carried out in a variety of modes by Baudelaire, Blanqui and Nietzsche. That doctrine conjured up the phantasmagoria of happiness, though in a very distinctive manner. The notion of

> the eternal return is an attempt to connect the two antinomical principles of happiness with one another: namely, that of eternity and that of 'once more' – The idea of the eternal return conjures up out of the calamity of time the speculative idea (or the phantasmagoria) of happiness. Nietzsche's heroism is a counterpart to Baudelaire's, which conjures up the phantasmagoria of modernity out of the calamity of humdrum routines.[403]

And lest it be thought that the eternal return of the ever-same only manifests itself at the higher cosmic level of, say, Blanqui's devastating inversion of bourgeois progress or Baudelaire's attack on the 'gloomy beacon' of progress, Benjamin insists that 'precisely in the minutiae of intermediary elements (*intermédiare*) the eternal same reveals itself'.[404] Similarly, Benjamin himself did not identify with these doctrines, however critical he was of the notion of progress in its bourgeois and socialist versions. Benjamin's messianic theological consciousness seldom led him into total despair.[405] His increasingly more developed Marxist position that coincides with the development of the Arcades Project and a greater confrontation with the Marxist standpoints of Brecht and later Korsch, as well as that of the members of the Frankfurt Institute, led him to take a critical stance not merely to that doctrine of despair but also to its political manifestations in the present.[406] In relation to the most developed version of the doctrine of the eternal return in Nietzsche's work, Benjamin detected its secret affinities: 'There exists an outline in which Caesar and not Zarathustra is the bearer of Nietzsche's doctrine . . . This is significant. It underlines the fact that Nietzsche had an inkling of the complicity of his doctrine with imperialism.'[407]

But all this should indicate that Benjamin's Arcades Project was in no way an orthodox historical project, not a history for 'idlers'. His construction of dialectical images of the prehistory of modernity was to proceed continuously 'until all of the past has been brought into the present in a historical *apocatastasis*'.[408] This restoration of the past out of forgottenness was to enable us to read the present out of the past, to awaken us into history. This 'coming awakening stands like the Greek's wooden horse in the Troy of the dream'.[409] In that horse was Benjamin himself; like Baudelaire, 'a secret agent – an agent of the secret discontent of his class with its own rule'[410] and, like Baudelaire, a 'destructive character'.

Conclusion

tempus fugit, aeternitas manet.

Boleslaw Prus, The Doll

There are no wholes in this world; rather, it consists of bits of chance events whose flow substitutes for meaningful continuity.

Siegfried Kracauer

In the fields with which we are concerned, knowledge comes only in flashes. The text is the thunder rolling long afterwards.

Walter Benjamin

In his 1939 Exposé for the Arcades Project, Benjamin declared that he would illuminate 'the new forms of life and the new creations' of the nineteenth century in the immediate forms in which they appeared – as phantasmagoria. For him, the world dominated by these phantasmagoria is modernity. His prehistory of modernity was to illuminate what he took to be the original site of modernity without, at the same time, denying that modernity reappears in various guises. Indeed, Benjamin declared that

> no epoch has existed that did not feel itself, in the most eccentric sense, to be 'modern' and consider itself to be standing immediately before an abyss. The despairing, wide-awake consciousness, standing immersed in a decisive crisis, is chronic in humanity. Every period appears to itself as unavoidably new. This 'modernity', however, is precisely that which is diverse just like the diverse aspects of one and the same kaleidoscope.[1]

Benjamin had gone in search of the original sense of modernity in the mid-nineteenth century in Paris. He had hoped to chart the decline of the arcades as a primal site at the turn of the century. Around the turn of the century, however, the *Jugendstil* movement in particular had declared its modernity, its adherence to the principles of an *art nouveau*. *This* site was investigated by Simmel as perhaps the first sociologist of modernity. His site was located firmly in Berlin, the capital of the 'new' Second German Reich. Three decades later, one of his students, Kracauer, re-examined the same site in the context of the city's development into a vanguard of modernity. The reactionary currents in this same modernity were destined, however, to contribute to that city's total destruction barely two decades later. Earlier, in fact, both Kracauer and Benjamin had been compelled to leave it.

Of the three figures investigating social dimensions of modernity, Simmel is the one whose work seems most totally bound up with Berlin, albeit in a very cosmopolitan circle within it.[2] Both Kracauer and Benjamin were to draw contrasts between Berlin and Paris. In Kracauer's case, his best Weimar work is arguably that associated with his analysis of the vanguard city of Berlin. For Benjamin, the first personal reawakening of the past was the reconstruction of his 'Berlin Childhood around Nineteen Hundred'. Around that time, the sober Baedeker's *Berlin and its Environs* had to concede that Berlin 'does not compete in antiquity or historical interest with the other great European capitals'. It did, however, point to 'its special and characteristic interest as the greatest purely modern city in Europe'. As a special attraction, which gave cause for both Kracauer and Benjamin to comment upon it in a very different manner, was the fact that 'its streets are a model of cleanliness'.[3] The sparklingly new and even the clean were amongst the 'diverse aspects' which the kaleidoscope of modernity revealed.

Though the traces and fragments of modernity were to be found everywhere in modern society – which meant, as often as not, that in their most obvious locations, their secrets remained undeciphered – there are nonetheless two locations which stand out above all others: the metropolis and capitalist social relations. For Simmel, Berlin at the turn of the century was his prime site; for Kracauer, Paris and, above all, Berlin in the Weimar period; and for Benjamin, at a personal level, that same Berlin but, in his most ambitious social theory of modernity, Paris in the mid-nineteenth century. With regard to capitalism, Simmel chose to emphasize the exchange and circulation process within the mature money economy; Kracauer highlighted the process of rationalization of production and social relations; and

Benjamin focused upon the process of commodity exchange and circulation and the attendant fetishism of commodities.

Simmel's examination of the metropolis as the social space within which the experiences of modernity are located is significant in a number of respects. As a complex, interwoven web or labyrinth of social relations, it is the location in which transitory, fleeting and fortuitous interactions take place that require only fragments of the individual personality to be involved. Indeed, the bombardment of the senses with a myriad of impressions and the constant juxtaposition to anonymous individuals produces an accentuated nervousness that requires modification by various forms of inward retreat and social distance, and even produces a state of complete indifference. Not surprisingly, therefore, this often provided the starting point for Simmel's pathbreaking sociology of the emotions and the senses. And as a sociologist preoccupied with forms of sociation and interaction, Simmel drew attention to the indefinite collectivities that assembled and dissolved within the social space of the city. Yet the crowd and other random configurations of people in the metropolis only gained significance through their confinement or dispersal within social space. Again, Simmel was one of the first to draw attention to that which, in a different manner, preoccupied both Kracauer and Benjamin – the social space of the metropolis.

Kracauer's analysis of the labyrinth of the metropolis, however, is one that is in many ways more precise and more threatening. He undertakes a rigorous investigation of the hieroglyphics of social space that focuses more directly upon the inanimate structures of the architectural and other spatial configurations of the metropolis. This 'forest of symbols' contains traces of meaning that require to be uncovered, fragments of lost experience that must be reconstructed. If, in the context of the secret symbolic world of the metropolis, Simmel chose to emphasize the protection of the nervous system by the creation of a quite conscious social distance (in a broader context, epitomized by the stranger) and the view of the city from above, as it were, Kracauer highlighted the 'dream-like expressive images' of the city that could only be deciphered by one who viewed things from below. In this respect, Benjamin's description of Kracauer as 'a ragpicker' is an apposite one – the collector of fortuitous images, of 'fortuitous creations' out of the configurations that, from the everyday standpoint, we choose to pass by and ignore. His contrast between Paris and Berlin brings out a further feature of this activity, namely the location of the fragments of spatial and other figurations within history in Paris and their location in Berlin within an unhistorical present in which the past is absent. The city thereby takes on the form of a temporal as well as a historical location. In his bleakest analyses of the vanguard city of Berlin, this temporal location is not merely that of the absolutely new but that of an empty, unhistorical time. Its facades hide the traces of history and humanity that could give meaning to its symbols. Kracauer's interiors, too, require an ideological–critical unmasking in order to become 'filled by reality itself', however barren it may be.

In Benjamin's case, it was Paris that originally provided him with the model of the metropolis as a labyrinth, both in terms of his own direct experiences in the course of his sojourns with Hessel and in the reflections stimulated by the surrealist visions of Aragon and others. But the mature concern with the metropolis as the site of lost or fragmentary remembrances was gained a few years later with his attempt to reconstruct his own childhood in Berlin at the turn of the century. Armed with that which Baudelaire declared to be 'the naive gaze of childhood' – which Benjamin had to restore – and his own concern for the redemption of the past, he turned once more to Paris as the site for the prehistory of modernity in the nineteenth century. Although never brought to fruition, Benjamin hoped to complete the circle, as it were, by extending that prehistory of modernity down to turn of the century and down to his own primal experiences of the city that were located in the deeper world of real objects of experience.

Yet this whole project was in no way construed as a celebration of the metropolis. For, as Benjamin observed in relation to Kracauer's study of white collar employees in Berlin, 'at the moment in which the first traces of an active love for the capital city reveals itself, one goes in search for the first time of its defects'.[4] If, in the Arcades Project, Benjamin wished to show how Baudelaire 'lies embedded in the nineteenth century', then a crucial part of that ground was 'Paris as *the* city of modernity'. The various layers of intersecting labyrinths constituted by the arcades and other 'dream houses', the streets themselves, the mythical nether world that lay beneath them, the masses who populated the streets and, finally, the labyrinth of human consciousness itself with its phantasmagoria of illusions all required careful excavation in order to reveal the primal site of modernity. In so doing, however, the metropolis became one site whose extension lay within capitalist social relations themselves.

This was stated quite explicitly at the end of Simmel's essay on the metropolis, except that what he had in mind was the social relations generated and transformed by a mature money economy. Money, and the exchange relations which it required, was significant because it was a means for 'the presentation of relations that exist between the most superficial, "realistic" and fortuitous phenomena and . . . the most profound currents of individual life and history'. Money relations could be readily viewed as fleeting, transitory and fortuitous. Yet although this was to recommend them to a social theory of modernity, their phenomenal forms were not Simmel's sole concern. He might start out with 'what is apparently most superficial and insubstantial', but his interest extended to 'the inner substance of life' and 'the essential forms of movements'. This did not, in the end, imply an analysis that economically went beyond the exchange and circulation spheres. Rather, in his later work, Simmel was to assert that 'the "fetishism" which Marx assigned to economic commodities represents only a special case of . . . [the] general fate of contents of culture', which followed their own 'immanent logic of development'. Since the future held in store an *eternally* tragic relationship between subjective and objective culture, the features of modernity which Simmel highlighted were condemned to be eternally present too.

Kracauer's analysis of modernity in relation to capitalism starts out in his early writings from a similar disjunction between the 'enormous material advance' of capitalism, and the attendant expansion of a restricted form of instrumental reason, and the impoverishment of individuality. Yet when, from the mid-1920s onwards, he came to develop his most powerful analysis of the 'insignificant superficial manifestations' of modernity, he focused not merely upon 'the thoroughly rationalised, civilised society' of capitalism but the manifestations and consequences of a concrete process of rationalization of production that permeated those spheres that were seemingly only indirectly related to the production process. Nonetheless, the 'daydreams' of this society, for example, did ultimately accord in a distorted manner with the maintenance of the essential social, economic and political relations of an increasingly contradictory social formation. In this respect, the experiences of modernity were located within an increasingly precarious present whose 'extremes' were the focal point for the illumination of modernity.

At times, Benjamin's analysis of capitalist social relations seems to possess affinities with that of Simmel, if we interpret the latter's focus upon capitalism in terms of the exchange and circulation of commodities (and not merely money). Certainly the production process only figures in a roundabout way in Benjamin's analysis of modernity, though the significance of his treatment of artistic production runs counter to this. However, what did become a central focus of Benjamin's analysis was the working out and exemplification of commodity fetishism within the fragments of modernity, in such a way that one could see beyond and behind the reified world of 'the commodity's halo'. Benjamin's exposure of the 'secret life' of the commodity rested upon a distinctive application of the theory of commodity fetishism that focused upon the dialectic of the ever-new face of the commodity and its ever-same circulation and exchange. Like Kracauer, Benjamin was fascinated by the fantasy world which such a process generated and reproduced. But his intention was not the celebration of this world of illusion. The search for the origins of modernity in the nineteenth century had as its goal the bringing to consciousness and destruction of phantasmagorias of capitalism. As Kracauer discerned in relation to the first of Benjamin's forays into modernity in *One-Way Street*, Benjamin had embarked upon his project because he wished 'to wake the world from its dream'. Long before Benjamin took his own life in 1940, that dream had become a nightmare.

For all three authors, the actual analysis of modernity was conceived in a novel and often radical manner. The discontinuity of modern experience, the recognition of its transitory, fleeting and arbitrary or fortuitous nature posed problems of investigation which, in their diverse ways, they sought to solve. They all sought, as it were, to complete the fragment, indeed to redeem it aesthetically, politically or historically. Viewed historically, modernity could be investigated as an eternal present, as a contradictory (and transitory) actuality and as a prehistory. For Simmel, Kracauer and Benjamin, this was not carried out in order to produce comprehensive, abstract theories of modernity, Simmel's 'fortuitous fragments of reality', Kracauer's 'insignificant superficial manifestations' and Benjamin's 'dialectical images' or 'monads' all redeemed the smallest, most insignificant traces of modernity in the everyday world. In their different ways, they each sought to decipher the secrets of modernity's fragments.

Each of their investigations of modernity is a testimony to that which Habermas has viewed as being absent in the work of more comprehensive theories of modernization, namely attention to and regard for the actual modes of experiencing modernity in everyday life. Since Simmel saw modernity as the translation of the world of experience into an inner world, he not merely went in search of 'the delicate, invisible threads' of experience of modern forms of interaction but also became preoccupied with the development of a social theory of the senses and the emotions. In other words, inner experience itself became the subject of social investigations.

For Kracauer, the world of modernity was one in which its various components had either been robbed of indigenous meaning or had been forced into a limited instrumental meaning. When Kracauer sought out the meanings residing in the profane fragments, he confronted two features not emphasized in Simmel's analysis of modernity. The first was the ideological responses within modernity in the form of 'daydreams' that accorded with a particular form of social domination. The second was the significance of mass symbols in understanding modernity's fragments, first announced in 'The Mass Ornament'. Kracauer went on to uncover the dark side of modernity, as it were, to reveal what lay hidden in 'the back courts of society'. Whereas Simmel could still conceive of the preservation of a quasi-autonomous sphere of creativity for the individual in the artistic and moral realms against the growing fragmenting power of objective culture, Kracauer maintained that the individual retreat from modernity was no longer possible. On the other hand, the future of the mass culture of modernity was rendered both ambiguous and precarious.

The world of modernity, for Benjamin, was a world of fantasy and illusion generated, ultimately, by the domination of commodity production, circulation and exchange. Even the poet of modernity, Baudelaire, could only give expression to this reified world allegorically since 'the allegorical perspective is always built upon a devalued phenomenal world' whose fundamental aspect was constituted by the commodity. With an increasing urgency, Benjamin sought to break through this reified world by means of his dialectical images in order to awaken the 'dreaming collectivity' from its dream. This could only be achieved by the remembrance of what had been forgotten about this reified world. Adorno hoped that Benjamin's theory of the experience of modernity would include 'the whole opposition between individual lived experience [*Erlebnis*] and concrete experience [*Erfahrung*] in a dialectical theory of forgetfulness. One might even say, in a theory of reification. For all reification is a form of forgetfulness [*ein Vergessen*]: objects become reified in that movement in which they are taken up, without being presently relevant in all their aspects, in which something about them is forgotten.'[5] The mere experience of the ever-new forgets that its fundamental precondition is the ever-same reproduction of the social relations necessary for the ever-new to appear. To speak of post-modernity, on this view, would therefore be premature.

Notes

INTRODUCTION

1. G. Simmel, *The Philosophy of Money*, translated by T. Bottomore and D. Frisby, London/Boston 1978 (second German edition 1907).
2. W. Benjamin, *One-Way Street*, translated by E. Jephcott and K. Shorter, New York 1978/London 1979.
3. Simmel, *Philosophy of Money*, p. 55.
4. S. Kracauer, *Das Ornament der Masse*, Frankfurt 1977, p. 50.
5. S. Kracauer, *Schriften*, 1, Frankfurt 1971, p. 207.
6. S. Kracauer, *Jacques Offenbach und das Paris seiner Seit*, Frankfurt 1976 (original edition Amsterdam 1937). English translation by G. David and E. Mosbacher, *Offenbach and the Paris of his Time*, London 1937.
7. T. W. Adorno, 'Benjamins "Einbahnstrasse"', in T. W. Adorno et al., *Über Walter Benjamin*, Frankfurt 1968, pp. 58–9.
8. W. Benjamin, *Charles Baudelaire: A Lyric Poet in the Era of High Capitalism*, translated by H. Zohn, London 1973.
9. Adorno, 'Charakteristik Walter Benjamins', in T. W. Adorno, *Über Walter Benjamin*, Frankfurt 1970, p. 26.
10. A. Salz, 'A Note from a Student of Simmel's', in K. H. Wolff (ed.), *Essays on Sociology, Philosophy and Aesthetics by Georg Simmel et al.*, Columbus, Ohio 1959, p. 235.
11. S. Kracauer, *Georg Simmel, Ein Beitrag zur Deutung desgeistigen Lebens unserer Zeit*, typescript, probably 1919, 147 pages, Siegfried Kracauer Nachlass, Deutsche Literaturarchiv, Marbach/Neckar, p. 92.
12. G. Scholem, *Walter Benjamin. The Story of a Friendship*, London 1982, p. 92.
13. W. Benjamin, *The Origins of German Tragedy*, translated by J. Osborne, London 1977.
14. T. W. Adorno, *Über Walter Benjamin*, Frankfurt 1970.
15. W. Benjamin, *Briefe*, 2, Frankfurt 1966, p. 808.
16. W. Benjamin, *Das Passagen-Werk*, Frankfurt 1982.
17. L. Coser, *Georg Simmel*, Englewood Cliffs 1965, p. 29 ff.

MODERNITÉ

1. J. Habermas, 'Die Moderne – ein unvollendetes Projekt', in *Kleine Politische Schriften*, (I-IV), Frankfurt 1981, pp. 444–64.
2. J.-F. Lyotard, *The Postmodern Condition: A Report on Knowledge*, Minnesota/Manchester 1984, p. 72.
3. Ibid., p. 79.
4. Ibid., p. 81.
5. F. Tönnies, *Community and Association*, translated by C. P. Loomis, London 1955, p. 4.
6. Habermas, 'Die Moderne', p. 446.
7. C. Baudelaire, 'The Painter of Modern Life', in C. Baudelaire, *The Painter of Modern Life and Other Essays*, translated and edited by J. Mayne, London 1964, pp. 1–40.
8. W. Benjamin, *Gesammelte Schriften*, (Werkausgabe), I, 3, Frankfurt 1980, p. 1152.
9. D. Oehler, *Pariser Bilder 1 (1830–1848). Antibourgeoise Ästhetik bei Baudelaire, Daumier und Heine*, Frankfurt 1979, p. 193.
10. Baudelaire, 'Painter of Modern Life', p. 1.
11. Ibid., p. 13.
12. Ibid., p. 3.
13. H. R. Jauss, 'Literarische Tradition und gegenwartiges Bewusstsein der Modernität', in his *Literaturgeschichte als Provokation*, Frankfurt 1970, pp. 11–66, especially p. 56.
14. Ibid.
15. Baudelaire, 'Painter of Modern Life', p. 4.
16. Ibid., p. 7.
17. Ibid., p. 8.
18. Ibid., p. 9.
19. Ibid., pp. 9–10.
20. Ibid., p. 11.
21. Ibid., p. 15.
22. Ibid., p. 18.
23. Ibid., p. 32.
24. Ibid., p. 12.
25. Oehler, *Pariser Bilder 1*, p. 248.
26. H. R. Jauss, 'Literarische Tradition', p. 53.
27. Baudelaire, 'Painter of Modern Life', p. 14.
28. Ibid., p. 29. On the significance of dandyism for modernity see Oehler, *Pariser Bilder 1*, pp. 199–200; I. Wohlfarth, '*Perte d'auréole*: The Emergence of the Dandy', *Modern Language Notes*, 48, 1970, pp. 529–71.
29. H. Lefebvre, *Einführung in die Modernität. Zwölf Präludien*, Frankfurt 1978, p. 201.

30. See Oehler, *Pariser Bilder 1*, and O. Sahlberg, *Baudelaire und seine Muse auf dem Weg zur Revolution*, Frankfurt 1980. On the whole literary and social context of the Revolution of 1848 see W. Feitkau, *Schwanengesang auf 1848. Ein Rendezvous am Louvre: Baudelaire, Marx, Proudhon und Victor Hugo*, Reinbek bei Hamburg 1978.
31. Oehler, *Pariser Bilder 1*, p. 261.
32. Ibid., p. 85.
33. W. Benjamin, *Illuminations*, translated by H. Zohn, New York 1969, p. 256. The context is Benjamin's 'Theses on the Philosophy of History' which he drafted in 1940.
34. M. Berman, *All That Is Solid Melts Into Air: The Experience of Modernity*, New York 1982/London 1983, p. 129.
35. K. Marx and F. Engels, 'The Communist Manifesto' in K. Marx, *The Revolutions of 1848*, Harmondsworth 1973, pp. 67–98, esp. pp. 70–3.
36. Berman, *All That Is Solid*, p. 89.
37. Berman, *All That Is Solid*, p. 95.
38. Marx and Engels, 'Communist Manifesto', p. 70.
39. Quoted in E. Pankoke, *Sociale Bewegung – Sociale Frage – Sociale Politik*, Stuttgart 1970, pp. 19–47. English translation, 'Social Movement', by D. Frisby, *Economy and Society*, 11, 2, 1982, pp. 317–46.
40. K. Marx, *Theories of Surplus Value*, Part III, London 1972, p. 514.
41. K. Marx, 'Preface to the First Edition' in K. Marx, *Capital*, vol. 1, Harmondsworth 1976, p. 89. For a detailed analysis of Marx's starting point see D. Sayer, *Marx's Method*, Brighton/Atlantic Heights, NJ, 1979.
42. Marx, *Capital*, vol. 1, p. 90.
43. Ibid., p. 163.
44. Ibid., pp. 168–9.
45. Ibid., p. 168.
46. Ibid., pp. 164–5.
47. Marx, *Surplus Value*, Part III, p. 453.
48. Marx, *Capital*, vol. 1, p. 175.
49. Ibid., p. 174.
50. Ibid.
51. Marx, *Surplus Value*, Part III, p. 514.
52. Marx, *Capital*, vol. 1, p. 187.
53. Marx, *Surplus Value*, Part III, p. 455.
54. Ibid., p. 458.
55. Ibid., p. 456.
56. Marx, Capital, vol. 3, Harmondsworth 1981, p. 953.
57. Ibid., p. 969.
58. Marx, *Surplus Value*, Part III, p. 503.
59. Ibid.
60. Habermas, 'Die Moderne', p. 447.

61. H. Fischer, *Nietzsche Apostata oder Die Philosophie des Ärgernisse*, Erfurt 1931, pp. 13f.
62. K. Marx, *Surveys from Exile*, Harmondsworth 1973, p. 171.
63. Ibid., p. 170.
64. Fischer, *Nietzsche Apostata*, p. 16.
65. F. Nietzsche, *Untimely Meditations*, translated by R. J. Hollingdale, Cambridge 1983, p. 216.
66. F. Nietzsche, *Sämtliche Werke. Kritische Studienausgabe*, edited by G. Colli and M. Montinari, Berlin/New York 1980, vol. 13, p. 238.
67. Ibid., p. 504.
68. On Nietzsche's relation to sociology and his 'anti-sociology' see H. B. Baier, 'Die Gesellschaft – ein langer Schatten des toten Gottes. Friedrich Nietzsche und die Entstehung der Soziologie aus dem Geist der decadence', *Nietzsche Studien*, 10/11, 1981/82, pp. 6–22.
69. Nietzsche, *Sämtliche Werke*, vol. 5, p. 52.
70. Nietzsche, *Untimely Meditations*, p. 229.
71. Ibid., pp. 148–9.
72. Ibid., p. 209.
73. Nietzsche, *Sämtliche Werke*, vol. 7, p. 817.
74. Ibid., pp. 814–5.
75. Ibid., p. 815.
76. See R. R. Wuthenow, *Muse, Maske, Meduse. Europäischer Ästhetizismus*, Frankfurt 1978, pp. 10f.
77. Nietzsche, *Untimely Meditations*, p. 221.
78. Ibid., p. 62.
79. Ibid., p. 66.
80. Ibid., p. 106.
81. Ibid., p. 120.
82. Ibid., p. 120.
83. Ibid., p. 94.
84. F. Nietzsche, *Twilight of the Idols. The Anti-Christ*, translated by R. J. Hollingdale, Harmondsworth 1968, p. 96.
85. Nietzsche, *Untimely Meditations*, pp. 92–3.
86. Nietzsche, *Sämtliche Werke*, vol. 13, p. 236.
87. Nietzsche, *Sämtliche Werke*, vol. 6, p. 27.
88. Nietzsche, *Twilight of the Idols*, pp. 93–4.
89. Ibid., p. 94.
90. Quoted in J. Stambaugh, *Nietzsche's Thought of Eternal Return*, Baltimore/London 1972, p. 17. I have found this a useful guide to Nietzsche's doctrine.
91. Ibid.
92. Ibid., p. 25.
93. Ibid., pp. 36–7.
94. Quoted in K. Lichtblau, 'Das "Pathos der Distanz". Präliminarien zur Nietzsche-Rezeption bei Georg Simmel' in H. J. Dahme and

O.Rammstedt (eds) *Georg Simmel und die Moderne*, Frankfurt 1984, pp. 231–81, esp. pp. 260–1.

95. The influence of Nietzsche upon Simmel has not yet been fully examined. The article by Lichtblau is a valuable exception. See also Simmel's most detailed treatment of Nietzsche in G. Simmel, *Schopenhauer und Nietzsche*, Leipzig, 1907.

96. M. Weber, *Economy and Society* edited by G. Roth and C. Wittich, Berkeley/Los Angeles/London 1978, p. 506.

97. On the neglected reception of Nietzsche's work by Benjamin see H. Pfotenhauer, 'Benjamin und Nietzsche' in B. Lindner (ed.) *'Links hatte noch alles sich zu enträtseln . . .' Walter Benjamin in Kontext*, Frankfurt 1978, pp. 100–26. Benjamin's major secondary source on Nietzsche's doctrine of the eternal return was K. Löwith, *Nietzsche's Philosophie der ewigen Wiederkunft des Gleichen*, Berlin 1935.

98. On the significance of Blanqui's work for Benjamin see F. Rella, 'Benjamin und Blanqui' in M. Brodersen, *Benjamin auf Italienisch. Aspekte einer Rezeption*, Frankfurt 1982, pp. 77–102.

99. See Pfotenhauer, 'Benjamin und Nietzsche'.

100. Quoted in W. Benjamin, *Das Passagen-Werk* (Gesammelte Schriften V), edited by R. Tiedemann, Frankfurt 1982, p. 173.

101. Benjamin, *Gesammelte Schriften*, I, p. 673.

102. Ibid., p. 683.

GEORG SIMMEL:
MODERNITY AS AN ETERNAL PRESENT

1. Berman, *All That Is Solid*, p. 28. There Berman adds that 'In Simmel – and later in his youthful followers Georg Lukács, T. W. Adorno and Walter Benjamin – dialectical vision and depth are always entangled, often in the same sentence, with monolithic cultural despair', thereby displaying the absence of a careful reading of Simmel's works and a misinterpretation of his 'followers', of whom Adorno was not one. Only Lukács actually studied with Simmel, whilst the latter's relationship to Benjamin is examined below.

2. See, for instance, 'The Concept and Tragedy of Culture', in G. Simmel, *The Conflict in Modern Culture and Other Essays*, translated and edited by P. K. Etzkorn, New York 1968, pp. 27–46.

3. On Simmel's early work see my 'Georg Simmel and Social Psychology', *Journal of the History of the Behavioral Sciences*, 20, 2, 1984, pp. 107–27. On Simmel's contribution to a sociology of the emotions see B. Nedelmann, 'Georg Simmel – Emotion und Wechselwirkung in intimen Gruppen', *Kölner Zeitschrift für Soziologie und Sozialpsychologie*, Sonderheft 25, 1983, pp. 174–209.

4. P. Fechter, 'Erinnerungen an Simmel', in K. Gassen and M. Landmann (eds), *Buch des Dankes an Georg Simmel*, Berlin 1958, p. 159.

5. F. Wolters, 'Erinnerungen an Simmel', in Gassen and Landmann (eds), *Buch des Dankes*, p. 195.

6. K. Jöel, 'Eine Zeitphilosophie', *Neue Deutsche Rundschau*, vol. 12, 1901, pp. 812–26.

7. D. Koigen, 'Sociologische Theorien', *Archiv für Sozialwissenschaft und Sozialpolitik*, vol. 31, 1910, p. 24.

8. E. Troeltsch, *Der Historismus und seine Probleme*, Tübingen 1922, p. 593.

9. E. Troeltsch, 'Der historische Entwicklungsbegriff in der modernen Geistes und Lebensphilosophie', *Historische Zeitschrift*, vol. 124, (1921), p. 431.

10. H. J. Becher, *Georg Simmel, Die Grundlagen seiner Soziologie*, Stuttgart 1971, pp. 23–4. From a different perspective, I have discussed Simmel's 'philosophy of the times' in my *Sociological Impressionism*, London 1981, ch. 5.

11. C. Baudelaire, 'Painter of Modern Life', p. 40.

12. G. Simmel, 'Das Problem des Stiles', *Dekorative Kunst* vol. 11, 7, 1908, p. 313.

13. H. G. Gadamer, *Truth and Method*, London 1975, p. 57.

14. In particular, see G. Simmel, *Rembrandt. Ein Kunstphilosophischer Versuch*, Leipzig 1916.

15. S. Kracauer, *Georg Simmel, Ein Beitrag zur Deutung des geistigen Lebens unserer Zeit*, typescript, probably 1919, 147 pages, Siegfried Kracauer Nachlass, Deutsche Literaturarchiv, Marbach/Neckar, p. 92.

16. G. Simmel, 'Tendencies in German Life and Thought since 1870', *International Monthly* (New York), 5, 1902, pp. 93–111, 166–84.

17. Ibid., p. 93.

18. Ibid., p. 95.

19. Ibid., p. 99.

20. Ibid., p. 101.

21. The levelling tendencies are examined in detail in G. Simmel *Philosophy of Money*, although the theme is already present in G. Simmel, *Über sociale Differenzierung*, Leipzig 1890. For a discussion of this early work see my *Georg Simmel* Chichester/London/New York 1984, pp. 76–93.

22. Simmel, 'Tendencies in German Life and Thought', pp. 176–7.

23. Ibid., p. 179.

24. F. Tönnies, 'Considérations sur l'histoire moderne', *Annales de l'institut international de sociologie*, vol. 1, 1895, pp. 245–52, esp. p. 246.

25. G. Simmel, 'Die Grossstädte und das Geistesleben', in *Jahrbuch der Gehe-Stiftung zu Dresden*, vol. 9, 1903, p. 187.

26. G. Simmel, 'Die Kunst Rodins und das Bewegungsmotiv in der Plastik', *Nord und Süd*, vol. 129, 1909, II, pp. 189–96; expanded version as G. Simmel, 'Rodin', in *Philosophische Kultur*, Leipzig 1911. All references are to the third edition (Potsdam 1923).

27. Simmel, 'Rodin', p. 196.

28. Ibid., p. 197.

29. Ibid., p. 188.
30. See my *Sociological Impressionism*, p. 102f.
31. M. Weber, *Wissenschaft als Beruf*, Munich/Leipzig 1919, p. 14.
32. Ibid., p. 15.
33. Becher, *Georg Simmel*, p. 14.
34. Simmel, *Philosophy of Money*, p. 53.
35. Ibid., p. 56.
36. Ibid., p. 55.
37. Ibid., p. 56.
38. G. Simmel, *Kant und Goethe*, Berlin 1906, p. 65.
39. Simmel, *Philosophy of Money*, pp. 494–5.
40. Simmel, *Rembrandt*, p. 2.
41. Ibid., p. 51.
42. See, for instance, H. J. Lieber and P. Furth, 'Zur Dialektik der Simmelschen Konzeption einer formalen Soziologie', in Gassen and Landmann (eds), *Buch des Dankes*, pp. 39–59.
43. Simmel, *Philosophy of Money*, p. 450.
44. Ibid., p. 451.
45. Ibid.
46. Ibid., p. 202.
47. Ibid.
48. Ibid., p. 53.
49. Ibid., p. 56.
50. M. Susman, *Die geistige Gestalt Georg Simmels*, Tübingen 1960, p. 36.
51. Simmel, *Philosophy of Money*, p. 452.
52. R. Bubner, 'Über einige Bedingungen gegenwartiger Ästhetik', *Neue Hefte für Philosophie*, 5, 1973, pp. 38–73, esp. p. 38.
53. Simmel, *Über soziale Differenzierung*, p. 13.
54. Ibid.
55. G. Simmel, 'Das Problem der Soziologie', *Jahrbuch für Gesetzgebung, Verwaltung und Volkswirtschaft*, vol. 16, 1894, p. 272.
56. G. Simmel, 'Exkurs über das Problem: wie ist Gesellschaft möglich?', in G. Simmel, *Soziologie*, Berlin 1908; in English as 'How is Society Possible?', in K. H. Wolff (ed.), *Essays on Sociology, Philosophy and Aesthetics by Georg Simmel*, Columbus 1959, pp. 337–56, esp. p. 352.
57. S. Kracauer, 'Georg Simmel', *Logos*, vol. 9, 1920, p. 314.
58. Ibid., pp. 324f.
59. G. Simmel, 'Soziologie der Sinne', *Die Neue Rundschau*, vol. 18, 2, 1907, pp. 1025–36. The passages quoted below from the opening and concluding remarks to this essay do not appear in its reworked version, 'Exkurs über die Soziologie der Sinne', in Simmel, *Soziologie*, 5th edn, Berlin 1968, pp. 483–93.
60. Simmel, 'Soziologie der Sinne', p. 1025.
61. Ibid.
62. Ibid., p. 1026.

63. Ibid.
64. Ibid., p. 1035.
65. Ibid., p. 1026.
66. Ibid., p. 1027.
67. B. Nedelmann, 'Georg Simmel – Emotion und Wechselwirkung in intimen Gruppen', *Kölner Zeitschrift für Soziologie und Sozialpsychologie*, Sonderheft 25, 1983, pp. 174–209.
68. E. Bloch, *Geist der Utopie*, 2nd edn, Frankfurt 1964, p. 93.
69. G. Simmel, 'Soziologische Aesthetik', *Die Zukunft*, vol. 17, 1896, p. 206. There is an English translation as 'Sociological Aesthetics' in K. P. Etzkorn (ed. and trans.), *Georg Simmel. The Conflict in Modern Culture and Other Essays*, New York 1968, p. 69. For similar passages elsewhere, see Simmel, *Philosophy of Money*, pp. 462f.
70. G. Simmel, 'The Metropolis and Mental Life', in Wolff (ed.) *Sociology of Georg Simmel*, p. 413.
71. Simmel, 'Soziologische Aesthetik', p. 204.
72. M. Frischeisen-Kohler, 'Georg Simmel', *Kantstudien*, vol. 24, 1920, p. 13.
73. C. Schmidt, 'Eine Philosophie des Geldes', *Sozialistische Monatshefte*, vol. 5, 1901, pp. 180–5.
74. E. Durkheim, 'Philosophie des Geldes', *L'Année Sociologique*, vol. 5, 1900–01, pp. 140–5.
75. T. W. Adorno, 'A Portrait of Walter Benjamin', in *Prisms*, translated by S. Weber and S. Weber, London 1967, p. 231.
76. Ibid.
77. R. Hamann, *Der Impressionismus in Leben und Kunst*, Cologne 1907, p. 130. Hamann's study contains a wealth of material on the relationship between impressionism, the metropolis and the money economy which substantiates other contemporary characterizations of Simmel as a sociological impressionist. The key work which Hamann himself relies upon is *The Philosophy of Money*.
78. Troeltsch, 'Der historische Entwicklungsbegriff' pp. 593–4.
79. Kracauer, 'Georg Simmel', p. 318.
80. Schmidt, 'Eine Philosophie des Geldes', p. 181.
81. Kracauer, 'Georg Simmel', p. 331.
82. Ibid., p. 320.
83. See note 23 above.
84. Simmel, 'Rodin', p. 196.
85. Ibid.
86. Ibid., p. 182.
87. Ibid., p. 188.
88. Ibid., p. 197.
89. G. Simmel, 'Philosophie des Abenteuers', *Der Tag*, Berlin, 7 and 8 June 1910. Reprinted with minor changes as 'Das Abenteuer' in G. Simmel,

Philosophische Kultur, Leipzig 1911. All references are to the third edition (Potsdam 1923).

90. Simmel, 'Das Abenteuer', p. 20.

91. See L. Coser 'The Stranger in the Academy' in L. Coser (ed.), *Georg Simmel*, Englewood Cliffs, NJ 1965.

92. See 'The Stranger' in D. Levine (ed.), *Georg Simmel on Individuality and Social Forms*, Chicago/London 1971, p. 143.

93. Simmel, 'Das Abenteuer', p. 14. The discussion of dreaming is also important in Benjamin's development of a theory of experience in relation to modernity. As well as his Baudelaire study, the following secondary sources are also useful: J.-M. Gagnebin, *Zur Geschichtsphilosophie Walter Benjamins*, Erlangen 1978, ch. 2; K. Greffrath, *Metaphorische Materialismus*, Stuttgart 1980.

94. Simmel, 'Das Abenteuers', p. 15.

95. Ibid., p. 17.

96. Ibid., pp. 26–7.

97. Simmel, 'Soziologische Aesthetik', pp. 215–6.

98. Ibid., p. 29. Here the contrast with surrealism and Benjamin's reception of it is most marked. See 'Surrealism' in W. Benjamin, *One-Way Street*, pp. 224–39.

99. Ibid., p. 16.

100. Benjamin, *Das Passagen-Werk*, p. 962.

101. W. Benjamin, *Charles Baudelaire: A Lyric Poet in the Era of High Capitalism*, p. 106.

102. A. Koppel, 'Für und wider Karl Marx', *Volkswirtschaftliche Abhandlungen der Badischen Hochschulen*, vol. 8, no. 1, Karlsruhe 1905, p. 20.

103. G. Simmel, 'Auszüge aus den Lebenserinnerungen', in H. Böhringer and K. Gründer (eds), *Ästhetik und Soziologie um die Jahrhundertwende: Georg Simmel* Frankfurt 1976, p. 265.

104. For discussion of Simmel's sociological impressionism, see my *Sociological Impressionism*, esp. chs. 3, 4.

105. Hamann, *Der Impressionismus in Leben und Kunst*, p. 134.

106. Susman, *Die geistige Gestalt Georg Simmels*, p. 2.

107. Joël, 'Eine Zeitphilosophie', p. 813.

108. Simmel, 'Auszüge aus den Lebenserinnerungen', p. 265.

109. See my *Sociological Impressionism*, ch. 3.

110. T. W. Adorno, 'Benjamins "Einbahnstrasse"', in T. W. Adorno, et al., *Über Walter Benjamin*, Frankfurt 1968, p. 59.

111. Kracauer, *Georg Simmel*, p. 36.

112. Benjamin, *Gesammelte Schriften*, III, p. 196.

113. Benjamin, *Charles Baudelaire*, p. 130, n. 44.

114. Simmel, *Philosophy of Money*, p. 484.

115. Ibid., p. 481.

116. Ibid., p. 479.

117. Simmel, 'Die Grossstädte und das Geistesleben' (see note 22 above). There exist two English translations of this essay: 'The Metropolis and Mental Life'. The first, by E. Shils, is available in D. Levine (ed.) *Georg Simmel on Sociability and Social Forms*, Chicago/London 1971, pp. 324–39; the second, by H. H. Gerth and C. Wright Mills, in Wolff (ed.), *The Sociology of Georg Simmel*, pp. 409–74.

118. Simmel, *Philosophy of Money*, p. 474.

119. Simmel, 'Soziologische Aesthetik', p. 78.

120. Simmel, 'Die Grossstädte und das Geistesleben', p. 193.

121. Simmel, *Philosophy of Money*, p. 256.

122. Ibid., p. 257.

123. Ibid.

124. G. Simmel, 'Berliner Gewerbe-Ausstellung', *Die Zeit* (Vienna), vol. 8, 25 July 1896. For a fuller discussion see below. Much earlier, Simmel had already pointed to this thirst for constant stimulation in art exhibitions and related it, amongst other things, to metropolitan life. See Simmel, 'Über Kunstausstellungen' (Druckbogen 1888), Staatsbibliothek Preussischer Kulturbesitz, Berlin.

125. Simmel, 'Die Grossstädte und das Geistesleben', p. 195.

126. G. Simmel, *Der Krieg und die geistigen Entscheidungen*, Munich/Leipzig 1917, p. 25.

127. Quoted in Troeltsch, 'Der historische Entwicklungsbegriff', p. 431.

128. S. P. Altmann, 'Simmel's Philosophy of Money', *AJS*, vol. 9, 1904, p. 46.

129. K. Joël, 'Georg Simmel', *Die Neue Rundschau*, vol. 30, I, 1919, p. 243.

130. Everett C. Hughes, Foreword to G. Simmel, *Conflict and the Web of Group Affiliation*, New York 1955, p. 9.

131. Wuthenow, *Muse, Maske, Meduse*, pp. 195–6.

132. Ibid., p. 200.

133. L. V. Wiese, 'Neuere Soziologische Literatur', *Archiv für Sozialwissenschaft und Sozialpolitik*, vol. 31, 1910, p. 300. Extract translated in Coser (ed.), *Georg Simmel*, p. 56.

134. G. Simmel, 'Soziologie des Raumes', *Jahrbuch für Gesetzgebung, Verwaltung und Volkswirtschaft*, vol. 27, 1903, pp. 27–71, esp. p. 35. Interestingly this important, neglected essay on the sociology of space appeared in the same year as the more famous essay on the metropolis. Reworked, it subsequently appeared as 'Der Raum und die räumlichen Ordnungen der Gesellschaft' in chapter 9 of Simmel, *Soziologie*, pp. 460–526.

135. Simmel, 'Soziologie des Raumes', p. 38.

136. Benjamin, *Charles Baudelaire*, p. 151.

137. Simmel, 'Soziologie des Raumes', p. 52.

138. Ibid., p. 61.

139. Ibid., p. 63.

140. Simmel, 'Die Grossstädte und das Geistesleben', p. 187. For a recent discussion of Simmel's theory of the metropolis see M. P. Smith, *The City and Social Theory*, New York 1979, ch. 3.
141. Simmel, *Soziologie*, p. 563.
142. See, for example, G. Simmel, 'Das Problem des Stiles', *Dekorative Kunst*, vol. 11, 7, 1908, p. 314.
143. Simmel, 'Die Grossstädte und das Geistesleben', pp. 203–4.
144. Ibid., p. 189.
145. Ibid., p. 199.
146. Ibid., p. 202.
147. Ibid., pp. 191–2.
148. Ibid., p. 190.
149. Hamann, *Der Impressionismus in Leben und Kunst*, p. 136.
150. Ibid., p. 201.
151. Ibid., p. 202.
152. Ibid., p. 216.
153. Ibid., p. 217.
154. G. Simmel, 'Soziologie der Geselligkeit', *Verhandlungen des Ersten Deutschen Soziologentages (1910)*, Tübingen 1911, pp. 1–16. Translated by E. C. Hughes as 'The Sociology of Sociability', *AJS*, vol. 55, no. 3, 1949, and reprinted in Levine (ed.), *Georg Simmel on Individuality and Social Forms*, p. 129.
155. Simmel, *Soziologie*, p. 570.
156. Kracauer, 'Georg Simmel', p. 330.
157. R. Goldscheid, 'Jahresbericht über Erscheinungen der Soziologie in den Jahren 1899–1904', *Archiv für systematische Philosophie*, vol. 10, 1904, p. 143.
158. G. Lukács, 'Georg Simmel', in Gassen and Landmann (eds) *Buch des Dankes*, p. 175.
159. G. Simmel, *Philosophy of Money*, p. 510.
160. Ibid., p. 102.
161. Ibid., p. 511.
162. Ibid.
163. Ibid., pp. 510–11.
164. Ibid., p. 511.
165. Ibid., p. 101.
166. Ibid., p. 129.
167. Ibid., p. 175.
168. For a fuller discussion of Simmel's economic categories see my 'Introduction to the Translation' in Simmel, *Philosophy of Money*, and my *Sociological Impressionism*. Also H. Brinkmann, *Methode und Geschichte*, Giessen 1974. This psychological dimension gives Simmel's analysis close affinities with contemporary political economy which, as one reviewer of Simmel's work indicated, had its basis in 'applied psychology'. See C. Bouglé, 'Les sciences sociales en Allemagne', in *Revue de Métaphysique et de Morale*, vol. 2, 1894, pp. 329–55, esp. p. 348.

169. Simmel, *Philosophy of Money*, p. 176.
170. Ibid.
171. Ibid., p. 454.
172. Ibid., p. 455.
173. Ibid., p. 456.
174. Ibid.
175. Ibid., p. 459.
176. Ibid., p. 465.
177. Ibid., p. 456.
178. Ibid., p. 455.
179. Ibid., p. 457.
180. Ibid., p. 459f.
181. Ibid., p. 460.
182. Ibid.
183. See note 122 above.
184. Simmel, 'Berliner Gewerbe-Ausstellung'.
185. Ibid.
186. Ibid.
187. Simmel, *Philosophy of Money*, pp. 461-2.
188. See G. Simmel, 'Fashion', *AJS*, vol. 62, 1957. Reprinted in Levine (ed.), *Georg Simmel on Individuality and Social Forms*, pp. 294-323.
189. G. Simmel, 'Die Mode', in G. Simmel, *Philosphische Kultur*, Potsdam 1923, pp. 31-64. All references are to this version.
190. Simmel, 'Die Mode', p. 31.
191. Ibid., p. 33.
192. Ibid., p. 35.
193. Ibid., p. 36.
194. Ibid., p. 39.
195. Ibid., p. 42.
196. Ibid.
197. Ibid.
198. Ibid., p. 43.
199. Ibid.
200. Ibid., pp. 44-5.
201. Ibid., p. 54.
202. Ibid., p. 57.
203. Ibid., p. 59.
204. Ibid., p. 60.
205. Ibid.
206. Simmel, *Philosophy of Money*, p. 462.
207. This last chapter was the one which he recommended the reader commence with, perhaps partly on the grounds that it had the most immediate relevance to modern life. He wrote to his friend Hermann Keyserling in 1908 after the second edition had appeared suggesting he should 'start with the last chapter and only then read further from the first chapter

onwards'. See Simmel's letter of 31 October 1908 in M. Landmann (ed.), *Georg Simmel, Das individuelle Gesetz*, Frankfurt 1968, p. 239.

208. See note 65 above.
209. See note 140 above.
210. Simmel, 'Das Problem des Stiles', p. 314.
211. Ibid., p. 314.
212. Simmel, *Philosophy of Money*, p. 431.
213. Ibid., pp. 483–4.
214. H. Böhringer, 'Die "Philosophie des Geldes" als ästhetische Theorie' in H. J. Dahme and O. Rammstedt (eds) *Georg Simmel und die Moderne*, Frankfurt 1984, pp. 178–82, esp. p. 182.
215. Simmel, *Philosophy of Money*, p. 449.
216. Habermas, 'Die Moderne', p. 446.
217. Ibid., p. 447.
218. Simmel, *Philosophy of Money*, p. 511.
219. H. Scheible, 'Georg Simmel und die "Tragodie der Kultur"', *Neue Rundschau*, 91, 2/3, 1980, pp. 133–64, esp. p. 158.
220. K. Marx, *Grundrisse*, Harmondsworth 1973, p. 790.
221. Ibid.
222. Ibid., p. 254–5.

SIEGFRIED KRACAUER:
'EXEMPLARY INSTANCES' OF MODERNITY

1. S. Kracauer, *History. The Last Things Before the Last*, New York/Oxford 1969, p. 5.
2. S. Kracauer, *Die Angestellten*, Frankfurt 1930. Reprinted in S. Kracauer, *Schriften I*, Frankfurt 1971. All references are to this later edition.
3. S. Kracauer, *Jacques Offenbach und das Paris seiner Zeit*, Amsterdam 1937. Reprinted Frankfurt 1976. All German references are to this later edition. English translation by G. David and E. Mosbacher as *Offenbach and the Paris of his Time*, London 1937.
4. Kracauer, *History*, p. 5.
5. Kracauer, *Schriften I*, p. 212.
6. Quoted in J. Bundschuh, 'Als dauere die Gegenwart eine Ewigkeit', in *Siegfried Kracauer. Text + Kritik*, 68, pp. 4–11, esp. p. 7.
7. I. Mülder, *Erfahrendes Denken. Zu den Schriften Siegfried Kracauers vom Ersten Weltkrieg bis zum Ende der Weimarer Republik*, dissertation Tübingen University 1984, p. 161. (Published in revised form Stuttgart 1985, all references are to the dissertation.) For the revised published version see I. Mülder, *Siegfried Kracauer – Grenzgänger zwischen Theorie und Literatur: Seine frühen Schriften 1913–1933*, Stuttgart 1985. Mülder's study is not merely the first excellent full-length examination of Kracauer's work as a whole in the Weimar period. It also contains the fullest biography to date of Kracauer's works, superceding that in *Text + Kritik*, 68.

8. K. Witte, Nachwort to S. Kracauer, *Das Ornament der Masse. Essays*, Frankfurt 1977, pp. 335–47, esp. pp. 336–7.

9. S. Kracauer, 'Vom Erleben des Krieges', *Preussische Jahrbuch*, 58, 1915, no. 3, pp. 410, 422.

10. S. Kracauer, *Das Leiden unter dem Wissen und die Sehnsucht nach der Tat. Eine Abhandlung aus dem Jahre 1917*, typescript, 260 pages, Siegfried Kracauer Nachlass, Deutsche Literaturarchiv, Marbach/Neckar.

11. S. Kracauer, *Über das Wesen der Persönlichkeit. Eine Abhandlung*, typescript, 178 pages, Universitätsbibliothek, Freie Universität, Berlin. (Mülder dates the manuscript as around 1917.)

12. S. Kracauer, *Über den Expressionismus. Wesen und Sinn einer Zeitbewegung*, typescript, 81 pages, Siegfried Kracauer Nachlass, Deutsche Literaturarchiv, Marbach/Neckar. (Mülder dates the manuscript from 1918.)

13. S. Kracauer, *Über die Pflichtethik*, manuscript, 1918, 91 pages, Siegfried Kracauer Nachlass, Deutsche Literaturarchiv, Marbach/Neckar.

14. S. Kracauer, 'Über die Freundschaft', *Logos*, 7, 1917/18, pp. 182–208. Reprinted in S. Kracauer, *Über die Freundschaft. Essays*, Frankfurt 1971, pp. 7–82.

15. The reader should consult Mülder, *Erfahrendes Denken*, for a fuller discussion.

16. S. Kracauer, *Die Entwicklung der Schmiedekunst in Berlin, Potsdam und einige Städten der Mark vom 17. Jahrhundert bis zum Beginn des 19. Jahrhunderts*, Worms 1915.

17. Anon., *Ginster. Von ihm selbst geschrieben*, Berlin 1928; 2nd edn (without the last chapter) as *Ginster*, Frankfurt 1963; complete in S. Kracauer, *Schriften 7*, Frankfurt 1973, which also contains the hitherto unpublished novel *Georg*.

18. Kracauer, 'Vom Erleben des Krieges', p. 414.

19. Ibid., p. 420.

20. See note 10 above.

21. Kracauer, *Das Leiden unter dem Wissen*, p. 41.

22. Ibid., p. 232.

23. Ibid., p. 240.

24. Ibid., p. 241.

25. Ibid., p. 242.

26. Kracauer, *Über den Expressionismus*, p. 11.

27. Ibid., p. 61.

28. Ibid., p. 67.

29. S. Kracauer, 'Die Wartenden', *Frankfurter Zeitung*, 12 March 1922. Reprinted in Kracauer, *Das Ornament der Masse*, pp. 106–19. All references are to this edition.

30. Kracauer, 'Die Wartenden', p. 106.

31. Ibid., p. 118.

32. M. Schröter, 'Weltzerfall und Rekonstruktion. Zur Physiognomik Siegfried Kracauers', in *Text + Kritik*, 68, pp. 18–40, esp. p. 22.

33. S. Kracauer, 'Georg von Lukács' Romantheorie', *Neue Blätter für Kunst und Literatur*, 4, 1921/22, no. 1, pp. 1–5; S. Kracauer, 'Lukács' Theorie des Romans', *Die Weltbühne*, 17. 1921, vol. 2, pp. 229–30.
34. See note 12, chapter 2 above.
35. See note 54, chapter 2 above.
36. Kracauer, *Georg Simmel*, p. 52.
37. Kracauer, 'Georg Simmel', p. 322.
38. Ibid., p. 314.
39. Kracauer, *Georg Simmel*, p. 37.
40. Kracauer, 'Georg Simmel', p. 331.
41. Ibid., p. 332.
42. Kracauer, *Georg Simmel*, pp. 45–6.
43. Ibid., p. 92.
44. Ibid., p. 126.
45. Ibid., p. 92.
46. S. Kracauer, 'Georg Simmel. "Zur Philosophie der Kunst"', *Frankfurter Zeitung*, 4 July 1923.
47. S. Kracauer, *Soziologie als Wissenschaft. Eine erkenntnistheoretische Untersuchung*, Dresden 1922. Reprinted in Kracauer, *Schriften 1*, pp. 9–101. All references are to this edition.
48. Kracauer, *Schriften 1*, p. 13.
49. Ibid., p. 62.
50. Ibid., p. 60.
51. S. Kracauer, 'Max Scheler', *Frankfurter Zeitung*, 22 May 1928.
52. S. Kracauer, 'Katholizismus und Relativismus', *Frankfurter Zeitung*, 19 November 1921. Reprinted in Kracauer, *Das Ornament der Masse*, pp. 187–96, esp. p. 196.
53. S. Kracauer, 'Der Bibel auf Deutsch', *Frankfurter Zeitung*, 27 and 28 April 1926. Reprinted in Kracauer, *Das Ornament der Masse*, pp. 173–86. For a fuller discussion of this translation and Kracauer's (and Benjamin's) response, see M. Jay, 'The Politics of Translation. Siegfried Kracauer and Walter Benjamin on the Buber–Rosenzweig Bible' in *Yearbook of the Leo Baeck Institute*, 21, London 1976, pp. 3–24.
54. Kracauer, *Das Ornament der Masse*, p. 183.
55. S. Kracauer, 'Zwei Arten der Mitteilung', typescript, 7 pages, Siegfried Kracauer Nachlass, esp. p. 3. (Mülder dates it as 1929/30.)
56. Ibid.
57. Ibid.
58. Ibid., p. 4.
59. See Mülder, *Erfahrendes Denken*, pp. 75f. Kracauer had already reviewed very critically Bloch's *Thomas Münzer*. See S. Kracauer, 'Prophetentum', *Frankfurter Zeitung*, 27 August 1922.
60. S. Kracauer to E. Bloch, 27 May 1926, Siegfried Kracauer Nachlass, Deutsche Literaturarchiv. What Kracauer has in mind here in his

critique of Lukács is the last chapter of G. Lukács, *History and Class Consciousness*, translated by R. Livingstone, London 1971.

61. M. Jay, 'The Extraterritorial Life of Siegfried Kracauer', *Salmagundi*, 31-2, 1975/76, pp. 49–106, esp. p. 62.
62. Kracauer to Bloch, 27 May 1926.
63. Ibid.
64. Ibid.
65. Ibid.
66. Jay, 'Extraterritorial Life', p. 62.
67. T. W. Adorno, 'Der wunderliche Realist', in T. W. Adorno, *Noten zur Literatur III*, Frankfurt 1965, pp. 83–108. Kracauer was outraged by this apparently positive but in many ways critical assessment of his work. See M. Jay, 'Adorno and Kracauer. Notes on a Troubled Friendship', *Salmagundi*, 40, 1978, pp. 42–66. More critically see also H. G. Helms, 'Der wunderliche Kracauer', *Neues Forum*, I, June/July 1971, pp. 27–9; II, October/November 1971, pp. 48–51; III, December 1971, pp. 27–30; IV, September/October 1972, pp. 55–8.
68. Kracauer to Bloch, 27 May 1926.
69. S. Kracauer to E. Bloch, 29 June 1926, Siegfried Kracauer Nachlass, Deutsche Literaturarchiv, Marbach/Neckar. In the same month. Kracauer reviewed briefly the work of the Marx–Engels Archive. See S. Kracauer, 'Marx–Engels-Archiv', *Frankfurter Zeitung*, 20 June 1926.
70. S. Kracauer, *Der Detektiv-Roman. Ein philosophische Traktat*, typescript, 1922 - 15 February 1925, Siegfried Kracauer Nachlass, Deutsche Literaturarchiv, Marbach/Neckar. First published in Kracauer, *Schriften 1*, pp. 103–204. All references are to this edition. The original manuscript is merely subtitled 'An Interpretation'. Omitted from the published text is a long opening quote from Baudelaire's *Journaux intimes* and a brief Goethe quote. The first chapter was originally entitled 'Transformation of Spheres'. The study as a whole is dedicated to Adorno, 'my friend'.
71. Kracauer, *Schriften 1*, pp. 105–6.
72. Hence the significance of the original title to this chapter. See note 70 above.
73. Kracauer, *Schriften 1*, pp. 116–7.
74. Ibid., p. 119.
75. Ibid., p. 124.
76. Ibid., p. 131.
77. Ibid., p. 136.
78. Ibid., p. 139.
79. Ibid., p. 150.
80. Ibid., p. 162.
81. Ibid., p. 181.
82. Ibid., p. 187.
83. Ibid., p. 188.

84. Ibid., pp. 197–8.
85. Ibid., p. 204.
86. Kracauer, *Das Ornament der Masse*, p. 280.
87. Kracauer, *History*, pp. 83–4.
88. Jay, 'Extraterritorial Life', p. 50.
89. Many of these are assembled in the collection, S. Kracauer, *Strassen in Berlin und anderswo*, Frankfurt 1964.
90. S. Kracauer, 'Neue Detektivromane', *Frankfurter Zeitung*, 24 April 1927.
91. Mülder, *Erfahrendes Denken*, pp. 155–6.
92. Ibid., p. 14.
93. S. Kracauer, 'Berliner Landschaft', *Frankfurter Zeitung*, 8 November 1931. Retitled as 'Aus dem Fenster gesehen' in Kracauer, *Strassen in Berlin*, pp. 51–3. References are to this edition.
94. Kracauer, *Strassen in Berlin*, p. 51.
95. Ibid., p. 53.
96. Schröter, 'Weltzerfall und Rekonstruktion', p. 33.
97. Ibid., p. 32.
98. G. Zohlen, 'Text-Strassen. Zur Theorie der Stadtlektüre bei S. Kracauer', in *Text + Kritik*, 68, pp. 62–72, esp. pp. 63–4.
99. S. Kracauer, 'Pariser Beobachtungen', *Frankfurter Zeitung*, 13 February 1927.
100. Ibid.
101. S. Kracauer, 'Ein Paar Tagen Paris', *Frankfurter Zeitung*, 5 April 1932.
102. S. Kracauer, 'Analyse einer Stadtplans' (1928), in Kracauer, *Das Ornament der Masse*, pp. 14–17.
103. Ibid., p. 16.
104. S. Kracauer, 'Strassenvolk in Paris', *Frankfurter Zeitung*, 12 April 1927. Reprinted in Kracauer, *Strassen in Berlin*, pp. 127–31.
105. In S. Kracauer, 'Stehbars im Süden', *Frankfurter Zeitung*, 8 October 1926, reprinted in Kracauer, *Strassen in Berlin*, pp. 66–8, esp. p. 68.
106. S. Kracauer, 'Erinnerung an einer Pariser Strasse', *Frankfurter Zeitung*, 9 November 1930. Reprinted in S. Kracauer, *Strassen in Berlin*, pp. 9–15; also in *Text + Kritik*, 68, pp. 55–8. References are to this reprint.
107. Ibid., p. 58.
108. S. Kracauer, 'Zwei Flächen', *Frankfurter Zeitung*, 26 September 1926. Reprinted in Kracauer, *Das Ornament der Masse*, pp. 11–13, esp. p. 12.
109. S. Kracauer, 'Die Berührung', *Frankfurter Zeitung*, 18 November 1928.
110. Ibid.
111. S. Kracauer, 'Berlin in Deutschland', *Frankfurter Zeitung*, 14 August 1932.
112. S. Kracauer, 'Strasse ohne Erinnerung', *Frankfurter Zeitung*, 16 December 1932. Reprinted in Kracauer, *Strassen in Berlin*, pp. 19–23; also in *Text + Kritik*, 68, pp. 59–61. References are to this reprint.
113. Ibid., p. 61.

L

114. G. Zohlen, 'Text-Strassen' in *Text + Kritik*, 68, pp. 65–6.
115. Ibid., p. 64.
116. S. Kracauer, 'Wiederholung', *Frankfurter Zeitung*, 29 May 1932.
117. Ibid.
118. S. Kracauer, 'Ansichtspostkarte', *Frankfurter Zeitung*, 26 May 1930.
119. Ibid.
120. S. Kracauer, 'Die Unterführung', *Frankfurter Zeitung*, 11 March 1932. Reprinted in Kracauer, *Strassen in Berlin*, pp. 48–50.
121. Kracauer, 'Zwie Flächen', p. 26.
122. S. Kracauer, 'Schreie auf der Strasse', *Frankfurter Zeitung*, 19 July 1930. Reprinted in Kracauer, *Strassen in Berlin*, pp. 27–9. References are to this reprint.
123. Ibid., p. 28.
124. Ibid., p. 29.
125. S. Kracauer, 'Unter der Oberfläche', *Frankfurter Zeitung*, 11 July 1931.
126. S. Kracauer, 'Abschied von der Lindenpassage', *Frankfurter Zeitung*, 21 December 1930. Reprinted in Kracauer, *Das Ornament der Masse*, pp. 326–32.
127. S. Kracauer, 'Über Arbeitsnachweise. Konstruktion eines Raumes', *Frankfurter Zeitung*, 17 June 1930. Reprinted in Kracauer, *Strassen in Berlin*, pp. 69–78; also in *Text + Kritik*, 68, pp. 12–17. References are to this reprint. In the same direction, see also S. Kracauer, 'Wärmehallen', *Frankfurter Zeitung*, 18 January 1931; reprinted in Kracauer, *Strassen in Berlin*, pp. 79–84.
128. S. Kracauer, 'Über Arbeitsnachweise', p. 12.
129. See, for instance, S. Kracauer, 'Glück und Schicksal', *Frankfurter Zeitung*, 10 October 1931 and 'Kino in der Münzstrasse', *Frankfurter Zeitung*, 2 April 1932. Both reprinted in Kracauer, *Strassen in Berlin*, pp. 85–8 and 92–4.
130. See, for example, S. Kracauer, 'Unter Palmen', *Frankfurter Zeitung*, 19 October 1930 (on exotic settings in cafés in Berlin) or S. Kracauer, 'Aus einem französischen Seebad', *Frankfurter Zeitung*, 14 September 1932.
131. See, for example, S. Kracauer, 'Im Luxushotel' *Frankfurter Zeitung*, 17 April 1932.
132. See, for example, S. Kracauer, 'Café im Berliner Westen', *Frankfurter Zeitung*, 17 April 1932.
133. S. Kracauer, 'Das Mittelgebirge', *Frankfurter Zeitung* (c.1926). Reprinted in Kracauer, *Strassen in Berlin*, pp. 122–5.
134. Helms, 'Der wunderliche Kracauer', III, p. 30.
135. Kracauer, 'Über Arbeitsnachweise', p. 12.
136. Cited in Mülder, *Erfahrendes Denken*, p. 259, note 17.
137. Kracauer, 'Über Arbeitsnachweise', p. 14.
138. Helms, 'Der wunderliche Kracauer', III, p. 27.
139. Kracauer, 'Über Arbeitsnachweise', p. 16.

140. S. Kracauer, 'Das Ornament der Masse', *Frankfurter Zeitung*, 9 and 10 June 1927. Reprinted in Kracauer, *Das Ornament der Masse*, pp. 50–63. English translation by B. Cowell and J. Zipes as 'The Mass Ornament', *New German Critique*, 2, 1975, pp. 67–76.

141. S. Kracauer, 'Kult der Zerstreuung', *Frankfurter Zeitung*, 4 March 1926. Reprinted in Kracauer, *Das Ornament der Masse*, pp. 311–17. All references are to the reprint.

142. S. Kracauer, 'Sie sporten', *Frankfurter Zeitung*, 13 January 1927.

143. S. Kracauer, 'Film und Gesellschaft', *Frankfurter Zeitung*, 11 and 19 March 1927. Reprinted as 'Die kleinen Ladenmädchen gehen ins Kono' in Kracauer, *Das Ornament der Masse*, pp. 279–94. All references are to the reprint.

144. S. Kracauer, 'Die Photographie', *Frankfurter Zeitung*, 28 October 1927. Reprinted in Kracauer, *Das Ornament der Masse*, pp. 21–39. All references are to the reprint.

145. Kracauer, 'Das Ornament der Masse', p. 50.

146. Schröter, 'Weltzerfall und Rekonstruktion', p. 26.

147. Kracauer, 'Das Ornament der Masse', p. 53.

148. Ibid., p. 54.

149. S. Kracauer, 'Girls und Krise', *Frankfurter Zeitung*, 26 May 1931.

150. Quoted in K. Witte, 'Introduction to Siegfried Kracauer's "The Mass Ornament"', in *New German Critique*, 2, 1975, pp. 63–4.

151. Kracauer, 'Das Ornament der Masse', p. 62.

152. Witte, 'Introduction to "The Mass Ornament"', p. 66.

153. Kracauer, 'Das Ornament der Masse', p. 63.

154. This process is discussed critically in H. Lethen, *Neue Sachlichkeit. 1924–1932. Studien zur Literatur des 'Weissen Sozialismus'*, Stuttgart, 1975, 2nd edn, pp. 102f.

155. Quoted in Witte, Nachwort to *Das Ornament der Masse*, p. 337.

156. On the disintegration of ornamentation in architecture see M. Müller, *Die Verdrängung des Ornaments. Zum Verhältnis von Architektur und Lebenspraxis*, Frankfurt 1977. On Kracauer cf. pp. 49f.

157. Lethen, *Neue Sachlichkeit*, pp. 43f.

158. See Kracauer, 'Die Photographie'.

159. Ibid., p. 32.

160. Ibid., p. 34.

161. Ibid.

162. Ibid., p. 35.

163. Mülder, *Erfahrendes Denken*, p. 105.

164. For a critical discussion of Kracauer's film theory see J. Beyse, *Film und Widerspeigelung. Interpretation und Kritik der Theorie Siegfried Kracauers*, dissertation, Cologne, 1977.

165. Cf. Kracauer, 'Kult der Zerstreuung'.

166. Schröter, 'Weltzerfall und Rekonstruktion', p. 32.

167. Kracauer, 'Die kleinen Ladenmädchen gehen ins Kino', p. 280.

168. Ibid.
169. S. Kracauer, 'Film 1928' in *Das Ornament der Masse*, p. 299.
170. S. Kracauer, 'Über die Aufgabe des Filmkritikers', *Frankfurter Zeitung*, 23 May 1932. Reprinted in Kracauer, *Kino. Essays, Glossen zum Film*, Frankfurt 1974, p. 9.
171. S. Kracauer, 'Not und Zerstreuung', *Frankfurter Zeitung*, 15 July 1931.
172. Kracauer, 'Über die Aufgabe des Filmkritikers', p. 11.
173. Mülder, *Erfahrendes Denken*, p. 143.
174. W. Benjamin, 'Ein Aussenseiter macht sich bemerkbar', in W. Benjamin, *Gesammelte Schriften III*, Werkausgabe 8, Frankfurt 1980, pp. 219–25.
175. Ibid., pp. 219–20.
176. S. Kracauer, 'Ideologie und Utopie', *Frankfurter Zeitung*, 23 April 1929.
177. S. Kracauer, 'Über den Schriftsteller', *Die Neue Rundschau*, vol. 42, 1931, 1, pp. 860–2.
178. Ibid., p. 862.
179. S. Kracauer, 'Minimalforderung an die Intellektuellen', *Die Neue Rundschau*, vol. 42, 1931, 2, pp. 71–5.
180. Such reflections upon the journalist, the writer and the intellectual arise directly out of Kracauer's increasingly precarious position in the last years of Weimar Germany. Significantly, the articles cited above did not and could not appear in the *Frankfurter Zeitung* of which Kracauer was the Berlin review editor from 1930 to 1933. (I. G. Farben secured a 49.5 per cent interest in the newspaper in 1929/30. Not unconnected with this development, Kracauer increasingly came into conflict with the editorial leadership. His 'promotion' to Berlin was the consequence, along with an increasingly insecure position on the newspaper and a not infrequent rejection of his articles.) For further details see the opening section of Mülder, *Erfahrendes Denken*.
181. Kracauer, *Die Angestellten*, p. 212.
182. Ibid., p. 298.
183. Ibid.
184. This summary of the correspondence is contained in Jay, 'Adorno and Kracauer', pp. 46–7.
185. Cited in Jay, 'Extraterritorial Life', p. 57.
186. Ibid.
187. T. W. Adorno, 'Der wunderliche Realist', p. 96.
188. W. Benjamin, 'S. Kracauer. Die Angestellten', in Benjamin, *Gesammelte Schriften III*, p. 226.
189. E. Bloch, 'Kunstliche Mitte. Zu S. Kracauer's "Die Angestellten"', *Die Neue Rundschau*, vol. 41, 1930, 2, pp. 861–2, esp. p. 861.
190. Ibid.
191. Kracauer, *Die Angestellten*, p. 216. In a later review, Kracauer speaks of literary reportage's '*illusory concretion*' which, instead of presenting real people, presents 'puppets'. See S. Kracauer, 'Zu einem Roman

aus der Konfektion. Nebst einem Exkurs über die soziale Roman-reportage', *Frankfurter Zeitung*, 5 June 1932.

192. Ibid.

193. Ibid., p. 207.

194. H. G. Helms, 'Vom Proletkult zum Bio-Interview' in R. Hübner and E. Schutz (eds), *Literatur als Praxis? Aktualität und Tradition operativen Schreibens*, Opladen 1976, pp. 71–95, esp. p. 93, note 22. For an overview of the relationship between Kracauer's study and reportage see E. Köhn, 'Konstruktion und Reportage. Anmerkungen zum literaturtheoretischen Hintergrund von Siegfried Kracauers Untersuchung "Die Angestellten" (1930)', in *Text und Kontext*, vol. 5, no. 2, 1977, pp. 107–23.

195. Ibid.

196. S. Kracauer, 'Der operierender Schriftsteller', *Frankfurter Zeitung*, 17 February 1932.

197. Kracauer, *Die Angestellten*, p. 215.

198. Ibid., pp. 215–16.

199. Schröter, 'Weltzerfall und Konstruktion', pp. 35–6.

200. E. Lederer and J. Marshak, 'Der neue Mittelstand', *Grundriss der Sozialökonomik*, 9, 1, 1926.

201. E. Lederer, 'Die Umschichtung des Proletariats', *Die Neue Rundschau*, vol. 40, 1929.

202. Mülder, *Erfahrendes Denken*, p. 175.

203. Kracauer, *Die Angestellten*, p. 223.

204. Ibid., p. 224.

205. Ibid., p. 273.

206. Ibid., pp. 282–3.

207. Ibid., p. 284.

208. Ibid., pp. 286–7.

209. Ibid., p. 287.

210. Ibid., p. 304.

211. Benjamin, 'Ein Aussenseiter', p. 225.

212. S. Kracauer, 'Die geistige Entscheidung des Unternehmertums', *Frankfurter Zeitung*, 2 September 1930.

213. S. Kracauer, 'Aufruhr der Mittelschichten', *Frankfurter Zeitung*, 10 December 1931. Reprinted in Kracauer, *Das Ornament der Masse*, pp. 81–105.

214. S. Kracauer, 'Mädchen im Beruf', *Der Querschnitt*, vol. 12, 1932, pp. 238–43.

215. Ibid., p. 242.

216. S. Kracauer, *Masse und Propaganda. Eine Untersuchung über faschistische Propaganda. Exposé*, typescript, 1936, 9 pages, Siegfried Kracauer Nachlass, Deutsche Literaturarchiv, Marbach/Neckar.

217. Correspondence of 20 August 1938, quoted in Jay 'Adorno and Kracauer', p. 50.

218. Quoted in K. Witte, Nachwort to S. Kracauer, *Jacques Offenbach und das Paris seiner Zeit.*

219. Letter from Benjamin to Scholem 9 August 1935 in G. Scholem (ed.), *Walter Benjamin/Gershom Scholem. Briefwechsel 1933–1940*, Frankfurt 1980, p. 203.

220. S. Kracauer, Vorwort to *Jacques Offenbach und das Paris seiner Zeit*, p. 9.

221. S. Kracauer, 'Die Biographie als neubürgerliche Kunstform', *Frankfurter Zeitung*, 29 June 1930. Reprinted in Kracauer, *Das Ornament der Masse*, pp. 75–80. References are to this reprint.

222. Kracauer, 'Die Biographie', p. 79. Interestingly, Kracauer points to 'one single biography that is not subject to these criticisms: that of Leon Trotsky'.

223. Kracauer, *Offenbach*, p. 9.

224. Ibid., p. 10.

225. T. W. Adorno, 'Kracauer, Siegfried, Jacques Offenbach und das Paris seiner Zeit' in *Zeitschrift für Sozialforschung*, vol. 6, 1937, pp. 697–9, esp. p. 698.

226. Kracauer, *Offenbach*, p. 270.

227. Ibid., p. 64.

228. Ibid., p. 74.

229. Ibid., p. 174.

230. Ibid., p. 156.

231. Ibid., p. 273.

232. Ibid., pp. 273–4.

233. T. W. Adorno, 'Kracauer, Siegfried, Offenbach', p. 698.

234. N. Nagler, 'Jacques Offenbach's musikalische Utopie: die Sehnsucht nach der Herrschaftsarmen Heimat. Reflexionen zu Siegfried Kracauers Gesellschaftsbiographie des Second Empire' in *Musik-Konzepte, 13, Jacques Offenbach*, 1980, pp. 71–86.

235. Ibid., p. 94. The reference to the destruction of aura recalls Benjamin, who occasionally quoted from Kracauer's Offenbach study. In a short review of Kraus on Offenbach, he also expressed the affinity between some of Offenbach's operettas and 'the moral configurations' that shone through the 'transparency' of 'the senseless night life' in works such as 'La vie parisienne'. See W. Benjamin, 'Karl Kraus liest Offenbach' in Benjamin, *Gesammelte Schriften*, IV, 1, 2, pp. 515–17.

236. G. Lukács, *The Theory of the Novel*, translated by A. Bostock, London 1971, pp. 61–2.

237. This is one of Bloch's criticisms of *History and Class Consciousness*, in E. Bloch, 'Aktualität und Utopie', *Der Neue Merkur*, 7, 1923/4, p. 474.

238. A. Münster (ed.), *Tagträume vom aufrechten Gang. Sechs Interviews mit Ernst Bloch*, Frankfurt 1977, p. 48.

239. S. Kracauer, 'Die Reise und der Tanz', *Frankfurter Zeitung*, 15 March 1925, reprinted in Kracauer, *Das Ornament der Masse*, pp. 40–9.

240. S. Kracauer, 'Sie Sporten', *Frankfurter Zeitung*, 13 January 1927. Kracauer ridicules the 'unlimited claim of sport and its fantastic ideology' as a 'definite trait of the physiognomy of the times'.
241. Kracauer, 'Über Arbeitsnachweise', pp. 16–17.
242. Kracauer, 'Lichtreklame', *Frankfurter Zeitung*, 15 January 1928. The shrill colours of neon advertising announce 'the ruthlessness of American commercial methods . . . what is chic rules on earth and in heaven the advertisement'.
243. Benjamin, 'Ein Aussenseiter', pp. 219–25.
244. Ibid., p. 220.
245. The ragpicker is one of the motifs of Benjamin's work that illustrates an important dimension of his historical method too. See I. Wohlfarth, 'Et cetera? Der Historiker als Lumpensammler' in N. Bolz and B. Witte (eds), *Passagen. Walter Benjamins Urgeschichte des neunzehnten Jahrhunderts*, Munich 1984, pp. 70–95, esp. pp. 80f.

WALTER BENJAMIN: PREHISTORY OF MODERNITY

1. See B. Witte, 'Benjamins Baudelaire. Rekonstruktion und Kritik eines Torsos', *Text und Kritik* 31/32, pp. 81–90.
2. T. W. Adorno, 'Charakteristik Walter Benjamins' in T. W. Adorno, *Über Walter Benjamin*, Frankfurt 1970, pp. 11–29, esp. p. 26. Some of the problems associated with the reconstruction of the Arcades Project are examined in S. Buck-Morss, 'Benjamin's Revolutionary Pedagogy', *New Left Review*, 128, pp. 50–75; S. Buck-Morss, 'Walter Benjamin – Revolutionary Writer', *New Left Review*, 129, pp. 77–95; Bolz and Witte (eds), *Passagen*. The fragments which were to make up the Arcades Project have now been assembled – though they too are incomplete – thanks to the exhaustive editorial work of Rolf Tiedemann, in Benjamin, *Das Passagen-Werk* (see note 99, chapter 1 above).
3. Adorno, 'Charakteristik Walter Benjamins', p. 26.
4. Benjamin, *Das Passagen-Werk*, p. 1030.
5. Ibid., p. 1014.
6. W. Benjamin, 'Ausgraben und Erinnern' in Benjamin, *Gesammelte Schriften*, IV, 1, pp. 400–1.
7. W. Benjamin, 'Der destruktive Charakter' in Benjamin, *Gesammelte Schriften*, IV, 1, pp. 396–8; in English as 'The Destructive Character' in W. Benjamin, *One-Way Street and Other Writings*, New York 1978, London 1979, pp. 157–9.
8. Benjamin, 'The Destructive Character', p. 159.
9. W. Benjamin, 'Der Surrealismus' in *Gesammelte Schriften*, II, 1, pp. 295–310; translated in Benjamin, *One-Way Street*, pp. 225–39.
10. Benjamin, *Das Passagen-Werk*, p. 575.

11. See W. Benjamin, 'Über einige Motive bei Baudelaire', *Zeitschrift für Sozialforschung*, 8, 1939, pp. 50–89; in English in Benjamin, *Charles Baudelaire (see note 98, chapter 2 above)*. pp. 107–54.

12. See Benjamin, *Das Passagen Werk*.

13. See R. Tiedemann, 'Zeugnisse zur Entstehungsgeschichte' in Benjamin, *Das Passagen-Werk*, p. 1081. The original unwritten article was to have been for the journal *Querschnitt*. In 'A Berlin Chronicle' (1932) Benjamin mentions his first guide to Paris: 'The city . . . whose guardian at that time was Franz Hessel, was a maze not only of paths but of tunnels. I cannot think of the underworld of the Metro and the North–South line opening their hundreds of shafts all over the city, without recalling my endless *flâneries.*' See W. Benjamin, 'A Berlin Chronicle' in Benjamin *One-Way Street*, p. 299.

14. T. W. Adorno, 'Benjamin's "Einbahnstrasse"' in *Über Walter Benjamin*, Frankfurt 1968, pp. 58–9.

15. Ibid., pp. 59–60.

16. E. Bloch, *Erbschaft dieser Zeit*, Zurich 1935, pp. 276–9.

17. This is suggested in W. Fuld, *Walter Benjamin. Zwischen den Stuhlen*, Frankfurt 1981, p. 189. Fuld's study remains the only existing biography of Benjamin. A major source for biographical details remains the often over-edited collection of correspondence, W. Benjamin, *Briefe* 2 vols, edited by G. Scholem and T. W. Adorno, Frankfurt 1966, to be supplemented by G. Scholem, *Walter Benjamin – die Geschichte einer Freundschaft*, Frankfurt 1975; *Walter Benjamin/Gershom Scholem: Briefwechsel 1933–1940*, edited by G. Scholem, Frankfurt 1980; Walter Benjamin, *Moskauer Tagebuch*, edited by G. Smith, Frankfurt 1980; G. Scholem, *Walter Benjamin und sein Engel*, Frankfurt 1983. Additional correspondence relating to the Arcades Project is contained in R. Tiedemann, 'Zeugnisse zur Entstehungsgeschichte', in Benjamin, *Das Passagen-Werk*, pp. 1081–205. In English, the following should be consulted: G. Scholem, *Walter Benjamin. The Story of a Friendship*, London 1982; J. Roberts, *Walter Benjamin*, London/Basingstoke 1982; R. Wolin, *Walter Benjamin. An Aesthetic of Redemption*, New York 1982.

18. Benjamin, *Briefe*, I, p. 47.

19. The documentation of Benjamin's Moscow visit is now available in Benjamin, *Moskauer Tagebuch*. *One-Way Street* is dedicated to Asja Lacis: 'This street is named Asja Lacis Street after her who as an engineer cut it through the author'. Cf. *One-Way Street*, p. 45. For Lacis's view of Benjamin, see A. Lacis, *Revolutionär im Beruf*, Munich 1971.

20. Benjamin, *Moskauer Tagebuch*, p. 108.

21. Appended to Benjamin, *Moskauer Tagebuch*, p. 213.

22. See S. Kracauer, 'Pariser Beobachtungen', *Frankfurter Zeitung*, 13 February 1927.

23. S. Kracauer, 'Zu den Schriften Walter Benjamins', *Frankfurter Zeitung*, 15 July 1928. Reprinted in Kracauer, *Das Ornament der Masse*,

pp. 249–55, esp. p. 249. For the study to which Kracauer is referring see W. Benjamin, *Ursprung des deutschen Trauerspiels*, Frankfurt 1963. In English see W. Benjamin, *The Origins of German Tragedy*, translated by J. Osborne, London 1977.

24. Kracauer, 'Zu den Schriften Walter Benjamins', pp. 253–4.
25. See Benjamin, *Das Passagen-Werk*, pp. 1041–3.
26. Ibid., pp. 993–1038.
27. Ibid., p. 1002.
28. Ibid., p. 1001.
29. Ibid., p. 1007.
30. Ibid., p. 1010.
31. Ibid.
32. Benjamin, *Briefe*, 1, p. 446.
33. Ibid., p. 455.
34. Ibid., p. 459.
35. Ibid., p. 462.
36. Ibid., p. 464.
37. Ibid., pp. 469–70.
38. Ibid., p. 471.
39. Ibid., p. 472.
40. Ibid., p. 478f.
41. See Fuld, *Walter Benjamin*, p. 211.
42. Benjamin, *Briefe*, 1, p. 483.
43. Ibid.
44. W. Benjamin, *Briefe*, 2, p. 491.
45. Ibid., p. 491.
46. Cited in Benjamin, *Das Passagen-Werk*, p. 1091.
47. W. Benjamin, *Briefe*, 2, p. 496.
48. Ibid., p. 502; for Benjamin's important review see 'Die Wiederkehr des Flaneurs', *Die Literarische Welt*, 5, 40, 4 October 1929. Reprinted in Benjamin, *Gesammelte Schriften*, III, pp. 194–9. Hessel's own work has recently been reprinted as F. Hessel, *Ein Flaneur in Berlin*, Berlin 1984.
49. Benjamin, *'Die Wiederkehr des Flaneurs'*, p. 198.
50. Benjamin, *Briefe*, 2, p. 506.
51. W. Benjamin, 'Pariser Tagebuch', in Benjamin, *Gesammelte Schriften*, IV, pp. 567–87, esp. p. 568.
52. See Benjamin, 'Ein Aussenseiter', and W. Benjamin, 'S. Kracauer, Die Angestellten', in Benjamin, *Gesammelte Schriften*, III, pp. 219–28.
53. Cited in Scholem, *Walter Benjamin – die Geschichte einer Freundschaft*, p. 208.
54. Benjamin, *Briefe*, 2, p. 531.
55. On the location and significance of this essay see I. Wohlfarth, 'Der "Destruktive Charakter". Benjamin zwischen den Fronten' in B. Lindner (ed.), *'Links hatte noch alles sich zu enträtseln . . .' Walter Benjamin im Kontext*, Frankfurt 1978, pp. 65–99.

56. Benjamin, *Briefe*, 2, pp. 541–2.
57. Scholem (ed.), *Benjamin/Scholem*, p. 28.
58. Ibid., p. 23.
59. W. Benjamin, *Deutsche Menschen*, Lucerne 1936.
60. See W. Benjamin, *Berliner Kindheit um Neunzehnhundert*, Frankfurt 1950. For a detailed study of the work's significance, see A. Stüssi, *Erinnerung an die Zukunft. Walter Benjamins 'Berliner Kindheit um Neunzehnhundert'*, Göttingen 1977. On its relevance for the Arcades Project see, most recently, B. Lindner, 'Das "Passagen-Werk", die "Berliner Kindheit" und die Archaologie des "Jüngstvergangenen"', in Bolz and Witte (eds), *Passagen*, pp. 27–48.
61. Scholem (ed.), *Benjamin/Sholem*, p. 28.
62. Benjamin, 'Ausgraben und Erinnern', pp. 400–1.
63. Benjamin, *Briefe*, 2, p. 596.
64. Scholem (ed.), *Benjamin/Scholem*, p. 123.
65. Benjamin, *Briefe*, 2, 602.
66. Scholem (ed.), *Benjamin/Scholem*, p. 127.
67. Ibid., p. 128.
68. On the relationship between Benjamin and Brecht see B. Lindner, 'Brecht/Benjamin/Adorno – Über Veränderungen der Kunstproduktion im wissenschaftlich-technischen Zeitalter' in *Text und Kritik, Bertolt Brecht* 1, Munich 1972, pp. 14–36; R. Tiedemann, 'Brecht oder die Kunst, in anderer Leute Kopfe zu denken', in R. Tiedemann, *Dialektik im Stillstand*, Frankfurt 1983, pp. 42–73.
69. Benjamin, *Briefe*, 2, p. 604.
70. Ibid., p. 605. Scholem offered Benjamin the possibility of an academic career in Palestine.
71. W. Benjamin, 'Der Autor als Produzent', in Benjamin, *Gesammelte Schriften*, II pp. 683–701. It was originally delivered as an address to the Institute for the Study of Marxism in Paris on 27 April 1934.
72. This large-ranging project was rejected by the *Institut für Sozialforschung*.
73. Benjamin, *Briefe*, 2, p. 626.
74. Ibid., p. 632.
75. Ibid., p. 653.
76. Ibid., p. 654.
77. Ibid.
78. Ibid.
79. W. Benjamin, 'Paris, die Hauptstadt des XIX. Jahrhunderts', in Benjamin, *Das Passagen-Werk*, pp. 45–59. In English in Benjamin, *Charles Baudelaire*, pp. 155–76.
80. Benjamin, *Briefe*, 2, p. 663.
81. See Wolin, *Walter Benjamin*, ch. 5., 'Benjamin and Brecht'.
82. See Benjamin, *Briefe*, 2, pp. 671–83. In English see Ernst Bloch *et al.*, *Aesthetics and Politics*, London 1977, pp. 100–41. On the confrontation between Adorno and Benjamin, see S. Buck-Morss, *The Origin of*

Negative Dialectics, New York 1977, chs. 9–11, Wolin, *Walter Benjamin*, ch. 6.

83. Cited in Benjamin, *Das Passagen-Werk*, p. 1143.
84. Scholem (ed.), *Benjamin/Scholem*, p. 202.
85. Ibid.
86. Benjamin, *Das Passagen-Werk*, p. 1145.
87. Ibid.
88. Benjamin, *Briefe*, 2, p. 690.
89. Ibid., p. 695.
90. Ibid., p. 700.
91. Ibid., p. 706.
92. W. Benjamin, 'Eduard Fuchs, der Sammler und der Historiker', in Benjamin, *Gesammelte Schriften*, II, pp. 465–505. In English as 'Eduard Fuchs, Collector and Historian', in Benjamin, *One-Way Street*, pp. 349–86.
93. Benjamin, *Briefe*, 2, p. 729.
94. Fuld, *Walter Benjamin*, p. 279.
95. Benjamin, *Das Passagen-Werk*, p. 1158.
96. This project on Jung's archetypes and Klage's archaic images was to have constituted a counterpoint to the concept of the dialectical image so central to the Arcades Project.
97. Benjamin, *Das Passagen-Werk*, p. 1160.
98. Scholem (ed.), *Benjamin/Scholem*, p. 240.
99. For its significance for the Arcades Project see F. Rella, 'Benjamin und Blanqui' in Brodersen (ed.), *Benjamin auf Italienisch*, pp. 77–102.
100. Benjamin, *Briefe*, pp. 741–2.
101. Ibid., p. 750.
102. Ibid., pp. 751–2.
103. Benjamin, *Das Passagen-Werk*, p. 1166.
104. Ibid., p. 1167.
105. Ibid. The book of the same title which has appeared in English is not this text which remained uncompleted.
106. See Benjamin, *Charles Baudelaire*, pp. 9–102.
107. Benjamin, *Gesammelte Schriften*, I, p. 1087.
108. Benjamin, *Briefe*, 2, pp. 769–70.
109. Ibid., p. 775.
110. Ibid., p. 778.
111. Ibid., p. 783.
112. Ibid., p. 785.
113. Ibid., p. 786.
114. Ibid., p. 794.
115. Ibid., p. 800. Among the personal factors was his sister's serious illness.
116. Ibid., p. 801.
117. Ibid., p. 805.
118. Ibid., p. 814.

119. W. Benjamin, *Das Passagen-Werk*, p. 1171.
120. Ibid., p. 1172.
121. Ibid., p. 1179.
122. Benjamin, 'Über einige Motive bei Baudelaire' (see note 11 above).
123. The 1939 *exposé* under the title 'Paris, Capitale du XIXème siècle' is to be found in Benjamin, *Das Passagen-Werk*, pp. 60–77. On its significance see B. Witte, 'Paris-Berlin-Paris' in Bolz and Witte (eds), *Passagen*, pp. 17–26, esp. pp. 24f.
124. On precisely this aspect of Benjamin's theory of aura see M. Stoessel, *Aura. Das vergessene Menschliche*, Munich 1983.
125. Benjamin, *Briefe*, 2, p. 850.
126. Benjamin, *Das Passagen-Werk*, p. 1181.
127. W. Benjamin, 'Zentralpark' in Benjamin, *Gesammelte Shriften*, I, pp. 657–90, esp. p. 683.
128. Benjamin, *Das Passagen-Werk*, p. 1010.
129. Ibid., pp. 993–1038.
130. R. Caillois, 'Paris, mythe moderne', *La nouvelle revue française*, 25, no. 284, pp. 682–99.
131. Benjamin, *Das Passagen-Werk*, p. 1002.
132. Ibid., p. 993.
133. Ibid., p. 1007.
134. L. Aragon, *Paris Peasant*, translated by S. W. Taylor, London 1980, p. 28.
135. Ibid., pp. 28–9.
136. The department store is, for Benjamin, the extension of the arcade. On Parisian stores see R. H. Williams, *Dream Worlds. Mass Consumption in Late Nineteenth Century France*, Berkeley/Los Angeles/London 1982; M. B. Miller, *The Bon Marché. Bourgeois Culture and the Department Store, 1869–1920*, Princeton/London 1981; more generally, K. Strohmeyer, *Warenhäuser*, Berlin 1980.
137. Benjamin, *Gesammelte Schriften*, III, p. 223.
138. This image of the labyrinth has been extended into the key to Benjamin's later experience as a writer. See H. Kaulen, 'Leben im Labyrinth. Walter Benjamins letzte Lebensjahre', *Neue Rundschau*, 93, 1, pp. 34–59.
139. W. Benjamin, 'James Ensor' in Benjamin, *Gesammelte Schriften*, IV, p. 567.
140. Benjamin, *Charles Baudelaire*, p. 103.
141. Benjamin, *Das Passagen-Werk*, p. 1034.
142. S. Kracauer, 'Zu den Schriften Walter Benjamins', in Kracauer, *Das Ornament der Masse*, p. 249.
143. Ibid., p. 252.
144. Ibid., pp. 253–4.
145. Ibid., p. 254.
146. E. Bloch, 'Ernst Bloch' in T. W. Adorno, *et al.*, *Über Walter Benjamin*, Frankfurt 1968, pp. 16–23, esp. p. 17.

147. Ibid., p. 18.
148. Benjamin, *Origins of German Tragedy*, p. 35.
149. Ibid., p. 29.
150. Ibid., p. 28.
151. Ibid., p. 44.
152. Benjamin, *Gesammelte Schriften*, III, p. 51.
153. Benjamin, *One-Way Street*, p. 337.
154. Benjamin, *Das Passagen-Werk*, p. 575.
155. Adorno, 'Charakteristik Walter Benjamins', p. 22.
156. W. Benjamin, 'N [Theoretics of Knowledge; Theory of Progress]', in *The Philosophical Forum*, XV, 1-2, pp. 1-40, esp. p. 23. This is a translation by L. Hafrey and R. Sieburth of Benjamin's notes to the projected epistemological introduction to the Arcades Project. For the original see Benjamin, *Das Passagen-Werk*, pp. 570-611.
157. Benjamin, *One-Way Street*, p. 45.
158. Benjamin, 'N', pp. 23-4.
159. Buck-Morss, *Origins of Negative Dialectics*, p. 106.
160. Benjamin, 'N', pp. 4-5.
161. Ibid., p. 2.
162. Ibid., p. 3.
163. Benjamin, *One-Way Street*, pp. 351-2.
164. Benjamin, 'N', p. 9.
165. Benjamin, *One-Way Street*, p. 352.
166. Benjamin, *Illuminations*, p. 256. There is an extensive discussion of Benjamin's philosophy of history. See P. Bulthaup (ed.), *Materialien zu Benjamin's Thesen 'Über den Begriff der Geschlichte'*, Frankfurt 1975, as well as the volumes by Greffrath and Gabnebin cited above.
167. Benjamin, *One-Way Street*, pp. 359-60.
168. Ibid., p. 168.
169. Ibid., p. 360.
170. Ibid., p. 362.
171. Benjamin, *Illuminations*, p. 255.
172. Ibid., p. 261.
173. Benjamin, 'N', p. 5.
174. Benjamin, *Illuminations*, p. 261.
175. Ibid., pp. 262-3.
176. Ibid., p. 263.
177. W. Benjamin, 'N', p. 18.
178. Ibid., p. 8.
179. Ibid.
180. Ibid. See also W. Benjamin, 'The Image of Proust', in Benjamin, *Illuminations*, pp. 201-15.
181. For Benjamin's later use of the significance of the dream see 'Some Motifs in Baudelaire', in Benjamin, *Charles Baudelaire*, esp. pp. 111ff. Benjamin's earlier notion of the dreaming collectivity had been

criticized by Adorno, largely on the grounds that the collectivity itself does not dream.

182. Benjamin, 'N', p. 22.
183. Ibid., p. 23.
184. Ibid., p. 17.
185. Ibid., p. 24.
186. Ibid., p. 7.
187. Ibid., p. 13.
188. Tiedemann, *Studien zur Philosophie Walter Benjamins*, p. 152.
189. Benjamin, *Das Passagen-Werk*, p. 177.
190. Benjamin, *Charles Baudelaire*, p. 172.
191. Benjamin, *Das Passagen-Werk*, pp. 1010–11.
192. Ibid., p. 1034.
193. Ibid., p. 1026.
194. Ibid., pp. 1026–7.
195. Ibid., p. 1015.
196. Benjamin, *Gesammelte Schriften*, IV, pp. 400–1. The original argument by Sagnol is to be found in M. Sagnol, 'La méthode archéologique de Walter Benjamin', *Les temps modernes*, 40, no. 444, July 1983, pp. 143–65.
197. Benjamin, *Gesammelte Schriften*, IV, p. 401.
198. Benjamin, *Das Passagen-Werk*, p. 140.
199. Benjamin, *One-Way Street*, p. 314.
200. Ibid., p. 337.
201. Benjamin, *Das Passagen-Werk*, p. 511.
202. A. Stüssi, *Erinnerung an der Zukunft*, p. 25.
203. Cited in Stüssi, *Erinnerung an der Zukunft*, p. 26.
204. Benjamin, *Das Passagen-Werk*, p. 273.
205. Ibid., p. 271.
206. Ibid.
207. Ibid., p. 279.
208. Ibid., p. 278.
209. Ibid., p. 279.
210. Benjamin, *One-Way Street*, p. 371.
211. J.-M. Gagnebin, *Zur Geschichtsphilosophie Walter Benjamins*, Erlangen 1978, p. 38.
212. Benjamin, *Charles Baudelaire*, p. 104.
213. Benjamin, 'Zentralpark', p. 660.
214. Bloch, 'Ernst Bloch', p. 19.
215. I. Wohlfarth, 'Et cetera? Der Historiker als Lumpensammler', in Bolz and Witte (eds), *Passagen*, pp. 70–95.
216. Ibid., p. 80.
217. Benjamin, *Das Passagen-Werk*, p. 274.
218. Ibid., p. 272.
219. Ibid., p. 274.

220. Bloch, 'Ernst Bloch', p. 21.
221. Benjamin, *Charles Baudelaire*, p. 170. Translation slightly amended.
222. Ibid.
223. The book has been reprinted with a new title. See F. Hessel, *Ein Flaneur in Berlin*, Berlin 1984.
224. Ibid., p. 7.
225. Benjamin, *One-Way Street*, p. 298.
226. Benjamin, *Das Passagen-Werk*, p. 541.
227. Benjamin, *Gesammelte Schriften*, III, p. 195.
228. Benjamin, *Das Passagen-Werk*, p. 437.
229. Ibid., p. 531.
230. Benjamin, *Gesammelte Schriften*, III, p. 196.
231. Ibid., p. 198.
232. Benjamin, *Das Passagen-Werk*, p. 528.
233. Benjamin, 'N', p. 2.
234. Benjamin, *Illuminations*, p. 234.
235. Benjamin, *Das Passagen-Werk*, p. 491.
236. Ibid., p. 493.
237. Ibid., p. 494.
238. Ibid., p. 491.
239. Ibid.
240. Benjamin, *Gesammelte Schriften*, IV, p. 357.
241. Ibid., p. 425.
242. Benjamin, *Das Passagen-Werk*, p. 1031.
243. Ibid., p. 134.
244. Ibid.
245. Benjamin, *Charles Baudelaire*, p. 176.
246. Pausanias, *Guide to Greece*, 2 vols., translated and introduced by P. Levi, Harmondsworth 1971.
247. J. G. Frazer, *Pausanias and Other Greek Sketches*, London/New York 1900, p. 22.
248. Ibid., p. 34.
249. Benjamin, *Das Passagen-Werk*, p. 135.
250. Ibid.
251. Ibid., pp. 134–5.
252. Benjamin, *Gesammelte Schriften*, I, p. 1173.
253. Benjamin, *Das Passagen-Werk*, p. 419.
254. Ibid., p. 423.
255. Ibid., p. 422.
256. Ibid., p. 423.
257. Benjamin, *Gesammelte Schriften*, I, p. 666.
258. Benjamin, *Das Passagen-Werk*, p. 377.
259. Ibid., p. 439.
260. Ibid., p. 463.
261. Ibid., p. 470.

262. Ibid., p. 309.
263. Ibid., p. 405.
264. Benjamin, *Gesammelte Schriften*, I, p. 681.
265. Ibid., pp. 1164–5.
266. Ibid., p. 1236.
267. Benjamin, *One-Way Street*, p. 243.
268. Benjamin, *Charles Baudelaire*, p. 132.
269. Benjamin, *One-Way Street*, pp. 243–4.
270. Ibid., p. 251.
271. Ibid., pp. 177–8.
272. Ibid., p. 318.
273. Benjamin, *Das Passagen-Werk*, p. 1166.
274. Benjamin, *Charles Baudelaire*, p. 158. For a full examination of their architectural significance see J. Geist, *Passagen*, Munich 1971.
275. Ibid., p. 513.
276. Ibid., p. 86.
277. Ibid., pp. 668–9.
278. Ibid., p. 1030.
279. Ibid., p. 1050.
280. Ibid., p. 280.
281. Ibid., p. 670.
282. Ibid., p. 993.
283. Ibid., p. 617.
284. Ibid., p. 1034.
285. Ibid., p. 140.
286. Ibid., pp. 1001–2.
287. Ibid., p. 1045.
288. Benjamin, *Charles Baudelaire*, p. 161. For a study of the panoramas and their variants see S. Oettermann, *Das Panorama. Die Geschichte eines Massenmediums*, Frankfurt 1980.
289. Benjamin, *Charles Baudelaire*, p. 161.
290. Ibid., p. 162.
291. Benjamin, *Das Passagen-Werk*, p. 661.
292. Ibid., p. 656.
293. Benjamin, *Charles Baudelaire*, p. 35.
294. Benjamin, *Das Passagen-Werk*, p. 513.
295. Ibid., p. 522.
296. Benjamin, *Charles Baudelaire*, pp. 173–4.
297. Ibid., pp. 174–5.
298. Benjamin, *Charles Baudelaire*, p. 85.
299. Benjamin, *Das Passagen-Werk*, p. 208.
300. See F. Engels, 'The Housing Question' in K. Marx and F. Engels, *Selected Works*, Moscow 1962, pp. 557–635, esp. pp. 607–8. Quoted by Benjamin in *Das Passagen-Werk*, p. 206.
301. Benjamin, *Charles Baudelaire*, p. 174.

302. Ibid.
303. Ibid., p. 87.
304. Ibid., pp. 88–9.
305. Ibid., p. 90.
306. Ibid., p. 176.
307. Ibid., p. 175.
308. Ibid., pp. 167–8.
309. Benjamin, *Das Passagen-Werk*, p. 281.
310. Ibid., p. 286.
311. Ibid.
312. Ibid., p. 289.
313. Ibid., pp. 288–9.
314. Ibid., p. 282.
315. Ibid., p. 286.
316. Ibid., pp. 291–2.
317. Benjamin, *Charles Baudelaire*, p. 46.
318. Ibid.
319. Benjamin, *Das Passagen-Werk*, p. 292.
320. Ibid.
321. Benjamin, *Charles Baudelaire*, p. 169.
322. Ibid., p. 40.
323. Benjamin, *Das Passagen-Werk*, p. 559.
324. Ibid., p. 437.
325. Ibid., p. 535.
326. Ibid.
327. Benjamin, *Charles Baudelaire*, pp. 62–3.
328. F. Engels, *The Condition of the Working Class in England in 1844*, translated by F. K. Wischnewetzky, London 1952, pp. 24–5.
329. Benjamin, *Charles Baudelaire*, pp. 38–9.
330. Benjamin, *Das Passagen-Werk*, p. 469.
331. Ibid., p. 421.
332. Benjamin, *Gesammelte Schriften*, I, p. 686.
333. Benjamin, *Charles Baudelaire*, p. 60.
334. Ibid., p. 96.
335. Ibid., p. 97.
336. Benjamin, *Charles Baudelaire*, p. 129.
337. Benjamin, *Gesammelte Schriften*, I, p. 685.
338. Benjamin, *Charles Baudelaire*, p. 132.
339. Ibid., p. 54.
340. Ibid., p. 55.
341. Benjamin, *Das Passagen-Werk*, p. 565.
342. Ibid., p. 967. On the connection between these figures and their later development see S. Buck-Morss, 'Der Flaneur, der Sandwichman und die Hure. Dialektische Bilder und die Politik des Müssiggangs', in Bolz and Witte (eds), *Passagen*, pp. 96–113.

343. Benjamin, *Charles Baudelaire*, p. 54.
344. Benjamin, *Das Passagen-Werk*, p. 93.
345. Ibid., p. 108.
346. Benjamin, *Charles Baudelaire*, pp. 104–5.
347. Ibid., p. 105.
348. Benjamin, *Das Passagen-Werk*, p. 267.
349. Benjamin, *Charles Baudelaire*, p. 165.
350. Benjamin, *Das Passagen-Werk*, p. 239. On the history of art museums see W. Grasskamp, *Museumsgründer und Museumsstürmer: Zur Sozialgeschichte des Kunstmuseums*, Munich 1981.
351. Benjamin, *Das Passagen-Werk*, p. 247.
352. Benjamin, *Charles Baudelaire*, p. 171.
353. Ibid., p. 172, amended translation.
354. Benjamin, *Das Passagen-Werk*, p. 436.
355. Ibid., p. 464.
356. Ibid., pp. 678–9.
357. Benjamin, *Gesammelte Schriften*, I, p. 677.
358. Benjamin, *Das Passagen-Werk*, p. 112.
359. Ibid., p. 113.
360. Benjamin, *Gesammelte Schriften*, I, p. 680.
361. Benjamin, *Das Passagen-Werk*, p. 232.
362. Ibid., p. 236.
363. Ibid., p. 438. On the significance of Benjamin's treatment of allegory in this context see the valuable study, W. Menninghaus, *Walter Benjamins Theorie der Sprachmagie*, Frankfurt 1980, esp. ch. 2.
364. Benjamin, *Gesammelte Schriften*, I, p. 1151.
365. Benjamin, *Das Passagen-Werk*, pp. 438–9.
366. Benjamin, *Gesammelte Schriften*, I, p. 671.
367. Ibid.
368. Benjamin, *Das Passagen-Werk*, pp. 614–5. In this context Benjamin does not cite Simmel's discussion of prostitution that is to be found in *The Philosophy of Money*.
369. Benjamin, *Das Passagen-Werk*, p. 437.
370. Benjamin hoped to complete his projected Baudelaire book with an analysis of the *Jugendstil* movement. There are many notes in *Das Passagen-Werk* and elsewhere on the female imagery of this movement. For a study of Benjamin on women which takes account of their position within his theory of modernity see the interesting study by C. Buci-Glucksmann, *Walter Benjamin und die Utopie des Weiblichen*, Hamburg 1984.
371. Wolin, *Walter Benjamin*, pp. 187–8. On the concept of aura see also F. Fuld, 'Die Aura', *Akzente*, 26, 1979, pp. 352–70. On the work of art study see also Buck-Morss *Origin of Negative Dialectics*, and on Benjamin's general response to modern media, Lindner (ed.), *'Links hatte noch alles sich zu enträtseln'*, pp. 171–323.

372. Cited in Wolin, *Walter Benjamin*, p. 189.
373. See Lichtblau, 'Das "Pathos der Distanz"', note 93, chapter 1 above.
374. Benjamin, *Das Passagen-Werk*, p. 425.
375. Ibid., p. 433.
376. Ibid., p. 475.
377. Benjamin, *Gesammelte Schriften*, I, p. 673.
378. Benjamin, *Das Passagen-Werk*, p. 414.
379. Ibid., p. 448.
380. Quoted in *Das Passagen-Werk*, p. 173.
381. Ibid., p. 429.
382. Ibid., p. 420.
383. Ibid., p. 488.
384. Benjamin, *Charles Baudelaire*, p. 110. For a fascinating attempt to develop some of Benjamin's insights on the changes in experience and perception in the nineteenth century see C. Asendorf, *Batterien der Lebenskraft. Zur Geschichte der Dinge und ihrer Wahrnehmung im 19. Jahrhundert*, Giessen 1984.
385. Benjamin, *Charles Baudelaire*, p. 113.
386. Ibid. On the relation between Benjamin's 'The Storyteller' and his theory of experience see Wolin, *Walter Benjamin*, ch. 7.
387. Benjamin, *Charles Baudelaire*, p. 113.
388. Ibid., p. 112.
389. Ibid., p. 110.
390. Ibid., p. 117.
391. Ibid., pp. 134–5.
392. Benjamin, *Gesammelte Schriften*, I, p. 1179.
393. Benjamin, *Charles Baudelaire*, p. 140.
394. Ibid., p. 141.
395. Greffrath, *Metaphorische Materialismus*, p. 57.
396. Benjamin, *Das Passagen-Werk*, p. 164.
397. C. Baudelaire, *Art in Paris. 1845–1862*, translated and edited by J. Mayne, Oxford 1965, p. 117.
398. Benjamin, *Das Passagen-Werk*, p. 455.
399. E. Durkheim, *Suicide*, translated by J. A. Spaulding and G. Simpson, London 1952, pp. 365ff. More generally on melancholy, see the study by W. Lepenies, *Melancholie und Gesellschaft*, Frankfurt 1969.
400. Benjamin, *Gesammelte Schriften*, I, p. 664.
401. Benjamin, *Das Passagen-Werk*, p. 466.
402. Ibid., p. 169.
403. Benjamin, *Gesammelte Schriften*, I. pp. 682–3.
404. Benjamin, *Das Passagen-Werk*, p. 677.
405. The Theological and Messianic dimension of Benjamin's work is emphasized by Scholem. See the collection by Scholem, *Walter Benjamin und sein Engel* (note 17 above). In relation to Benjamin's philosophy of history see the essays in Bulthaup (ed.), *Materialien*, (note 166 above).

406. On the development of Benjamin's Marxism see the volumes by Buck-Morss and Wolin. Also C. Hering, *Der Intellektuelle als Revolutionär*, Munich 1979; J. Roberts, *Walter Benjamin*, London and Basingstoke, 1982, esp. ch. 3.
407. Benjamin, *Das Passagenwerk*, p. 175.
408. Ibid., p. 573.
409. Ibid., p. 495.
410. Benjamin, *Charles Baudelaire*, p. 104.

CONCLUSION

1. Benjamin, *Das Passagen-Werk*, p. 677.
2. On Berlin at this time see *Berlin um 1900*, Catalogue of exhibition in Akademie der Künste Berlin 1984.
3. K. Baedeker, *Berlin and its Environs*, 5th ed., Leipzig 1912, pp. v and 54.
4. Benjamin, *Gesammelte Schriften*, III, p. 198.
5. Benjamin, *Gesammelte Schriften*, I, p. 1131.

Bibliography

Since this study has been largely concerned with the works of three authors – Georg Simmel, Siegfried Kracauer and Walter Benjamin – existing bibliographies of their works are provided at the outset.

For Georg Simmel, the most extensive bibliography of his work, together with reviews and secondary literature to 1958, is provided by Kurt Gassen in Kurt Gassen and Michael Landmann (eds), *Buch des Dankes an Georg Simmel*, Duncker and Humblot, Berlin, 1958, pp. 311–65.

For Siegfried Kracauer, there are two sources. The first selective bibliography by Eckhardt Köhn and Stefan Oswald is contained in *Text + Kritik*, 68, October 1980, (Siegfried Kracauer), pp. 84–9. A more comprehensive and accurate bibliography is to be found in Inka Mülder, *Siegfried Kracauer-Grenzgänger zwischen Theorie und Literatur*, Metzler, Stuttgart, 1985, pp. 210–37.

For Walter Benjamin, his collected writings should be consulted. To date, five volumes have been published and a sixth is planned. Excluding *Das Passagen-Werk*, which constitutes volume V of the collected works, most useful is the 'Inhaltsverzeichnis Band I-IV' in Tillman Rexroth (ed.), *Walter Benjamin. Gesammelte Schriften*, IV, Suhrkamp, Frankfurt, 1972, pp. 1135–57.

Adorno, Theodor, W., 'Kracauer, Siegfried, Jacques Offenbach und das Paris seiner Zeit', *Zeitschrift für Sozialforschung*, 6, 1937, pp. 697–9.
—— *Noten zur Literatur*, III, Suhrkamp, Frankfurt, 1965.
—— *Prisms*, translated by S. Weber and S. Weber, Neville Spearman, London, 1967.
—— et al., *Über Walter Benjamin*, Suhrkamp, Frankfurt, 1968.
—— *Über Walter Benjamin*, Suhrkamp, Frankfurt, 1970.

310   *Bibliography*

Aragon, Louis, *Paris Peasant*, translated by S. W. Taylor, Picador, London, 1980.

Asendorf, Christoph, *Batterien der Lebenskraft. Zur Geschichte der Dinge und ihrer Wahrnehmung im 19. Jahrhundert*, Anabas, Giessen, 1984.

Baedeker, Karl, *Berlin and its Environs*, 5th edn, Baedeker, Leipzig, 1912.

Bahr, Hermann, *Zur Überwindung des Naturalismus*, Kohlhammer, Stuttgart/Berlin/Cologne/Mainz, 1968.

Baier, Horst, 'Die Gesellschaft – ein langer Schatten des toten Gottes. Friedrich Nietzsche und die Entstehung der Soziologie aus dem Geist der Decadence', *Nietzsche Studien*, 10/11, 1981/82, pp. 6–22.

Baudelaire, Charles, *The Painter of Modern Life and Other Essays*, translated and edited by J. Mayne, Phaidon, London, 1964.

—— *Art in Paris 1845–1862*, translated and edited by J. Mayne, Phaidon, London, 1965.

Becher, Heribert J., *Georg Simmel. Die Grundlagen seiner Soziologie*, Encke, Stuttgart, 1971.

Benjamin, Walter, *Gesammelte Schriften*, I, edited by R. Tiedemann and H. Schweppenhäuser, Suhrkamp, Frankfurt, 1974.

—— *Gesammelte Schriften*, II, edited by R. Tiedermann and H. Schweppenhäuser, Suhrkamp, Frankfurt, 1977.

—— *Gesammelte Schriften*, III, edited by H. Tiedermann-Bartels, Suhrkamp, 1972.

—— *Gesammelte Schriften*, IV, edited by T. Rexroth, Suhrkamp, Frankfurt, 1972.

—— *Gesammelte Schriften*, V, edited by R. Tiedermann, Suhrkamp, Frankfurt, 1982.

—— 'Uber einige Motive bei Baudelaire', *Zeitschrift für Sozialforschung*, 8, 1939, pp. 50–89.

—— *Berliner Kindheit um Neunzehnhundert*, Suhrkamp, Frankfurt, 1950.

—— *Briefe*, 2 vols., edited by G. Scholem and T. W. Adorno, Suhrkamp, Frankfurt, 1966.

—— *Illuminations*, translated by H. Zohn, Schocken, New York, 1969.

—— *Charles Baudelaire: A Lyric Poet in the Era of High Capitalism*, translated by H. Zohn, New Left Books, London, 1973.

—— *The Origins of German Tragedy*, translated by J. Osborne, New Left Books, London, 1977.

'Walter Benjamin', *Text + Kritik*, 2nd edn, 31/32, 1979.

—— *One-Way Street*, translated by E. Jephcott and K. Shorter, Harcourt Brace Jovanovich, 1978; New Left Books, London, 1979.

—— *Moskauer Tagebuch*, edited by G. Smith, Suhrkamp, Frankfurt, 1980.

—— *Ursprung des deutschen Trauerspiels*, Suhrkamp, Frankfurt, 1983.

Berman, Marshall, *All That Is Solid Melts Into Air: The Experience of Modernity*, Simon and Schuster, New York, 1982; New Left Books, London, 1983.

Beyse, Jochen, *Film und Wiederspiegelung. Interpretation und Kritik der Theorie Siegfried Kracauers*, dissertation, Cologne, 1977.

Bloch, Ernst, 'Kunstliche Mitte. Zu S. Kracauers "Die Angestellten"', *Die Neue Rundschau*, 41, 2, 1930, pp. 861–2.

—— *Erbschaft dieser Zeit*, Oprecht & Helbling, Zurich, 1935.

—— *Geist der Utopie*, 2nd edn, Suhrkamp, Frankfurt, 1964.

—— *et al.*, *Aesthetics and Politics*, New Left Books, London, 1977.

Böhringer, Hannes and Grunder, Karlfried, eds, *Ästhetik und Soziologie um die Jahrhundertwende: Georg Simmel*, Klostermann, Frankfurt, 1976.

Bolz, Norbert and Witte, Bernd, eds, *Passagen. Walter Benjamins Urgeschichte des neunzehnten Jahrhunderts*, Fink, Munich, 1984.

Brinkmann, Heinrich, *Methode und Geschichte. Die Analyse der Entfremdung in Georg Simmels 'Philosophie des Geldes'*, focus verlag, Giessen, 1974.

Bubner, Rüdiger, 'Uber einige Bedingungen gegenwärtiger Ästhetik', *Neue Hefte für Philosophie*, 5. 1973, pp. 38–73.

Buci-Glucksmann, Christine, *Walter Benjamin und die Utopie des Weiblichen*, VSA Verlag, Hamburg, 1984.

Buck-Morss, Susan, *The Origin of Negative Dialectics*, Free Press, New York, 1977.

—— 'Benjamin's Revolutionary Pedagogy', *New Left Review*, 128, pp. 50–75.

—— 'Walter Benjamin – Revolutionary Writer', *New Left Review*, 129, pp. 77–95.

Bulthaup, Peter, ed., *Materialien zu Benjamins Thesen 'Über den Begriff der Geschichte'*, Suhrkamp, Frankfurt, 1975.

Caillois, Robert, 'Paris, mythe moderne', *La nouvelle revue Française*, 25, 284, pp. 682–99.

Coser, Lewis, *Georg Simmel*, Free Press, Englewood Cliffs, NJ, 1965.

Durkheim, Emile, 'Philosophie des Geldes', *L'Année sociologique*, 5, 1900–1, pp. 150–5.

—— *Suicide*, translated by J. A. Spaulding and G. Simpson, Free Press, Englewood Cliffs, NJ, Routledge, London, 1950.

Engels, Friedrich, *The Condition of the Working Class in England in 1844*, translated by F. K. Wischnewetzky, Allen & Unwin, London, 1952.

Feikau, Wolfgang, *Schwanengesang auf 1848. Ein Rendezvous am Louvre: Baudelaire, Marx, Proudhon und Victor Hugo*, Rowohlt, Reinbeck bei Hamburg, 1978.

Fischer, Hugo, *Nietzsche Apostata oder die Philosophie des Ärgernisse*, Kurt Stenger, Erfurt, 1931.

Frazer, James G., *Pausanias and other Greek Sketches*, Macmillan, London/New York, 1900.

Frisby, David, *Sociological Impressionism. A Reassessment of Georg Simmel's Social Theory*, Heinemann, London, 1981.

—— 'Georg Simmel and Social Psychology', *Journal of the History of the Behavioral Sciences*, 20, 3, 1984, pp. 107–27.

—— 'Georg Simmels Theorie der Moderne' in H. J. Dahme and O. Rammstedt eds, *Georg Simmel und die Moderne*, Suhrkamp, Frankfurt, 1984, pp. 9–79.

────── *Georg Simmel*, Ellis Horwood/Tavistock/Methuen Inc., Chichester/
London/New York, 1984.

Fuld, Werner, 'Die Aura', *Akzente*, 26, 1979, pp. 352–70.

────── *Walter Benjamin: Zwischen den Stuhlen*, Fischer, Frankfurt, 1981.

Gagnebin, Jeanne-M., *Zur Geschichtsphilosophie Walter Benjamins*, Palm &
Enke, Erlangen, 1978.

Gassen, Kurt and Landmann, Michael, *Buch des Dankes an Georg Simmel*,
Duncker und Humblot, Berlin, 1958.

Gebhardt, Peter, *et al.*, *Walter Benjamin – Zeitgenosse der Moderne*, Scriptor,
Kronberg/Taunus, 1976.

Geist, Johann F., *Passagen*, Prestel, Munich, 1971.

Grasskamp, Walter, *Museumsgründer und Museumstürmer: Zur Geschichte des
Kunstmuseums*, C. H. Beck, Munich, 1981.

Greffrath, Krista R., *Metaphorische Materialismus*, Wilhelm Fink, Munich,
1980.

Habermas, Jürgen, 'Die Moderne – ein unvollendetes Projekt', in *Kleine
Politische Schriften*, (I-IV), Suhrkamp, Frankfurt, 1981, pp. 444–64.

────── 'Simmel als Zeitdiagnostiker', in Georg Simmel, *Philosophische Kultur*,
Klaus Wagenbach, Berlin, 1983, pp. 243–53.

Hamann, Richard, *Der Impressionismus in Leben und Kunst*, Dumont, Cologne,
1907.

Helms, Hans G., 'Der wunderliche Kracauer', *Neues Forum*, I, June/July
1971, pp. 27–9; October/November 1971, pp. 48–51; III, December 1971,
pp. 27–30; IV, September/October 1972, pp. 55–8.

────── 'Vom Proletkult zum Bio-Interview' in R. Hubner and E. Schutz,
eds, *Literatur als Praxis? Aktualität und Tradition operativen Schreibens*,
Westdeutscher Verlag, Opladen, 1976, pp. 71–95.

Hering, Christoph, *Der Intellektuelle als Revolutionär*, Wilhelm Fink, Munich,
1979.

Hessel, Franz, *Ein Flaneur in Berlin*, Arsenal, Berlin, 1984.

Hübner-Funk, Sibylle, *Georg Simmels Konzeption von Gesellschaft*, Pahl-
Rugenstein, Cologne, 1982.

Jauss, Hans-Robert, *Literaturgeschichte als Provokation*, Suhrkamp, Frankfurt,
1970.

Jay, Martin, 'The Extraterritorial Life of Siegfried Kracauer', *Salmagundi*,
31/32, 1975/76, pp. 49–106.

────── 'The Politics of Translation. Siegfried Kracauer and Walter Benjamin
on the Buber–Rosenzweig Bible', *Yearbook of the Leo Baeck Institute*, 21,
1976, pp. 3–24.

────── 'Adorno and Kracauer. Notes on a Troubled Friendship', *Salmagundi*,
40, 1978, pp. 42–66.

Joël, Karl, 'Eine Zeitphilosophie', *Neue Deutsche Rundschau*, 12, 1901,
pp. 812–26.

Kaulen, Heinrich, 'Walter Benjamins letzte Lebensjahre', *Neue Rundschau*,
93, 1, 1982, pp. 34–59.

Koigen, David, 'Soziologische Theorien', *Archiv für Sozialwissenschaft und Sozialpolitik*, 31, 1910, pp. 908–24.

Koppel, August, 'Für und wider Karl Marx', *Volkswirtschaftliche Abhandlungen der Badischen Hochschulen*, 8, 1, 1905.

Korsch, Karl, *Karl Marx. Marxistische Theorie und Klassenbewegung*, Rowohlt, Reibeck bei Hamburg, 1981.

Kracauer, Siegfried, 'Vom Erleben des Krieges', *Preussische Jahrbuch*, 58, 3, 1915, pp. 410–22.

—— *Das Leiden unter dem Wissen und die Sehnsucht nach der Tat. Eine Abhandlung aus dem Jahre 1917*, unpublished manuscript, Siegfried Kracauer Nachlass, Deutsche Literaturarchiv, Marbach/Neckar.

—— *Über die Pflichtethik*, unpublished manuscript, Siegfried Kracauer Nachlass, Deutsche Literaturarchiv, Marbach/Neckar.

—— *Über den Expressionismus. Wesen und Sinn einer Zeitbewegung*, unpublished manuscript, Siegfried Kracauer Nachlass, Deutsche Literaturarchiv, Marbach/Neckar.

—— *Über das Wesen der Personlichkeit. Eine Abhandlung*, unpublished manuscript, Universitätsbibliothek, Freie Universität Berlin.

—— *Georg Simmel. Ein Beitrag zur Deutung des geistigen Lebens unserer Zeit*, unpublished manuscript, Siegfried Kracauer Nachlass, Deutsche Literaturarchiv, Marbach/Neckar, c.1920.

—— 'Lukács Theorie des Romans', *Die Weltbühne*, 17, 2, 1921, pp. 229–30.

—— 'Georg von Lukács Romantheorie', *Neue Blätter für Kunst und Literatur*, 4, 1, 1921/22, pp. 105.

—— 'Prophetentum', *Frankfurter Zeitung*, 27 August 1922.

—— 'Georg Simmel. "Zur Philosophie der Kunst"', *Frankfurter Zeitung*, 4 July 1923.

—— 'Marx–Engels-Archiv', *Frankfurter Zeitung*, 20 June 1926.

—— 'Sie sporten', *Frankfurter Zeitung*, 13 January 1927.

—— 'Pariser Beobachtungen', *Frankfurter Zeitung*, 13 February 1927.

—— 'Neue Detektivromane', *Frankfurter Zeitung*, 24 April 1927.

—— 'Lichtreklame', *Frankfurter Zeitung*, 15 January 1928.

—— 'Max Scheler', *Frankfurter Zeitung*, 22 May 1928.

—— 'Die Berührung', *Frankfurter Zeitung*, 18 November 1928.

—— 'Ideologie und Utopie', *Frankfurter Zeitung*, 23 April 1929.

—— 'Zwei Arten der Mitteilung', ms. Siegfried Kracauer Nachlass.

—— *Die Angestellten*, Societäts Verlag, Frankfurt, 1930. Reprinted in Kracauer, Siegfried, *Schriften*, 1, Suhrkamp, Frankfurt, 1971.

—— 'Die geistige Entscheidung des Unternehmertums', *Frankfurter Zeitung*, 19 October 1930.

—— 'Unter Palmen', *Frankfurter Zeitung*, 19 October 1930.

—— 'Uber den Schriftsteller', *Die Neue Rundschau*, 42, 1, 1932, pp. 860–62.

—— 'Der operierender Schriftsteller', *Frankfurter Zeitung*, 17 February 1932.

—— 'Ein Paar Tagen Paris', *Frankfurter Zeitung*, 5 April 1932.

—— 'Café im Berliner Westen', Frankfurter Zeitung, 17 April 1932.

—— 'Im Luxushotel', *Frankfurter Zeitung*, 17 April 1932.

—— 'Girls und Krise', *Frankfurter Zeitung*, 26 May 1931.

—— 'Wiederholung', *Frankfurter Zeitung*, 29 May 1932.

—— 'Zu einem Roman aus der Konfektion', *Frankfurter Zeitung*, 5 June 1932.

—— 'Unter der Oberfläche', *Frankfurter Zeitung*, 11 July 1931.

—— 'Not und Zerstreuung', *Frankfurter Zeitung*, 15 July 1931.

—— 'Berlin in Deutschland', *Frankfurter Zeitung*, 14 August 1932.

—— 'Aus einem französischen Seebad', *Frankfurter Zeitung*, 14 September 1932.

——*Jacques Offenbach und das Paris seiner Zeit*, Albert de Lange, Amsterdam, 1937.

—— *Offenbach and the Paris of his Times*, translated by G. David and E. Mosbacher, Constable, London, 1937.

—— *Masse und Propaganda. Eine Untersuchung über faschistische Propaganda. Exposé*, unpublished manuscript, Siegfried Kracauer Nachlass.

—— *Strassen in Berlin und anderswo*, Suhrkamp, Frankfurt, 1964.

—— *History. The Last Things Before the Last*, Oxford University Press, Oxford/New York, 1969.

—— *Über die Freundschaft. Essays*, Suhrkamp, Frankfurt, 1971.

—— *Schriften*, 1, (*Soziologie als Wissenschaft, Der Detektiv-Roman, Die Angestellten*), Suhrkamp, Frankfurt, 1971.

—— *Kino. Essays, Glossen zum Film*, Suhrkamp, Frankfurt, 1974.

—— 'The Mass Ornament', translated by B. Cowell and J. Zipes, *New German Critique*, 2, 1975, pp. 67–76.

—— *Schriften*, 8, (*Jacques Offenbach und das Paris seiner Zeit*), Suhrkamp, Frankfurt, 1976.

—— *Schriften*, 7, (*Ginster, Georg*), Suhrkamp, Frankfurt, 1977.

—— *Das Ornament der Masse. Essays*, Suhrkamp, Frankfurt, 1977.

'Siegfried Kracauer', *Text + Kritik*, 68, October 1980.

Lacis, Asja, *Revolutionär im Beruf*, Hanser, Munich, 1971.

Landmann, Michael, ed., *Georg Simmel. Das individuelle Gesetz*, Suhrkamp, Frankfurt, 1968.

Lefebvre, Henri, *Einführung in die Modernität. Zwölf Präludien*, Suhrkamp, Frankfurt, 1978.

Lepenies, Wolf, *Melancholie und Gesellschaft*, Suhrkamp, Frankfurt, 1969.

Lethen, Helmuth, *Neue Sachlichkeit: 1924–1932. Studien zur Literatur des 'Weissen Socialismus'*, Metzler, Stuttgart, 1975.

Levine, Donald, ed., *Georg Simmel on Individuality and Social Forms*, Chicago University Press, Chicago/London, 1971.

Lichtblau, Klaus, 'Das "Pathos der Distanz". Präliminarien zur Nietzsche-Rezeption bei Georg Simmel', in H. J. Dahme and O. Rammstedt, eds, *Georg Simmel und die Moderne*, Suhrkamp, Frankfurt, 1984, pp. 231–81.

Löwith, Karl, *Nietzsches Philosophie der ewigen Wiederkunft des Gleichen*, Die Runde, Berlin, 1935.

Lukács, Georg, *The Theory of the Novel*, translated by A. Bostock, Merlin, London, 1971.

—— *History and Class Consciousness*, translated by R. Livingstone, Merlin, London, 1971.

Lyotard, Jean-Francois, *The Postmodern Condition: A Report on Knowledge*, translated by G. Bennington and B. Massumi, Manchester University Press, Manchester, 1984.

Marx, Karl, and Engels, Friedrich, *Selected Works*, Progress Publishers, Moscow, 1962.

Marx Karl, *Theories of Surplus Value*, Part III, Lawrence & Wishart, London, 1972.

—— *Grundrisse*, edited by M. Nichlaus, Penguin, Harmondsworth, 1973.

—— *Surveys from Exile*, edited by D. Fernbach, Penguin, Harmondsworth, 1973.

—— *The Revolutions of 1848*, edited by D. Fernbach, Penguin, Harmondsworth, 1973.

—— *Early Writings*, edited by L. Coletti, Penguin, Harmondsworth, 1975.

—— *Capital*, vol. 1, translated by B. Fowkes, Penguin, Harmondsworth, 1976.

Menninghaus, Winfried, *Walter Benjamins Theorie der Sprachmagie*, Suhrkamp, Frankfurt, 1980.

Miller, Michael B., *The Bon Marché. Bourgeois Culture and the Department Store*, Princeton University Press, Princeton; Allen & Unwin, London, 1981.

Mülder, Inka, *Erfahrendes Denken. Zu den Schriften Siegfried Kracauers vom Ersten Weltkrieg bis zum Ende der Weimarer Republik*, dissertation, Tübingen University, 1984.

—— *Siegfried Kracauer-Grenzgänger zwischen Theorie und Literatur: Seine frühen Schriften 1913–1933*, Metzler, Stuttgart, 1985.

Müller, Michael, *Die Verdrängung des Ornaments. Zum Verhältnis von Architektur und Lebenspraxis*, Suhrkamp, Frankfurt, 1977.

Münster, Arno, ed., *Tagträume vom aufrechten Gang. Sechs Interviews mit Ernst Bloch*, Suhrkamp, Frankfurt, 1977.

Nagler, Norbert, 'Jacques Offenbach musikalische Utopie: die Sehnsucht nach der herrschaftsarmen Heimat. Reflexionen zu Siegfried Kracauers Gesellschaftsbiographie des Second Empires', *Musik Konzepte*, 13, 1980, pp. 71–86.

Nedelmann, Birgitta, 'Georg Simmel – Emotion und Wechselwirkung in intimen Gruppen', *Kölner Zeitschrift für Soziologie und Socialpsychologie*, Sonderheft 25, 1983, pp. 174–209.

Nietzsche, Friedrich, *Twilight of the Idols. The Anti-Christ*, translated by R. J. Hollingdale, Penguin, Harmondsworth, 1968.

—— *Sämtliche Werke. Kritische Studienausgabe*, 15 vols., edited by G. Colli and M. Montinari, DTV, de Gruyter, Munich/Berlin/New York, 1980.

—— *Untimely Meditations*, translated by R. J. Hollingdale, Cambridge University Press, Cambridge, 1983.

Oehler, Dolf, *Pariser Bilder I (1830–1848). Antibourgeoise Ästhetik bei Baudelaire, Daumier und Heine*, Suhrkamp, Frankfurt, 1979.

Oettermann, Stephan, *Das Panorama. Die Geschichte eines Massenmediums*, Syndikat, Frankfurt, 1980.

Pankoke, Eckart, 'Social Movement', translated by D. Frisby, *Economy and Society*, 11, 2, 1982, pp. 317–46.

Pausanias, *Guide to Greece*, translated by P. Levi, 2 vols., Penguin Books, Harmondsworth, 1971.

Pfotenhauer, Herbert, 'Benjamin und Nietzsche', in B. Lindner, ed., *'Links hatte noch sich alles zu enträtseln . . .' Walter Benjamin in Kontext*, Syndikat, Frankfurt, 1978, pp. 100–26.

Rella, Franco, 'Benjamin und Blanqui', in M. Brodersen, *Benjamin auf Italienisch: Aspekte einer Rezeption*, Neue Kritik, Frankfurt, 1982, pp. 77–102.

Roberts, Julien, *Walter Benjamin*, Macmillan, London/Basingstoke, 1982.

Sagnol, Marc, 'La méthode archéologique de Walter Benjamin', *Les temps modernes*, 40, 444, 1983, pp. 143–65.

Sayer, Derek, *Marx's Method*, Harvester, Brighton; Humanities, Atlantic Heights, NJ, 1979.

Scheible, Helmuth, 'Georg Simmel und die Tragödie der Kultur', *Neue Rundschau*, 91, 2/3, 1980, pp. 133–64.

Schmidt, Conrad, 'Eine Philosophie des Geldes', *Sozialistische Monatshefte*, 5, 1901, pp. 180–5.

Scholem, Gershom, ed., *Walter Benjamin/Gershom Scholem. Briefwechsel 1933–1940*, Suhrkamp, Frankfurt, 1980.

—— *Walter Benjamin. The Story of a Friendship*, Faber, London, 1982.

—— *Walter Benjamin und sein Engel*, Suhrkamp, Frankfurt, 1983.

Simmel, Georg, *Über sociale Differenzierung*, Duncker und Humblot, Leipzig, 1890.

—— 'Tendencies in German Life and Thought since 1870', *International Monthly* (New York), 5, 1902, pp. 93–111 and 166–84.

—— 'Soziologie des Raumes', *Jahrbuch für Gesetzgebung, Verwaltung und Volkswirtschaft*, 27, 1903, pp. 27–71.

—— 'Die Grossstädte und das Geistesleben', *Jahrbuch der Gehe-Stiftung zu Dresden*, 9, 1903, pp. 227–42.

—— *Kant und Goethe*, Kurt Wolff, Berlin, 1906.

—— 'Soziologie der Sinne', *Die Neue Rundschau*, 18, 2, 1907, pp. 1025–36.

—— *Schopenhauer und Nietzsche*, Duncker und Humblot, Leipzig, 1907.

—— 'Das Problem des Stiles', *Dekorative Kunst*, 11, 7, 1908, pp. 307–16.

—— *Philosophische Kultur*, W. Klinkhardt, Leipzig, 1911.

—— *Rembrandt: Ein kunstphilosophischer Versuch*, Kurt Wolff, Leipzig, 1916.

—— *Der Krieg und die geistigen Entscheidungen*, Duncker und Humblot, Munich/Leipzig, 1917.

—— *Conflict and the Web of Group Affiliations*, translated by K. H. Wolff and R. Bendix, Free Press, Englewood Cliffs, NJ, 1955.

—— *The Conflict in Modern Culture and Other Essays*, translated and edited by P. K. Etzkorn, Teachers Press, New York, 1968.

—— *The Philosophy of Money*, translated by T. Bottomore and D. Frisby, Routledge, London/Boston, 1978.

Stambaugh, Joan, *Nietzsche's Thought of Eternal Return*, John Hopkins University Press, Baltimore/London, 1972.

Stoessel, Maria, *Aura. Das vergessene Meschliche*, Hanser, Munich, 1983.

Strohmeyer, Klaus, *Warenhäuser*, Klaus Wagenbach, Berlin, 1980.

Stüssi, Anna, *Erinnerung an die Zukunft. Walter Benjamins "Berliner Kindheit um Neunzehnhundert"*, Vandenhoeck & Ruprecht, Göttingen, 1977.

Susman, Margaretta, *Die geistige Gestalt Georg Simmels*, Mohr, Tübingen, 1960.

Tönnies, Ferdinand, 'Considérations sur l'histoire moderne', *Annales de l'institut international de sociologie*, 1, 1895, pp. 245–52.

—— *Community and Association*, translated by C. P. Loomis, Routledge, London, 1955.

Tiedemann, Rolf, *Studien zur Philosophie Walter Benjamins*, Suhrkamp, Frankfurt, 1973.

—— *Dialektik im Stillstand*, Suhrkamp, Frankfurt, 1983.

Troeltsch, Ernst, 'Der historische Entwicklungsbegriff in der modernen Geistes-und Lebensphilosophie', *Historische Zeitschrift*, 124, 1921, pp. 424–86.

—— *Der Historismus und seine Probleme*, Mohr, Tübingen, 1922.

Unseld, Siegfried, ed., *Zur Aktualität Walter Benjamins*, Suhrkamp, Frankfurt, 1972.

Weber, Max, *Wissenschaft als Beruf*, Duncker und Humblot, Munich/Leipzig, 1919.

—— *Economy and Society*, edited by G. Roth and C. Wittich, University of California Press, Berkeley/Los Angeles/London, 1978.

Wohlfarth, Irving, '*Perte d'auréole*: The Emergence of the Dandy', *Modern Language Notes*, 48, 1970, pp. 529–71.

Wolff, Kurt H., ed., *The Sociology of Georg Simmel*, Free Press, Englewood Cliffs, NJ, 1950.

—— ed., *Essays on Sociology, Philosophy and Aesthetics by Georg Simmel*, Ohio University Press, Columbus, 1959.

Williams, Rosalind H., *Dream World. Mass Consumption in Late Nineteenth Century France*, University of California Press, Berkeley/Los Angeles/London, 1982.

Witte, Bernd, *Walter Benjamin – Der Intellektuelle als Kritiker*, Metzler, Stuttgart, 1976.

Wolin, Richard, *Walter Benjamin*, Columbia University Press, New York/London, 1982.

Wuthenow, Ralph-Rainer, *Muse, Maske, Meduse. Europäischer Ästhetizismus*, Suhrkamp, Frankfurt, 1978.

Index

Adorno, Theodor W., 59, 145, 161, 163, 176, 182, 188, 191, 200, 204–5, 215
antiquity, 208, 232–6
Aragon, Louis, 188, 189, 194, 209, 240
arcades, 143–4, 209, 240–2
Arcades Project, 7, 68, 187–206, 269
archaeology, 223–5, 232
art, 32, 42, 45, 47, 53, 62–4, 214–15, 258
art nouveau, 77, 82, 83, 101–2, 190, 204, 248, 256–7, 261
aura, 258–9, 261

Baudelaire, Charles, 6, 14–20, 36, 37, 40–1, 45–6, 190, 202–4, 206, 235–6, 259, 260, 262, 263, 264, 265
Balzac, Honoré de, 232–3
Becher, Heribert, 40, 48
Benjamin Walter, 3, 4, 5, 7, 8–9, 15, 36–7, 61, 68, 78, 174, 185–6, 187–265, 266, 269, 270–1, 272
Berlin, 7, 69–70, 110, 136, 137, 139–47, 164–71, 185, 267
Berman, Marshall, 21, 38
Blanqui, August, 36, 37, 202
Bloch, Ernot, 57, 122–6, 162, 183–4, 191, 213–14, 228
Böhringer, Hannes, 104–5
Brecht, Bertolt, 198

Bubner, Rudiger, 53
Buck-Morss, Susan, 217

capitalism, 21–7, 91–2, 107–8, 113, 148–50, 231, 269–71
collector, 217, 225–8
commodity fetishism, 23–7, 182, 210, 254–60, 270, 271
consumption, 87, 92–3, 169–70, 240–1, 252–5
crowd, 17, 249–52

detective novel, 126–34
dialectical images, 219–20
Dickens, Charles, 86
division of labour, 90–2
Durkheim, Emile, 263

Engels, Friedrich, 244

fascism, 172–3, 201
fashion, 18–19, 95–101, 153, 256
film, 155–8
Fischer, Hugo, 28–9
flâneur, 16–17, 18, 70–1, 158, 205, 210, 228–30, 242, 250–2, 255
fragments, 23, 31, 33, 48–51, 55–8, 87, 183–4, 185, 188, 189, 212–16, 271–2
Frazer, James G. 233
Fuld, Werner, 201

George, Stefan, 76–7

Habermas, Jürgen, 12, 13, 27, 105, 106, 271
Hamann, Richard, 59, 83–5
Haussmann, Baran, 179, 242, 243–6
Helms, Hans G. 146, 163
Hessel, Franz, 190–1, 192, 195, 229
historicism, 153–4, 218–19
Hofmannsthal, Hugo, 193
Holz, Hans H., 152
Horkheimer, Max, 191, 198, 200, 202, 203

intellectuals, 151, 159–61, 171
interieur, 243, 244, 246–9

Jauss Hans-Robert, 16
Jay, Martin, 134, 161
Joel, Karl, 76

Kitsch, 132–3, 143
Kracauer, Siegfried, 3, 4, 5, 6–7, 8, 41, 54, 60–1, 71, 86, 109–86, 191–2, 195, 213, 214, 215, 248, 267, 268–9, 270, 272

labyrinth, 86, 87, 88, 134, 192–3, 208–9, 210–11, 225, 232–4, 237, 243, 268
Lacis, Asja, 191, 194
Lukács, Georg, 86, 117, 120, 123–4, 126, 127, 183, 214
Lyotard, Jean-François, 12

Marx, Karl, 14, 20–7, 28–9, 36, 107–8, 117, 122–6, 191, 230, 262
masses, 147–52, 211, 249–54
metropolis, 18, 20, 70–2, 72–86, 100, 134–47, 208, 267–70
money, 88–9, 90, 103–5, 106–7, 180, 257–8, 269–70
Mulder, Inka, 135, 136, 155, 158
myth, 208, 233–4

neurasthenia, 72–7
Nietzsche, Friedrich, 14, 28–37, 44, 202, 258, 259, 264

Oehler, Dolf, 15–16, 18, 20
Offenbach, Jacques, 174, 176–82

Pausanias, 232–4
Paris, 7, 137–9, 175–81, 190–1, 192–3, 198–9, 202–3, 229, 230, 231–33, 234–46
photography, 153–5, 237–8
prehistory of modernity, 219–23, 230–2, 241, 263, 266

ragpicker, 186, 227
reification, 90, 212
Rodin, August, 47, 62–4

Sagnol, Marc, 223
Scheler, Max, 120–1
Schmidt, Conrad, 60
Scholem, Gershom, 191, 192, 194, 196, 198, 200, 205
Schröter, Michael, 136, 156, 165
Simmel, Georg, 2–3, 4, 5, 6, 35, 38–108, 114, 118–19, 247, 258, 267, 268, 269–70
sport, 170–1, 185
Stein, Lorenz von, 22
Stussi, Anna, 225
surrealism, 188–9, 194–5
Susman, Margarete, 52, 69

Tönnies, Ferdinand, 13, 46
totality, 48–52, 118, 204, 213, 214
Troeltsch, Ernst, 39–40, 59–60, 75

Weber, Max, 2, 35–6, 47–8, 114–15, 149
white-collar workers, 162–71
Witte, Bernd, 187, 206
Witte, Carsten, 151
world exhibitions, 94–5, 254

Zohlen, Gerwin, 136–7, 140–1